Essential Readings on Rhetoric

Essential Readings on Rhetoric

Joseph P. Zompetti, editor

International Debate Education Association

New York, London & Amsterdam

Published by
The International Debate Education Association
105 East 22nd Street
New York, NY 10010

Library of Congress Cataloging-in-Publication Data
Essential readings on rhetoric / Joseph P. Zompetti, editor.
    pages cm
    ISBN 978-1-61770-069-9
    1. Rhetoric—Study and teaching.   2. Discourse analysis—Study and teaching.   3. Composition (Language arts)—Study and teaching.   I. Zompetti, Joseph P., 1970– editor of compilation.   II. International Debate Education Association.
    P53.27.E88 2013
    808—dc23   2012047627

Composition by Brad Walrod/Kenoza Type, Inc.
Printed in the USA

 IDEBATE Press

Acknowledgments

This book would not have been possible without the help and support of a number of people. I cannot possibly list them all here, but some that readily come to mind are Marcin Zaleski, Noel Selegzi, Eleanora von Dehsen, Martin Greenwald, Buffy Ryan, Alauna Akins, Lee Anne Hale, Steve Hunt, Lance Lippert, my dad, and my four-legged daughter, Midnight.

I am grateful for all of their help, support, advice, and friendship. I truly hope that the material in this book will be as inspirational to its readers as these people have been to me.

Contents

Introduction

Unfortunately, the word "rhetoric" is often misunderstood and given a negative connotation. If we watch any television show about politics, we are likely to hear a commentator opine "we need to focus more on policies and less on rhetoric," or "that's just rhetoric." These and other references portray rhetoric, at best, as hot air, fluff, discourse lacking substance, meaningless banter or, worse, as trickery, deception, or skillful verbal manipulation. While these characterizations can be true in some cases, "rhetoric" also has a more positive meaning. Although rhetoric can be abused, it can also educate, bring joy to its listeners, memorialize the dead, advocate policy, defend justice, and stir the imagination.

Our modern conception of rhetoric owes a great deal to the writers, teachers, and orators who came before us. Revered men of Ancient Greece and Rome spent considerable time—some their entire lives—studying, teaching, and defending the core principles of rhetoric. We know, for example, that Greeks in antiquity wrote about and debated the proper use of rhetoric (also termed "eloquence"), cautioning against using it for abusive and unethical purposes. Much of the heated discussions about the Greek Sophists, for instance, centered on this very concept of teaching rhetoric as a skill for any purpose, including manipulation and deceit.

Rhetoric can be seen as a tool, skill, talent, or artifice. Aristotle defined rhetoric as "the faculty of discovering the possible *means* of persuasion in reference to any subject whatever" (Aristotle, 1926, p. 1355, emphasis added). Aristotle and other writers of his time clearly stressed the method and the way rhetoric is used . Knowing the "means of persuasion" can help us to understand the context of using rhetoric in specific ways and in certain circumstances; in other words, we can develop a grasp of the strategies used to persuade audiences. But, we should also note that the most important component of defining rhetoric is captured in the word "persuasion." As the Greek philosopher and rhetorician Gorgias remarked when asked by Socrates to explain his profession, "persuasion is the chief end of rhetoric."

Throughout history, the nature of rhetoric—its purpose, its relationship with dialectic (logic), its impact on argumentation, and the role of the audience—has been discussed virtually ad nauseum. Scholars have also debated if rhetoric is teachable, if rhetorical style can match an occasion, and if rhetoric must be intentional in its purpose to persuade. All of these questions have interesting implications for our everyday lives and on specific fields of study. For example, if rhetorical ability is innate, we should not bother studying it at all, for only a select few can deploy it effectively. Further, if rhetoric must be intentional, how do we account for unintended outcomes? For example, politicians give speeches asking for votes but turn voters off instead.

Regardless of where we stand on the issues relating to rhetoric, one thing is certain: rhetoric surrounds us and constantly affects us on a number of levels. Rhetorical strategies are used in our interpersonal relationships—for example, when parents explain to their teenage children that they should avoid parties during school nights. In business, workers use rhetoric to argue and advocate for better conditions. In religion, law, and public policy, rhetoric functions as a means of proposing positions and refuting opposing viewpoints. When we respond to TV commercials, listen to certain music, are moved by messages in film, we are experiencing the power of rhetoric. Since rhetoric is practically omnipresent—especially if we consider that rhetoric exists in verbal and non-verbal situations—we would do well to study its history, its principles, its use, and its ability to influence audiences.

This anthology helps us in this pursuit. It reminds us of the long and celebrated tradition of rhetoric. It also reminds us that much of our contemporary communication—despite all our technological advancements—functions in a fashion similar to the way Romans and Greeks communicated more than 2,500 years ago. Yet, as the readings below indicate, rhetoric has also changed over the centuries. Aristotle, Cicero, and Isocrates mention the origins of the study of rhetoric with Corax of Syracuse and Tisias, his student. The Greeks and Romans taught rhetoric as an oratorical skill, primarily to be used in ceremonial (epideictic), legal (forensic), and policy (deliberative) speeches. Over time, the occasions for speeches expanded to include all areas of speech making, and then later to cover all verbal communication related to persuasion. In the Middle Ages, for example, those interested in rhetoric, like St. Augustine, argued for favoring rhetoric in discussing theological issues, especially in sermons and evangelizing.

In addition to speeches, writing persuasive messages also fell under the purview of rhetorical studies. Aristotle, then Horace after him, described the relationship between *ars rhetorica* and *ars poetica,* thereby cementing a bond between oratorical and written persuasion. This is particularly important when we consider that the oral tradition of narratives and poetry—many of which were persuasive in nature—were the first to experience the transition to inscribing communicative messages in clay or wax tablets and writing them on paper. The advent of the printing press made the role of persuasion in written communication even more important to study since persuasive texts became far more readily available. The topic of style, while discussed at length by Cicero in the context of speeches, became still more emphasized when exploring rhetoric in writing. As we will see with writers such as Erasmus, the stylistic considerations of rhetoric garnered greater attention in the Middle Ages.

In the readings below, the reader will notice references to "dialectic." In Ancient Greece, dialectic was the study and use of formal logic to demonstrate a proof or law or concept. For the most part, dialectic in Ancient Greece was viewed as a distinct practice from rhetoric—dialectic was more scientific, rhetoric was more artistic. At times the distinction is less clear. Later in history, when we study the Enlightenment with George Campbell and Hugh Blair, we shall see that dialectic becomes an accepted part of rhetoric.

Although some scholars argue about the primacy of oral over written rhetoric (Wichelns, 1925), and vice versa (Derrida, 1967), much of the rhetorical techniques of invention, arrangement, and style are shared by both kinds of communication. When we consider the manner of presenting rhetorical points, many of the devices and strategies are similar regardless if one speaks or writes them (Campbell, 1868). As such, studying rhetoric is not just about learning about speeches—it is about examining the techniques of persuasion in a variety of contexts and forms.

Essential Readings on Rhetoric provides insight into the history of rhetoric so that we may tease out important concepts and then see how those concepts inform our contemporary rhetorical practices. It offers a compendium of key primary works from Ancient Greece and Rome, the Middle Ages, and the Enlightenment as well as a brief examination of contemporary rhetorical thought. Our inclusion of these sources is deliberate—to allow the reader an opportunity to see the evolution of thinking about rhetoric. We can see, for example, how the focus on rhetoric changes from teaching students how to persuade others in legal and public affairs, to viewing rhetoric as an art, to seeing it as an ethical discursive practice for the benefit of the community or state, to acknowledging its usefulness for religious practices, to noting elements of style, and to displaying the need to conjoin argument studies with rhetoric. Today, contemporary rhetoricians study rhetoric in all of these areas, highlighting the work that previous scholars—such as the ones presented in this volume—have contributed.

To our knowledge, no other book includes all of these selections. There are, of course, books that have original excerpts from Ancient Greece, Ancient Rome, and the Middle Ages, but none chronicle the trajectory of rhetoric through these centuries. The readings here are useful to students and teachers, scholars and practitioners of persuasion, as well as novice and veteran rhetoricians. Anyone interested in philosophy, history, language, and, of course, rhetoric and persuasion will find this book useful.

Of course, many of the readings in this volume use language that is different from our modern parlance; some of the examples used in the essays might not be familiar to contemporary readers. Today's reader may need to consult other online or print resources to appreciate some of the allusions or references, but many can be understood by considering their context. While many readers may find the language and examples used challenging, nothing really substitutes for reading this original material.

We hope readers will find this text useful as they explore the field of rhetoric. Of course, we also hope that readers will use the valuable information included here for beneficial, ethical purposes. Persuasion is a powerful force in communication, and the skills learned from the essays in this anthology will enhance the skills of persuasion of anyone who reads it.

SECTION ONE

Ancient Greece

The ancient Greeks had a profound influence on rhetoric. They were the first to make rhetoric a formal part of education, to suggest that teaching the skills of persuasion were important for the proper functioning of the city-state, and to write on the theory and practice of rhetoric.

Aristotle's *The Rhetoric* is the first complete treatise on rhetoric that has survived. We know that other manuals predate Aristotle's, but they exist only in fragments, if at all. For example, even Aristotle acknowledges the significance of the manual written by Corax (Korax), from Syracuse, who taught rhetoric to students long before Aristotle and Socrates. Aristotle quotes from an obscure source:

> "Korax, what did you undertake to teach me?"
>
> "To persuade anyone you please."
>
> "If so, I now persuade you to receive no fee; if not, you have failed to teach me to persuade you: in either case, I owe you nothing."
>
> Korax retorts with a similar dilemma: "If you persuade me, I have taught you the art; if not, you have failed to persuade me to remit the fee: in either case, you are bound to pay." (Aristotle, 1909)

Unfortunately, the writings of Corax and Tisias, his student, are believed to have been destroyed by a fire; as a result, our knowledge of them comes from references found in the writings of others.

The Greeks were also the first to debate the role and uses of rhetoric (also termed "eloquence"), a debate that continues today. For example, the Sophists emphasized practical rhetoric and taught students to argue any side of an issue regardless of the morality of the perspective. The Sophists, while often criticized at the time, were instrumental in the progression of rhetoric as a discipline, since they were the first to elevate rhetoric to a field of educational study. Isocrates and Aristotle, on the other hand, argued that an effective orator needs integrity if he is to be persuasive and that rhetoric must be allied with virtue. Plato castigated the Sophists on other grounds. For Plato, only the privileged elite should be considered effective persuaders, since the elite were considered to be the moral defenders of the polis—the Greek city-state. Thus, for Plato, the Sophist contention that anyone could learn rhetoric was demeaning to the nature of rhetoric.

The Greeks did not find the teaching of rhetoric in itself problematic. Isocrates and Aristotle, for example, argued that teaching the skills of persuasion were important for the proper functioning of the city-state. Their criticism, of course, was directed primarily against the unprincipled pedagogy of rhetoric without any allegiance to virtue. In the selections chosen for this book, we have included passages that discuss the reasons for the ethical teaching of rhetoric.

The Greeks laid important groundwork for understanding rhetoric to enhance speeches as well as criticize them. Today, we have rhetorical scholars who are also rhetorical *critics*—they evaluate the strengths and weaknesses of rhetoric. Understanding the strengths and weaknesses of rhetoric is similar to knowing the components that are used to create effective rhetoric; so, the composition and critique of rhetoric are two sides of the same coin. For example, Isocrates mentions the components needed for an effective oratory that were the precursors to Cicero's "Five Canons of Rhetoric" (see section 2). These components and canons are instructive for writing a speech as well as for evaluating someone else's speech.

Finally, with Aristotle, we have the introduction of logos, pathos, and ethos—the use of reasoning, emotion, and credibility to persuade an audience. Aristotle called these elements "rhetorical proofs." They are the three cornerstone *means* that a speaker would use to persuade audiences. These concepts are emphasized by various writers throughout the ages and are still important for our understanding of rhetoric today.

For these reasons, we present the crucial contributions of the Greeks on rhetoric chronologically, beginning with Isocrates who argued for rhetoric's prominence as a central discipline. In his "Against the Sophists," he expressed disdain for the Sophists who, in his view, devalued rhetoric through their pay-for-hire teaching methods. Next, we include the complete "Gorgias" by Plato. The "Gorgias" presents a short discussion by men trying to ascertain the nature of rhetoric. After Plato, we have key passages from Aristotle's *The Art of Rhetoric*. For many reasons, Aristotle's *Rhetoric* has become the foundational text for all rhetorical studies. We end this section with *On Style* by Demetrius. *On Style* focuses on the different stylistic principles of persuasion. In all, the Greeks offer us insight into the teaching of rhetoric, its fundamental characteristics, and its primary strategies for influencing audiences, and its elements of style.

READINGS

Barney, Rachel. "*Gorgia's* Defense: Plato and His Opponents on Rhetoric and the Good." *Southern Journal of Philosophy* 48, no. 1 (2010): 95–121.

Benson, Thomas W., and Michael H. Prosser. *Readings in Classical Rhetoric*. Bloomington: Indiana University Press, 1969.

Chase, Kenneth R. "Constructing Ethics through Rhetoric: Isocrates and Piety." *Quarterly Journal of Speech* 95, no. 3 (2009): 239–262.

Cole, Thomas. *The Origins of Rhetoric in Ancient Greece*. Baltimore: Johns Hopkins University Press, 1991.

Crowley, Sharon, and Debra Hawhee. *Ancient Rhetorics for Contemporary Students*. 3rd ed. New York: Pearson, 2004.

Enos, Richard L., and Margaret Kantz. "A Selected Bibliography on Corax and Tisias." *Rhetoric Society Quarterly* 13 (1983): 71–74.

Futter, D. "*Gorgias* and the Psychology of Persuasion." *Akroterion* 56 (2011): 3–20.

Garver, Eugene. *Aristotle's Rhetoric: An Art of Character*. Chicago: University of Chicago Press, 1994.

Liebersohn, Yosef Z. "The Problem of Rhetoric's Materia in Plato's *Gorgias*." *Rhetorica: A Journal of the History of Rhetoric* 29, no. 1 (2011): 1–22.

Murphy, James J. "Aristotle's Rhetoric in the Middle Ages." *Quarterly Journal of Speech* 52, no. 2 (1966): 109–116.

Schenkeveld, Dirk M. "The Intended Public of Demetrius's *On Style*: The Place of the Treatise in the Hellenistic Educational System." *Rhetorica: A Journal of the History of Rhetoric* 18, no. 1 (2000): 29–48.

Chapter 1

Isocrates

Isocrates (436–338 BCE), a philosopher who established the first permanent institution for teaching the liberal arts, is significant in the history of rhetoric because of his efforts at elevating the discipline of rhetoric. In "Against the Sophists," he not only establishes his philosophy of teaching rhetoric but also articulates what he considers to be effective oratory. Isocrates distinguishes his views from those of the Sophists—who believed that anyone could learn rhetoric and that rhetoric could be used for any purpose, including manipulation and deceit. Isocrates was the first to maintain that effective orators must have natural abilities, but they need teaching to perfect their speaking talents. He also stressed that a good rhetorician must be knowledgeable in a wide variety of subjects—such as philosophy, art, and history—as well as be virtuous. With this latter point, Isocrates clashed with the Sophists, for Isocrates maintained that honesty of character is crucial for an effective orator. Isocrates also delineated the elements of a good speech: choosing the components of the topic, arranging them together, being aware of the demands of the occasion, and focusing on style with "flowing and melodious phrase." His analysis is the precursor to what is typically attributed to Cicero—the "Five Canons of Rhetoric" (invention, arrangement, style, delivery, and memory). Given his position vis-à-vis the Sophists, Isocrates is one of the most significant figures in our rhetorical history.

"Against the Sophists"

If all who are engaged in the profession of education were willing to state the facts instead of making greater promises than they can possibly fulfil, they would not be in such bad repute with the lay-public. As it is, however, the teachers who do no scruple to vaunt their powers with utter disregard of the truth have created the impression that those who choose a life of careless indolence are better advised than those who devote themselves to serious study.

Indeed, who can fail to abhor, yes to contemn, those teachers, in the first place, who devote themselves to disputation, since they pretend to search for truth, but straightway at the beginning of their professions attempt to deceive us with lies? For I think it is manifest to all that foreknowledge of future events is not vouchsafed to our human nature, but that we are so far removed from this prescience that Homer, who has been conceded the highest reputation for wisdom, has pictured even the gods as at times debating among themselves about the future—not that he knew their minds but that he desired to show us that for mankind this power lies in the realms of the impossible.

But these professors have gone so far in their lack of scruple that they attempt to persuade our young men that if they will only study under them they will know what to do in life and through this knowledge will become happy and prosperous. More than that, although they set themselves up as masters and dispensers of goods so precious, they are not ashamed of asking for them a price of three or four minae! Why, if they were to sell any other commodity for so trifling a fraction of its worth they would not deny their folly; nevertheless, although they set so insignificant a price on the whole stock of virtue and happiness, they pretend to wisdom and assume the right to instruct the rest of the world. Furthermore, although they say that they do not want money and speak contemptuously of wealth as "filthy lucre," they hold their hands out for a trifling gain and promise to make their disciples all but immortal! But what is most ridiculous of all is that they distrust those from whom they are to get this money—they distrust, that is to say, the very men to whom they are about to deliver the science of just dealing—and require that the fees advanced by their students be entrusted for safe keeping to those who have never been under their instruction, being well advised as to their security, but doing the opposite of what they preach. For it is permissible to those who give any other instruction to be exacting in matters open to dispute, since nothing prevents those who have been made adept in other lines of training from being dishonourable in the matter of contracts. But men who inculcate virtue and sobriety—is it not absurd if they do not trust in their own students before all others? For it is not to be supposed that men who are honourable and just-dealing with others will be dishonest with the very preceptors who have made them what they are.

When, therefore, the layman puts all these things together and observes that the teachers of wisdom and dispensers of happiness are themselves in great want but exact only a small fee from their students, that they are on the watch for contradictions in words but are blind to inconsistencies in deeds, and that, furthermore, they pretend to have knowledge of the future but are incapable either of saying anything pertinent or of giving any counsel regarding the present, and when he observes that those who follow their judgements are more consistent and more successful than those who profess to have exact knowledge, then he has, I think, good reason to contemn such studies and regard them as stuff and nonsense, and not as a true discipline of the soul.

But it is not these sophists alone who are open to criticism, but also those who profess to teach political discourse. For the latter have no interest whatever in the truth, but consider that they are masters of an art if they can attract great numbers of students by the smallness of their charges and the magnitude of their professions and get something out of them. For they are themselves so stupid and conceive others to be so dull that, although the speeches which they compose are worse than those which some laymen improvise, nevertheless they promise to make their students such clever orators that they will not overlook any of the possibilities which a subject affords. More than that, they do not attribute any of this power either to the practical experience or to the native ability of the student, but undertake to transmit the science of discourse as simply as they would teach the letters of the alphabet, not having taken trouble to examine into the nature of each kind of knowledge, but thinking that because of the extravagance of their promises they themselves will command admiration and the teaching of discourse will be held in higher esteem—oblivious of the fact that the arts are made great, not by those who are without scruple in boasting about them, but by those who are able to discover all of the resources which each art affords.

For myself, I should have preferred above great riches that philosophy had as much power as these men claim; for, possibly, I should not have been the very last in the profession nor had the least share, in its profits. But since it has no such power, I could wish that this prating might cease. For I note that the bad repute which results therefrom does not affect the offenders only, but that all the rest of us who are in the same profession share in the opprobium [sic].

But I marvel when I observe these men setting themselves up as instructors of youth who cannot see that they are applying the analogy of an art with hard and fast rules to a creative process. For, excepting these teachers, who does not know that the art of using letters remains fixed and unchanged, so that we continually and invariably use the same letters for the same purposes, while exactly the reverse is true of the art of discourse? For what has been said by one speaker is not equally useful for the speaker for the speaker who comes after him; on the contrary, he is accounted most skilled in this art who speaks in a manner worthy of his subject and yet is able to discover in its topics which are nowise the same as those used by others. But the greatest proof of the difference between these two arts is that oratory is good only if it has the qualities of originality of treatment, while in the case of letters there is no such need whatsoever. So that those who make use of such analogies ought more justly to pay out than to accept fees, since they attempt to teach others when they are themselves in great need of instruction.

However, if it is my duty not only to rebuke others, but also to set forth my own values, I think all intelligent people will agree with me that while many of those who have pursued philosophy have remained in private life, others, on the other hand, who have never taken lessons from any one of the sophists have become able orators and statesmen. For ability, whether in speech or in any other activity, is found in those who are well endowed by nature and have been schooled by practical experience. Formal training makes such men more skilful and more resourceful in discovering the possibilities of a subject; for it teaches them to take from a readier source the topics which they otherwise hit upon in haphazard fashion. But it cannot fully fashion men who are without natural aptitude into good debaters or writers, although it is capable of leading them on to self-improvement and to a greater degree of intelligence on many subjects.

But I desire, now that I have gone this far, to speak more clearly on these matters. For I hold that to obtain a knowledge of the elements out of which we make and compose all discourses is not so very difficult if anyone entrusts himself, not to those who make rash promises, but to those who have some knowledge of these things. But to choose from these elements those which should be employed for each subject, to join them together, to arrange them properly, and also, not to miss what the occasion demands but appropriately to adorn the whole speech with striking thoughts and to clothe it in flowing and melodious phrase—these things, I hold, require much study and are the task of a vigorous and imaginative mind: for this, the student must not only have the requisite aptitude but he must learn the different kinds of discourse and practice himself in their use; and the teacher, for his part, must so expound the principles of the art with the utmost possible exactness as to leave out nothing that can be taught, and, for the rest, he must in himself set such an example of oratory that the students who have taken form under his instruction and are able to pattern after him will, from the outset, show in their speaking a degree of grace and charm which is not found in others. When all of these requisites are found together, then the devotees of philosophy will achieve complete success; but according as any one of the things which I have mentioned is lacking, to this extent must their disciples of necessity fall below the mark.

Now as for the sophists who have lately sprung up and have very recently embraced these pretensions, even though they flourish at the moment, they will all, I am sure, come round to this position. But there remain to be considered those who lived before our time and did not scruple to write the so-called arts of oratory. These must not be dismissed without rebuke, since they professed to teach how to conduct law-suits, picking out the most discredited of terms, which the enemies, not the champions, of this discipline might have been expected to employ—and that too although this facility, in so far as it can be taught, is of no greater aid to forensic than to all other discourse. But they were much worse than those who dabble in disputation; for although the latter expounded such captious theories that were anyone to cleave to them in practice he would at once be in all manner of trouble, they did, at any rate, make professions of virtue and sobriety in their teaching, whereas the former, although exhorting others to study political discourse, neglected all the good things which this study affords, and became nothing more than professors of meddlesomeness and greed.

And yet those who desire to follow the true precepts of this discipline may, if they will, be helped more speedily towards honesty of character than towards facility of oratory. And let no one suppose that I claim that just living can be taught; for, in a word, I hold that there does not exist an art of the kind which can implant sobriety and justice in depraved natures. Nevertheless, I do think that the study of political discourse can help more than any other thing to stimulate and form such qualities of character.

But in order that I may not appear to be breaking down the pretensions of others while myself making greater claims than are within my powers, I believe that the very arguments by which I myself was convinced will make it clear to others also that these things are true.

Reprinted by permission of the publishers and the Trustees of the Loeb Classical Library from *Isocrates: On the Peace, Areopagiticus, Against the Sophists, Antidosis, Panathenaicus*, Loeb Classical Library, translated by George Norlin, pp. 163–177, Cambridge, MA: Harvard University Press, Copyright 1929, by the President and Fellows of Harvard College. Loeb Classical Library® is a registered trademark of the President and Fellows of Harvard College.

Chapter 2

Plato

Plato (424–348 BCE) was a key political theorist of his time; he is often credited for laying the foundation for our understanding of democracy. Given his interest in politics, it isn't surprising that he also valued the important contribution of rhetoric for the political leaders of Ancient Greece. As a student of Socrates, Plato was highly influenced by the so-called Socratic method (the back-and-forth exchange of opposing ideas to foster critical thinking and philosophical inquiry). He uses this method in the "Gorgias" to map out a debate on the nature of rhetoric between Socrates and Gorgias, a Sophist rhetorician. As such, rhetoric is defined as persuasion that occurs in discourse and defended by Gorgias from the probing questions of Socrates.

The "Gorgias" also speaks to the nature of rhetoric, the moral basis for rhetoric as Truth, and the value of rhetoric in the political context. In these ways, Plato is distinguishing his views of rhetoric from the Sophistic perspective of rhetoric as manipulation. This in itself secures the "Gorgias" as a crucial text for our study of rhetoric. During the debate, we learn that rhetoric can be seen as different than dialectic (formal logic); rhetoric is based on experience and is, as such, a form of art; rhetoric can be combined with knowledge of any other subject; rhetoric can be abused, but should be taught for virtuous purposes; and a rhetorician must consider his/her audience. Another important concept that emerges from this work is *kairos*, which essentially is when an opportune moment occurs so that a rhetor can seize the moment to his or her advantage. When Gorgias refers to using persuasion to speak on any subject, he is suggesting that a skillful rhetor can be persuasive on a topic at a moment's notice. The concept of *kairos* is important for us today partly because it became the premise behind the twentieth century concept of the "rhetorical situation," the idea that a specific context is either established or exploited by an effective rhetor (Bitzer, 1968).

"Gorgias"

CALLICLES: The wise man, as the proverb says, is late for a fray, but not for a feast.

SOCRATES: And are we late for a feast?

CALLICLES: Yes, and a delightful feast; for Gorgias has just been exhibiting to us many fine things.

SOCRATES: It is not my fault, Callicles; our friend Chaerephon is to blame; for he would keep us loitering in the Agora.

CHAEREPHON: Never mind, Socrates; the misfortune of which I have been the cause I will also repair; for Gorgias is a friend of mine, and I will make him give the exhibition again either now, or, if you prefer, at some other time.

CALLICLES: What is the matter, Chaerephon—does Socrates want to hear Gorgias?

CHAEREPHON: Yes, that was our intention in coming.

CALLICLES: Come into my house, then; for Gorgias is staying with me, and he shall exhibit to you.

SOCRATES: Very good, Callicles; but will he answer our questions? For I want to hear from him what is the nature of his art, and what it is which he professes and teaches; he may, as you [Chaerephon] suggest, defer the exhibition to some other time.

CALLICLES: There is nothing like asking him, Socrates; and indeed to answer questions is a part of his exhibition, for he was saying only just now, that any one in my house might put any question to him, and that he would answer.

SOCRATES: How fortunate! Will you ask him, Chaerephon—?

CHAEREPHON: What shall I ask him?

SOCRATES: Ask him who he is.

CHAEREPHON: What do you mean?

SOCRATES: I mean such a question as would elicit from him, if he had been a maker of shoes, the answer that he is a cobbler. Do you understand?

CHAEREPHON: I understand, and will ask him: Tell me, Gorgias, is our friend Callicles right in saying that you undertake to answer any questions which you are asked?

GORGIAS: Quite right, Chaerephon: I was saying as much only just now; and I may add, that many years have elapsed since any one has asked me a new one.

CHAEREPHON: Then you must be very ready, Gorgias.

GORGIAS: Of that, Chaerephon, you can make trial.

POLUS: Yes, indeed, and if you like, Chaerephon, you may make trial of me too, for I think that Gorgias, who has been talking a long time, is tired.

CHAEREPHON: And do you, Polus, think that you can answer better than Gorgias?

POLUS: What does that matter if I answer well enough for you?

CHAEREPHON: Not at all:—and you shall answer if you like.

POLUS: Ask:—

CHAEREPHON: My question is this: If Gorgias had the skill of his brother Herodicus, what ought we to call him? Ought he not to have the name which is given to his brother?

POLUS: Certainly.

CHAEREPHON: Then we should be right in calling him a physician?

POLUS: Yes.

CHAEREPHON: And if he had the skill of Aristophon the son of Aglaophon, or of his brother Polygnotus, what ought we to call him?

POLUS: Clearly, a painter.

CHAEREPHON: But now what shall we call him—what is the art in which he is skilled?

POLUS: O Chaerephon, there are many arts among mankind which are experimental, and have their origin in experience, for experience makes the days of men to proceed according to art, and inexperience according to chance, and different persons in different ways are proficient in different arts, and the best persons in the best arts. And our friend Gorgias is one of the best, and the art in which he is a proficient is the noblest.

SOCRATES: Polus has been taught how to make a capital speech, Gorgias; but he is not fulfilling the promise which he made to Chaerephon.

GORGIAS: What do you mean, Socrates?

SOCRATES: I mean that he has not exactly answered the question which he was asked.

GORGIAS: Then why not ask him yourself?

SOCRATES: But I would much rather ask you, if you are disposed to answer: for I see, from the few words which Polus has uttered, that he has attended more to the art which is called rhetoric than to dialectic.

POLUS: What makes you say so, Socrates?

SOCRATES: Because, Polus, when Chaerephon asked you what was the art which Gorgias knows, you praised it as if you were answering someone who found fault with it, but you never said what the art was.

POLUS: Why, did I not say that it was the noblest of arts?

SOCRATES: Yes, indeed, but that was no answer to the question: nobody asked what was the quality, but what was the nature, of the art, and by what name we were to describe Gorgias. And I would still beg you briefly and clearly, as you answered Chaerephon when he asked you at first, to say what this art is, and what we ought to call Gorgias: Or rather, Gorgias, let me turn to you, and ask the same question,—what are we to call you, and what is the art which you profess?

GORGIAS: Rhetoric, Socrates, is my art.

SOCRATES: Then I am to call you a rhetorician?

GORGIAS: Yes, Socrates, and a good one too, if you would call me that which, in Homeric language, 'I boast myself to be.'

SOCRATES: I should wish to do so.

GORGIAS: Then pray do.

SOCRATES: And are we to say that you are able to make other men rhetoricians?

GORGIAS: Yes, that is exactly what I profess to make them, not only at Athens, but in all places.

SOCRATES: And will you continue to ask and answer questions, Gorgias, as we are at present doing, and reserve for another occasion the longer mode of speech which Polus was attempting? Will you keep your promise, and answer shortly the questions which are asked of you?

GORGIAS: Some answers, Socrates, are of necessity longer; but I will do my best to make them as short as possible; for a part of my profession is that I can be as short as any one.

SOCRATES: That is what is wanted, Gorgias; exhibit the shorter method now, and the longer one at some other time.

GORGIAS: Well, I will; and you will certainly say, that you never heard a man use fewer words.

SOCRATES: Very good then; as you profess to be a rhetorician, and a maker of rhetoricians, let me ask you, with what is rhetoric concerned: I might ask with what is weaving concerned, and you would reply (would you not?), with the making of garments?

GORGIAS: Yes.

SOCRATES: And music is concerned with the composition of melodies?

GORGIAS: It is.

SOCRATES: By Here, Gorgias, I admire the surpassing brevity of your answers.

GORGIAS: Yes, Socrates, I do think myself good at that.

SOCRATES: I am glad to hear it; answer me in like manner about rhetoric: with what is rhetoric concerned?

GORGIAS: With discourse.

SOCRATES: What sort of discourse, Gorgias?—such discourse as would teach the sick under what treatment they might get well?

GORGIAS: No.

SOCRATES: Then rhetoric does not treat of all kinds of discourse?

GORGIAS: Certainly not.

SOCRATES: And yet rhetoric makes men able to speak?

GORGIAS: Yes.

SOCRATES: And to understand that about which they speak?

GORGIAS: Of course.

SOCRATES: But does not the art of medicine, which we were just now mentioning, also make men able to understand and speak about the sick?

GORGIAS: Certainly.

SOCRATES: Then medicine also treats of discourse?

GORGIAS: Yes.

SOCRATES: Of discourse concerning diseases?

GORGIAS: Just so.

SOCRATES: And does not gymnastic also treat of discourse concerning the good or evil condition of the body?

GORGIAS: Very true.

SOCRATES: And the same, Gorgias, is true of the other arts:—all of them treat of discourse concerning the subjects with which they severally have to do.

GORGIAS: Clearly.

SOCRATES: Then why, if you call rhetoric the art which treats of discourse, and all the other arts treat of discourse, do you not call them arts of rhetoric?

GORGIAS: Because, Socrates, the knowledge of the other arts has only to do with some sort of external action, as of the hand; but there is no such action of the hand in rhetoric which works and takes effect only through the medium of discourse. And therefore I am justified in saying that rhetoric treats of discourse.

SOCRATES: I am not sure whether I entirely understand you, but I dare say I shall soon know better; please do answer me a question:—you would allow that there are arts?

GORGIAS: Yes.

SOCRATES: As to the arts generally, they are for the most part concerned with doing, and require little or no speaking; in painting, and statuary, and many other arts, the work may proceed in silence; and of such arts I suppose you would say that they do not come within the province of rhetoric.

GORGIAS: You perfectly conceive my meaning, Socrates.

SOCRATES: But there are other arts which work wholly through the medium of language, and require either no action or very little, as, for example, the arts of arithmetic, of calculation, of geometry, and of play-ing draughts; in some of these speech is pretty nearly co-extensive with action, but in most of them the verbal element is greater—they depend wholly on words for their efficacy and power: and I take your meaning to be that rhetoric is an art of this latter sort?

GORGIAS: Exactly.

SOCRATES: And yet I do not believe that you really mean to call any of these arts rhetoric; although the precise expression which you used was, that rhetoric is an art which works and takes effect only through the medium of discourse; and an adversary who wished to be captious might say, 'And so, Gorgias, you call arithmetic rhetoric.' But I do not think that you really call arithmetic rhetoric any more than geometry would be so called by you.

GORGIAS: You are quite right, Socrates, in your apprehension of my meaning.

SOCRATES: Well, then, let me now have the rest of my answer:—seeing that rhetoric is one of those arts which works mainly by the use of words, and there are other arts which also use words, tell me what is that quality in words with which rhetoric is concerned:—Suppose that a person asks me about some of the arts which I was mentioning just now; he might say, 'Socrates, what is arithmetic?' and I should reply to him, as you replied to me, that arithmetic is one of those arts which take effect through words. And then he would proceed to ask: 'Words about what?' and I should reply, Words about odd and even numbers, and how many there are of each. And if he asked again: 'What is the art of calculation?' I should say, That also is one of the arts which is concerned wholly with words. And if he further said, 'Concerned with what?' I should say, like the clerks in the assembly, 'as aforesaid' of arithmetic, but with a difference, the difference being that the art of calculation considers not only the quantities of odd and even numbers, but also their numerical relations to themselves and to one another. And suppose, again, I were to say that astronomy is only words—he would ask, 'Words about what, Socrates?' and I should answer, that astronomy tells us about the motions of the stars and sun and moon, and their relative swiftness.

GORGIAS: You would be quite right, Socrates:

SOCRATES: And now let us have from you, Gorgias, the truth about rhetoric: which you would admit (would you not?) to be one of those arts which act always and fulfil all their ends through the medium of words?

GORGIAS: True.

SOCRATES: Words which do what? I should ask. To what class of things do the words which rhetoric uses relate?

GORGIAS: To the greatest, Socrates, and the best of human things.

SOCRATES: That again, Gorgias, is ambiguous; I am still in the dark: for which are the greatest and best of human things? I dare say that you have heard men singing at feasts the old drinking song, in which the singers enumerate the goods of life, first health, beauty next, thirdly, as the writer of the song says, wealth honestly obtained.

GORGIAS: Yes, I know the song; but what is your drift?

SOCRATES: I mean to say, that the producers of those things which the author of the song praises, that is to say, the physician, the trainer, the money-maker, will at once come to you, and first the physician will say: 'O Socrates, Gorgias is deceiving you, for my art is concerned with the greatest good of men and not his.' And when I ask, Who are you? He will reply, 'I am a physician.' What do you mean? I shall say. Do you mean that your art produces the greatest good? 'Certainly,' he will answer, 'for is not health the greatest good? What greater good can men have, Socrates?' And after him the trainer will come and say, 'I too, Socrates, shall be greatly surprised if Gorgias can show more good of his art than I can show of mine.' To him again I shall say, Who are you, honest friend, and what is your business? 'I am a trainer,' he will reply, 'and my business is to make men beautiful and strong in body.' When I have done with the trainer, there arrives the money-maker, and he, as I expect, will utterly despise them all. 'Consider, Socrates,' he will say, 'whether Gorgias or anyone else can produce any greater good than wealth.' Well, you and I say to him, and are you a creator of wealth? 'Yes,' he replies. And who are you? 'A money-maker.' And do you consider wealth to be the greatest good of man? 'Of course,' will be his reply. And we shall rejoin: Yes; but our friend Gorgias contends that his art produces a greater good than yours. And then he will be sure to go on and ask, 'What good? Let Gorgias answer.' Now I want you, Gorgias, to imagine that this question is asked of you by them and by me; What is that which, as you say, is the greatest good of man, and of which you are the creator? Answer us.

GORGIAS: That good, Socrates, which is truly the greatest, being that which gives to men freedom in their own persons, and to individuals the power of ruling over others in their several states.

SOCRATES: And what would you consider this to be?

GORGIAS: What is there greater than the word which persuades the judges in the courts, or the senators in the council, or the citizens in the assembly, or at any other political meeting?—if you have the power of uttering this word, you will have the physician your slave, and the trainer your slave, and the money-maker of whom you talk will be found to gather treasures, not for himself, but for you who are able to speak and to persuade the multitude.

SOCRATES: Now I think, Gorgias, that you have very accurately explained what you conceive to be the art of rhetoric; and you mean to say, if I am not mistaken, that rhetoric is the artificer of persuasion, having this and no other business, and that this is her crown and end. Do you know any other effect of rhetoric over and above that of producing persuasion?

GORGIAS: No: the definition seems to me very fair, Socrates; for persuasion is the chief end of rhetoric.

SOCRATES: Then hear me, Gorgias, for I am quite sure that if there ever was a man who entered on the discussion of a matter from a pure love of knowing the truth, I am such a one, and I should say the same of you.

GORGIAS: What is coming, Socrates?

SOCRATES: I will tell you: I am very well aware that I do not know what, according to you, is the exact nature, or what are the topics of that persuasion of which you speak, and which is given by rhetoric; although I have a suspicion about both the one and the other. And I am going to ask—what is this power of persuasion which is given by rhetoric, and about what? But why, if I have a suspicion, do I ask instead of telling you? Not for your sake, but in order that the argument may proceed in such a manner as is most likely to set forth the truth. And I would have you observe, that I am right in asking this further question: If I asked, 'What sort of a painter is Zeuxis?' and you said, 'The painter of figures,' should I not be right in asking, 'What kind of figures, and where do you find them?'

GORGIAS: Certainly.

SOCRATES: And the reason for asking this second question would be, that there are other painters besides, who paint many other figures?

GORGIAS: True.

SOCRATES: But if there had been no one but Zeuxis who painted them, then you would have answered very well?

GORGIAS: Quite so.

SOCRATES: Now I want to know about rhetoric in the same way;—is rhetoric the only art which brings persuasion, or do other arts have the same effect? I mean to say—Does he who teaches anything persuade men of that which he teaches or not?

GORGIAS: He persuades, Socrates,—there can be no mistake about that.

SOCRATES: Again, if we take the arts of which we were just now speaking:—do not arithmetic and the arithmeticians teach us the properties of number?

GORGIAS: Certainly.

SOCRATES: And therefore persuade us of them?

GORGIAS: Yes.

SOCRATES: Then arithmetic as well as rhetoric is an artificer of persuasion?

GORGIAS: Clearly.

SOCRATES: And if anyone asks us what sort of persuasion, and about what,—we shall answer, persuasion which teaches the quantity of odd and even; and we shall be able to show that all the other arts of which we were just now speaking are artificers of persuasion, and of what sort, and about what.

GORGIAS: Very true.

SOCRATES: Then rhetoric is not the only artificer of persuasion?

GORGIAS: True.

SOCRATES: Seeing, then, that not only rhetoric works by persuasion, but that other arts do the same, as in the case of the painter, a question has arisen which is a very fair one: Of what persuasion is rhetoric the artificer, and about what?—is not that a fair way of putting the question?

GORGIAS: I think so.

SOCRATES: Then, if you approve the question, Gorgias, what is the answer?

GORGIAS: I answer, Socrates, that rhetoric is the art of persuasion in courts of law and other assemblies, as I was just now saying, and about the just and unjust.

SOCRATES: And that, Gorgias, was what I was suspecting to be your notion; yet I would not have you wonder if by-and-by I am found repeating a seemingly plain question; for I ask not in order to confute you, but as I was saying that the argument may proceed consecutively, and that we may not get the habit of anticipating and suspecting the meaning of one another's words; I would have you develop your own views in your own way, whatever may be your hypothesis.

GORGIAS: I think that you are quite right, Socrates:

SOCRATES: Then let me raise another question; there is such a thing as 'having learned'?

GORGIAS: Yes.

SOCRATES: And there is also 'having believed'?

GORGIAS: Yes.

SOCRATES: And is the 'having learned' the same as 'having believed,' and are learning and belief the same things?

GORGIAS: In my judgment, Socrates, they are not the same.

SOCRATES: And your judgment is right, as you may ascertain in this way:— If a person were to say to you, 'Is there, Gorgias, a false belief as well as a true?'—you would reply, if I am not mistaken, that there is.

GORGIAS: Yes.

SOCRATES: Well, but is there a false knowledge as well as a true?

GORGIAS: No.

SOCRATES: No, indeed; and this again proves that knowledge and belief differ.

GORGIAS: Very true.

SOCRATES: And yet those who have learned as well as those who have believed are persuaded?

GORGIAS: Just so.

SOCRATES: Shall we then assume two sorts of persuasion,—one which is the source of belief without knowledge, as the other is of knowledge?

GORGIAS: By all means.

SOCRATES: And which sort of persuasion does rhetoric create in courts of law and other assemblies about the just and unjust, the sort of persuasion which gives belief without knowledge, or that which gives knowledge?

GORGIAS: Clearly, Socrates, that which only gives belief.

SOCRATES: Then rhetoric, as would appear, is the artificer of a persuasion which creates belief about the just and unjust, but gives no instruction about them?

GORGIAS: True.

SOCRATES: And the rhetorician does not instruct the courts of law or other assemblies about things just and unjust, but he creates belief about them; for no one can be supposed to instruct such a vast multitude about such high matters in a short time?

GORGIAS: Certainly not.

SOCRATES: Come, then, and let us see what we really mean about rhetoric; for I do not know what my own meaning is as yet. When the assembly meets to elect a physician or a shipwright or any other craftsman, will the rhetorician be taken into counsel? Surely not. For at every election he ought to be chosen who is most skilled; and, again, when walls have to be built or harbours or docks to be constructed, not the rhetorician but the master workman will advise; or when generals have to be chosen and an order of battle arranged, or a position taken, then the military will advise and not the rhetoricians: what do you say, Gorgias? Since you profess to be a rhetorician and a maker of rhetoricians, I cannot do better than learn the nature of your art from you. And here let me assure you that I have your interest in view as well as my own. For likely enough someone or other of the young men present might desire to become your pupil, and in fact I see some, and a good many too, who have this wish, but they would be too modest to question you. And therefore when you are interrogated by me, I would have you imagine that you are interrogated by them. 'What is the use of coming to you, Gorgias?' they will say—'about what will you teach us to advise the state?—about the just and unjust only, or about those other things also which Socrates has just mentioned?' How will you answer them?

GORGIAS: I like your way of leading us on, Socrates, and I will endeavour to reveal to you the whole nature of rhetoric. You must have heard, I think, that the docks and the walls of the Athenians and the plan of the harbour were devised in accordance with the counsels, partly of Themistocles, and partly of Pericles, and not at the suggestion of the builders.

SOCRATES: Such is the tradition, Gorgias, about Themistocles; and I myself heard the speech of Pericles when he advised us about the middle wall.

GORGIAS: And you will observe, Socrates, that when a decision has to be given in such matters the rhetoricians are the advisers; they are the men who win their point.

SOCRATES: I had that in my admiring mind, Gorgias, when I asked what is the nature of rhetoric, which always appears to me, when I look at the matter in this way, to be a marvel of greatness.

GORGIAS: A marvel, indeed, Socrates, if you only knew how rhetoric comprehends and holds under her sway all the inferior arts. Let me offer you a striking example of this. On several occasions I have been with my brother Herodicus or some other physician to see one of his patients, who would not allow the physician to give him medicine, or apply the knife or hot iron to him; and I have persuaded him to do for me what he would not do for the physician just by the use of rhetoric. And I say that if a rhetorician and a physician were to go to any city, and had there to argue in the Ecclesia or any other assembly as to which of them should be elected state-physician, the physician would have no chance; but he who could speak would be chosen if he wished; and in a contest with a man of any other profession the rhetorician more than anyone would have the power of getting himself chosen, for he can speak more persuasively to the multitude than any of them, and on any subject. Such is the nature and power of the art of rhetoric! And yet, Socrates, rhetoric should be used like any other competitive art, not against everybody,—the rhetorician ought not to abuse his strength any more than a pugilist or pancratiast or other master of fence;—because he has powers which are more than a match either for friend or enemy, he ought not therefore to strike, stab, or slay his friends. Suppose a man to have been trained in the palestra and to be a skilful boxer,—he in the fulness of his strength goes and strikes his father or mother or one of his familiars or friends; but that is no reason why the trainers or fencing-masters should be held in detestation or banished from the city;—surely not. For they taught their art for a good purpose, to be used against enemies and evil-doers, in self-defence not in aggression, and others have perverted their instructions, and turned to a bad use their own strength and skill. But not on this account are the teachers bad, neither is the art in fault, or bad in itself; I should rather say that those who make a bad use of the art are to blame. And the same argument holds good of rhetoric; for the rhetorician can speak against all men and upon any subject,—in short, he can persuade the multitude better than any other man of anything which he pleases, but he should not therefore seek to defraud the physician or any other artist of his reputation merely because he has the power; he ought to use rhetoric fairly, as he would also use his athletic powers. And if after having become a rhetorician he makes a bad use of his strength and skill, his instructor surely ought not on that account to be held in detestation or banished. For he was intended by his teacher to make a good use of his instructions, but he abuses them. And therefore he is the person who ought to be held in detestation, banished, and put to death, and not his instructor.

SOCRATES: You, Gorgias, like myself, have had great experience of disputations, and you must have observed, I think, that they do not always terminate in mutual edification, or in the definition by either party of the subjects which they are discussing; but disagreements are apt to arise— somebody says that another has not spoken truly or clearly; and then they get into a passion and begin to quarrel, both parties conceiving that their opponents are arguing from personal feeling only and jealousy of themselves, not from any interest in the question at issue. And sometimes they will go on abusing one another until the company at last are quite vexed at themselves for ever listening to such fellows. Why do I say this? Why, because I cannot help feeling that you are now saying what is not quite consistent or accordant with what you were saying at first about rhetoric. And I am afraid to point this out to you, lest you should think that I have some animosity against you, and that I speak, not for the sake of discovering the truth, but from jealousy of you. Now if you are one of my sort, I should like to cross-examine you, but if not I will let you alone. And what is my sort? You will ask. I am one of those who are very willing to be refuted if I say anything which is not true, and very willing to refute anyone else who says what is not true, and quite as ready to be refuted as to refute; for I hold that this is the greater gain of the two, just as the gain is greater of being cured of a very great evil than of curing another. For I imagine that there is no evil which a man can endure so great as an erroneous opinion about the matters of which we are speaking; and if you claim to be one of my sort, let us have the discussion out, but if you would rather have done, no matter;—let us make an end of it.

GORGIAS: I should say, Socrates, that I am quite the man whom you indicate; but, perhaps, we ought to consider the audience, for, before you came, I had already given a long exhibition, and if we proceed the argument may run on to a great length. And therefore I think that we should consider whether we may not be detaining some part of the company when they are wanting to do something else.

CHAEREPHON: You hear the audience cheering, Gorgias and Socrates, which shows their desire to listen to you; and for myself, heaven forbid that I should have any business on hand which would take me away from a discussion so interesting and so ably maintained.

CALLICLES: By the gods, Chaerephon, although I have been present at many discussions, I doubt whether I was ever so much delighted before, and therefore if you go on discoursing all day I shall be the better pleased.

SOCRATES: I may truly say, Callicles, that I am willing, if Gorgias is.

GORGIAS: After all this, Socrates, I should be disgraced if I refused, especially as I have promised to answer all comers; in accordance with the wishes of the company, then, do you begin, and ask of me any question which you like.

SOCRATES: Let me tell you then, Gorgias, what surprises me in your words; though I dare say that you may be right, and I may have misunderstood your meaning. You say that you can make any man, who will learn of you, a rhetorician?

GORGIAS: Yes.

SOCRATES: Do you mean that you will teach him to gain the ears of the multitude on any subject, and this not by instruction but by persuasion?

GORGIAS: Quite so.

SOCRATES: You were saying, in fact, that the rhetorician will have greater powers of persuasion than the physician even in a matter of health?

GORGIAS: Yes, with the multitude,—that is.

SOCRATES: You mean to say, with the ignorant; for with those who know he cannot be supposed to have greater powers of persuasion.

GORGIAS: Very true.

SOCRATES: But if he is to have more power of persuasion than the physician, he will have greater power than he who knows?

GORGIAS: Certainly.

SOCRATES: Although he is not a physician:—is he?

GORGIAS: No.

SOCRATES: And he who is not a physician must, obviously, be ignorant of what the physician knows.

GORGIAS: Clearly.

SOCRATES: Then, when the rhetorician is more persuasive than the physician, the ignorant is more persuasive with the ignorant than he who has knowledge?—is not that the inference?

GORGIAS: In the case supposed:—yes.

SOCRATES: And the same holds of the relation of rhetoric to all the other arts; the rhetorician need not know the truth about things; he has only to discover some way of persuading the ignorant that he has more knowledge than those who know?

GORGIAS: Yes, Socrates, and is not this a great comfort?—not to have learned the other arts, but the art of rhetoric only, and yet to be in no way inferior to the professors of them?

SOCRATES: Whether the rhetorician is or is not inferior on this account is a question which we will hereafter examine if the enquiry is likely to be of any service to us; but I would rather begin by asking, whether he is or is not as ignorant of the just and unjust, base and honourable, good and evil, as he is of medicine and the other arts; I mean to say, does he really know anything of what is good and evil, base or honourable, just or unjust in them; or has he only a way with the ignorant of persuading them that he not knowing is to be esteemed to know more about these things than someone else who knows? Or must the pupil know these things and come to you knowing them before he can acquire the art of rhetoric? If he is ignorant, you who are the teacher of rhetoric will not teach him—it is not your business; but you will make him seem to the multitude to know them, when he does not know them; and seem to be a good man, when he is not. Or will you be unable to teach him rhetoric at all, unless he knows the truth of these things first? What is to be said about all this? By heaven, Gorgias, I wish that you would reveal to me the power of rhetoric, as you were saying that you would.

GORGIAS: Well, Socrates, I suppose that if the pupil does chance not to know them, he will have to learn of me these things as well.

SOCRATES: Say no more, for there you are right; and so he whom you make a rhetorician must either know the nature of the just and unjust already, or he must be taught by you.

GORGIAS: Certainly.

SOCRATES: Well, and is not he who has learned carpentering a carpenter?

GORGIAS: Yes.

SOCRATES: And he who has learned music a musician?

GORGIAS: Yes.

SOCRATES: And he who has learned medicine is a physician, in like manner? He who has learned anything whatever is that which his knowledge makes him.

GORGIAS: Certainly.

SOCRATES: And in the same way, he who has learned what is just is just?

GORGIAS: To be sure.

SOCRATES: And he who is just may be supposed to do what is just?

GORGIAS: Yes.

SOCRATES: And must not the just man always desire to do what is just?

GORGIAS: That is clearly the inference.

SOCRATES: Surely, then, the just man will never consent to do injustice?

GORGIAS: Certainly not.

SOCRATES: And according to the argument the rhetorician must be a just man?

GORGIAS: Yes.

SOCRATES: And will therefore never be willing to do injustice?

GORGIAS: Clearly not.

SOCRATES: But do you remember saying just now that the trainer is not to be accused or banished if the pugilist makes a wrong use of his pugilistic art; and in like manner, if the rhetorician makes a bad and unjust use of his rhetoric, that is not to be laid to the charge of his teacher, who is not to be banished, but the wrong-doer himself who made a bad use of his rhetoric—he is to be banished—was not that said?

GORGIAS: Yes, it was.

SOCRATES: But now we are affirming that the aforesaid rhetorician will never have done injustice at all?

GORGIAS: True.

SOCRATES: And at the very outset, Gorgias, it was said that rhetoric treated of discourse, not [like arithmetic] about odd and even, but about just and unjust? Was not this said?

GORGIAS: Yes.

SOCRATES: I was thinking at the time, when I heard you saying so, that rhetoric, which is always discoursing about justice, could not possibly be an unjust thing. But when you added, shortly afterwards, that the rhetorician might make a bad use of rhetoric I noted with surprise the inconsistency into which you had fallen; and I said, that if you thought, as I did, that there was a gain in being refuted, there would be an advantage in going on with the question, but if not, I would leave off. And in the course of our investigations, as you will see yourself, the rhetorician has been acknowledged to be incapable of making an unjust use of rhetoric or of willingness to do injustice. By the dog, Gorgias, there will be a great deal of discussion, before we get at the truth of all this.

POLUS: And do even you, Socrates, seriously believe what you are now saying about rhetoric? What! because Gorgias was ashamed to deny that the rhetorician knew the just and the honourable and the good, and admitted that to anyone who came to him ignorant of them he could teach them, and then out of this admission there arose a contradiction—the thing which you so dearly love, and to which not he, but you, brought the argument by your captious questions—[do you seriously believe that there is any truth in all this?] For will anyone ever acknowledge that he does not know, or cannot teach, the nature of justice? The truth is that there is great want of manners in bringing the argument to such a pass.

SOCRATES: Illustrious Polus, the reason why we provide ourselves with friends and children is, that when we get old and stumble, a younger generation may be at hand to set us on our legs again in our words and in our actions: and now, if I and Gorgias are stumbling, here are you who should raise us up; and I for my part engage to retract any error into which you may think that I have fallen—upon one condition:

POLUS: What condition?

SOCRATES: That you contract, Polus, the prolixity of speech in which you indulged at first.

POLUS: What! Do you mean that I may not use as many words as I please?

SOCRATES: Only to think, my friend, that having come on a visit to Athens, which is the most free-spoken state in Hellas, you when you got there, and you alone, should be deprived of the power of speech—that would be hard indeed. But then consider my case:—shall not I be very hardly used, if, when you are making a long oration, and refusing to answer what you are asked, I am compelled to stay and listen to you, and may not go away? I say rather, if you have a real interest in the argument, or, to repeat my former expression, have any desire to set it on its legs, take back any statement which you please; and in your turn ask and answer, like myself and Gorgias—refute and be refuted: for I suppose that you would claim to know what Gorgias knows—would you not?

POLUS: Yes.

SOCRATES: And you, like him, invite any one to ask you about anything which he pleases, and you will know how to answer him?

POLUS: To be sure.

SOCRATES: And now, which will you do, ask or answer?

POLUS: I will ask; and do you answer me, Socrates, the same question which Gorgias, as you suppose, is unable to answer: What is rhetoric?

SOCRATES: Do you mean what sort of an art?

POLUS: Yes.

SOCRATES: To say the truth, Polus, it is not an art at all, in my opinion.

POLUS: Then what, in your opinion, is rhetoric?

SOCRATES: A thing which, as I was lately reading in a book of yours, you say that you have made an art.

POLUS: What thing?

SOCRATES: I should say a sort of experience.

POLUS: Does rhetoric seem to you to be an experience?

SOCRATES: That is my view, but you may be of another mind.

POLUS: An experience in what?

SOCRATES: An experience in producing a sort of delight and gratification.

POLUS: And if able to gratify others, must not rhetoric be a fine thing?

SOCRATES: What are you saying, Polus? Why do you ask me whether rhetoric is a fine thing or not, when I have not as yet told you what rhetoric is?

POLUS: Did I not hear you say that rhetoric was a sort of experience?

SOCRATES: Will you, who are so desirous to gratify others, afford a slight gratification to me?

POLUS: I will.

SOCRATES: Will you ask me, what sort of an art is cookery?

POLUS: What sort of an art is cookery?

SOCRATES: Not an art at all, Polus.

POLUS: What then?

SOCRATES: I should say an experience.

POLUS: In what? I wish that you would explain to me.

SOCRATES: An experience in producing a sort of delight and gratification, Polus.

POLUS: Then are cookery and rhetoric the same?

SOCRATES: No, they are only different parts of the same profession.

POLUS: Of what profession?

SOCRATES: I am afraid that the truth may seem discourteous; and I hesitate to answer, lest Gorgias should imagine that I am making fun of his own profession. For whether or no this is that art of rhetoric which Gorgias practises I really cannot tell:—from what he was just now saying, nothing appeared of what he thought of his art, but the rhetoric which I mean is a part of a not very creditable whole.

GORGIAS: A part of what, Socrates? Say what you mean, and never mind me.

SOCRATES: In my opinion then, Gorgias, the whole of which rhetoric is a part is not an art at all, but the habit of a bold and ready wit, which knows how to manage mankind: this habit I sum up under the word 'flattery;' and it appears to me to have many other parts, one of which is cookery, which may seem to be an art, but, as I maintain, is only an experience or routine and not an art:—another part is rhetoric, and the art of attiring and sophistry are two others: thus there are four branches, and four different things answering to them. And Polus may ask, if he likes, for he has not as yet been informed, what part of flattery is rhetoric: he did not see that I had not yet answered him when he proceeded to ask a further question: Whether I do not think rhetoric a fine thing? But I shall not tell him whether rhetoric is a fine thing or not, until I have first answered, 'What is rhetoric?' For that would not be right, Polus; but I shall be happy to answer, if you will ask me, What part of flattery is rhetoric?

POLUS: I will ask, and do you answer? What part of flattery is rhetoric?

SOCRATES: Will you understand my answer? Rhetoric, according to my view, is the ghost or counterfeit of a part of politics.

POLUS: And noble or ignoble?

SOCRATES: Ignoble, I should say, if I am compelled to answer, for I call what is bad ignoble:—though I doubt whether you understand what I was saying before.

GORGIAS: Indeed, Socrates, I cannot say that I understand myself.

SOCRATES: I do not wonder, Gorgias; for I have not as yet explained myself, and our friend Polus, colt by name and colt by nature, is apt to run away.

GORGIAS: Never mind him, but explain to me what you mean by saying that rhetoric is the counterfeit of a part of politics.

SOCRATES: I will try, then, to explain my notion of rhetoric, and if I am mistaken, my friend Polus shall refute me. We may assume the existence of bodies and of souls?

GORGIAS: Of course.

SOCRATES: You would further admit that there is a good condition of either of them?

GORGIAS: Yes.

SOCRATES: Which condition may not be really good, but good only in appearance? I mean to say, that there are many persons who appear to be in good health, and whom only a physician or trainer will discern at first sight not to be in good health.

GORGIAS: True.

SOCRATES: And this applies not only to the body, but also to the soul: in either there may be that which gives the appearance of health and not the reality?

GORGIAS: Yes, certainly.

SOCRATES: And now I will endeavour to explain to you more clearly what I mean: The soul and body being two, have two arts corresponding to them: there is the art of politics attending on the soul; and another art attending on the body, of which I know no single name, but which may be described as having two divisions, one of them gymnastic, and the other medicine. And in politics there is a legislative part, which answers to gymnastic, as justice does to medicine; and the two parts run into one another, justice having to do with the same subject as legislation, and medicine with the same subject as gymnastic, but with a difference. Now, seeing that there are these four arts, two attending on the body and two on the soul for their highest good; flattery knowing, or rather guessing their natures, has distributed herself into four shams or simulations of them; she puts on the likeness of some one or other of them, and pretends to be that which she simulates, and having no regard for men's highest interests, is ever making pleasure the bait of the unwary, and deceiving them into the belief that she is of the highest value to them. Cookery simulates the disguise of medicine, and pretends to know what food is the best for the body; and if the physician and the cook had to enter into a competition in which children were the judges, or men who had no more sense than children, as to which of them best understands the goodness or badness of food, the physician would be starved to death. A flattery I deem this to be and of an ignoble sort, Polus, for to you I am now addressing myself, because it aims at pleasure without any thought of the best. An art I do not call it, but only an experience, because it is unable to explain or to give a reason of the nature of its own applications. And I do not call any irrational thing an art; but if you dispute my words, I am prepared to argue in defence of them.

Cookery, then, I maintain to be a flattery which takes the form of medicine; and tiring, in like manner, is a flattery which takes the form of gymnastic, and is knavish, false, ignoble, illiberal, working deceitfully by the help of lines, and colours, and enamels, and garments, and making men affect a spurious beauty to the neglect of the true beauty which is given by gymnastic.

I would rather not be tedious, and therefore I will only say, after the manner of the geometricians, (for I think that by this time you will be able to follow,)

as tiring : gymnastic : : cookery : medicine;

or rather,

as tiring : gymnastic : : sophistry : legislation;

and

as cookery : medicine : : rhetoric : justice.

And this, I say, is the natural difference between the rhetorician and the sophist, but by reason of their near connection, they are apt to be jumbled up together; neither do they know what to make of themselves, nor do other men know what to make of them. For if the body presided over itself, and were not under the guidance of the soul, and the soul did not discern and discriminate between cookery and medicine, but the body was made the judge of them, and the rule of judgment was the bodily delight which was given by them, then the word of Anaxagoras, that word with which you, friend Polus, are so well acquainted, would prevail far and wide: 'Chaos' would come again, and cookery, health, and medicine would mingle in an indiscriminate mass.

And now I have told you my notion of rhetoric, which is, in relation to the soul, what cookery is to the body. I may have been inconsistent in making a long speech, when I would not allow you to discourse at length. But I think that I may be excused, because you did not understand me, and could make no use of my answer when I spoke shortly, and therefore I had to enter into an explanation. And if I show an equal inability to make use of yours, I hope that you will speak at equal length; but if I am able to understand you, let me have the benefit of your brevity, as is only fair: And now you may do what you please with my answer.

Plato. "Gorgias." *The Dialogues of Plato.* 3rd ed. Translated by Ben Jowett. London: Oxford University Press, 1892, http://oll.libertyfund.org/index.php?option=com_staticxt&staticfile=show.php%3Ftitle=766&Itemid=27

Chapter 3

Aristotle

Aristotle (c. 384–322 BCE) is arguably the most important figure in the discipline of rhetoric. A student of Plato, he wrote extensively on philosophy, history, and what we would today consider to be the field of "literature," especially about poetry, tragedy, comedy, and the like. Most important for our purposes, Aristotle wrote the first complete treatise on the nature of rhetoric; more specifically, he described the techniques useful for improving the power of persuasion. We cannot include the entire treatise—it is a book in itself— but we include the key passages that support Aristotle's perspective on the nature of rhetoric: his definition of the term; the discussion of ethos, pathos, and logos; the main speeches where persuasion occurs; and the importance of considering the audience when developing persuasive messages.

In *The Art of Rhetoric*, a treatise that had a profound influence on rhetoric for the next 2,000 years, Aristotle concentrates on the nature of persuasion or, as he defines rhetoric: "the faculty of discovering the possible means of persuasion in reference to any subject whatever." The book is a discourse on how to compose effective persuasive speeches as well as techniques for judging and criticizing rhetorical messages.

Aristotle goes to great lengths to explain the key elements that constitute effective persuasion, namely reasoning (logos), appeals to emotion (pathos), and the speaker's credibility and integrity (ethos). These elements are important to speeches involving forensics (law), deliberation (policymaking), and what Aristotle calls "*epideictic*" occasions (ceremonial speeches). Like Gorgias, Aristotle discusses at length how an effective rhetor should be able to discuss any subject at a moment's notice. In fact, Aristotle provides a taxonomy of techniques, which he calls *topoi* (topics), that a speaker can use regardless of the subject. Although not included in this excerpt, *topoi* are extremely valuable for any student of rhetoric and became an important teaching tool used by later writers, who gave them different appellations such as "*loci*" and "common places."

In the selection provided here, we see another of Aristotle's invaluable contributions to our study of rhetoric—the enthymeme. An enthymeme is a truncated syllogism, which is a formal argument—taken from dialectic—comprising two premises and a conclusion. An enthymeme is missing either a premise or a conclusion, thus encouraging the audience to supply the missing piece of the argument. The enthymeme revolutionized the nuances of rhetoric as well as provided a vital tool for critics of rhetoric. For example, when we analyze rhetoric today, most persuasive discourse occurs in enthymematic forms, which often leads to fallacies, manipulation, and knee-jerk decisions unless analyzed carefully.

The Art of Rhetoric

[...]

1. Rhetoric is a counterpart of Dialectic; for both have to do with matters that are in a manner within the cognizance of all men and not confined to any special science. Hence all men in a manner have a share of both; for all, up to a certain point, endeavour to criticize or uphold an argument, to defend themselves or to accuse. Now, the majority of people do this either at random or with a familiarity arising from habit. But since both these ways are possible, it is clear that matters can be reduced to a system, for it is possible to examine the reason why some attain their end by familiarity and others by chance; and such an examination all would at once admit to be the function of an art.

Now, previous compilers of "Arts" of Rhetoric have provided us with only a small portion of this art, for proofs are the only things in it that come within the province of art; everything else is merely an accessory. And yet they say nothing about enthymemes which are the body of proof, but chiefly devote their attention to matters outside the subject; for the arousing of prejudice, compassion, anger, and similar emotions has no connexion [sic] with the matter in hand, but is directed only to the diecast. The result would be that, if all trials were now carried on as they are in some States, especially those that are well administered, there would be nothing left for the rhetorician to say. For all men either think that all the laws ought so to prescribe, or in fact carry out the principle and forbid speaking outside the subject, as in the court of Aeropagus, and in this they are right. For it is wrong to warp the dicast's feelings, to arouse him to anger, jealousy, or compassion, which one intended to use. Further, it is evident that the only business of the litigant is to prove that the fact in question is or is not so, that it has happened or not; whether it is important or unimportant, just or unjust, in all cases in which the legislator has not laid down a ruling, is a matter for the dicast himself to decide; it is not the business of the litigants to instruct him.

First of all, therefore, it is proper that laws, properly enacted, should themselves define the issue of all cases as far as possible, and leave as little as possible to the discretion of the judges; in the first place, because it is easier to find one or a few men of good sense, capable of framing laws and pronouncing judgements, than a large number; secondly, legislation is the result of long consideration, whereas judgements are delivered on the spur of the moment,

41

so that it is difficult for the judges properly to decide questions of justice or expediency. But what is most important of all is that the judgement of the legislator does not apply to a particular case, but is universal and applies to the future, whereas the member of the public assembly and the dicast have to decide present and definite issues, and in their case love, hate, or personal interest is often involved, so that they are no longer capable of discerning the truth adequately, their judgement being obscured by their own pleasure or pain.

[...]

Hence, although the method of deliberative and forensic Rhetoric is the same, and although the pursuit of the former is nobler and more worthy of a statesman than that of the latter, which is limited to transactions between private citizens, they say nothing about the former, but without exception endeavour to bring forensic speaking under the rules of art. The reason of this is that in public speaking it is less worthwhile to talk of what is outside the subject, and that deliberative oratory lends itself to trickery less than forensic, because it is of more general interest. For in the assembly the judges decide upon their own affairs, so that the only thing necessary is to prove the truth of the statement of one who recommends a measure, but in the law courts this is not sufficient; there it is useful to win over the hearers, for the decision concerns other interests than those of the judges, who, having only themselves to consider and listening merely for their own pleasure, surrender to the pleaders but do not give a real decision. That is why, as I have said before, in many places the law prohibits speaking outside the subject in the law courts, whereas in the assembly the judges themselves take adequate precautions against this.

It is obvious, therefore, that a system arranged according to the rules of art is only concerned with proofs; that proof is a sort of demonstration, since we are most strongly convinced when we suppose anything to have been demonstrated; that rhetorical demonstration is an enthymeme, which, generally speaking, is the strongest of rhetorical proofs; and lastly, that the enthymeme is a kind of syllogism. Now, as it is the function of Dialectic as a whole, or of one of its parts, to consider every kind of syllogism in a similar manner, it is clear that he who is most capable of examining the matter and forms of a syllogism will be in the highest degree a master of rhetorical argument, if to this he adds a knowledge of the subjects with which enthymemes deal and the differences between them and logical syllogisms. For, in fact, the true and that which resembles it come under the purview of the same faculty, and at the same time men have sufficient natural capacity for the truth and indeed in most cases attain to it; wherefore one who divines well in regard to the truth will also be able to divine well in regard to probabilities.

It is clear, then, that all other rhetoricians bring under the rules of art what is outside the subject, and have rather inclined to the forensic branch of oratory. Nevertheless, Rhetoric is useful, because the true and the just are naturally superior to their opposites, so that, if decisions are improperly made, they must owe their defeat to their own advocates; which is reprehensible. Further, in dealing with certain persons, even if we possessed the most accurate scientific knowledge, we should not find it easy to persuade them by the employment of such knowledge. For scientific discourse is concerned with instruction, but in the case of such persons instruction is impossible; our proofs and arguments must rest on generally accepted principles, as we said in the *Topics*, when speaking of converse with the multitude. Further, the orator should be able to prove opposites, as in logical arguments; not that we should do both (for one ought not to persuade people to do what is wrong), but that the real state of the case may not escape us, and that we ourselves may be able to counteract false arguments, if another makes an unfair use of them. Rhetoric and Dialectic alone of all the arts prove opposites; for both are equally concerned with them. However, it is not the same with the subject matter, but, generally speaking, that which is true and better is naturally always easier to prove and more likely to persuade. Besides, it would be absurd if it were considered disgraceful not to be able to defend oneself with the help of the body, but not disgraceful as far as speech is concerned, whose use is more characteristic of man than that of the body. If it is argued that one who makes an unfair use of such faculty of speech may do a great deal of harm, this objection applies equally to all good things except virtue, and above all to those things which are most useful, such as strength, health, wealth, generalship; for as these, rightly used, may be of the greatest benefit, so, wrongly used, they may do an equal amount of harm.

It is thus evident that Rhetoric does not deal with any one definite class of subjects, but, like Dialectic, [is of general application]; also, that it is useful; and further, that its function is not so much to persuade, as to find out in each case the existing means of persuasion. The same holds good in respect to all other arts. For instance, it is not the function of medicine to restore a patient to health, but only to promote this end as far as possible; for even those whose recovery is impossible may be properly treated. It is further evident that it belongs to Rhetoric to discover the real and apparent means of persuasion, just as it belongs to Dialectic to discover the real and apparent syllogism. For what makes the sophist is not the faculty but the moral purpose. But there is a difference: in Rhetoric, one who acts in accordance with sound argument, and one who acts in accordance with moral purpose, are both called rhetoricians; but in Dialectic it is the moral purpose that makes the sophist, the dialectician being one whose arguments rest, not on moral purpose but on the faculty.

Let us now endeavour to treat of the method itself, to see how and by what means we shall be able to attain our objects. And so let us as it were start again, and having defined Rhetoric anew, pass on to the remainder of the subject.

2. Rhetoric then may be defined as the faculty of discovering the possible means of persuasion in reference to any subject whatever. This is the function of no other of the arts, each of which is able to instruct and persuade in its own special subject; thus, medicine deals with health and sickness, geometry with the properties of magnitudes, arithmetic with number, and similarly with all the other arts and sciences. But Rhetoric, so to say, appears to be able to discover the means of persuasion in reference to any given subject That is why we say that as an art its rules are not applied to any particular definite class of things.

[. . .]

Now the proofs furnished by the speech are of three kinds. The first depends upon the moral character of the speaker, the second upon putting the hearer into a certain frame of mind, the third upon the speech itself, in so far as it proves or seems to prove.

The orator persuades by moral character when his speech is delivered in such a manner as to render him worthy of confidence; for we feel confidence in a greater degree and more readily in persons of worth in regard to everything in general, but where there is no certainty and there is room for doubt, our confidence is absolute. But this confidence must be due to the speech itself, not to any preconceived idea of the speaker's character; for it is not the case, as some writers of rhetorical treatises lay down in their "Art," that the worth of the orator in no way contributes to his powers of persuasion; on the contrary, moral character, so to say, constitutes the most effective means of proof. The orator persuades by means of his hearers, when they are roused to emotion by his speech; for the judgements we deliver are not the same when we are influenced by joy or sorrow, love or hate; and it is to this alone that, as we have said, the present-day writers of treatises endeavour to devote their attention. (We will discuss these matters in detail when we come to speak of the emotions.) Lastly, persuasion is produced by the speech itself, when we establish the true or apparently true from the means of persuasion applicable to each individual subject.

Now, since proofs are effected by these means, it is evident that, to be able to grasp them, a man must be capable of logical reasoning, of studying characters and the virtues, and thirdly the emotions—the nature and character of each, its origin, and the manner in which it is produced. Thus it appears that Rhetoric is as it were an offshoot of Dialectic and of the science of Ethics, which may be reasonably called Politics. That is why Rhetoric assumes the character of Politics, and those who claim to possess it, partly from ignorance, partly from boastfulness, and partly from other human weaknesses, do the same. For, as we said at the outset, Rhetoric is a sort of division or likeness of Dialectic, since neither of them is a science that deals with the nature of any definite subject, but they are merely faculties of furnishing arguments. We have now said nearly enough about the faculties of these arts and their mutual relations.

But for purposes of demonstration, real or apparent, just as Dialectic possesses two modes of argument, induction and the syllogism, real or apparent, the same is the case in Rhetoric; for the example is induction, and the enthymeme a syllogism, and the apparent enthymeme an apparent syllogism. Accordingly I call an enthymeme a rhetorical syllogism, and an example a rhetorical induction. Now all orators produce belief by employing as proofs either examples or enthymemes and nothing else; so that if, generally speaking, it is necessary to prove any fact whatever either by syllogism or by induction—and that this is so clear from the *Analytics*—each of the two former must be identical with each of the latter. The difference between example and enthymeme is evident from the *Topics*, where, in discussing syllogism and induction, it has previously been said that the proof from a number of particular cases that such is the rule, is called Dialectic induction, in Rhetoric example; but when, certain things being posited, something different results by reason of them, alongside of them, from their being true, either universally or in most cases, such a conclusion in Dialectic is called a syllogism, in Rhetoric an enthymeme.

It is evident that Rhetoric enjoys both these advantages—for what has been said in the *Methodica* holds good also in this case—for rhetorical speeches are sometimes characterized by examples and sometimes by enthymemes, and orators themselves may be similarly distinguished by their fondness for one or the other. Now arguments that depend on examples are not less calculated to persuade, but those which depend upon enthymemes meet with greater approval. Their origin and the way in which each should be used will be discussed later; for the moment let us define more clearly these proofs themselves.

Now, that which is persuasive is persuasive in reference to some one, and is persuasive and convincing either at once and in and by itself, or because it appears to be proved by propositions that are convincing; further, no art has the particular in view, medicine for instance what is good for Socrates or Callias, but what is good for this or that class of persons (for this is a matter that comes within the province of an art, whereas the particular is infinite and cannot be the subject of a true science); similarly, therefore, Rhetoric will not consider what seems probably in each individual case, for instance to Socrates or Hippias, but that which seems probable to this or that class of persons. It is the same with Dialectic, which does not draw conclusions from an random premises—for even madmen have some fancies—but it takes its material from subjects which demand reasoned discussion, as Rhetoric does from those which are common subjects of deliberation.

The functions of Rhetoric, then, is to deal with things about which we deliberate, but for which we have no systematic rules; and in the presence of such hearers as are unable to take a general view of many stages, or to follow a lengthy chain of argument. But we only deliberate about things which seem to admit of issuing in two ways; as for those things which cannot in the past, present, or future be otherwise, no one deliberates about them, if he supposes that they are such; for nothing would be gained by it. Now, it is possible to draw conclusions and inferences partly from what has been previously demonstrated syllogistically, partly from what has not, which however needs demonstration, because it is not probable. The first of these methods is necessarily difficult to follow owing to its length, for the judge is supposed to be a simple person; the second will obtain little credence, because it does not depend upon what is either admitted or probable. The necessary result then is that the enthymeme and the example are concerned with things which may, generally speaking, be other than they are, the example being a kind of induction and the enthymeme a kind of syllogism, and deduced from few premises, often from fewer than the regular syllogism; for if any one of these is well known, there is no need to mention it, for the hearer can add it himself. For instance, to prove that Dorieus was the victor in a contest at which the prize was a crown, it is enough to say that he won a victory at the

Olympic games; there is no need to add that the prize at the Olympic games is a crown, for everybody knows it.

[…]

Such then are the materials which we must employ in exhorting and dissuading, praising and blaming, accusing and defending, and such are the opinions and propositions that are useful to produce conviction in these circumstances; for they are the subject and source of enthymemes, which are specially suitable to each class (so to say) of speeches. But since the object of Rhetoric is judgement—for judgements are pronounced in deliberative rhetoric and judicial proceedings are a judgement—it is not only necessary to consider how to make the speech itself demonstrative and convincing, but also that the speaker should show himself to be of a certain character and should know how to put the judge into a certain frame of mind. For it makes a great difference with regard to producing conviction—especially in demonstrative, and, next to this, in forensic oratory—that the speaker should show himself to be possessed of certain qualities and that his hearers should think that that he is disposed in a certain way towards them; and further, that they themselves should be disposed in a certain way towards him. In deliberative oratory, it is more useful that the orator should appear to be of a certain character, in forensic, that the hearer should be disposed in a certain way; for opinions vary, according as men love or hate, are wrathful or mild, and things appear either altogether different, or different in degree; for when a man is favourably disposed towards one on whom he is passing judgement, he either thinks that the accused has committed no wrong at all or that his offence is trifling; but if he hates him, the reverse is the case. And if a man desires anything and has good hopes of getting it, if what is to come is pleasant, he thinks that it is sure to come to pass and will be good; but if a man is unemotional or not hopeful it is quite the reverse.

For the orator to produce conviction three qualities are necessary; for, independently of demonstrations, the things which induce belief are three in number. These qualities are good sense, virtue, and goodwill; for speakers are wrong both in what they say and in the advice they give, because they lack either all three or one of them. For either through want of sense they form incorrect opinions, or, if their opinions are correct, through viciousness they do not say what they think, or, if they are sensible and good, they lack goodwill; wherefore it may happen that they do not give the best advice, although they know what it is. These qualities are all that are necessary, so that the speaker who appears to possess all three will necessarily convince his hearers. The means whereby he may appear sensible and good must be inferred from the classification of the virtues; for to make himself appear such he would employ the same means as he would in case of others.

[...]

There are three things which require special attention in regard to speech: first, the sources of proofs; secondly, style; and thirdly, the arrangement of the parts of the speech. We have already spoken of proofs and stated that they are three in number, what is their nature, and why there are only three; for in all cases persuasion is the result either of the judges themselves being affected in a certain manner, or because they consider the speakers to be of a certain character, or because something has been demonstrated. We have also stated the sources from which enthymemes should be derived—some of them being special, the others general commonplaces.

We have therefore next to speak of style; for it is not sufficient to know what one ought to say, but one must also know how to say it, and this largely contributes to making the speech appear of a certain character. In the first place, following the natural order, we investigated that which first presented itself—what gives things themselves their persuasiveness; in the second place, their arrangement by styles; and in the third place, delivery, which is of the greatest importance, but has not yet been treated of by any one. In fact, it only made its appearance late in tragedy and rhapsody, for at first the poets themselves acted their tragedies. It is clear, therefore, that there is something of the sort in rhetoric as well as in poetry, and it has been dealt with by Glaucon of Teos among others. Now delivery is a matter of voice, as to the mode in which it should be used for each particular emotion; when it should be loud, when low, when intermediate; and how the tones, that is, shrill, deep, and intermediate, should be used; and what rhythms are adapted to each subject. For there are three qualities that are considered—volume, harmony, rhythm. Those who use these properly nearly always carry off the prizes in dramatic contests, and as at the present day actors have greater influence on the stage than the poets, it is the same in political contests, owing to the corruptness of our forms of government. But no treatise has yet been composed on delivery, since the matter of style itself only lately came into notice; and rightly considered it is though vulgar. But since the whole business of Rhetoric is to influence opinion, we must pay attention to it, not as being right, but necessary; for, as a matter of right, one should aim at nothing more in a speech than how to avoid exciting pain or pleasure.

For justice should consist in fighting the case with the facts alone, so that everything else that is beside demonstration is superfluous; nevertheless, as we have just said, it is of great importance owing to the corruption of the hearer. However, in every system of instruction there is some slight necessity to pay attention to style; for it does make a difference, for the purpose of making a thing clear, to speak in this or that manner; still, the difference is not so very great, but all these things are mere outward show for pleasing the hearer; wherefore no on teaches geometry in this way.

Now, when delivery comes into fashion, it will have the same effect as acting. Some writers have attempted to say a few words about it, as Thrasymachus, in his *Eleoi*; and in fact, a gift for acting is a natural talent and depends less upon art, but in regard to style it is artificial. Wherefore people who excel in this in their turn obtain prizes, just as orators who excel in delivery; for written speeches owe their effect not so much to the sense as to the style.

Chapter 4

Demetrius

Demetrius (350–280 BCE) was an Athenian orator and statesman who used his practical experience as a politician and speaker to discuss the impact of rhetorical style. While others in Ancient Greece mentioned style, Demetrius was the first to emphasize style as a valuable component of persuasive effectiveness. As the title suggests, *On Style* focuses on the use of different literary and grammatical styles to emphasize the force of rhetoric. To highlight his contribution to elocutionary style in persuasion, we have included passages that describe the concept of style, examples of effective style, and ways of incorporating style in persuasive messaging.

On Style

[…]

240. We now come to the quality of force. It is clear, from what has already been said, that force also, like the styles previously described, may have three sources. Some things are forcible in themselves, so that those who give utterance to them seem to be forcible, even if they do not speak forcibly. Theopompus, for instance, in a certain passage describes the flute-girls in the Peiraeus, the stews, and the sailors who pipe and sing and dance; and through employing all this strong language he seems to be forcible, although his style is really feeble.

241. In respect of composition this type of style requires, first of all, phrases in place of members. Prolixity paralyses vigour, while much meaning conveyed in a brief form is the more forcible. An example is the message of the Lacedaemonians to Philip: 'Dionysius at Corinth.' If they had expanded the thought at full length, saying 'Dionysius has been deposed from his sovereignty and is now a beggarly schoolmaster at Corinth,' the result would have been a bit of narrative rather than a taunt.

242. The Lacedaemonians had a natural turn for brevity of speech under all circumstances. Brevity is, indeed, more forcible and peremptory, while prolixity is suited for begging and praying.

243. For this reason symbolic expressions are forcible, as resembling brief utterances. We are left to infer the chief of the meaning from a short statement, as though it were a sort of riddle. Thus the saying 'your cicalas shall chirp from the ground' is more forcible in this figurative form than if the sentence had simply run 'your trees shall be hewed down'

244. In this style the periods should be brought to a definite point at the end. The periodic form is forcible, while looseness of structure is more naive and betokens an innocent nature. This is true of all old-fashioned style, the ancients being distinguished by naivete.

245. It follows that, in the forcible style, we must avoid old-fashioned traits both of character and of rhythm, and regard the forcible style at present in vogue as our special goal. Now, for the members, cadences of the following kind, 'I have agreed to plead, to the best of my ability, my clients' case' keep closest to the rhythm I have mentioned.

246. Even violence conveys a certain impression of energy in composition. Yes, in many passages harshness gives all the effect of vehemence; as though we were jolted on rough roads. Demosthenes' words are a case in point: '(he has deprived) you of the bestowal—you of the prerogative.'

247. We should avoid antitheses and exact parallelisms of words in the period, since in place of force they render the style laboured and often frigid. Theopompus, for example, when inveighing against the intimates of Philip, enfeebled his invective by the following antithesis: 'men-slayers in nature, they were men-harlots in life.' The hearer, having his attention fixed on this elaboration, or rather affectation, forgets to be angry.

248. We shall often find ourselves constrained by the very nature of the subject-matter to construct sentences which are rounded, indeed, but forcible too, as in the following passage of Demosthenes: 'Just as you would not have made this proposal if any of the former parties had been convicted, so if you are convicted now no one will do so in future ' This particular arrangement obviously grew naturally out of the subject and the order of words evoked by it. Not even by violent perversion could a writer easily have framed the sentence otherwise. There are many topics in handling which we are swept along by the subject itself, just as though we were running down a slope.

249. It also conduces to force to place the most forcible expression at the end. If this be surrounded and enveloped, its point is blunted. Let the following sentence of Antisthenes serve as an example: 'almost torment will be caused by a man from brushwood started.' If a writer were to change the order thus, 'almost will a man from brushwood started cause torment/he will be saying the same thing but will no longer be believed to be saying the same.

250. Excessive antithesis, already condemned in the case of Theopompus, is out of place even in Demosthenes, as in the following passage: 'You were initiating, I was initiated; you taught, I attended classes; you took minor parts in the theatre, I was a spectator; you broke down, I hissed '" The elaborate parallelism of clauses produces the impression of false artifice; of trifling, rather than of honest indignation.

251. An uninterrupted series of periods, although inappropriate in other styles, is favourable to force. Its crowded succession will convey the impression of line recited after line,—forcible lines like the choliambic.

252. These massed periods should, however, be short (of two members, say), since many-membered periods will produce the feeling of beauty rather than of force.

253. Conciseness is so favourable to this style that a sudden lapse into silence is often yet more forcible, as when Demosthenes says: 'I could on my part . . . but I do not desire to say anything offensive; only, my opponent accuses at a great advantage.' The orator's reserve is here more effective than any possible retort could have been.

254. And (strange though it may seem) obscurity often produces force, since what is distantly hinted is more forcible, while what is plainly stated is held cheap.

255. Occasionally cacophony produces vigour, especially if the subject requires harshness of sound, as in Homer's line:—'Then shuddered the Trojans, beholding the writhing serpent'. It would have been possible to construct the line more euphoniously, without violating the metre, thus:—'Then shuddered the Trojans, the writhing serpent beholding.' But there would then have seemed to be nothing terrific whether in the speaker or in the serpent itself.

[. . .]

258. Force of style will also mark a sentence of this kind: 'He turned upside down, in his folly and his impiety too, things sacred and things holy too.' As a general rule, smoothness and a pleasant cadence are characteristic of the elegant rather than the forcible style; and these two styles seem to be direct opposites.

[. . .]

263. We shall next show how force can be secured by rhetorical figures. It can be secured by figures conveying the speaker's thought. Take, for instance, that which is called 'praetermission,' e.g. 'I pass over Olynthus, Methone, Apollonia, and the two-and-thirty towns on the confines of Thrace.' In these words the orator has said everything he wished, while professing to have passed everything over in his desire to proceed to weightier matters.

264. The figure 'aposiopesis' already mentioned, which partakes of the same character, will also make expression more forcible.

265. Another figure of thought—the so-called 'proso-popoeia'—may be employed to produce energy of style, as in the words: 'Imagine that your ancestors, or Hellas, or your native land, assuming a woman's form, should address such and such reproaches to you.'

[. . .]

268. The same thing is true of the figure 'anaphora,' as in the words: 'against yourself you summon him; against the laws you summon him; against the democracy you summon him.' Here the figure in question is threefold. It is, as has been already said, an 'epanaphora,' because of the repetition of the' same word at the commencement of each clause; an 'asyndeton,' because of the absence of conjunctions; and a 'homoeoteleuton,' because of the recurring termination 'you summon him.' And force is the cumulative result of the three figures. Were we to write 'against yourself and the laws and the democracy you summon him,' the force would vanish together with the figures.

[...]

271. In a word, the figures of speech help the speaker in delivery and in debate; lending especially the effect of abruptness,—in other words, of energy.—With regard to both kinds of figures what has been said must suffice.

[...]

Demetrius. *On Style*. Translated by W. Rhys Roberts. Cambridge: Cambridge University Press, 1902, http://archive.org/stream/demetriusonstyleoodemeuoft/demetriusonstyleoodemeuoft_djvu.txt

SECTION TWO

Ancient Rome

Much has been written about Ancient Rome's contribution to rhetoric. When Roman rhetoric is mentioned, we might think of the actual Roman speeches, such as the oratory of Julius Cesar made famous by Shakespeare or the famed "rostrum" where speeches were given in front of the Roman Senate, but the most important impetus the Romans gave to rhetoric was spreading the value of rhetoric across the Empire, emphasizing the virtue of integrity, providing a template for producing a persuasive speech, and acknowledging the persuasive potential inherent in poetry.

The Romans owed much to their Greek predecessors. For example, in the selections below, Cicero, Rome's greatest orator, emphasizes the five components of persuasive speaking, known as the "Five Canons of Rhetoric": invention, arrangement, style, delivery, and memory. As we have seen, we can trace these back to Isocrates but, because Cicero codified them, he is typically credited with the idea. Although Aristotle wrote about the value of poetry, the Roman poet Horace actually articulated how we can persuade by using poetry. And, with Quintilian, we see stress given to the concept of integrity and honesty by effective rhetors, a theoretical concept akin to Aristotle's description of ethos.

The importance of the Romans in the history of rhetoric lies not in their original thought but in their ability to disseminate their ideas, and the Greek ideas that underlie them, throughout their vast Empire. And, of course, because of the Roman dominance, many of the Greek ideas were also preserved. We should remember that with the spread of the Roman Empire, Latin became the primary language throughout the world, especially for nobility and religious leaders. Since virtually all communication was conducted in Latin, the Romans were able to spread their contributions to rhetoric all over the Empire. When we ponder the influence of Cicero, Horace, and Quintilian, it will be important for us to remember that the Empire provided an infrastructure for projecting ideas. The Roman imperial legacy will also be significant when we think about the role of rhetoric in the Middle Ages. What will become clear is the profound mark that Roman writers left on the study of rhetoric.

READINGS

Brinton, Alan. "Quintilian, Plato, and the *Vir Bonus*." *Philosophy & Rhetoric* 16, no. 3 (1983): 167–184.

Clarke, Martin L. *Rhetoric at Rome*. London: Cohen & West, 1953.

Enos, Richard L. *Roman Rhetoric: Revolution and the Greek Influence*. Prospect Heights, IL: Waveland Press, 1995.

Golden, James L. "Cicero and Quintilian on the Formation of an Orator." *Speech Journal* 6 (1969): 29–34.

Howell, Wilbur S. "Aristotle and Horace on Rhetoric and Poetics." *Quarterly Journal of Speech* 54, no. 4 (1968): 325–340.

Kennedy, George. *The Art of Rhetoric in the Roman World: 300 B.C.–A.D. 300*. Princeton, NJ: Princeton University Press, 1972.

Murphy, James J. "Cicero's Rhetoric in the Middle Ages." *Quarterly Journal of Speech* 53, no. 4 (1967): 334–342.

Oliensis, Ellen. *Horace and the Rhetoric of Authority*. Cambridge, UK: Cambridge University Press, 1998.

Sinclair, Patrick. "The Sententia in *Rhetorica ad Herennium*: A Study in the Sociology of Rhetoric." *American Journal of Philology* 114, no. 4 (1993): 561–581.

Ward, John O. "The Catena Commentaries on the Rhetoric of Cicero and Their Implications for Development of a Teaching Tradition in Rhetoric." *Studies in Medieval and Renaissance Teaching* 6, no. 2 (1998): 79–95.

Chapter 5

Cicero

Roman philosopher, lawyer, statesman, and political theorist, Marcus Tullius Cicero (106–43 BCE) was Rome's most significant rhetorical scholar. No one really knows why, but at a young age Cicero traveled to Greece where he studied philosophy and was influenced by Greek rhetoric. In his *De Inventione* and *De Oratore*, both included here, Cicero acknowledges Aristotle's contribution to his thinking on eloquence (rhetoric).

Cicero is best known in the history of rhetoric for his classification of the "Five Canons of Rhetoric": invention, arrangement, delivery, style, and memory. They are called "canons" because they form the pillars for effective oratory. *Invention* is the process of finding a topic and formulating contentions; it is where elements of logos and pathos are employed as persuasive appeals. *Arrangement* is the structure of the speech. Rhetors must carefully consider the organization of their arguments so that they have the most persuasive impact. *Delivery* requires making use of voice and gestures for effective presentation. *Style* includes using certain words, phrases, tonality, etc., to stir emotions. Finally, *memory* addresses the rehearsed memorization of a speech, but it also includes the knowledge retained of subjects to be discussed in persuasive oratory. As we have seen, Cicero did not originate these concepts, but his approach to studying them and the emphasis he gave them are certainly unique and worthy of recognition.

Another important contribution from Cicero is his discussion of the exordium, the introduction of a persuasive speech. As we see in *De Inventione* and the *Rhetorica ad Herennium*, Cicero describes a direct, subtle approach to introductions to generate good will with an audience, engage the audience's attention, and influence an audience's argumentative belief toward the matter at hand. No other writer spends as much time or deals with exordium in as much detail as Cicero.

The *Rhetorica ad Herennium*, which has long been attributed to Cicero, deals with the structure and uses of rhetoric. It is the Roman version of Aristotle's *The Art of Rhetoric*—a systematic guide to how to craft a persuasive message. It also solidifies the idea that persuasive appeals—like ethos, pathos, and logos—are essential strategies for the discipline of rhetoric.

With *De Oratore*, Cicero reiterates many of his positions from his other works, including why rhetorical oratory should be respected as an art. He also goes to great length in describing the use of logos, especially the different types of deductive arguments. As we shall see, Cicero's contribution to our understanding of rhetoric, even if not completely original, is impressive and valuable. These three selections offer us a glimpse into Cicero's influence on rhetoric. In short, he introduces us to the Five Canons, he stresses the value of rhetoric, and he describes the utility of logos in convincing audiences about important matters of the day.

De Inventione

[…]

Therefore the material of the art of rhetoric seems to me to be that which we said Aristotle approved. The parts of it, as most authorities have stated, are Invention, Arrangement, Expression, Memory, Delivery. Invention is the discovery of valid or seemingly valid arguments to render one's cause plausible. Arrangement is the distribution of arguments thus discovered in the proper order. Expression is the fitting of the proper language to the invented matter. Memory is the firm mental grasp of matter and words. Delivery is the control of voice and body in a manner suitable to the dignity of the subject matter and the style.

[…]

An exordium is a passage which brings the mind of the auditor into a proper condition to receive the rest of the speech. This will be accomplished if he becomes well-disposed, attentive, and receptive. Therefore one who wishes his speech to have a good exordium must make a careful study beforehand of the kind of case which he has to present. There are five kinds of cases: honourable, difficult, mean, ambiguous, obscure. An honourable case is one which wins favour in the mind of the auditor at once without any speech of ours: the difficult is one which has alienated the sympathy of those who are about to listen to the speech. The mean is one which the auditor makes light of and thinks unworthy of serious attention; the ambiguous is one in which the point for decision is doubtful, or the case is partly honourable and partly discreditable so that it engenders both good-will and ill-will; the obscure case is one in which either the auditors are slow of wit, or the case involves matters which are rather difficult to grasp. Hence, since the kinds of cases are so diverse, it is necessary to construct the exordium on a different plan in each kind of case. The exordium is, then, divided into two species, *introduction* and *insinuation*. An introduction is an address which directly and in plain language makes the auditor well-disposed, receptive, and attentive. Insinuation is an address which by dissimulation and indirection unobtrusively steals into the mind of the auditor.

In the difficult case, if the auditors are not completely hostile, it will be permissible to try to win their good-will by an introduction; if they are violently opposed it will be necessary to have recourse to the insinuation. For if amity and good-will are sought from auditors who are in a rage, not only is the desired result not obtained, but their hatred is increased and fanned into a flame. In the mean case, on the other hand, it is necessary to make the audience attentive in order to remove their disdain. If an ambiguous case has a doubtful point for the judge's decision, the exordium must being with a discussion of this very point. But if the case is partly honourable and partly discreditable, it will be proper to try to win good-will so that the case may seem to be transferred to the honourable class. When, however, the case is really in the honourable class, it will be possible either to pass over the introduction or, if it is convenient, we shall being with the narrative or with a law or some very strong argument which supports our plea: if, on the contrary, it is desirable to use the introduction, we must use the topics designed to produce good-will, that the advantage which already exists may be increased. In a case of the obscure kind the introduction must be used to make the audience receptive.

Now that it has been stated what results the orator ought to accomplish by the exordium, it remains to show by what means each result can be obtained.

Good-will is to be had from four quarters: from our own person, from the person of the opponents, from the persons of the jury, and from the case itself. We shall win good-will from our own person if we refer to our own acts and services without arrogance; if we weaken the effect of charges that have been preferred, or of some suspicion of less honourable dealing which has been cast upon us; if we dilate on the misfortunes which have befallen us or the difficulties which still beset us; if we use prayers and entreaties with a humble and submissive spirit. Good-will is acquired from the person of the opponents if we can bring them into hatred, unpopularity, or contempt. They will be hated if some act of theirs is presented which is base, haughty, cruel, or malicious; they will become unpopular if we present their power, political influence, wealth, family connexions [sic], and their arrogant and intolerable use of these advantages, so that they seem to rely on these rather than on the justice of their case. They will be brought into contempt if we reveal their laziness, carelessness, sloth, indolent pursuits or luxurious idleness. Good-will will be sought from the persons of the auditors if an account is given of acts which they have performed with courage, wisdom, and mercy, but so as not to show excessive flattery: and if it is shown in what honourable esteem they are held and how eagerly their judgement and opinion are awaited. Good-will may come from the circumstances themselves if we praise and exalt our own case, and depreciate our opponent's with contemptuous allusions.

We shall make our audience attentive if we show that the matters which we are about to discuss are important, novel, or incredible, or that they concern all humanity or those in the audience or some illustrious men or the immortal gods or the general interest of the state; also if we promise to prove our own case briefly and explain the point to be decided or the several points if there are to be more than one. We shall make the auditors receptive if we explain the essence of the case briefly and in plain language, that is, the point on which the controversy turns. For when you wish to make an auditor receptive, you should also at the same time render him attentive. For he is most receptive who is prepared to listen most attentively.

Now I think we should discuss secondly the proper method of handling insinuations. The insinuation, then, is to be used when the case is difficult, that is, as I said above, when the spirit of the audience is hostile. This hostility arises principally from three causes: if there is something scandalous in the case, or if those who have spoken first seem to have convinced the auditor on some point, or if the chance to speak comes at a time when those who ought to listen have been wearied by listening. For sometimes the mind of the auditor takes offence at an orator no less form this last cause than from the first two. If the scandalous nature of the case occasions offence, it is necessary to substitute for the person at whom offence is taken another who is favoured, or for a thing at which offence is taken, another which is approved, or a person for a thing or a thing for a person, in order that the attention of the auditor may be shifted from what he hates to what he favours. Also, you must conceal your intention of defending the point which you are expected to defend. After that, when the audience has now become more tractable, approach the defence little by little and say that the things which displease your opponents are also displeasing to you. Next, after pacifying the audience, show that none of these charges apply to you and assert that you will say nothing about your opponents, neither this nor that, so as not openly to attack those who are favoured, and yet, by working imperceptibly, as far as possible to win the good-will of the audience away from your opponents. Also you may offer a decision or opinion of some authorities in a similar case as worthy of imitation; then show that in the present case the same question is to be decided, or one like it or one of greater or lesser importance.

On the other hand, if the speeches of your opponents seem to have won conviction among the audience—a result which will easily be apprehended by one who knows the means by which conviction is won—it behoves you to promise to discuss first the argument which the opponents thought was their strongest and which the audience have especially approved. Or you may begin by a reference to what has been said by your opponent, preferably to something that he has said recently. Or you may express doubt as to what to say first, or which passage to answer before all others, at the same time showing perplexity and astonishment. For when the audience see that he whom they think is shaken by the opponent's speech is ready to speak in reply with confidence and assurance, they generally think that they have assented too readily rather than that he is confident without good cause. If, in the third place, weariness has alienated the sympathy of the auditor from your case, it is a help to promise that you will speak more briefly than you were prepared to speak; that you will not imitate your opponent.

If the case permits, it is not unprofitable to begin with some new topic, or a jest, either one which is extemporaneous—a kind which meets with uproarious applause and shouts of approval—or one already prepared containing a fable, or a story, or some laughable incident. Or, if the seriousness of the occasion denies an opportunity for a jest, it is not disadvantageous to insert something appalling, unheard of, or terrible at the very beginning. For, just as a loathing and distaste for food is relieved by some morsel with a bit of a tang, or appeased by a sweet, so a mind wearied by listening is strengthened by astonishment or refreshed by laughter.

This is about all that is seemed necessary to say concerning the introduction and the insinuation separately: now it seems desirable to state some brief rules which will apply to both alike.

The *exordium* ought to be sententious to a marked degree and of a high seriousness, and, to put it generally, should contain everything which contributes to dignity, because the best thing to do is that which especially commends the speaker to his audience. It should contain very little brilliance, vivacity, or finish of style, because these give rise to a suspicion of preparation and excessive ingenuity. As a result of this most of all the speech loses conviction and the speaker, authority.

The following are surely the most obvious faults of *exordia*, which are by all means to be avoided: it should not be general, common, interchangeable, tedious, unconnected, out of place, or contrary to the fundamental principles. A *general* exordium is one which can be tacked to many cases, so as to seem to suit them all. A *common* exordium is one equally applicable to both sides of the case. The *interchangeable* can with slight changes be used by the opponent in a speech on the other side. The *tedious* exordium is one which is spun out beyond all need with a superabundance of words or ideas.

The *unconnected* is one which is not derived from the circumstances of the case nor closely knit with the rest of the speech, as a limb to a body. It is *out of place* if it produces a result different from what the nature of the case requires: for example, if it makes the audience receptive when the case calls for good-will, or uses an introduction when the situation demands an insinuation. It is contrary to fundamental principles when it achieves none of the purposes for which rules are given about exordia, that is, when it renders the audience neither well-disposed, nor attentive, nor receptive, or produces the opposite result; and nothing surely can be worse than that. This is enough to say about the exordium.

Reprinted by permission of the publishers and the Trustees of the Loeb Classical Library from *Cicero: De Inventione, De Optimo Genere Oratorum, Topica,* Loeb Classical Library, translated by H. M. Hubbell, pages 19–21, 41–53, Cambridge, MA: Harvard University Press, Copyright 1949, by the President and Fellows of Harvard College. Loeb Classical Library® is a registered trademark of the President and Fellows of Harvard College.

Rhetorica ad Herennium

[...]

I. My private affairs keep me so busy that I can hardly find enough leisure to devote to study, and the little that is vouchsafed to me I have usually preferred to spend on philosophy. Yet your desire, Gaius Herennius, has spurred me to compose a work on the Theory of Public Speaking, lest you should suppose that in a matter which concerns you I either lacked the will or shirked the labour. And I have undertaken this project the more gladly because I knew that you had good grounds in wishing to learn rhetoric, for it is true that copiousness and facility in expression bear abundant fruit, if controlled by proper knowledge and a strict discipline of the mind.

That is why I have omitted to treat those topics which, for the sake of futile self-assertion, Greek writers have adopted. For they, from fear of appearing to know too little, have gone in quest of notions irrelevant to the art, in order that the art might seem more difficult to understand. I, on the other hand, have treated those topics which seemed pertinent to the theory of public speaking. I have not been moved by hope of gain or desire for glory as the rest have been, in undertaking to write, but have done so in order that, by my painstaking work, I may gratify your wish. To avoid prolixity, I shall now begin my discussion of the subject, as soon as I have given you this one injunction: Theory without continuous practice in speaking is of little avail; from this you may understand that the precepts of theory here offered ought to be applied in practice.

II. The task of the public speaker is to discuss capably those matters which law and custom have fixed for the uses of citizenship, and to secure as far as possible the agreement of his hearers. There are three kinds of causes which the speaker must treat: Epideictic, Deliberative, and Judicial. The epideictic kind is devoted to the praise or censure of some particular person. The deliberative consists in the discussion of policy and embraces the persuasion and dissuasion. The judicial is based on legal controversy, and comprises criminal prosecution or civil suit, and defence.

Now I shall explain what faculties the speaker should possess, and then show the proper means of treating these causes.

The speaker, then, should possess the faculties of Invention, Arrangement, Style, Memory, and Delivery. Invention is the devising of the matter, true or plausible, that would make the case convincing. Arrangement is the ordering and distribution of the matter, making it clear the place to which each thing is to be assigned. Style is the adaptation of suitable words and sentences to the matter devised. Memory is the firm retention in the mind of the matter, words, and arrangement. Delivery is the graceful regulation of voice, countenance, and gesture.

All these faculties we can acquire by three means: Theory, Imitation, and Practice. By theory is meant a set of rules that provide a definite method and system of speaking. Imitation stimulates us to attain, in accordance with a studied method, the effectiveness of certain models in speaking. Practice is assiduous exercise and experience in speaking.

Since, then, I have shown what causes the speaker should treat and what kinds of competence he should possess, it seems that I now need to indicate how the speech can be adapted to the theory of the speaker's function.

III. Invention is used for the six parts of a discourse: the Introduction, Statement of Facts, Division, Proof, Refutation, and Conclusion. The Introduction is the beginning of the discourse, and by it the hearer's mind is prepared for attention. The Narration or Statement of Facts sets forth the events that have occurred or might have occurred. By means of the Division we make clear what matters are agreed upon and what are contested, and announce what points we intend to take up. Proof is the presentation of our arguments, together with their corroboration. Refutation is the destruction of our adversaries' arguments. The Conclusion is the end of the discourse, formed in accordance with the principles of the art.

Along with the speaker's functions, in order to make the subject easier to understand, I have been led also to discuss the parts of a discourse, and to adapt these to the theory of Invention. It seems, then, that I must at this juncture first discuss the Introduction.

Given the cause, in order to be able to make a more appropriate Introduction, we must consider what kind of cause it is. The kinds of causes are four: honourable, discreditable, doubtful, and petty. A cause is regarded as of the honourable kind when we either defend what seems to deserve defence by all men, or attack what all men seem in duty bound to attack; for example, when we defend a hero, or prosecute a parricide. A cause is understood to be of the discreditable kind when something honourable is under attack or when something discreditable is being defended. A cause is of the doubtful kind when it is partly honourable and partly discreditable.

A cause is of the petty kind when the matter brought up is considered unimportant.

IV. In view of these considerations, it will be in point to apply the theory of Introductions to the kind of cause. There are two kinds of Introduction: the Direct Opening, in Greek called the *Prooimion,* and the Subtle Approach, called the *Ephodos.* The Direct Opening straightway prepares the hearer to attend to our speech. Its purpose is to enable us to have hearers who are attentive, receptive, and well-disposed. If our cause is of the doubtful kind, we shall build the Direct Opening upon goodwill, so that the discreditable part of the cause cannot be prejudicial to us. If our cause is of the petty kind, we shall make our hearers attentive. If our cause is of the discreditable kind, unless we have hit upon a means of capturing goodwill by attacking our adversaries, we must use the Subtle Approach, which I shall discuss later. And finally, if our cause is of the honourable kind, it will be correct either to use the Direct Opening or not to use it. If we wish to use it, we must show why the cause is honourable, or else briefly announce what matters we are going to discuss. But if we do not wish to use the Direct Opening, we must begin our speech with a law, a written document, or some argument supporting our cause.

Since, then, we wish to have our hearer receptive, well-disposed, and attentive, I shall disclose how each state can be brought about. We can have receptive hearers if we briefly summarize the cause and make them attentive; for the receptive hearer is one who is willing to listen attentively. We shall have attentive hearers by promising to discuss important, new, and unusual matters, or such as appertain to the commonwealth, or to the hearers themselves, or to the worship of the immortal gods; by bidding them listen attentively; and by enumerating the points we are going to discuss. We can by four methods make our hearers well-disposed: by discussing our own person, the person of our adversaries, that of our hearers, and the facts themselves.

V. From the discussion of our own person we shall secure goodwill by praising our services without arrogance and revealing also our past conduct toward the republic, or toward our parents, friends, or the audience, and by making some reference to ... provided that all such references are pertinent to the matter in question; likewise by setting forth our disabilities, need, loneliness, and misfortune, and pleading for our hearers' aid, and at the same time showing that we have been unwilling to place our hope in anyone else.

From the discussion of the person of our adversaries we shall secure goodwill by bringing them into hatred, unpopularity, or contempt. We shall force hatred upon them by adducing some base, high-handed, treacherous, cruel, impudent, malicious, or shameful act of theirs. We shall make our adversaries unpopular by setting forth their violent behaviour, their dominance, factiousness, wealth, lack of self-restraint, high birth, clients, hospitality, club allegiance, or marriage alliances, and by making clear that they rely more upon these supports than upon the truth. We shall bring our adversaries into contempt by presenting their idleness, cowardice, sloth, and luxurious habits.

From the discussion of the person of our hearers goodwill is secured if we set forth the courage, wisdom, humanity, and nobility of past judgements they have rendered, and if we reveal what esteem they enjoy and with what interest their decision is awaited.

From the discussion of the facts themselves we shall render the hearer well-disposed by extolling our own cause with praise and by contemptuously disparaging that of our adversaries.

VI. Now I must explain the Subtle Approach. There are three occasions on which we cannot use the Direct Opening, and these we must consider carefully: (1) when our cause is discreditable, that is, when the subject itself alienates the hearer from us; (2) when the hearer has apparently been won over by the previous speakers of the opposition; (3) or when the hearer has become wearied by listening to the previous speakers.

If the cause has a discreditable character, we can make our Introduction with the following points: that the agent, not the action, ought to be considered; that we ourselves are displeased with the acts which our opponents say have been committed, and that these are unworthy, yes, heinous. Next, when we have for a time enlarged this idea, we shall show that nothing of the kind has been committed by us. Or we shall set forth the judgement rendered by others in an analogous cause, whether that cause be of equal, or less, or greater importance; then we shall gradually approach our own cause and establish the analogy. The same result is achieved if we deny an intention to discuss our opponents or some extraneous matter and yet, by subtly inserting the words, do so.

If the hearers have been convinced, if our opponent's speech has gained their credence—and this will not be hard for us to know, since we are well aware of the means by which belief is ordinarily effected—if, then, we think belief has been effected, we shall make our Subtle Approach to the cause by the following means: the point which our adversaries have regarded as their strongest support we shall promise to discuss first; we shall begin with a statement made by the opponent, and particularly with that which he has made last; and we shall use Indecision, along with an exclamation of astonishment: "What had I best say?" or "To what point shall I first reply?"

If the hearers have been fatigued by listening, we shall open with something that may provoke laughter—a fable, a plausible fiction, a caricature, an ironical inversion of the meaning of a word, an ambiguity, innuendo, banter, a naïvety, an exaggeration, a recapitulation, a pun, an unexpected turn, a comparison, a novel tale, a historical anecdote, a verse, or a challenge or a smile of approbation directed at some one. Or we shall promise to speak otherwise than as we have prepared, and not to talk as others usually do; we shall briefly explain what the other speakers do and what we intend to do.

[...]

In what I have thus far said I believe that I agree with the other writers on the art of rhetoric except for the innovations I have devised on Introductions by the Subtle Approach. I alone, in contrast with the rest, have distinguished three occasions for the Subtle Approach, so as to provide us with a thoroughly sure method and a lucid theory of Introductions.

[...]

Since it is through the Arrangement that we set in order the topics we have invented so that there may be a definite place for each in the delivery, we must see what kind of method one should follow in the process of arranging. The kinds of Arrangement are two: one arising from the principles of rhetoric, the other accommodated to particular circumstances.

[...]

There are, then, three kinds of style, called types, to which discourse, if faultless, confines itself: the first we call the Grand; the second, the Middle; the third, the Simple. The Grand type consists of a smooth and ornate arrangement of impressive words. The Middle type consists of words of a lower, yet not of the lowest and most colloquial, class of words. The Simple type is brought down even to the most current idiom of standard speech.

A discourse will be composed in the Grand style if to each idea are applied the most ornate words that can be found for it, whether literal or figurative; if impressive thoughts are chosen, such as are used in Amplification and Appeal to Pity; and if we employ figures of thought and figures of diction which have grandeur—these I shall discuss later.

De Oratore

[...]

I. When, as often happens, brother Quintus, I think over and recall the days of old, those men always seem to me to have been singularly happy who, with the State at her best, and while enjoying high distinctions and the fame of their achievements, were able to maintain such a course of life that they could either engage in activity that involved no risk or enjoy a dignified repose. And time was when I used to imagine that I too should become entitled, with wellnigh universal approval, to some opportunity of leisure and of again directing my mind to the sublime pursuits beloved of us both, when once, the career of office complete and life too taking the turn towards its close, the endless toil of public speaking and the business of canvassing should have come to a standstill. The hopes so born of my thoughts and plans have been cheated, alike by the disastrous times of public peril and by my manifold personal misfortunes. For the time of life which promised to be fullest of quiet and peace proved to be that during which the greatest volume of vexations and the most turbulent tempests arose. And notwithstanding my desire, and indeed my profound longing, no enjoyment of leisure was granted me, for the cultivation and renewed pursuit, in your company, of those arts to which from boyhood you and I have been devoted. For in my early years I came just upon the days when the old order was overthrown; then by my consulship I was drawn into the midst of a universal struggle and crisis, and my whole time ever since that consulship I have spent in stemming those billows which, stayed by my efforts from ruining the nation, rolled in a flood upon myself. But none the less, though events are thus harassing and my time so restricted, I will hearken to the call of our studies, and every moment of leisure allowed me by the perfidy of my enemies, the advocacy of my friends and my political duties, I will dedicate first and foremost to writing. And when you, brother, exhort and request me, I will not fail you, for no man's authority or wish can have greater weight with me than yours.

II. And now I must bring back to mind the recollection of an old story, not, I admit, as clear in detail as it might be, but, to my thinking, suited to what you ask; so that you may learn what men renowned above all others for eloquence have thought about the whole subject of oratory. For it is your wish, as you have often told me, that—since the unfinished and crude essays, which slipped out of the notebooks of my boyhood, or rather of my youth, are hardly worthy of my present time of life and of my experience gained form the numerous and grave causes in which I have been engaged—I should publish something more polished and complete on these same topics; and generally you disagree with me, in our occasional discussions of this subject, because I hold that eloquence is dependent upon the trained skill of highly educated men, while you consider that it must be separated from the refinements of learning and made to depend on a sort of natural talent and on practice.

And, for my own part, when, as has often happened, I have been contemplating men of the highest eminence and endowed with the highest abilities, it has seemed to me to be a matter for inquiry, why it was that more of them should have gained outstanding renown in all other pursuits, than have done so in oratory. For in whatever direction you turn your mind and thoughts, you will find very many excelling in every kind, not merely of ordinary arts, but of such as are almost the greatest. Who, for instance, in seeking to measure the understanding possessed by illustrious men, whether by the usefulness or the grandeur of their achievements, would not place the general above the orator? Yet who could doubt that, from this country alone, we could cite almost innumerable examples of leaders in war of the greatest distinction, but of men excelling in oratory a mere handful? Nay further, among the men who by their counsel and wisdom could control and direct the helm of state, many have stood out in our own day, and still more in the history of our fathers and even of our remoter ancestors, and yet through lengthy ages no good orator is to be found, and in each successive generation hardly a single tolerable one. And that no one may think that other pursuits, which have to do with abstruse branches of study, and what I may call the varied field of learning, should be compared with this art of oratory, rather than the merits of a commander or the wisdom of a statesman-like senator, let him turn his attention to these very kinds of art, and look around to see who, and how many, have been distinguished therein; in this way he will most readily judge how scarce orators are now, and ever have been.

III. For indeed you cannot fail to remember that the most learned men hold what the Greeks call "philosophy" to be the creator and mother, as it were, of all of the reputable arts, and yet in this field of philosophy it is difficult to count how many men there have been, eminent for their learning and for the variety and extent of their studies, men whose efforts were devoted, not to one separate branch of study, but who have mastered everything they could whether by scientific investigation or by the methods of dialectic. Who does not know, as regards the so-called mathematicians, what very obscure subjects, and how abstruse, manifold, and exact an art they are engaged in?

Yet in this pursuit so many men have displayed outstanding excellence, that hardly one seems to have worked in real earnest at this branch of knowledge without attaining the object of his desire. Who has devoted himself wholly to the cult of the Muses, or to this study of literature, which is professed by those who are known as men of letters, without bringing within the compass of his knowledge and observation the almost boundless range and subject-matter of those arts?

I think I shall be right in affirming this, that out of all those who have been engaged in the infinitely copious studies and learning pertaining to these arts, the smallest number of distinguished men is found among poets and orators; and even in this small number—within which a man of excellence very rarely emerges—if you will make a careful comparison of our own national supply and that of Greece, far fewer good orators will be found even than good poets. And this should seem even more marvelous because the subjects of the other arts are derived as a rule from hidden and remote sources, while the whole art of oratory lies open to the view, and is concerned in some measure with the common practice, custom, and speech of mankind, so that, whereas in all other arts that is most excellent which is farthest removed from the understanding and mental capacity of the untrained, in oratory the very cardinal sin is to depart from the language of everyday life, and the usage approved by the sense of the community.

IV. And yet it cannot truly be said either that more men devote themselves to the other arts, or that those who do so are stimulated to close study by greater pleasure, higher hopes, or more splendid rewards. In fact, to say nothing of Greece, which has ever claimed the leading part in eloquence, and of Athens, that discoverer of all learning, where the supreme power of oratory was both invented and perfected, in this city of our own assuredly no studies have ever had a more vigorous life than those having to do with the art of speaking.

For as soon as our world-empire had been established, and an enduring peace had assured us leisure, there was hardly a youth, a thirst for fame, who did not deem it his duty to strive with might and main after eloquence. At first indeed, in their complete ignorance of method, since they thought there was no definite course of training or any rules of art, they used to attain what skill they could by means of their natural ability and of reflection. But later, having heard the Greek orators, gained acquaintance with their literature and called in Greek teachers, our people were fired with a really incredible enthusiasm for eloquence. The importance, variety, and frequency of current suits of all sorts aroused them so effectually, that, to the learning which each man had acquired by his own efforts, plenty of practice was added, as being better than the maxims of all the masters. In those days too, as at present, the prizes open to this study were supreme, in the way of ability again—there are many things to show it—our fellow-countrymen have far excelled the men of every other race. And considering all this, who would not rightly marvel that, in all the long record of ages, times, and states, so small a number of orators is to be found?

But the truth is that this oratory is a greater thing, and has its sources in more arts and branches of study, than people suppose.

[…]

Under my whole oratorical system and that very readiness in speaking which Crassus just now lauded to the skies, lie three principles, as I said before, first the winning of men's favour, secondly their enlightenment, thirdly their excitement. Of these three the first calls for gentleness of style, the second for acuteness, the third for energy. For, of necessity, the arbitrator who is to decide in our favour must either lean to our side by natural inclination, or be won over by the arguments for the defence, or constrained by stirring his feelings.

[…]

"But, to recall Oratory to the point at which this digression started, do you observe that, of those three most illustrious philosophers, who visited Rome as you told us, it was Diogenes who claimed to be teaching an art of speaking well, and of distinguishing truth from error, which art he called by the Greek name of dialectic? This art, if indeed it be an art, contains no directions for discovering the truth, but only for testing it. For as to every proposition that we enunciate with an affirmation of its truth or falsity, if it be affirmed without qualification, the dialecticians undertake to decide whether it be true or false; and, if again it be stated hypothetically, with collateral propositions annexed, then they decide whether these others are properly annexed, and whether the conclusion drawn from each and every reasoning is correct: and in the end they prick themselves with their own barbs, and by wide investigation discover not only difficulties such as they themselves can no longer solve, but also others by which webs already attacked, or rather well-nigh unwound, are tangled up again. In this connexion [sic] then that eminent Stoic is of no help to us, since he does not teach me how to discover what to say; and he actually hinders me, by finding many difficulties which he pronounces quite insoluble, and by introducing a kind of diction that is not lucid, copious and flowing, but meagre, spiritless, cramped and paltry; and, if any man commands this style, it will only be with the qualification that it is unsuitable to an orator. For this oratory of ours must be adapted to the ears of the multitude, for charming or urging their minds to approve of proposals, which are weighed in no goldsmith's balance, but in what I may call common scales.

"Let us therefore renounce entirely that art which has too little to say when proofs are being thought out, and too much when they are being assessed. That Critolaus, whose visit in company with Diogenese you recall, might have been more useful, I think, in this pursuit of ours. For he was a follower of your Aristotle, from whose doctrines you think my own differ but a little. And between this Aristotle (I read also that book of his, setting forth the rhetorical theories of all his forerunners, and those other works containing sundry observations of his own on the same art), and these true professors of this art, there seemed to me to be this difference—that he surveyed these concerns of the art of rhetoric, which he disdained, with that same keen insight, by which he had discerned the essential nature of all things; whereas those others, considering this the only thing worth cultivating, have dwelt upon the treatment of this single subject, without his sagacity, but, in this one instance, with larger practice and closer application. As for Carneades, however, the extraordinary power and diversity of his oratory would be extremely to our liking; since, in those debates of his he supported no contention without proving it, and attacked none which he did not overthrow. But this is rather more than should be asked of the authors and teachers of these maxims.

"For my part, if just now I were to want a complete novice trained up to oratory, I should rather entrust him to these untiring people, who hammer day and night on the same anvil at their one and only task, for them to put into his mouth none but the most delicate morsels—everything chewed exceedingly small—in the manner of wet nurses feeding baby-boys. But should he, whom I have had liberally educated in theory, and who by this time has some tincture of practice, show also signs of sufficient natural acuteness, I will hurry him off to that source where no sequestered pool is land-locked, but from it bursts forth a general flood; to that teacher who will point out to him the very homes of all proofs, so to speak, illustrating these briefly and defining them in terms. For in what respect could a speaker be at a loss, who has contemplated everything to be employed in a speech, for purposes of either proof or disproof, or to be derived from the essential nature of the case, or adopted from without? Intrinsic arguments, when the problem concerns the character of the subject as a whole, or of part of it, or the name it is to bear, or anything whatever relating to the subject; extrinsic arguments, on the other hand, when topics are assembled form without and are not inherent in the nature of the case.

"If the problem concerns the whole subject, the general idea of it has to be made plain by definition; for example: 'If sovereignty by the grandeur and glory of the State, it was violated by the man who delivered up to the enemy an army of the Roman People, not by him who delivered the man that did it into the power of the Roman People.' But if only a part is being dealt with, its nature must be explained by distribution, as follows: 'The right course, in a situation affecting the welfare of the State, was to obey the Senate, or to set up another advisory body, or to act on his own initiative: to set up another body would have been insolence, to follow his own counsel, arrogance; therefore he should have taken the advice of the Senate.' If the argument turns on a word, remember Carbo's 'If a consul's duty is to consult the interests of his native land, what else has Opimius done?' If it turns on something correlated with the subject, the proofs come from several sources or common-places; for we shall investigate connected terms, and general heads with their sub-divisions, and resemblances and differences, and opposites, and corresponding and concurrent circumstances, and so-called antecedents, and contradictories, and we shall track down the causes of things, and the effects proceeding from causes, and investigate things of relatively greater, equal or lesser significance.

"An instance of proof deduced from connected terms is: 'If the highest praise is due to loyalty, you should be stirred at the sight of Quintus Metellus mourning so loyally.' One of deduction from a general term is: 'If the magistracies ought to be under the control of the Roman People, why impeach Norbanus, whose conduct as tribune was subservient to the will of the community?'

"As a deduction from a subdivision of a general head take: 'If we are bound to esteem all who make the interests of the State their care, surely our commanders-in-chief stand foremost, by whose strategy, valour and hazards we preserve both our own security and the grandeur of our sovereignty.' Then, as a deduction from resemblance, we have: 'If the wild beasts cherish their young, what tenderness ought we to bear to our children!' One from difference, on the other hand, is: 'If it be the mark of uncivilized folk to live but for the day, our own purposes should contemplate all time.' And, in cases involving both resemblance and difference, analogies are found in the deeds or the words or the fate of other people, and feigned tales must often be cited. Again, as deduction from an opposite, take: 'If Gracchus did wickedly, Opimius did nobly.' And, as one from corresponding circumstances: 'If he was killed by a sword, and you, his enemy, were caught on the very spot with a bloody blade, and none other than yourself was seen there or had any motive, and you were ever a man of violence, what doubt could we feel as to the crime?' And, to illustrate deduction from concurrent circumstances, antecedents and contradictories, we remember Crassus arguing in his youth: 'This tribunal, Carbo, is not going to deem you a patriotic citizen just because you defended Opimius: clearly you were only pretending, and had some other end in view, inasmuch as in your harangues you frequently lamented the death of Tiberius Gracchus, and you were a party to the murder of Publius Africanus, and you brought in that statute during your tribuneship, and always disagreed with the patriotic.' And a deduction from the causes of things is: 'If you would abolish covetousnous, you must abolish its mother, profusion.' And one from the effects of causes is: 'If we are using the funds of the Treasury to aid war and beautify peace, let us become the slaves of taxation.' And to show how we shall compare things of relatively greater, lesser and equal significance, a deduction from the greater is: 'If good repute is above riches, and money is so keenly desired, how far more keenly should fame be desired?' For one from the lesser take:

> Just for a slender acquaintance!
> So heartfelt his grief at her death!
> What had he loved her? What sorrow
> Will he show for his father—for me?

For one from the equal we have: 'It is one and the same man's part to snatch the State's money and lavish it to her detriment.'

Finally, proofs adopted from outside are such as rest upon no intrinsic force of their own but upon external authority, instances being: 'This is true, for Quintus Lutatius said so': 'This evidence is false, for torture has been employed': 'This must inevitably follow, for I am reading from the documents.' Of all this kind of thing I spoke just now.

"I have sketched these topics as shortly as possible. For if I wished to reveal to somebody gold that was hidden here and there in the earth, it should be enough for me to point out to him some marks and indications of its positions, with which knowledge he could do his own digging, and find what he wanted, with very little trouble and no chance of mistake: so I know these indications of proofs, which reveal to me their whereabouts when I am looking for them; all the rest is dug out by dint of careful consideration. But what type of proofs best befits each type of case needs not consummate art to dictate, but only ordinary talent to decide. For our immediate task is not to display any system of speaking, but to hand on to highly educated men certain lessons, as I may call them, learned from our own practice. Accordingly, with these commonplaces firmly established in his mind and memory, and roused into activity with every topic proposed for discussion, nothing will be able to elude the orator, either in our own contentions at the Bar, or in any department whatever of speaking. If however he shall succeed in appearing, to those before whom he is to plead, to be such a man as he would desire to seem, and in touching their hearts in such fashion as to be able to lead or drag them whithersoever he pleases, he will assuredly be completely furnished for oratory.

Reprinted by permission of the publishers and the Trustees of the Loeb Classical Library from *Cicero: Volumes III–IV, De Oratore, Books I–III*, Loeb Classical Library, translated by E. W. Sutton & H. Rackham, pages 3–13, 291, 311–323, Cambridge, MA: Harvard University Press, Copyright 1942, by the President and Fellows of Harvard College. Loeb Classical Library® is a registered trademark of the President and Fellows of Harvard College.

Chapter 6

Horace

Horace (65–8 BCE), a Roman poet and eloquent spokesman for the Empire, included poetry in the list of key rhetorical devices. Since he was both a lyricist and a politician, Horace bridged the gap between poetry and rhetoric. Horace is best known for writing many satires, much poetry, and many letters (epistles). Like Cicero, Horace went to Greece during his adolescence and studied the Greek traditions of eloquence (rhetoric), but paid particular attention to Greek tragedies, comedies, and lyrical poems. In *Ars Poetica*, which is the selection here, Horace discusses how effective poetry must be cohesive, with a balance of harmony and words that evoke strong feelings. He mentions how poetry can be persuasive, especially when it commands that attention be given to certain characters, the meanings of their arguments, and the emphasis provided by certain plots. And, of course, the *Ars Poetica* is a piece of rhetoric itself, arguing for the value of poetry. In these ways, Horace plays an important part in our understanding of rhetorical history.

Ars Poetica

Suppose some painter, as a tour de force,
Should couple head of man with neck of horse,
Invest them both with feathers, 'stead of hair,
And tack on limbs picked up from here and there,
So that the figure, when complete, should show
A maid above, a hideous fish below:
Should you be favoured with a private view,
You'd laugh, my friends, I know, and rightly too.
Yet trust me, Pisos, not less strange would look,
To a discerning eye, the foolish book
Where dream-like forms in sick delirium blend,
And nought is of a piece from end to end.
"Poets and painters (sure you know the plea)
Have always been allowed their fancy free."
I own it; 'tis a fair excuse to plead;
By turns we claim it, and by turns concede;
But 'twill not screen the unnatural and absurd,
Unions of lamb with tiger, snake with bird.

When poets would be lofty, they commence
With some gay patch of cheap magnificence:
Of Dian's altar and her grove we read,
Or rapid streams meandering through the mead;
Or grand descriptions of the river Rhine,
Or watery bow, will take up many a line.
All in their way good things, but not just now:
You're happy at a cypress, we'll allow;
But what of that? you're painting by command
A shipwrecked sailor, striking out for land:
That crockery was a jar when you began;
It ends a pitcher: you an artist, man!

Make what you will, in short, so, when 'tis done,
'Tis but consistent, homogeneous, one.

Ye worthy trio! we poor sons of song
Oft find 'tis fancied right that leads us wrong.
I prove obscure in trying to be terse;
Attempts at ease emasculate my verse;
Who aims at grandeur into bombast falls;
Who fears to stretch his pinions creeps and crawls;
Who hopes by strange variety to please
Puts dolphins among forests, boars in seas.
Thus zeal to 'scape from error, if unchecked
By sense of art, creates a new defect.
Fix on some casual sculptor; he shall know
How to give nails their sharpness, hair its flow;
Yet he shall fail, because he lacks the soul
To comprehend and reproduce the whole.
I'd not be he; the blackest hair and eye
Lose all their beauty with the nose awry.

Good authors, take a brother bard's advice:
Ponder your subject o'er not once nor twice,
And oft and oft consider, if the weight
You hope to lift be or be not too great.
Let but our theme be equal to our powers,
Choice language, clear arrangement, both are ours.
Would you be told how best your pearls to thread?
Why, say just now what should just now be said,
But put off other matter for to-day,
To introduce it later by the way.

In words again be cautious and select,
And duly pick out this, and that reject.
High praise and honour to the bard is due
Whose dexterous setting makes an old word new.

Nay more, should some recondite subject need
Fresh signs to make it clear to those who read,
A power of issuing terms till now unused,
If claimed with modesty, is ne'er refused.
New words will find acceptance, if they flow
Forth from the Greek, with just a twist or so.
But why should Rome capriciously forbid
Our bards from doing what their fathers did?
Or why should Plautus and Caecilius gain
What Virgil or what Varius asks in vain?
Nay, I myself, if with my scanty wit
I coin a word or two, why grudge me it,
When Ennius and old Cato boldly flung
Their terms broadcast, and amplified our tongue?
To utter words stamped current by the mill
Has always been thought right and always will.

When forests shed their foliage at the fall,
The earliest born still drops the first of all:
So fades the elder race of words, and so
The younger generations bloom and grow.
Death claims humanity and human things,
Aye, e'en "imperial works and worthy kings:"
What though the ocean, girdled by the shore,
Gives shelter to the ships it tossed before?
What though the marsh, once waste and watery, now
Feeds neighbour towns, and groans beneath the plough?
What though the river, late the corn-field's dread,
Rolls fruit and blessing down its altered bed?
Man's works must perish: how should words evade
The general doom, and flourish undecayed?
Yes, words long faded may again revive,
And words may fade now blooming and alive,
If usage wills it so, to whom belongs
The rule, the law, the government of tongues.

For metres, Homer shows you how to write
Heroic deeds and incidents of fight.

Complaint was once the Elegiac's theme;
From thence 'twas used to sing of love's young dream:
But who that dainty measure first put out,
Grammarians differ, and 'tis still in doubt.

Archilochus, inspired by fiery rage,
Called forth Iambics: now they tread the stage
In buskin or in sock, conduct discourse,
Lead action on, and awe the mob perforce.

The glorious gods, the gods' heroic seed,
The conquering boxer, the victorious steed,
The joys of wine, the lover's fond desire,
Such themes the Muse appropriates to the lyre.

Why hail me poet, if I fail to seize
The shades of style, its fixed proprieties?
Why should false shame compel me to endure
An ignorance which common pains would cure?

A comic subject steadily declines
To be related in high tragic lines.
The Thyestean feast no less disdains
The vulgar vehicle of comic strains.
Each has its place allotted; each is bound
To keep it, nor invade its neighbour's ground.
Yet Comedy sometimes will raise her note:
See Chremes, how he swells his angry throat!
And when a tragic hero tells his woes,
The terms he chooses are akin to prose.
Peleus or Telephus, suppose him poor
Or driven to exile, talks in tropes no more;

His yard-long words desert him, when he tries
To draw forth tears from sympathetic eyes.

Mere grace is not enough: a play should thrill
The hearer's soul, and move it at its will.
Smiles are contagious; so are tears; to see
Another sobbing, brings a sob from me.
No, no, good Peleus; set the example, pray,
And weep yourself; then weep perhaps I may:
But if no sorrow in your speech appear,
I nod or laugh; I cannot squeeze a tear.
Words follow looks: wry faces are expressed
By wailing, scowls by bluster, smiles by jest,
Grave airs by saws, and so of all the rest.
For nature forms our spirits to receive
Each bent that outward circumstance can give:
She kindles pleasure, bids resentment glow,
Or bows the soul to earth in hopeless woe;
Then, as the tide of feeling waxes strong,
She vents it through her conduit-pipe, the tongue.

Unless the speaker's words and fortune suit,
All Rome will join to jeer him, horse and foot.
Gods should not talk like heroes, nor again
Impetuous youth like grave and reverend men;
Lady and nurse a different language crave,
Sons of the soil and rovers o'er the wave;
Assyrian, Colchian, Theban, Argive, each
Has his own style, his proper cast of speech.

In painting characters, adhere to fame,
Or study keeping in the type you frame:
If great Achilles figure in the scene,
Make him impatient, fiery, ruthless, keen;
All laws, all covenants let him still disown,
And test his quarrel by the sword alone.

Still be Medea all revenge and scorn,
Ino still sad, Ixion still forsworn,
Io a wanderer still, Orestes still forlorn.

If you would be original, and seek
To frame some character ne'er seen in Greek,
See it be wrought on one consistent plan,
And end the same creation it began.
'Tis hard, I grant, to treat a subject known
And hackneyed so that it may look one's own;
Far better turn the Iliad to a play
And carve out acts and scenes the readiest way,
Than alter facts and characters, and tell
In a strange form the tale men know so well.
But, with some few precautions, you may set
Your private mark on public chattels yet:
Avoid careering and careering still
In the old round, like carthorse in a mill;
Nor, bound too closely to the Grecian Muse,
Translate the words whose soul you should transfuse,
Nor act the copyist's part, and work in chains
Which, once put on by rashness, shame retains.

Don't open like the cyclic, with a burst:
"Troy's war and Priam's fate are here rehearsed."
What's coming, pray, that thus he winds his horn?
The mountain labours, and a mouse is born.
Far better he who enters at his ease,
Nor takes your breath with empty nourishes:
"Sing, Muse, the man who, after Troy was burned,
Saw divers cities, and their manners learned."
Not smoke from fire his object is to bring,
But fire from smoke, a very different thing;
Yet has he dazzling miracles in store,
Cyclops, and Laestrygons, and fifty more.
He sings not, he, of Diomed's return,

Starting from Meleager's funeral urn,
Nor when he tells the Trojan story, begs
Attention first for Leda and her eggs.
He hurries to the crisis, lets you fall
Where facts crowd thick, as though you knew them all,
And what he judges will not turn to gold
Beneath his touch, he passes by untold.
And all this glamour, all this glorious dream,
Truth blent with fiction in one motley scheme,
He so contrives, that, when 'tis o'er, you see
Beginning, middle, end alike agree.

Now listen, dramatists, and I will tell
What I expect, and all the world as well.
If you would have your auditors to stay
Till curtain-rise and plaudit end the play,
Observe each age's temper, and impart
To each the grace and finish of your art.

Note first the boy who just knows how to talk
And feels his feet beneath him in his walk:
He likes his young companions, loves a game,
Soon vexed, soon soothed, and not two hours the same.

The beardless youth, at last from tutor freed,
Loves playing-field and tennis, dog and steed:
Pliant as wax to those who lead him wrong,
But all impatience with a faithful tongue;
Imprudent, lavish, hankering for the moon,
He takes things up and lays them down as soon.

His nature revolutionized, the man
Makes friends and money when and how he can:
Keen-eyed and cool, though on ambition bent,
He shuns all acts of which he may repent.

Grey hairs have many evils: without end
The old man gathers what he dares not spend,
While, as for action, do he what he will,
'Tis all half-hearted, spiritless, and chill:
Inert, irresolute, his neck he cranes
Into the future, grumbles, and complains,
Extols his own young years with peevish praise,
But rates and censures these degenerate days.

Years, as they come, bring blessings in their train;
Years, as they go, take blessings back again:
Yet haste or chance may blink the obvious truth,
Make youth discourse like age, and age like youth:
Attention fixed on life alone can teach
The traits and adjuncts which pertain to each.

Sometimes an action on the stage is shown,
Sometimes 'tis done elsewhere, and there made known.
A thing when heard, remember, strikes less keen
On the spectator's mind than when 'tis seen.
Yet 'twere not well in public to display
A business best transacted far away,
And much may be secluded from the eye
For well-graced tongues to tell of by and by.
Medea must not shed her children's blood,
Nor savage Atreus cook man's flesh for food,
Nor Philomel turn bird or Cadmus snake,
With people looking on and wide awake.
If scenes like these before my eyes be thrust,
They shock belief and generate disgust.

Would you your play should prosper and endure?
Then let it have five acts, nor more nor fewer.
Bring in no god save as a last resource,
Nor make four speakers join in the discourse.

An actor's part the chorus should sustain
And do their best to get the plot in train:
And whatsoe'er between the acts they chant
Should all be apt, appropriate, relevant.
Still let them give sage counsel, back the good,
Attemper wrath, and cool impetuous blood,
Praise the spare meal that pleases but not sates,
Justice, and law, and peace with unbarred gates,
Conceal all secrets, and the gods implore
To crush the proud and elevate the poor.

Not trumpet-tongued, as now, nor brass-belayed,
The flute was used to lend the chorus aid:
Simple and slight and moderately loud,
It charmed the ears of not too large a crowd,
Which, frugal, rustic, primitive, severe,
Flocked in those early days to see and hear.

Then, when the city gained increase of land,
And wider walls its waxing greatness spanned,
When the good Genius, frolicsome and gay,
Was soothed at festivals with cups by day,
Change spread to scenic measures: breadth, and ease,
And freedom unrestrained were found in these:
For what (said men) should jovial rustic, placed
At random 'mid his betters, know of taste?

So graceful dance went hand in hand with song,
And robes of kingly splendour trailed along:
So by the side of music words upgrew,
And eloquence came rolling, prompt and new:
Shrewd in things mundane, wise in things divine,
Its voice was like the voice of Delphi's shrine.

The aspiring bard who served the tragic muse,
A paltry goat the summit of his views,

Soon brought in Satyrs from the woods, and tried
If grave and gay could nourish side by side,
That the spectator, feasted to his fill,
Noisy and drunk, might ne'ertheless sit still.

Yet, though loud laugh and frolic jest commend
Your Satyr folk, and mirth and morals blend,
Let not your heroes doff their robes of red
To talk low language in a homely shed,
Nor, in their fear of crawling, mount too high,
Catching at clouds and aiming at the sky.
Melpomene, when bidden to be gay,
Like matron dancing on a festal day,
Deals not in idle banter, nor consorts
Without reserve with Satyrs and their sports.

In plays like these I would not deal alone
In words and phrases trite and too well known,
Nor, stooping from the tragic height, drop down
To the low level of buffoon and clown,
As though pert Davus, or the saucy jade
Who sacks the gold and jeers the gull she made,
Were like Silenus, who, though quaint and odd,
Is yet the guide and tutor of a god.
A hackneyed subject I would take and treat
So deftly, all should hope to do the feat,
Then, having strained and struggled, should concede
To do the feat were difficult indeed.
So much may order and arrangement do
To make the cheap seem choice, the threadbare new.

Your rustic Fauns, methinks, should have a care
Lest people deem them bred in city air;
Should shun the cant of exquisites, and shun
Coarse ribaldry no less and blackguard fun.
For those who have a father or a horse

Or an estate will take offence of course,
Nor think they're bound in duty to admire
What gratifies the vetch-and-chestnut-buyer

The Iambic foot is briefly thus defined:
Two syllables, a short with long behind:
Repeat it six times o'er, so quick its beat,
'Tis trimeter, three measures for six feet:
At first it ran straight on; but, years ago,
Its hearers begged that it would move more slow;
On which it took, with a good-natured air,
Stout spondees in, its native rights to share,
Yet so that none should ask it to resign
The sixth, fourth, second places in the line.
But search through Attius' trimeters, or those
Which Ennius took such pleasure to compose,
You'll rarely find it: on the boards they groan,
Laden with spondees, like a cart with stone,
And brand our tragedy with want of skill
Or want of labour, call it which you will.
What then? false rhythm few judges can detect,
And Roman bards of course are all correct.

What shall a poet do? make rules his sport,
And dash through thick and thin, through long and short?
Or pick his steps, endeavour to walk clean,
And fancy every mud-stain will be seen?
What good were that, if though I mind my ways
And shun all blame, I do not merit praise?
My friends, make Greece your model when you write,
And turn her volumes over day and night.

"But Plautus pleased our sires, the good old folks;
They praised his numbers, and they praised his jokes."
They did: 'twas mighty tolerant in them
To praise where wisdom would perhaps condemn;

That is, if you and I and our compeers
Can trust our tastes, our fingers, and our ears,
Know polished wit from horse-play, and can tell
What verses do, and what do not, run well.

Thespis began the drama: rumour says
In travelling carts he carried round his plays,
Where actors, smeared with lees, before the throng
Performed their parts with gesture and with song.
Then Aeschylus brought in the mask and pall,
Put buskins on his men to make them tall,
Turned boards into a platform, not too great,
And taught high monologue and grand debate.
The elder Comedy had next its turn,
Nor small the glory it contrived to earn:
But freedom passed into unbridled spite,
And law was soon invoked to set things right:
Law spoke: the chorus lost the power to sting,
And (shame to say) thenceforth refused to sing.

Our poets have tried all things; nor do they
Deserve least praise, who follow their own way,
And tell in comedy or history-piece
Some story of home growth, not drawn from Greece.
Nor would the land we love be now more strong
In warrior's prowess than in poet's song,
Did not her bards with one consent decline
The tedious task, to alter and refine.
Dear Pisos! as you prize old Numa's blood,
Set down that work, and that alone, as good,
Which, blurred and blotted, checked and counter-checked,
Has stood all tests, and issued forth correct.

Because Democritus thinks fit to say,
That wretched art to genius must give way,
Stands at the gate of Helicon, and guards

Its precinct against all but crazy bards,
Our witlings keep long nails and untrimmed hair,
Much in brown studies, in the bath-room rare.
For things are come to this; the merest dunce,
So but he choose, may start up bard at once,
Whose head, too hot for hellebore to cool,
Was ne'er submitted to a barber's tool.
What ails me now, to dose myself each spring?
Else had I been a very swan to sing.
Well, never mind: mine be the whetstone's lot,
Which makes steel sharp, though cut itself will not.
Although no writer, I may yet impart
To writing folk the precepts of their art,
Whence come its stores, what trains and forms a bard,
And how a work is made, and how 'tis marred.

Of writing well, be sure, the secret lies
In wisdom: therefore study to be wise.
The page of Plato may suggest the thought,
Which found, the words will come as soon as sought.
The man who once has learned to comprehend
His duty to his country and his friend,
The love that parent, brother, guest may claim.
The judge's, senator's, or general's aim,
That man, when need occurs, will soon invent
For every part its proper sentiment.
Look too to life and manners, as they lie
Before you: these will living words supply.
A play, devoid of beauty, strength, and art,
So but the thoughts and morals suit each part,
Will catch men's minds and rivet them when caught
More than the clink of verses without thought.

To Greece, fair Greece, ambitious but of praise,
The Muse gave ready wit, and rounded phrase.
Our Roman boys, by puzzling days and nights,

Bring down a shilling to a hundred mites.
Come, young Albinus, tell us, if you take
A penny from a sixpence, what 'twill make.
Fivepence. Good boy! you'll come to wealth one day.
Now add a penny. Sevenpence, he will say.
O, when this cankering rust, this greed of gain,
Has touched the soul and wrought into its grain,
What hope that poets will produce such lines
As cedar-oil embalms and cypress shrines?

A bard will wish to profit or to please,
Or, as a *tertium quid,* do both of these.
Whene'er you lecture, be concise: the soul
Takes in short maxims, and retains them whole:
But pour in water when the vessel's filled,
It simply dribbles over and is spilled.

Keep near to truth in a fictitious piece,
Nor treat belief as matter of caprice.
If on a child you make a vampire sup,
It must not be alive when she's ripped up.
Dry seniors scout an uninstructive strain;
Young lordlings treat grave verse with tall disdain:
But he who, mixing grave and gay, can teach
And yet give pleasure, gains a vote from each:
His works enrich the vendor, cross the sea,
And hand the author down to late posterity.

Some faults may claim forgiveness: for the lyre
Not always gives the note that we desire;
We ask a flat; a sharp is its reply;
And the best bow will sometimes shoot awry.
But when I meet with beauties thickly sown,
A blot or two I readily condone,
Such as may trickle from a careless pen,
Or pass unwatched: for authors are but men.

What then? the copyist who keeps stumbling still
At the same word had best lay down his quill:
The harp-player, who forever wounds the ear
With the same discord, makes the audience jeer:
So the poor dolt who's often in the wrong
I rank with Choerilus, that dunce of song,
Who, should he ever "deviate into sense,"
Moves but fresh laughter at his own expense:
While e'en good Homer may deserve a tap,
If, as he does, he drop his head and nap.
Yet, when a work is long, 'twere somewhat hard
To blame a drowsy moment in a bard.

Some poems, like some paintings, take the eye
Best at a distance, some when looked at nigh.
One loves the shade; one would be seen in light,
And boldly challenges the keenest sight:
One pleases straightway; one, when it has passed
Ten times before the mind, will please at last.

Hope of the Pisos! trained by such a sire,
And wise yourself, small schooling you require;
Yet take this lesson home; some things admit
A moderate point of merit, e'en in wit.
There's yonder counsellor; he cannot reach
Messala's stately altitudes of speech,
He cannot plumb Cascellius' depth of lore,
Yet he's employed, and makes a decent score:
But gods, and men, and booksellers agree
To place their ban on middling poetry.
At a great feast an ill-toned instrument,
A sour conserve, or an unfragrant scent
Offends the taste: 'tis reason that it should;
We do without such things, or have them good:
Just so with verse; you seek but to delight;
If by an inch you fail, you fail outright.

He who knows nought of games abstains from all,
Nor tries his hand at quoit, or hoop, or ball,
Lest the thronged circle, witnessing the play,
Should laugh outright, with none to say them nay:
He who knows nought of verses needs must try
To write them ne'ertheless. "Why not?" men cry:
"Free, gently born, unblemished and correct,
His means a knight's, what more can folks expect?"
But you, my friend, at least have sense and grace;
You will not fly in queen Minerva's face
In action or in word. Suppose some day
You should take courage and compose a lay,
Entrust it first to Maecius' critic ears,
Your sire's and mine, and keep it back nine years.
What's kept at home you cancel by a stroke:
What's sent abroad you never can revoke.

Orpheus, the priest and harper, pure and good,
Weaned savage tribes from deeds and feasts of blood,
Whence he was said to tame the monsters of the wood.
Amphion too, men said, at his desire
Moved massy stones, obedient to the lyre,
And Thebes arose. 'Twas wisdom's province then
To judge 'twixt states and subjects, gods and men,
Check vagrant lust, give rules to wedded folk,
Build cities up, and grave a code in oak.
So came great honour and abundant praise,
As to the gods, to poets and their lays.
Then Homer and Tyrtaeus, armed with song,
Made manly spirits for the combat strong:
Verse taught life's duties, showed the future clear,
And won a monarch's favour through his ear:
Verse gave relief from labour, and supplied
Light mirth for holiday and festal tide.
Then blush not for the lyre: Apollo sings
In unison with her who sweeps its strings.

But here occurs a question some men start,
If good verse comes from nature or from art.
For me, I cannot see how native wit
Can e'er dispense with art, or art with it.
Set them to pull together, they're agreed,
And each supplies what each is found to need.

The youth who suns for prizes wisely trains,
Bears cold and heat, is patient and abstains:
The flute-player at a festival, before
He plays in public, has to learn his lore.
Not so our bardlings: they come bouncing in—
"I'm your true poet: let them laugh that win:
Plague take the last! although I ne'er was taught,
Is that a cause for owning I know nought?"

As puffing auctioneers collect a throng,
Rich poets bribe false friends to hear their song:
Who can resist the lord of so much rent,
Of so much money at so much per cent.?
Is there a wight can give a grand regale,
Act as a poor man's counsel or his bail?
Blest though he be, his wealth will cloud his view,
Nor suffer him to know false friends from true.
Don't ask a man whose feelings overflow
For kindness that you've shown or mean to show
To listen to your verse: each line you read,
He'll cry, "Good! bravo! exquisite indeed!"
He'll change his colour, let his eyes run o'er
With tears of joy, dance, beat upon the floor.
Hired mourners at a funeral say and do
A little more than they whose grief is true:
'Tis just so here: false flattery displays
More show of sympathy than honest praise.
'Tis said when kings a would-be friend will try,
With wine they rack him and with bumpers ply:

If you write poems, look beyond the skin
Of the smooth fox, and search the heart within.

Read verses to Quintilius, he would say,
"I don't like this and that: improve it, pray:"
Tell him you found it hopeless to correct;
You'd tried it twice or thrice without effect:
He'd calmly bid you make the three times four,
And take the unlicked cub in hand once more.
But if you chose to vindicate the crime,
Not mend it, he would waste no further time,
But let you live, untroubled by advice,
Sole tenant of your own fool's paradise.

A wise and faithful counsellor will blame
Weak verses, note the rough, condemn the lame,
Retrench luxuriance, make obscureness plain,
Cross-question this, bid that be writ again:
A second Aristarch, he will not ask,
"Why for such trifles take my friend to task?"
Such trifles bring to serious grief ere long
A hapless bard, once flattered and led wrong.

See the mad poet! never wight, though sick
Of itch or jaundice, moon-struck, fanatic,
Was half so dangerous: men whose mind is sound
Avoid him; fools pursue him, children hound.
Suppose, while spluttering verses, head on high,
Like fowler watching blackbirds in the sky,
He falls into a pit; though loud he shout
"Help, neighbours, help!" let no man pull him out:
Should someone seem disposed a rope to fling,
I will strike in with, "Pray do no such thing:
I'll warrant you he meant it," and relate
His brother bard Empedocles's fate,
Who, wishing to be thought a god, poor fool,

Leapt down hot Aetna's crater, calm and cool.
"Leave poets free to perish as they will:
Save them by violence, you as good as kill.
'Tis not his first attempt: if saved to-day,
He's sure to die in some outrageous way.
Beside, none knows the reason why this curse
Was sent on him, this love of making verse,
By what offence heaven's anger he incurred,
A grave denied, a sacred boundary stirred:
So much is plain, he's mad: like bear that beats
His prison down and ranges through the streets,
This terrible reciter puts to flight
The learned and unlearned left and right:
Let him catch one, he keeps him till he kills,
As leeches stick till they have sucked their fills."

Horace. *Satires, Epistles, and Ars Poetica.* Translated by John Conington. Cambridge: University of Oxford Press, 1878 & 2004, http://archive.org/stream/thesatiresepistlo5419gut/hrcst10.txt

Chapter 7

Quintilian

Quintilian (Marcus Fabius Quintilianus [35–100 CE]) was a renowned educator and famous rhetorician who stressed the importance of virtue and integrity in rhetoric. Indeed, he defined rhetoric as *vir bonus, dicendi peritus*, the "good man speaking well." Quintilian believed that rhetoric could be taught through imitation—students should seek good examples of oratory and emulate those examples and combine them with their own style and voice. Quintilian argued that it was not only important to study the examples of good speeches, but that it was also crucial to emulate the virtues of model speakers. Thus, Quintilian emphasized the concept of ethos as an effective method for persuading audiences.

The *Institutio Oratoria*, vol. 1

[...]

The custom has prevailed and is daily growing commoner of sending boys to the schools of rhetoric much later than is reasonable: this is always the case as regards Latin rhetoric and occasionally applies to Greek as well. The reason for this is twofold: the rhetoricians, more especially our own, have abandoned certain of their duties and the teachers of literature have undertaken tasks which rightly belong to others. For the rhetorician considers that his duty is merely to declaim and give instruction in the theory and practice of declamation and confines his activities to deliberative and judicial themes, regarding all others as beneath the dignity of his profession; while the teacher of literature is not satisfied to take what is left him (and we owe him a debt of gratitude for this), but even presumes to handle declamations in character and deliberative themes, tasks which impose the very heaviest burden on the speaker. Consequently subjects which once formed the first stages of rhetoric have come to form the final stages of a literary education, and boys who are ripe for more advanced study are kept back in the inferior school and practice rhetoric under the direction of teachers of literature. Thus we get the absurd result that a boy is not regarded as fit to go on to the schools of declamation till he knows how to declaim.

The two professions must each be assigned their proper sphere. *Grammatice,* which we translate as the science of letters, must learn to know its own limits, especially as it has encroached so far beyond the boundaries to which its unpretentious name should restrict it and to which its earlier professors actually confined themselves. Springing from a tiny fountain-head, it has gathered strength from the historians and critics and has swollen to the dimensions of a brimming river, since, not content with the theory of correct speech, no inconsiderable subject, it has usurped the study of practically all the highest departments of knowledge. On the other hand rhetoric, which derives its name from the power of eloquence, must not shirk its peculiar duties nor rejoice to see its own burdens shouldered by others. For the neglect of these is little less than a surrender of its birthright. I will of course admit that there may be a few professors of literature who have acquired sufficient knowledge to be able to teach rhetoric as well; but when they do so, they are performing their duties of the rhetorician, not their own.

A further point into which we must enquire concerns the age at which a boy may be considered sufficiently advanced to profit by the instructions of the rhetorician. In this connexion [sic] we must consider not the boy's actual age, but the progress he has made in his studies. To put it briefly, I hold that the best answer to the question "When should a boy be sent to the school of rhetoric?" is this, "When he is fit." But this question is really dependent on that previously raised. For if the duties of the teacher of literature are prolonged to include instruction in deliberative declamation, this will postpone the need for the rhetorician. On the other hand if the rhetorician does not refuse to undertake the first duties of his task, his instruction will be required from the moment the boy begins to compose narratives and his first attempts at passages of praise or denunciation. We know that the orators of earlier days improved their eloquence by declaiming themes and common-places and other forms of rhetorical exercises not involving particular circumstances or persons such as provide the material for real or imaginary causes. From this we can clearly see what a scandalous dereliction of duty it is for the schools of rhetoric to abandon this department of their work, which was not merely its first, but for a long time its sole task. What is there in those exercises of which I have just spoken that does not involve matters which are the special concern of rhetoric and further are typical of actual legal cases? Have we not to narrate facts in the law-courts? Indeed I am not sure that this is not the most important department of rhetoric in actual practice. Are not eulogy and denunciation frequently introduced in the course of the contests in the courts? Are not common-places frequently those which we find in the works of Cicero, they are directed against vice, or, like those published by Quintus Hortensius, deal with questions of general interest such as "whether small points of argument should carry weight," or are employed to defend or impugn the credibility of witnesses? These are weapons which we should always have stored in our armoury ready for immediate use as occasion may demand. The critic who denies that such matters concern an orator is one who will refuse to believe that a statue is being begun when its limbs are actually being cast. Some will think that I am in too great a hurry, but let no one accuse me of thinking that the pupil who has been entrusted to the rhetorician should forthwith be withdrawn from the teacher of literature. The latter will still have certain hours allotted him, and there is no reason to fear that a boy will be overloaded by receiving instruction from two different masters. It will not mean any increase of work, but merely the division among two masters of the studies which were previously indiscriminately combined under one: and the efficiency of either teacher will be increased. This method is still in vogue among the Greeks, but has been abandoned by us, not perhaps without some excuse, as there were others ready to step into the rhetorician's shoes.

[. . .]

I shall now proceed to indicate what I think should be the first subjects in which the rhetorician should give instruction, and shall postpone for a time our consideration of the art of rhetoric in the narrow sense in which that term is popularly used. For in my opinion it is most desirable that we should commence with something resembling the subjects already acquired under the teacher of literature.

Now there are three forms of narrative, without counting the type used in actual legal cases. First there is the fictitious narrative as we get it in tragedies and poems, which is not merely not true but has little resemblance to truth. Secondly, there is the realistic narrative as presented by comedies, which, though not true, has yet a certain verisimilitude. Thirdly there is the historical narrative, which is an exposition of actual fact. Poetic narratives are the property of the teacher of literature. The rhetorician therefore should begin with the historical narrative, whose force is in proportion to its truth. I will, however, postpone my demonstration of what I regard as the best method of narration till I come to deal with narration as required in the courts. In the meantime, it will be sufficient to urge that it should be neither dry nor jejune (for why spend so much labour over our studies if a bald and naked statement of fact is regarded as sufficiently expressive?); nor on the other hand must it be tortuous or revel in elaborate descriptions, such as those in which so many are led to indulge by a misguided imitation of poetic license. Both these extremes are faults; but that which springs from poverty of wit is worse than that which is due to imaginative excess. For we cannot demand or expect a perfect style from boys. But there is greater promise in a certain luxuriance of mind, in ambitious effort and an ardour that leads at times to ideas bordering on the extravagant. I have no objection to a little exuberance in the young learner.

Reprinted by permission of the publishers and the Trustees of the Loeb Classical Library from *Quintilian: The Institutio Oratoria of Quintilian*, volume 1, Loeb Classical Library, translated by H. E. Butler, pages 205–211; 225–227, Cambridge, MA: Harvard University Press, Copyright 1922, by the President and Fellows of Harvard College. Loeb Classical Library® is a registered trademark of the President and Fellows of Harvard College.

The *Institutio Oratoria,* vol. 4

[...]

But presently when I entered on the task of setting forth a theory of eloquence which I had been newly discovered and rarely essayed, I found but
few that had ventured so far from harbour. And finally now that the ideal
orator, whom it was my design to mould, has been dismissed by his masters
and is either proceeding on his way borne onward by his own impetus, or
seeking still mightier assistance from the innermost shrine of wisdom, I begin
to feel how far I have been swept into the great deep. Now there is "Nothing before and nothing behind but the sky and the Ocean." One only can
I discern in all the boundless waste of waters, Marcus Tullius Cicero, and
even he, though the ship in which he entered these seas is of such size and
so well found, begins to lessen sail and to row a slower stroke, and is content
to speak merely of the kind of speech to be employed by the perfect orator.
But my temerity is such that I shall essay to form my orator's character and
to teach him his duties. Thus I have no predecessor to guide my steps and
must press far, far on, as my theme may demand. Still an honourable ambition is always deserving of approval, and it is all the less hazardous to dare
greatly, when forgiveness is assured us if we fail.

1. The orator then, whom I am concerned to form, shall be the orator
as defined by Marcus Cato, "a good man, skilled in speaking." But above
all he must possess the quality which Cato places first and which is in the
very nature of things the greatest and most important, that is, he must be
a good man. This is essential not merely on account of the fact that, if the
powers of eloquence serve only to lend arms to crime, there can be nothing
more pernicious than eloquence to public and private welfare alike, while I
myself, who have laboured to the best of my ability to contribute something
of value to oratory, shall have rendered the worst of services to mankind,
if I forge there weapons not for a soldier, but for a robber. But shy speak of
myself? Nature herself will have proved not a mother, but a stepmother
with regard to what we deem her greatest gift to man, the gift that distinguishes us from other living things, if she devised the power of speech to
be the accomplice of crime, the foe to innocency and the enemy of truth.
For it had been better for men to be born dumb and devoid of reason than
to turn the gifts of providence to their mutual destruction. But this conviction of mine goes further. For I do not merely assert that the ideal orator

should be a good man, but I affirm that no man can be an orator unless he is a good man. For it is impossible to regard those men as gifted with intelligence who on being offered the choice between the two paths of virtue and of vice choose the latter, nor can we allow them prudence, when by the unforeseen issue of their own actions they render themselves liable not merely to the heaviest penalties of the laws, but to the inevitable torment of an evil conscience. But if the view that a bad man is necessarily a fool is not merely held by philosophers, but is the universal belief of ordinary men, the fool will most assuredly never become an orator. To this must be added the fact that the mind will not find leisure even for the study of the noblest of tasks, unless it first be free from vice. The reasons for this are, first, that vileness and virtue cannot jointly inhabit in the selfsame heart and that it is impossible for one and the same mind to harbour good and evil thoughts as it is for one man to be at once both good and evil: and secondly, that if the intelligence is to be concentrated on such a vast subject as eloquence it must be free from all other distractions, among which must be included even those preoccupations which are free from blame. For it is only when it is free and self-possessed, with nothing to divert it or lure it elsewhere, that it will fix its attention solely on that goal, the attainment of which is the object of its preparations. If on the other hand inordinate care for the development of our estates, excess of anxiety over household affairs, passionate devotion to hunting or the sacrifice of whole days to the shows of the theatre, rob our studies of much of the time that is their due (for every moment that is given to other things involves a loss of time for study), what, think you, will be the results of desire, avarice, and envy, which waken such violent thoughts within our souls that they disturb our very slumbers and our dreams? There is nothing so preoccupied, so distracted, so rent and torn by so many and such varied passions as an evil mind. For when it cherishes some dark design, it is tormented with hope, care and anguish of spirit, and even when it has accomplished its criminal purpose, it is racked by anxiety, remorse and the fear of all manner of punishments. Amid such passions as these what room is there for literature or any virtuous pursuit? You might as well look for fruit in land that is choked with thorns and brambles. Well then, I ask you, is not simplicity of life essential if we are to be able to endure the toil entailed by study? What can we hope to get from lust or luxury? Is not the desire to win praise one of the strongest stimulants to a passion for literature? But does that mean that we are to suppose that praise is an object of concern to bad men? Surely every one of my readers must by now have realised that oratory is in the main concerned with the treatment of what is just and honourable? Can a bad and unjust man speak on such themes as the dignity of the subject demands? Nay, even if we exclude the most important aspects of the question now before us, and make the impossible concession that the best and worst of men may have the same talent, industry and learning, we are still confronted by the question as to which of the two is entitled to be called the better orator. The answer is surely clear enough: it will be he who is the better man. Consequently, the bad man and the perfect orator can never be identical.

[...]

However, let us fly in the face of nature and assume that a bad man has been discovered who is endowed with the highest eloquence. I shall none the less deny that he is an orator. For I should not allow that every man who has shown himself ready with his hands was necessarily a brave man, because true courage cannot be conceived of without the accompaniment of virtue. Surely the advocate who is called to defend the accused requires to be a man of honour, honour which greed cannot corrupt, influence seduce, or fear dismay. Shall we then dignify the traitor, the deserter, the turncoat with the sacred name of orator? But if the quality which is usually termed goodness is to be found even in quite ordinary advocates, why should not the orator, who has not yet existed, but may still be born, be no less perfect in character than in excellence of speech? It is no hack-advocate, no hireling pleader, nor yet, to use no harsher term, a serviceable attorney of the class generally known as *causidici*, that I am seeking to form, but rather a man who to extraordinary natural gifts has added a thorough mastery of all the fairest branches of knowledge, a man sent by heaven to be the blessing of mankind, one to whom all history can find no parallel, uniquely perfect in every detail and utterly noble alike in thought and speech. How small a portion of all these abilities will be required for the defence of the innocent, the repression of crime or the support of truth against falsehood in suits involving questions of money? It is true that our supreme orator will bear his part in such tasks, but his powers will be displayed with brighter splendour in greater matters than these, when he is called upon to direct the counsels of the senate and guide the people from the paths of error to better things. Was not this the man conceived by Virgil and described as quelling a riot when torches and stones have begun to fly: "Then, if before their eyes some statesman grave Stand forth, with virtue and high service crowned, Straight are they dumb and stand intent to hear." Here then we have one who is before all else a good man, and it is only after this that the poet adds that he is skilled in speaking: "His words their minds control, their passions soothe." Again, will not this same man, whom we are striving to form, if in time of war he be called upon to inspire his soldiers with courage for the fray, draw for his eloquence on the innermost precepts of philosophy? For how can men who stand upon the verge of battle banish all the crowding fears of hardship, pain and death from their minds, unless those fears be replaced by the sense of the duty that they owe their country, by courage and the lively image of a soldier's honour? And assuredly the man who will best inspire such feelings in others is he who has first inspired them in himself. For however we strive to conceal it, insincerity will always betray itself, and there was never in any man so great eloquence as would not begin to stumble and hesitate so soon as his words ran counter to his inmost thoughts. Now a bad man cannot help speaking things other than he feels. On the other hand, the good will never be at a loss for honourable words or fail to find matter full of virtue for utterance, since among his virtues practical wisdom will be one. And even though his imagination lacks artifice to lend it charm, its own nature will be ornament enough, for if honour dictate the words, we shall find eloquence there as well. Therefore, let those that are young, or rather let all of us, whatever our age, since it is never too late to resolve to follow what is right, strive with all our hearts and devote all our efforts to the pursuit of virtue and eloquence; and perchance it may be granted to us to attain to the perfection that we seek. For since nature does not forbid the attainment of either, why should not someone succeed in attaining both together? And why should not each of us hope to be that happy man? But if our powers are inadequate to such achievement, we shall still be the better for the double effort in proportion to the distance which we have advanced toward either goal. At any rate let us banish from our hearts the delusion that eloquence, the fairest of all things, can be combined with vice. The power of speaking is even to be accounted an evil when it is found in evil men; for it makes its possessors yet worse than they were before.

I think I hear certain persons (for there will always be some who had rather be eloquent than good) asking, "Why then is there so much art in connexion [sic] with eloquence? Why have you talked so much of 'glosses,' the methods of defence to be employed in difficult cases, and sometimes even of actual confession of guildt, unless it is the case that the power and force of speech at times triumphs over truth itself? For a good man will only plead good cases, and those might safely be left to truth to support without the aid of learning." Now, though my reply to these critics will in the first place be a defence of my own work, it will also explain what I consider to be the duty of a good man on occasions when circumstances have caused him to undertake the defence of the guilty. For it is by no means useless to consider how at times we should speak in defence of falsehood or even of injustice, if only for this reason, that such an investigation will enable us to detect and defeat them with the greater case, just as the physician who has a thorough knowledge of all that can injure the health will be all the more skilful in the prescription of remedies. For the Academicians, although they will argue on either side of a question, do not thereby commit themselves to taking one of these two views as their guide in life to the exclusion of the other, while the famous Carneades, who is said to have spoken at Rome in the presence of Cato the Censor, and to have argued against justice with no less vigour than he had argued for justice on the preceding day, was not himself an unjust man. But the nature of virtue is revealed by vice, its opposite, justice becomes yet more manifest from the contemplation of injustice, and there are many other things that are proved by their contraries. Consequently the schemes of his adversaries should be no less well known to the orator than those of the enemy to a commander in the field. But it is even true, although at first sight it seems hard to believe, that there may be sound reason why at times a good man who is appearing for the defence should attempt to conceal the truth from the judge.

[...]

For my purpose is not to assert that such tasks will often be incumbent on the orator whom I desire to form, but merely to show that, in the event of his being compelled to take such action, it will not invalidate our definition of an orator as a "good man, skilled in speaking." And it is necessary also both to teach and learn how to establish difficult cases by proof. For often even the best cases have a resemblance to bad and, the charges which tell heavily against an innocent person frequently have a strong resemblance to the truth. Consequently, the same methods of defence have to be employed that would be used if he were guilty. Further, there are countless elements which are common to both good cases and bad, such as oral and documentary evidence, suspicions and opinions, all of which have to be established or disposed of in the same way, whether they be true or merely resemble the truth. Therefore, while maintaining his integrity of purpose, the orator will modify his pleading to suit the circumstances.

Since then the orator is a good man, and such goodness cannot be conceived as existing apart from virtue, despite the fact that it is in part derived from certain natural impulses, will require to be perfected by instruction. The orator must above all things devote his attention to the formation of moral character and must acquire a complete knowledge of all that is just and honourable. For without this knowledge no one can be either a good man or skilled in speaking, unless indeed we agree with those who regard morality as intuitive and as owing nothing to instruction: indeed they go so far as to acknowledge that handicrafts, not excluding even those which are most despised among them, can only be acquired by the result of teaching, whereas virtue, which of all gifts to man is that which makes him most near akin to the immortal gods, comes to him without search or effort, as a natural concomitant of birth. But can the man who does not know what abstinence is, claim to be truly abstinent? Or brave, if he has never purged his soul of the fears of pain, death and superstition? Or just, if he has never, in language approaching that of philosophy, discussed the nature of virtue and justice, or of the laws that have been given to mankind by nature or established among individual peoples and nations? What a contempt it argues for such themes to regard them as being so easy of comprehension! However, I pass this by; for I am sure that no one with the least smattering of literary culture will have the slightest hesitation in agreeing with me. I will proceed to my next point, that no one will achieve sufficient skill even in speaking, unless he makes a thorough study of all the workings of nature and forms his character to the precepts of philosophy and the dictates of reason. For it is with good cause that Lucius Crassus, in the third book of the *de Oratore*, affirms that all that is said concerning equity, justice, truth and the good, and their opposites, forms part of the studies of an orator, and that the philosophers, when they exert their powers of speaking to defend these virtues, are using the weapons of rhetoric, not their own. But he also confesses that the knowledge of these subjects must be sought from the philosophers for the reason that, in his opinion, philosophy has more effective possession of them. And it is for the same reason that Cicero in several of his books and letters proclaims that eloquence has its fountain-head in the most secret springs of wisdom, and that consequently for a considerable time the instructors of morals and of eloquence were identical. Accordingly this exhortation of mine must not be taken to mean that I wish the orator to be a philosopher, since there is no other way of life that is further removed from the duties of a statesman and the tasks of an orator. For what philosopher has ever been a frequent speaker in the courts or won renown in public assemblies? Nay, what philosopher has ever taken a prominent part in the government of the state, which forms the most frequent theme of their instructions? None the less I desire that he, whose character I am seeking to mould, should be a "wise man" in the Roman sense, that is, one who reveals himself as a true statesman, not in the discussions of the study, but in the actual practice and experience of life. But inasmuch as the study of philosophy has been deserted by those who have turned to the pursuit of eloquence, and since philosophy no longer moves in its true sphere of action and in the broad daylight of the forum, but has retired first to porches and gymnasia and finally to the gatherings of the schools, all that is essential for an orator, and yet is not taught by the professors of eloquence, must undoubtedly be sought from those persons in whose possession it has remained. The authors who have discoursed on the nature of virtue must be read through and through, that the life of the orator may be wedded to the knowledge of things human and divine. But how much greater and fairer would such subjects appear if those who taught them were also those who could give them most eloquent expression! O that the day may dawn when the perfect orator of our heart's desire shall claim for his own possession that science that has lost the affection of mankind through the arrogance of its claims and the vices of some that have brought disgrace upon its virtues, and shall restore it to its place in the domain of eloquence, as though he had been victorious in a trial for the restoration of stolen goods! And since philosophy falls into three divisions, physics, ethics, and dialectic, which, I ask you, of these departments is not closely connected with the task of the orator?

SECTION THREE
The Middle Ages

The Middle Ages (c. 500–1500) is often considered to be a bridge between Antiquity and the modern era. It was marked by several notable developments—the spread of Christianity, the founding of universities, the invention of the printing press, debates over theology, and disputes about theories of astronomy and geometry. Central to these issues and debates was rhetoric, although rhetoric was not generally thought to be an important practice or art during this time. In the Middle Ages, human history underwent a communication transition from oral to handwritten to print. The role of rhetoric was primarily seen to be legitimate in religious contexts, elements of style, and teaching.

We have included selections from St. Augustine, Dante Alighieri, and Erasmus to provide a sense of the rhetorical tradition during this era as well as to highlight some of the key issues in rhetoric throughout the Middle Ages. These issues include the teaching and use of rhetoric for religious purposes (Augustine), the power of language (Dante), and elements of style (Erasmus). Just as the Middle Ages are a transition period in human history, so, too, do they provide an important connection for our understanding of rhetoric. The classical concepts of rhetoric are not forgotten during this time—but neither are they emphasized. In some respects, this era consists of 10 centuries of theoretical limbo in terms of our knowledge about rhetoric.

READINGS

McLaughlin, Thomas. *Street Smarts and Critical Theory: Listening to the Vernacular.* Madison: University of Wisconsin Press, 1996.

Miller, Joseph M., Michael H. Prosser, and Thomas W. Benson. *Readings in Medieval Rhetoric.* Bloomington: Indiana University Press, 1974.

O'Donnell, Anne M. "Rhetoric and Style in Erasmus." *Studies in Philology* 77, no. 1 (1980): 26–50.

Ono, Kent A., and John M. Sloop. "Commitment to Telos—a Sustained Critical Rhetoric." *Communication Monographs* 59 (1992): 48–60.

Ramsey, Shawn D. "*Consilium*: A System to Address Deliberative Uncertainty in the Rhetoric of the Middle Ages." *Advances in the History of Rhetoric* 15, no. 2 (2012): 204–221.

Chapter 8

Augustine

St. Augustine (354–430 CE), bishop of Hippo in Africa, was one of the most influential Christian thinkers of all time. His primary contribution to our study of rhetoric is his contention that Christian leaders and teachers should be taught the principles of rhetoric so they can spread the Christian faith and defend orthodox doctrine against heresy.

Augustine expounds on these ideas in *De Doctrina Christiana*, his four-volume theological text on how to interpret and teach scripture. The first three volumes discuss doctrine, but in volume four he describes the relationship between Christian doctrine and rhetoric, stressing that preachers should use rhetoric to impart wisdom.

In the selections here, Augustine spends considerable time discussing style both in terms of enhancing eloquence (rhetoric) and in relation to effective teaching. He argues that there are three types of style—the subdued (for instruction), the elegant (for praise), and the majestic (for exhortation)—and suggests that styles can overlap and mingle depending on the audience and occasion. Here we have an allusion to the Greek concept of *kairos*, although Augustine does not explicitly refer to it by name. Even though he claims that *De Doctrina Christina* is not a "treatise on rhetoric," he goes to great lengths to argue that clergy need to be skilled in the art and techniques of rhetoric. By extension, he is also making the case for why all of us should be knowledgeable about rhetoric.

55. This art, however, when it is learnt, is not to be used so much for ascertaining the meaning as for setting forth the meaning when it is ascertained. But the art previously spoken of, which deals with inferences, and definitions, and divisions, is of the greatest assistance in the discovery of the meaning, provided only that men do not fall into the error of supposing that when they have learnt these things they have learnt the true secret of a happy life. Still, it sometimes happens that men find less difficulty in attaining the object for the sake of which these sciences are learnt, than in going through the very intricate and thorny discipline of such rules. It is just as if a man wishing to give rules for walking should warn you not to lift the hinder foot before you set down the front one, and then should describe minutely the way you ought to move the hinges of the joints and knees. For what he says is true, and one cannot walk in any other way; but men find it easier to walk by executing these movements than to attend to them while they are going through them, or to understand when they are told about them. Those, on the other hand, who cannot walk, care still less about such directions, as they cannot prove them by making trial of them. And in the same way a clever man often sees that an inference is unsound more quickly than he apprehends the rules for it. A dull man, on the other hand, does not see the unsoundness, but much less does he grasp the rules. And in regard to all these laws, we derive more pleasure from them as exhibitions of truth, than assistance in arguing or forming opinions, except perhaps that they put the intellect in better training. We must take care, however that they do not at the same time make it more inclined to mischief or vanity,—that is to say, that they do not give those who have learnt them an inclination to lead people astray by plausible speech and catching questions, or make them think that they have attained some great thing that gives them an advantage over the good and innocent.

[…]

Chap. 1: This Work Not Intended as a Treatise on Rhetoric.

1. This work of mine, which is entitled On Christian Doctrine, was at the commencement divided into two parts. For, after a preface, in which I answered by anticipation those who were likely to take exception to the work, I said, "There are two things on which all interpretation of Scripture

depends: the mode of ascertaining the proper meaning, and the known, the meaning." As, then, I have already said a great deal about the mode of ascertaining the meaning, and have given three books to this one part of the subject, I shall only say a few things about the mode of making known the meaning, in order of four books.

2. In the first place, then, I wish by this preamble to put a stop to the expectations of readers who may think that I am about to lay down rules of rhetoric such as I have learnt and taught too, in the secular schools, and to warn them that they need not look for any such from me. Not that I think such rules of no use, but that whatever use they have is to be learnt elsewhere; and if any good man should happen to have leisure for learning them, he is not to ask me to teach them either in this work or any other.

Chap. 2: It Is Lawful For a Christian Teacher To Use the Art of Rhetoric.

3. Now, the art of rhetoric being available for the enforcing either of truth or falsehood, who will dare to say that truth in the person of its defenders is to take its stand unarmed against falsehood? For example, that those who are trying to persuade men of what is false are to know how to introduce their subject, so as to put the hearer into a friendly, or attentive, or teachable frame of mind, while the defenders of the truth shall be ignorant of that art? That the former are to tell their falsehoods briefly, clearly, and plausibly, while the latter shall tell the truth in such a way that it is tedious to listen to, hard to understand, and, in fine, not easy to believe it? That the former are to oppose them to melt, to enliven, and to rouse them, while the latter shall in defence of the truth be sluggish, and frigid, and somnolent? Who is such a fool as to think this wisdom? Since, then, the faculty of eloquence is available for both sides, and is of very great service in the enforcing either of wrong or right, why do not good men study to engage it on the side of truth, when bad men use it to obtain the triumph of wicked and worthless causes, and to further injustice and error?

Chap. 3: The Proper Age and the Proper Means for Acquiring Rhetorical Skill.

4. But the theories and rules on this subject (to which, when you add a tongue thoroughly skilled by exercise and habit in the use of many words and many ornaments of speech, you have what is called eloquence or oratory)

may be learnt apart from these writings of mine, if a suitable space of time be set aside for the purpose at a fit and proper age. But only by those who can learn them any one who cannot learn this art quickly can never thoroughly learn it at all. Whether this be true or not, why need we inquire? For even if this art can occasionally be in the end mastered by men of slower intellect, I do not think it of so much importance as to wish men who have arrived at mature age to spend time in learning it. It is enough that boys should give attention to it; and even of these, not all who are to be fitted for usefulness in the Church, but only those who are not yet engaged in any occupation of more urgent necessity, or which ought evidently to take precedence of it. For men of quick intellect and glowing temperament find it easier to become eloquent by reading and listening to eloquent speakers than by following rules for eloquence. And even outside the canon, which to our great advantage is fixed in a place of secure authority, there is no want of ecclesiastical writings, in reading which a man of ability will acquire a tinge of the eloquence with which they are written, even though he does not aim at this, but is solely intent on the matters treated of; especially, of course, if in addition he practise himself in writing, or dictating, and at last also in speaking, the opinions he has formed on grounds of piety them, and who speak with fluency and elegance, cannot always think of them when they are speaking so as to speak in accordance with them, unless they are discussing the rules themselves. Indeed, I think there are scarcely any who can do both things—that is, speak well, and; in order to do this, think of the rules of speaking while they are speaking. For we must be careful that what we have got to say does not escape us whilst we are thinking about saying it according to the rules of art. Nevertheless, in the speeches of eloquent men, we find rules of eloquence carried out which the speakers did not think of as aids to eloquence at the time when they were speaking, whether they had ever learnt them, or whether they had never even met with them. For it is because they are eloquent that they exemplify these rules; it is not that they use them in order to be eloquent.

5. And, therefore, as infants cannot learn to speak except by learning words and phrases from those who do speak, why should not men become eloquent without being taught any art of speech, simply by reading and learning the speeches of eloquent men, and by imitating them as far as they can? And what do we find from the examples themselves to be the case in this respect? We know numbers who, without acquaintance with rhetorical rules, are more eloquent than many who have learnt these; but we know no one who is eloquent without having read and listened to the speeches and debates

of eloquent men. For even the art of grammar, which teaches correctness of speech, need not be learnt by boys, if they have the advantage of growing up and living among men who speak correctly. For without knowing the names of any of the faults, they will, from being accustomed to correct speech, lay hold upon whatever is faulty in the speech of any one they listen to, and avoid it; just as city-bred men, even when illiterate, seize upon the faults of rustics.

Chap. 4: The Duty of the Christian Teacher.

6. It is the duty, then, of the interpreter and teacher of Holy Scripture the defender of the true faith and the opponent of error, both to teach what is right and to refute what is wrong, and in the performance of this task to conciliate the hostile, to rouse the careless, and to tell the ignorant both what is occurring at present and what is probable in the future. But once that his hearers are friendly, attentive, and ready to learn, whether he has found them so, or has himself made them so the remaining objects are to be carried out in whatever way the case requires. If the hearers need teaching, the matter treated of must be made fully known by means of narrative. On the other hand, to clear up points that are doubtful requires reasoning and the exhibition of proof. If, however, the hearers require to be roused rather than instructed, in order that they may be diligent to do what they already know, and to bring their feelings into harmony with the truths they admit, greater vigor of speech is needed. Here entreaties and reproaches, exhortations and upbraidings, and all the other means of rousing the emotions, are necessary.

7. And all the methods I have mentioned are constantly used by nearly everyone in cases where speech is the agency employed.

Chap. 5: Wisdom of More Importance Than Eloquence to the Christian Teacher.

But as some men employ these coarsely, inelegantly, and frigidly, while others use them with acuteness, elegance, and spirit, the work that I am speaking of ought to be undertaken by one who can argue and speak with wisdom, if not with eloquence, and with profit to his hearers, even though he profit them less than he would if he could speak with eloquence too. But we must beware of the man who abounds in eloquent nonsense, and so much the more if the hearer is pleased with what is not worth listening to, and thinks that because the speaker is eloquent what he says must be true. And this opinion is held even by those who think that the art of rhetoric should be taught; for they confess that "though wisdom without eloquence is of little service to states, yet eloquence without wisdom is frequently a positive injury, and is of service never." If, then, the men who teach the principles of eloquence have been forced by truth to confess this in the very books which treat of eloquence, though they were ignorant of the true, that is, the heavenly wisdom which comes down from the Father of Lights, how much more ought we to feel it who are the sons and the ministers of this higher wisdom! Now a man speaks with more or less wisdom just as he has made more or less progress in the knowledge of Scripture; I do not mean by reading them much and committing them to memory, but by understanding them aright and carefully searching into their meaning. For there are who read and yet neglect them; they read to remember the words, but are careless about knowing the meaning. It is plain we must set far above these the men who are not so retentive of the words, but see with the eyes of the heart into the heart of Scripture. Better than either of these, however, is the man who, when he wishes, can repeat the words, and at the same time correctly apprehends their meaning.

8. Now it is especially necessary for the man who is bound to speak wisely, even though he cannot speak eloquently, to retain in memory the words of Scripture. For the more he discerns the poverty of his own speech, the more he ought to draw on the riches of Scripture, so that what he says in his own words he may prove by the words of Scripture; and he himself, though small and weak in his own words, may gain strength and power from the confirming testimony of great men. For his proof gives pleasure when he cannot please by his mode of speech. But if a man desire to speak not only with wisdom, but with eloquence also (and assuredly he will prove of greater service if he can do both), I would rather send him to read, and listen to, and exercise himself in imitating, eloquent men, than advise him to spend time with the teachers of rhetoric; especially if the men he reads and listens to are justly praised as having spoken, or as being accustomed to speak, not only with eloquence, but with wisdom also. For eloquent speakers are heard with pleasure; wise speakers with profit. And, therefore, Scripture does not say that the multitude of the eloquent, but "the multitude of the wise is the welfare of the world." And as we must often swallow wholesome bitters, so we must always avoid unwholesome sweets. But what is better than wholesome sweetness or sweet wholesomeness? For the sweeter we try to make such things, the easier it is to make their wholesomeness serviceable. And so there are writers of the Church who have expounded the Holy Scriptures, not only with wisdom, but with eloquence as well; and there is not more time

for the reading of these than is sufficient for those who are studious and at leisure to exhaust them.

Chap. 6: The Sacred Writers Unite Eloquence with Wisdom.

9. Here, perhaps, someone inquires whether the authors whose divinely-inspired writings constitute the canon, which carries with it a most wholesome authority, are to be considered wise only, or eloquent as well. A question which to me, and to those who think with me, is very easily settled. For where I understand these writers, it seems to me not only that nothing can be wiser, but also that nothing can be more eloquent. And I venture to affirm that all who truly understand what these writers say, perceive at the same time that it could not have been properly said in any other way. For as there is a kind of eloquence that is more becoming in youth, and a kind that is more becoming in old age, and nothing can be called eloquence if it be not suitable to the person of the speaker, so there is a kind of eloquence that is becoming in men who justly claim the highest authority, and who are evidently inspired of God. With this eloquence they spoke; no other would have been suitable for them; and this itself would be unsuitable in any other, for it is in keeping with their character, while it mounts as far above that of others (not from empty inflation, but from solid merit) as it seems to fall below them. Where, however, I do not understand these writers, though their eloquence is then less apparent, I have no doubt but that it is of the same kind as that I do understand. The very obscurity, too, of these divine and wholesome words was a necessary element in eloquence of a kind that was designed to profit our understandings, not only by the discovery of truth, but also by the exercise of their powers.

10. I could, however, if I had time, show those men who cry up their own form of language as superior to that of our authors (not because of its majesty, but because of its inflation), that all those powers and beauties of eloquence which they make their boast, are to be found in the sacred writings which God in His goodness has provided to mould our characters, and to guide us from this world of wickedness to the blessed world above. But it is not the qualities which these writers have in common with the heathen orators and poets that give me such unspeakable delight in their eloquence; I am more struck with admiration at the way in which, by an eloquence peculiarly their own, they so use this eloquence of ours that it is not conspicuous either by its presence or its absence: for it did not become them either to condemn

it or to make an ostentatious display of it; and if they had shunned it, they would have done the former; if they had made it prominent. They might have appeared to be doing the latter. And in those passages where the learned do note its presence, the matters spoken of are such, that the words in which they are put seem not so much to be sought out by the speaker as spontaneously to suggest themselves; as if wisdom were walking out of its house,—that is, the breast of the wise man, and eloquence, like an inseparable attendant, followed it without being called for.

[...]

Chap. 12: The Aim of the Orator, According to Cicero, Is to Teach, to Delight, and to Move. of These, Teaching Is the Most Essential.

27. Accordingly a great orator has truly said that "an eloquent man must speak so as to teach, to delight, and to persuade." Then he adds: "To teach is a necessity, to delight is a beauty, to persuade is a triumph." Now of these three, the one first mentioned, the teaching, which is a matter of necessity, depends on what we say; the other two on the way we say it. He, then, who speaks with the purpose of teaching should not suppose that he has said what he has to say as long as he is not understood; for although what he has said be intelligible to himself it is not said at all to the man who does not understand it. If, however, he is understood, he has said his say, whatever may have been his manner of saying it. But if he wishes to delight or persuade his hearer as well, he will not accomplish that end by putting his thought in any shape no matter what, but for that purpose the style of speaking is a matter of importance. And as the hearer must be pleased in order to secure his attention, so he must be persuaded in order to move him to action. And as he is pleased if you speak with sweetness and elegance, so he is persuaded if he be drawn by your promises, and awed by your threats; if he reject what you condemn, and embrace what you commend; if he grieve when you heap up objects for grief, and rejoice when you point out an object for joy; if he pity those whom you present to him as objects of pity, and shrink from those whom you set before him as men to be feared and shunned. I need not go over all the other things that can be done by powerful eloquence to move the minds of the hearers, not telling them what they ought to do, but urging them to do what they already know ought to be done.

28. If, however, they do not yet know this, they must of course be instructed before they can be moved. And perhaps the mere knowledge of their duty

will have such an effect that there will be no need to move them with greater strength of eloquence. Yet when this is needful, it ought to be done. And it is needful when people, knowing what they ought to do, do it not. Therefore, to teach is a necessity. For what men know, it is in their own hands either to do or not to I do. But who would say that it is their duty to do what they do not know? On the same principle, to persuade is not a necessity: for it is not always called for; as, for example, when the hearer yields his assent to one who simply teaches or gives pleasure. For this reason also to persuade is a triumph, because it is possible that a man may be taught and delighted, and yet not give his consent. And what will be the use of gaining the first two ends if we fail in the third? Neither is it a necessity to give pleasure; for when, in the course of an address, the truth is clearly pointed out (and this is the true function of teaching), it is not the fact, nor is it the intention, that the style of speech should make the truth pleasing, or that the style should of itself give pleasure; but the truth itself, when exhibited in its naked simplicity, gives pleasure, because it is the truth. And hence even falsities are frequently a source of pleasure when they are brought to light and exposed. It is not, of course, their falsity that gives pleasure; but as it is true that they are false, the speech which shows this to be true gives pleasure.

Chap. 13: The Hearer Must Be Moved As Well As Instructed.

29. But for the sake of those who are so fastidious that they do not care for truth unless it is put in the form of a pleasing discourse, no small place has been assigned in eloquence to the art of pleasing. And yet even this is not enough for those stubborn-minded men who both understand and are pleased with the teacher's discourse, without deriving any profit from it. For what does it profit a man that he both confesses the truth and praises the eloquence, if he does not yield his consent, when it is only for the sake of securing his consent that the speaker in urging the truth gives careful attention to what he says? If the truths taught are such that to believe or to know them is enough, to give one's assent implies nothing more than to confess that they are true. When, however, the truth taught is one that must be carried into practice, and that is taught for the very purpose of being practised, it is useless to be persuaded of the truth of what is said, it is useless to be pleased with the manner in which it is said, if it be not so learnt as to be practised. The eloquent divine, then, when he is urging a practical truth, must not only teach so as to give instruction, and please so as to keep up the attention, but he must also sway the mind so as to subdue the will. For

if a man be not moved by the force of truth, though it is demonstrated to his own confession, and clothed in beauty of style, nothing remains but to subdue him by the power of eloquence.

Chap. 14: Beauty of Diction to be in Keeping with the Matter.

30. And so much labor has been spent by men on the beauty of expression here spoken of, that not only is it not our duty to do, but it is our duty to shun and abhor, many and heinous deeds of wickedness and baseness which wicked and base men have with great eloquence recommended, not with a view to gaining assent, but merely for the sake of being read with pleasure. But may God avert from His Church what the prophet Jeremiah says of the synagogue of the Jews: "A wonderful and horrible thing is committed in the land: the prophets prophesy falsely, and the priests applaud them with their hands; and my people love to have it so: and what will ye do in the end thereof?" O eloquence, which is the more terrible from its purity, and the more crushing from its solidity! Assuredly it is "a hammer that breaketh the rock in pieces." For to this God Himself has by the same prophet compared His own word spoken through His holy prophets. God forbid, then, God forbid that with us the priest should applaud the false prophet, and that God's people should love to have and so. God forbid, I say, that with us there should be such terrible madness! For what shall we do in the end thereof? And assuredly it is preferable, even though what is said should be less intelligible, less pleasing, and less persuasive, that truth be spoken, and that what is just, not what is iniquitous, be listened to with pleasure. But this, of course, cannot be, unless what is true and just be expressed with elegance.

31. In a serious assembly, moreover, such as is spoken of when it is said, "I will praise Thee among much people," no pleasure is derived from that species of eloquence which indeed says nothing that is false, but which buries small and unimportant truths under a frothy mass of ornamental words, such as would not be graceful or dignified even if used to adorn great and fundamental truths. And something of this sort occurs in a letter of the blessed Cyprian, which, I think, came there by accident, or else was inserted designedly with this view, that posterity might see how the wholesome discipline of Christian teaching had cured him of that redundancy of language, and confined him to a more dignified and modest form of eloquence, such as we find in his subsequent letters, a style which is admired without effort, is sought after with eagerness, but is not attained without great difficulty. He says, then, in

one place," Let us seek this abode: the neighboring solitudes afford a retreat where, whilst the spreading shoots of the vine trees, pendulous and intertwined, creep amongst the supporting reeds, the leafy covering has made a portico of vine." There is wonderful fluency and exuberance of language here; but it is too florid to be pleasing to serious minds. But people who are fond of this style are apt to think that men who do not use it, but employ a more chastened style, do so because they cannot attain the former, not because their judgment teaches them to avoid it. Wherefore this holy man shows both that he can speak in that style, for he has done so once, and that he does not choose, for he never uses it again.

Chap. 17: Threefold Division of the Various Styles of Speech.

34. He then who, in speaking, aims at enforcing what is good, should not despise any of those three objects, either to teach, or to give pleasure, or to move, and should pray and strive, as we have said above, to be heard with intelligence, with pleasure, and with ready compliance· And when he does this with elegance and propriety, he may justly be called eloquent, even though he do not carry with him the assent of his hearer. For it is these three ends, viz., teaching, giving pleasure, and moving, that the great master of Roman eloquence himself seems to have intended that the following three directions should subserve: "He, then, shall be eloquent, who can say little things in a subdued style, moderate things in a temperate style, and great things in a majestic style:" as if he had taken in also the three ends mentioned above, and had embraced the whole in one sentence thus: "He, then, shall be eloquent, who can say little things in a subdued style, in order to give instruction, moderate things in a temperate style, in order to give pleasure, and great things in a majestic style, in order to sway the mind."

[…]

Chap. 19: The Christian Teacher Must Use Different Styles on Different Occasions.

38. And yet, while our teacher ought to speak of great matters, he ought not always to be speaking of them in a majestic tone, but in a subdued tone when he is teaching, temperately when he is giving praise or blame. When, however, something is to be done, and we are speaking to those who ought, but are not willing, to do it, then great matters must be spoken of with power, and in a manner calculated to sway the mind. And sometimes the

same important matter is treated in all these ways at different times, quietly when it is being taught, temperately when its importance is being urged, and powerfully when we are forcing a mind that is averse to the truth to turn and embrace it. For is there anything greater than God Himself? Is nothing, then, to be learnt about Him? Or ought he who is teaching the Trinity in unity to speak of it otherwise than in the method of calm discussion, so that in regard to a subject which it is not easy to comprehend, we may understand as much as it is given us to understand? Are we in this case to seek out ornaments instead of proofs? Or is the hearer to be moved to do something instead of being instructed so that he may learn something? But when we come to praise God, either in Himself, or in His works, what a field for beauty and splendor of language opens up before man, who can task his powers to the utmost in praising Him whom no one can adequately praise, though there is no one who does not praise Him in some measure! But if He be not worshipped, or if idols, whether they be demons or any created being whatever, be worshipped with Him or in preference to Him, then we ought to speak out with power and impressiveness, show how great a wickedness this is, and urge men to flee from it.

[...]

Chap. 22: The Necessity of Variety in Style.

51. But we are not to suppose that it is against rule to mingle these various styles: taste. For when we keep monotonously to one style, we fail to retain the hearer's attention; but when we pass from one style to another, the discourse goes off more gracefully, even though it extend to greater length. Each separate style, again, has varieties of its own which prevent the hearer's attention from cooling or becoming languid. We can bear the subdued style, however, longer without variety than the majestic style. For the mental emotion which it is necessary to stir up in order to carry the hearer's feelings with us, when once it has been sufficiently excited, the higher the pitch to which it is raised, can be maintained the shorter time. And therefore we must be on our guard, lest, in striving to carry to a higher point the emotion we have excited, we rather lose what we have already gained. But after the interposition of matter that we have to treat in a quieter style, we can return with good effect to that which must be treated forcibly, thus making the tide of eloquence to ebb and flow like the sea. It follows from this, that the majestic style, if it is to be long continued, ought not to be unvaried, but

should alternate at intervals with the other styles; the speech or writing as a whole, however, being referred to that style which is the prevailing one.

Chap. 23: How The Various Styles Should Be Mingled.

52. Now it is a matter of importance to determine what style should be alternated with what other, and the places where it is necessary that any particular style should be used. In the majestic style, for instance, it is always, or almost always, desirable that the introduction should be temperate. And the speaker has it in his discretion to use the subdued style even where the majestic would be allowable, in order that the majestic when it is used may be the more majestic by comparison, and may as it were shine out with greater brilliance from the dark background. Again, whatever may be the style of the speech or writing, when knotty questions turn up for solution, accuracy of distinction is required, and this naturally demands the subdued style. And accordingly this style must be used in alternation with the other two styles whenever questions of that sort turn up; just as we must use the temperate style, no matter what may be the general tone of the discourse, whenever praise or blame is to be given without any ulterior reference to the condemnation or acquittal of any one, or to obtaining the concurrence of any one in a course of action. In the majestic style, then, and in the quiet likewise, both the other two styles occasionally find place. The temperate style, on the other hand, not indeed always, but occasionally, needs the quiet style; for example, when, as I have said, a knotty question comes up to be settled, or when some points that are susceptible of ornament are left unadorned and expressed in the quiet style, in order to give greater effect to certain exuberances (as they may be called) of ornament. But the temperate style never needs the aid of the majestic; for its object is to gratify, never to excite, the mind.

[...]

Chap. 25: How The Temperate Style Is to Be Used.

55. From all this we may conclude, that the end arrived at by the two styles last mentioned is the one which it is most essential for those who aspire to speak with wisdom and eloquence to secure. On the other hand, what the temperate style properly aims at, viz., to please by beauty of expression, is not in itself an adequate end; but when what we have to say is good and useful,

and when the hearers are both acquainted with it and favorably disposed towards it, so that it is not necessary either to instruct or persuade them, beauty of style may have its influence in securing their prompter compliance, or in making them adhere to it more tenaciously. For as the function of all eloquence, whichever of these three forms it may assume, is to speak persuasively, and its object is to persuade, an eloquent man will speak persuasively, whatever style he may adopt; but unless he succeeds in persuading, his eloquence has not secured its object. Now in the subdued style, he persuades his hearers that what he says is true; in the majestic style, he persuades them to do what they are aware they ought to do, but do not; in the temperate style, he persuades them that his speech is elegant and ornate. But what use is there in attaining such an object as this last? They may desire it who are vain of their eloquence and make a boast of panegyrics, and such-like performances, where the object is not to instruct the hearer, or to persuade him to any course of action, but merely to give him pleasure. We, however, ought to make that end subordinate to another, viz., the effecting by this style of eloquence what we aim at effecting when we use the majestic style. For we may by the use of this style persuade men to cultivate good habits and give up evil ones, if a good course; we may induce them to pursue a good course, we may induce them to pursue it more zealously, and to persevere in it with constancy. Accordingly, even in the temperate style we must use beauty of expression not for ostentation, but for wise ends; not contenting ourselves merely with pleasing the hearer, but rather seeking to aid him in the pursuit of the good end which we hold out before him.

Augustine. *De Doctrina, Nicene and Post-Nicene Fathers*. Series 1, vol. 2. Translated by Philip Schaff. Grand Rapids, MI: Christian Classics Ethereal Library, 1887 & 2004, http://www9.georgetown.edu/faculty/jod/augustine/ddc.html

Chapter 9

Dante

Dante (Dante Alighieri [1265–1321]) is most famous for his *Divine Comedy*, an allegorical vision of the afterlife. Most people who have read the epic poem are aware of its literary beauty, historical and religious allusions, and significant linguistic devices. An important contribution of which most are unaware, however, is that the *Divine Comedy* was the first major literary work written in Italian—although Latin was still the primary language of the time, especially for the clergy and the aristocracy.

In a small manuscript titled *De Vulgari Eloquentia* (*On Speaking in the Vernacular* [c. 1302–1305]), Dante justified writing in the vernacular, which he considered more natural and more appropriate for art. He discusses the communicative power of language and argues for the use of the vernacular so that those who could not read Latin or who had been denied the opportunity to learn it would not remain powerless and subject to the mercy of the Latin-speaking elite. The issue of the political power of language is one that contemporary rhetorical scholars address with some regularity.

De Vulgari Eloquentia

Now, however, it becomes necessary to explain why what we have found should be given the epithets 'illustrious', 'cardinal', 'aulic', and 'curial'; and by so doing I shall reveal more clearly what the phenomenon is in itself. First of all, therefore, I shall explain what I mean when I use the term 'illustrious', and why it is applied to the vernacular. Now when we call something 'illustrious', we mean that it gives off light or reflects the light that it receives from elsewhere: and we call men 'illustrious' in this sense, either because, enlightened by power, they shine forth justice and charity upon other people, or because, excellently taught, they teach most excellently, like Seneca or Numa Pompilius. And this vernacular of which I speak is both sublime in learning and power, and capable of exalting those who use it in honour and glory. That it is sublime in learning is clear when we see it emerge, so outstanding, so lucid, so perfect and so civilized, from among so many ugly words used by Italians, so many convoluted constructions, so many defective formations, and so many barbarous pronunciations—as Cino da Pistoia and his friend show us in their canzoni. That it is exalted in power is plain. And what greater power could there be than that which can melt the hearts of human beings, so as to make the unwilling willing and the willing unwilling, as it has done and still does? That it raises to honour is readily apparent. Does not the fame of its devotees exceed that of any king, marquis, count or warlord? There is no need to prove this. And I myself have known how greatly it increases the glory of those who serve it, I who, for the sake of that glory's sweetness, have the experience of exile behind me. For all these reasons we are right to call this vernacular 'illustrious'.

Nor are we without justification if we adorn this illustrious vernacular with our second epithet, by calling it 'cardinal'. For, just as the whole structure of a door obeys its hinge, so that in whatever direction the hinge moves, the door moves with it, whether it opens towards the inside or the outside, so the whole flock of languages spoken in the cities of Italy turns this way or that, moves or stands still, at the behest of this vernacular, which thus shows itself to be the true head of their family. Does it not daily dig up thorn-bushes growing in the Italian forest? Does it not daily make new grafts or prick out seedlings? What else do its gardeners do, if they are not uprooting or planting, as I said earlier? For this reason it has fully earned the right to deck itself out with so noble an epithet. The reason for calling this vernacular 'aulic' [royal court], on the other hand, is that if we Italians had a royal court, it would make its home in the court's palace. For if the court is the shared home of the entire kingdom, and the honoured governor of every part of it, it is fitting that everything that is common to all yet owned by none should frequent the court and live there; and indeed no other dwelling-place would be worthy of such a resident. And this certainly seems to be true of this vernacular of which I speak. So this is why those who frequent any royal court always speak an illustrious vernacular; it is also why our illustrious vernacular wanders around like a homeless stranger, finding hospitality in more humble homes—because we have no court. It is right to call this vernacular 'curial' [law-court], because the essence of being curial is no more than providing a balanced assessment of whatever has to be dealt with; and because the scales on which this assessment is carried out are usually found only in the most authoritative of tribunals, whatever is well balanced in our actions is called 'curial'. Therefore, since this vernacular has been assessed before the most excellent tribunal in Italy, it deserves to be called 'curial'. Yet it seems contradictory to say that it has been assessed in the most excellent tribunal in Italy, since we have no such tribunal. The answer to this is simple. For although it is true that there is no such tribunal in Italy—in the sense of a single institution, like that of the king of Germany—yet its constituent elements are not lacking. And just as the elements of the German tribunal are united under a single monarch, so those of the Italian have been brought together by the gracious light of reason. So it would not be true to say that the Italians lack a tribunal altogether, even though we lack a monarch, because we do have one, but its physical components are scattered.

So now we can say that this vernacular, which has been shown to be illustrious, cardinal, aulic, and curial, is the vernacular that is called Italian. For, just as one vernacular can be identified as belonging to Cremona, so can another that belongs to Lombardy; and just as one can be identified that belongs to Lombardy, so can another that belongs to the whole left-hand side of Italy; and just as all these can be identified in this way, so can that which belongs to Italy as a whole. And just as the first is called Cremonese, the second Lombard, and the third half-Italian, so this last, which belongs to all Italy, is called the Italian vernacular. This is the language used by the illustrious authors who have written vernacular poetry in Italy, whether they came from Sicily, Apulia, Tuscany Romagna, Lombardy, or either of the Marches. And since my intention, as I promised at the beginning of this work, is to teach a theory of the effective use of the vernacular, I have begun with this form of it, as being the most excellent; and I shall go on, in the following books, to discuss the following questions: whom I think worthy of using this language, for what purpose, in what manner, where, when, and what audience they should address. Having clarified all this, I shall attempt to throw some light on the question of the less important vernaculars, descending step by step until I reach the language that belongs to a single family.

Alighieri, Dante. *De Vulgari Eloquentia*. Translated by Steven Botterill. London: Cambridge University Press, 1996, http://alighieri.scarian.net/translate_english/alighieri_dante_de _vulgari_eloquentia.html

Chapter 10

Erasmus

Desiderius Erasmus (1466–1536) was a theologian, educator, philosopher, and social critic whose impact on rhetoric was felt most strongly in his emphasis on style. Unlike Dante, Erasmus was what we would consider a "classical Latinist," meaning he wrote in a classical Latin style. Thus, his writing is careful, technically proficient, and replete with analogies and examples. His meticulous use of language reinforces his perspective on rhetorical style—it should be crisp, precise, and well-argued. As a humanist, he places confidence in our ability to reason and use evidence to resolve problems.

In his rhetorical manual *On Copia of Words and Ideas*, Erasmus takes this humanistic approach by stressing the use of reasoning and by offering a systematic, rational approach to the use of language when attempting to persuade. Erasmus discusses the concept of "asseverations" in rhetorical style. Asseverations are similar to arguments in that they are positive and stern declarations that affirm a position. When combined with evidentiary proof, according to Erasmus, one's persuasive appeal is much more effective. Similarly, Erasmus argues that certain words and phrases can be added for emphasis, or what he calls "amplification," to produce more forceful and compelling conclusions. Erasmus offers us a rhetorical treatise that suggests we combine style with logic.

On Copia of Words and Ideas

[...]

Just as there is nothing more admirable or more splendid than a speech with a rich copia of thoughts and words overflowing in a golden stream, so it is, assuredly, such a thing as may be striven for at no slight risk, because, according to the proverb, "Not every man has the luck to go to Corinth." Whence we see it befalls not a few mortals that they strive for this divine excellence diligently, indeed, but unsuccessfully, and fall into a kind of futile and amorphous loquacity, as with a multitude of inane thoughts and words thrown together without discrimination, they alike obscure the subject and burden the ears of their wretched hearers. To such a degree is this true that a number of writers, having gone so far as to deliver precepts concerning this very thing, if it please the gods, seem to have accomplished nothing else than, having professed copia (abundance) to have betrayed their poverty. And in truth this thing has so disturbed us, that partly selecting those from among the precepts of the art of Rhetoric suitable to this purpose, and partly adapting those which we have learned by a now long-continued experience in speaking and writing and have observed in our varied reading of a great many authors, we here set forth concerning each kind of copia, a number of principles, examples, and rules.

[...]

Further, lest anyone think this is a modern device and to be disdained as lately born at our home, let him know that this method of diversifying speech is touched on lightly in a number of places by a very learned and likewise very diligent man, Quintilian, and that many noted Sophists have showed the way to the advantages of condensing speech. And they would not by any means have been able to do this without pointing out also a method of amplification; and if their books were extant, or if, as Quintilian suggests, they had been willing to expound their doctrines fully, there would have been no need at all for these modest precepts of mine. It is a further recommendation of this thing that eminent men in every branch of learning have eagerly and diligently practiced this one. Thus there still survive several admirable efforts of Vergil about a mirror, about a stream frozen by the cold, about Iris, about the rising of the sun, about the four seasons of the year, about the heavenly constellations. That Aesopic fable about the fox and the crow which Apuleius narrates briefly with a wonderful economy of words, and also amplifies as fully as possible with a great many words, doubtless to exercise and display his genius, shows the same thing fully. But come, who could find fault with this study when he sees that Cicero, that father of all eloquence, was so given to this exercise that he used to compete with his friend, the mimic actor, Roscius, to see whether the latter might express the same idea more times by means of various gestures, or he himself render it more often in speech varied through copia of eloquence.

[...]

Elegance consists partly in words used by suitable authors; partly in using the right word; and partly in using it in the right expression. What clothing is to our body, diction is to the expression of our thoughts. For just as the fine appearance and dignity of the body are either set off to advantage or disfigured by dress and habit, just so thought is by words. Accordingly, they err greatly who think that it matters nothing in what words something is expressed, provided only it is in some way understandable. And the reason for changing clothes and for varying speech is one and the same. Consequently, let this be the primary concern, that the clothes not be dirty, or ill fitting, or improperly arranged. For it would be a shame if a figure good in itself should be displeasing because degraded by dirty clothes. And it would be ridiculous for a man to appear in public in a woman's dress, and unseemly for anyone to be seen with his clothes turned backside to and inside out. Therefore, if anyone should wish to strive for copia before he has acquired competence in the Latin language, that one, in my opinion at least, would be acting no less ridiculously than a pauper who did not own a single garment that he could wear without great shame, and who, suddenly changing his clothes, should appear in the forum covered by assorted rags, ostentatiously exhibiting his poverty instead of his riches. And will he not appear more senseless the more often he does this? I think he will. And yet no less absurdly do some of those who strive for copia act, who, although they are not able to express their thoughts even in one way in elegant phrases, nevertheless, just as if they were ashamed to appear insufficiently stammering, variously rephrase their stuttering in such a way as to make it more stuttering; as if they have undertaken a contest with themselves to speak as barbarously as possible. I want the furnishings of a rich house to exhibit the greatest variety; but I want it to be altogether in good taste, not with every corner crammed with willow and fig and Samian ware. At a splendid banquet I want various kinds of food to be served, but who could endure anyone serving a hundred different dishes not one of which but would move to nausea? I have deliberately given this warning at length, because I know the rash presumption of very many people who prefer to omit the fundamentals and (as the saying goes) with dirty feet to hasten to the heights straightaway. Nor do they sin much less seriously who, mixing the sordid with the elegant, disfigure the purple with rags, and intersperse glass among precious stones, and combine garlic with Attic sweetmeats. Now we shall set forth formulas for varying, those of course that pertain to copia of words.

[...]

Now that we have stated our ideas on copia of words as briefly as we were able, it remains for us to touch upon copia of thought briefly. And so, to begin this part of the work with those matters that are most nearly related to the former, the first way to embellish thought is to relate at length and treat in detail something that could be expressed summarily and in general. And this, in fact, is the same as if one should display merchandise first through latticework, or rolled up in carpets, then should unroll the carpets and disclose the merchandise, exposing it completely to sight. An example of this method follows: "He lost everything through excess." This expression, complete in itself, and, as it were, all rolled up, may be developed by enumerating a great many kinds of possessions, and by setting forth various ways of losing property. Whatever had come by inheritance from father or mother, whatever had come by death of other relatives, whatever had been added from his wife's dowry, which was not at all mean, whatever had accrued from bequests (and considerable had accrued), whatever he had received from the liberality of his prince, whatever private property he had procured, all money, military equipment, clothes, estates, fields, together with farms and herds, in short, everything, whether movable or real estate, and finally even his immediate household property, in a short time he so consumed, wasted, and devoured in foulest passion for harlots, in daily banquets, in sumptuous entertainments, nightly drinking bouts, low taverns, delicacies, perfumes, dice, and gaming that what remained to him would not equal a farthing. In this case the words *everything* and *he lost by excess* are developed in detail. We will add yet another: "He has finished his education."

This is a general statement. You will be able to develop this by recounting one by one the individual disciplines—every field of learning. There is no branch of learning at all in which he has not been elaborately trained, no discipline which he has not learned thoroughly to the smallest detail, and has so learned that he seems to have worked in that one alone. Further, he knows wonderfully well all the stories of the poets; and more, he has a rich fund of the ornaments of the rhetoricians, and has also studied the difficult canons of the grammarians. He is versed in the subtleties of the dialecticians; he has traced out the mysteries of natural philosophy, he has conquered the difficulties of metaphysics, he has penetrated the abstruseness of the theologians, he has learned the demonstrations of mathematics, likewise he is versed in the movements of the stars, the systems of numbers, the surveying of land, the location of cities, mountains, rivers and springs, their names and the distances between them, the harmonies and intervals of tones. Further, whatever of history there is, both ancient and modern, he knows. Whatever there is of good authors, of antiquity or of modern times, all that he has. Add to these an equal competence in Greek and Latin literature and languages; finally, whatever learning of any time has been acquired and handed down by eminent authors, all that, this man has completely comprehended and learned and holds in his mind.

[…]

Now, besides the methods of enriching we have pointed out above, proofs are amplified by undermining an opponent's argument in advance and by asseveration. We undermine an argument in two ways: First, by proposition, by which I mean not those statements that compass the whole of a subject, but, for example, the summaries of individual parts, or conclusions, which it is the habit of orators to place at the beginning of arguments and to repeat more emphatically at the end in an appeal to the emotions or as an epilogue. […] Furthermore, we can set these forth in such a way that by this figure of speech we either destroy belief or win it. An example is found in Cicero's *For Milo*: "But before I come to that part of my speech which deals specifically with the question before us, I think those associations which have been constantly tossed about in the Senate by enemies and in public meetings by scoundrels, and just now even by the prosecutors, etc." By using the term enemies and scoundrels, he has already destroyed much belief in his opponent's proposition. Then by use of irony he disparages the proposition itself: "They say that he who confesses the slaying of a man has no right to look upon the light of day." For those harsh words, "they say that he has no right to look upon the light of day," must be uttered in mockery for "he should be punished." Secondly, preparations of this sort are joined to the separate parts of arguments: since indeed in the same place Cicero, on the point of refuting the proposition by means of *exempla*, prepares the way thus: "In what city, indeed, can you find men stupid enough to make this claim?" Then he adds the *exemplum* of M. Horatius, who, when he had slain his sister, was acquitted. Different from these are asseverations, which although they are not arguments, yet often have the weight of an argument if they are intermingled with the proofs; as, who is so blind that he does not see this? Who so shameless that he denies it? And, he is too foolish to need rebuttal, for who does not understand, etc.; and, put aside all shame; and, dare to deny; since this is the case and this after all is shamelessness, etc. Individual arguments are enriched by special epilogues which recall to the hearer in a few words the whole reasoning just brought to his attention so that the conclusion follows with greater force; this is a frequent practice of Cicero's because he develops the point of his argument in considerable detail. An example of this type would be that from his oration *For the Manilian Law*: "Therefore consider whether you ought to hesitate to enter with all zeal upon this war to defend the glory of your name, the safety of your allies, your greatest tribute, and the fortunes of a great number of citizens, together with the State." Then those arguments are enlarged by amplification in digressions, so that we may add to individual proofs their own appeal to the emotions, for which a conclusion has been fittingly chosen. If we wish that to be copious, we may make this conclusion double, so that the chief arguments are at the same time recapitulated in an epilogue and every sort of appeal to the emotions is employed throughout.

Erasmus, Desiderius. *On Copia of Words and Ideas*. Translated by Donald B. King and H. David Rix. Milwaukee, WI: Marquette University Press, 1963. Pages 11–12, 18–19, 43–44, 101–102.

Reprinted by permission.

SECTION FOUR

The Enlightenment

Whereas the Middle Ages saw a close relationship between religion and rhetoric, the Enlightenment of the seventeenth and eighteenth centuries stressed the importance of logic, reason, and the advancement of knowledge through science and observation over tradition and faith. During these centuries, many intellectuals rejected the principles of Christian dogma, especially in matters external to religious beliefs. Faith in science, in many ways, replaced faith in God. Many scientific advancements were achieved, with the Enlightenment paving the way for the Industrial Revolution. Consequently, during the Enlightenment, the role of formal logic (dialectic) became more pronounced in rhetorical theory. Scholars presumed that to persuade effectively, logic and reasoning were more important than emotional or ethical appeals. Interestingly, one of the leaders was Richard Whately, an Anglican archbishop who stressed the use of logic in all matters relating to persuasion. Whately influenced two other significant rhetoricians and Anglican priests of the time—Hugh Blair and George Campbell, who also stressed the use of logos. That these men of the cloth tried to use reasoning to spread the word of God to audiences who generally rejected faith in favor of science and rationality is testament to reasoning's importance as a form of persuasion.

READINGS

Golden, James L., and Edward P. J. Corbett. *The Rhetoric of Blair, Campbell, and Whately.* Carbondale: Southern Illinois University, 1990.

Leathers, Dale G. "Whately's Logically Derived 'Rhetoric': A Stranger in Its Time." *Western Speech* 33, no. 1 (1969): 48–58.

McKerrow, Raymie E. "Method of Composition: Whately's Earliest 'Rhetoric.'" *Philosophy & Rhetoric* 11, no. 1 (1978): 43–58.

Walzer, Arthur E. *George Campbell: Rhetoric in the Age of Enlightenment.* Albany: State University of New York Press, 2003.

———. "Blair's Ideal Orator: Civic Rhetoric and Christian Politeness in Lectures 25–34." *Rhetorica: A Journal of the History of Rhetoric* 25, 3 (2007): 269–295.

Chapter 11

Richard Whately

During an era wherein religion faced serious competition with science and rationality, Richard Whately's (1787–1863 CE) *Elements of Logic* discussed the utility of formal and informal logic in all persuasive matters, including topics related to the Church of Ireland (Whately was the archbishop of Dublin). He also spends a great deal of time tracing the history and development of logic, discussing the systematic rules of logic, answering those who oppose the use of logic, and explaining the use of fallacies. In the tradition of Aristotle, Whately's manuscript not only resurrects the importance of reasoning in the persuasion process, but it also lays the groundwork for other contemporaries to favor logos over other rhetorical techniques (Leathers 1969; McKerrow 1978).

Elements of Logic

Logic, in the most extensive sense in which it has been thought advisable to employ the name, may be considered as the Science, and also as the Art, of Reasoning. It investigates the principles on which argumentation is conducted, and furnishes such rules as may be derived from those principles, for guarding against erroneous deductions. Its most appropriate office, however, is that of instituting an analysis of the process of the mind in Reasoning; and in this point of view it is, as I have said, strictly a *Science*; while, considered in reference to the practical rules above mentioned, it may be called the *Art* of Reasoning. For it is to be remembered, that as a science is conversant about speculative *knowledge only*, and *art* is the *application* of knowledge to *practice*, hence Logic (as well as any other system of knowledge) becomes, when applied to practice, an *art*; while confined to the theory of reasoning, it is strictly a *science*: and it is as such that it occupies the higher place in point of dignity, since it professes to develop some of the most interesting and curious intellectual phenomena.

Considering how early Logic attracted the attention of philosophers, it may appear surprising that so little progress should have been made, as is confessedly the case, in developing its principles, and perfecting the detail of the system; and this circumstance has been brought forward as a proof of the barrenness and futility of the study. But a similar argument might have been urged with no less plausibility, at a period not very remote, against the study of Natural Philosophy; and, very recently, against that of Chemistry. No science can be expected to make any considerable progress, which is not cultivated on right principles. Whatever may be the inherent vigor of the plant, it will neither be flourishing nor fruitful till it meet with a suitable soil and culture: and in no case is the remark more applicable than in the present; the greatest mistakes having always prevailed respecting the nature of Logic; and its province having in consequence been extended by many writers to subjects with which it has no proper connection. Indeed, with the exception perhaps of Aristotle, (who is himself, however, not entirely exempt from the errors in question,) hardly a writer on Logic can be mentioned who has clearly perceived, and steadily kept in view throughout, its real nature and object. Before his time, no distinction was drawn between the science of which we are speaking, and that which is now usually called Metaphysics; a circumstance which alone shows how small was the progress made in earlier times. Indeed, those who first turned their attention to the subject, hardly thought of inquiring into the process of Reasoning itself, but confined themselves almost entirely to certain preliminary points, the discussion of which is (if logically considered) subordinate to that of the main inquiry.

[...]

But if I felt myself as fully competent to the task of writing such a history of Logic as I have alluded to, as I am conscious of not being so, I should still decidedly prefer keeping such a work altogether distinct from a treatise on the science; because the combination of the two in a single volume would render it the more difficult to avoid the blending of them confusedly together; and also because, on such a plan, the distinction could not be so easily preserved between Logic, in the sense in which I am here using that title, and various metaphysical disquisitions to which several writers have given the same name.

For these reasons I have thought it best to take only a slight and rapid glance of the series of logical writers down to the present day, and of the general tendency of their labors.

[...]

Dialectics, divided his work into three parts; the first of which (upon Consequences) is censured by Socrates [Plato] for obscurity and confusion. In his second part, however, he furnished that interrogatory method of disputation which Socrates adopted, and which has since borne his name. The third part of his work was devoted to what may not be improperly termed the art of wrangling, which supplied the disputant with a collection of sophistical questions, so contrived, that the concession of some point, that seemed unavoidable, immediately involved some glaring absurdity. This, if it is to be esteemed as at all falling within the province of Logic, is certainly not to be regarded (as some have ignorantly or heedlessly represented it) as its principal or proper business. The Greek philosophers generally have unfortunately devoted too much attention to it; but we must beware of falling into the vulgar error of supposing the ancients to have regarded as a serious and intrinsically important study, that which in fact they considered as an ingenious recreation. The disputants diverted themselves in their leisure hours by making trial of their own and their adversary's acuteness, in the endeavor mutually to perplex each other with subtle fallacies; much in the same way as men amuse themselves with propounding and guessing riddles, or with the game of chess; to each of which diversions the sportive disputations of the ancients bore much resemblance. They were closely analogous to the wrestling and other exercises of the Gymnasium; these last being reckoned conducive to bodily vigor and activity, as the former were to habits of intellectual acuteness; but the immediate object in each was a sportive, not a serious contest; though doubtless fashion and emulation often occasioned an undue importance to be attached to success in each.

Zeno, then, is hardly to be regarded as any further a logician than as to what respects his *erotetic* method of disputation; a course of argument constructed on this principle being properly a hypothetical Sorites, which may easily be reduced into a series of syllogisms.

To Zeno succeeded Euclid of Megara, and Antisthenes; both pupils of Socrates. The former of these prosecuted the subject of the third part of his predecessor's treatise, and is said to have been the author of many of the fallacies attributed to the Stoical school. Of the writings of the latter nothing certain is known; if, however, we suppose the above-mentioned sect to be his disciples in this study, and to have retained his principles, he certainly took a more correct view of the subject than Euclid. The Stoics divided... everything that could be said—into three classes; 1st, the Simple Term; 2d, the Proposition; 3d, the Syllogism; *viz.* the hypothetical; for they seem to have had little notion of a more rigorous analysis of argument than into that familiar form.

[…]

In every instance in which we *reason*, in the strict sense of the word, i.e. make use of arguments, (I mean *real*, i.e. *valid* arguments) whether for the sake of refuting an adversary, or of conveying instruction, or of satisfying our own minds on any point, whatever may be the subject we are engaged on, a certain process takes place in the mind which is one and the same in all cases, provided it be correctly conducted.

Of course it cannot be supposed that everyone is even conscious of this process in his own mind; much less, is competent to explain the principles on which it proceeds. This indeed is, and cannot but be, the case with every other process respecting which any system has been formed; the practice not only may exist independently of the theory, but must have preceded the theory. There must have been Language before a system of Grammar could be devised; and musical compositions, previous to the Science of Music. This, by the way, will serve to expose the futility of the popular objection against Logic, that then may reason very well who know nothing of it. The parallel instances adduced, show that such an objection might be applied in many other cases, where its absurdity would be obvious; and that there is no ground for deciding thence, either that the system has no tendency to improve practice, or that even if it had not, it might not still be a dignified and interesting pursuit.

One of the chief impediments to the attainment of a just view of the nature and object of Logic, is the not fully understanding, or not sufficiently keeping in mind, the sameness of the reasoning-process in all cases. If, as the ordinary mode of speaking would seem to indicate. Mathematical reasoning, and Theological, and Metaphysical, and Political, etc., were essentially different from each other, i.e. different *kinds* of *reasoning,* it would follow, that supposing there could be at all any such science as we have described Logic, there must be so many different species, or at least different branches, of Logic. And such is perhaps the most prevailing notion. Nor is this much to be wondered at: since it is evident to all, that some men converse and write, in an argumentative way, very justly on one subject, and very erroneously on another; in which again others excel, who fail in the former. This error may be at once illustrated and removed, by considering the parallel instance of Arithmetic; in which everyone is aware that the process of a calculation is not affected by the nature of the objects, whose numbers are before us: but that (e.g.) the multiplication of a number is the very same operation, whether it be a number of 'men, of miles, or of pounds; though nevertheless persons may perhaps be found who are accurate in the results of their calculations relative to natural-philosophy, and incorrect in those of political-economy, from their different degrees of skill in the subjects of these two sciences; not surely because there are different arts of Arithmetic applicable to each of these respectively.

Others again, who are aware that the simple system of Logic may be applied to all subjects whatever, are yet disposed to view it as a *peculiar method* of reasoning, and not, as it is, a method of unfolding and analyzing our reasoning: whence many have been led (e.g. the author of the Philosophy of Rhetoric) to talk of comparing Syllogistic- reasoning with Moral-reasoning; taking it for granted that it is possible to reason correctly without reasoning logically; which is, in fact, as great a blunder as if any one were to mistake grammar for a peculiar *language*, and to suppose it possible to speak, correctly without speaking grammatically. They have in short considered Logic as an *art* of reasoning; whereas (so far as it is an art) it is *the* art of reasoning; the logician's object being, not to lay down principles by which one *may* reason, but, by which all *must* reason, even though they are not distinctly aware of them: —to lay down rules, not which *may* be followed with advantage, but which cannot possibly be *departed* from in sound reasoning. These misapprehensions and objections being such as lie on the very threshold of the subject, it would have been hardly possible, without noticing them, to convey any just notion of the nature and design of the logical system.

Supposing it then to have been perceived that the operation of Reasoning is in all cases the same, the analysis of that operation could not fail to strike the mind as an interesting matter of inquiry. And moreover, since (apparent) arguments which are unsound and inconclusive, are so often employed, either from error or design; and since even those who are not misled by these fallacies, are so often at a loss to detect and expose them in a manner satisfactory to others, or even to themselves; it could not but appear desirable to lay down some general rules of reasoning applicable to all cases; by which a person might be enabled the more readily and clearly to state the grounds of his own conviction, or of his objection to the arguments of an opponent; instead of arguing at random, without any fixed and acknowledged principles to guide his procedure. Such rules would be analogous to those of Arithmetic, which obviate the tediousness and uncertainty of calculations in the head; wherein, after much labor, different persons might arrive at different results, without any of them being able distinctly to point out the error of the rest. A system of such rules, it is obvious, must, instead of deserving to be called the "art of wrangling," be more justly characterized as the "art of cutting short wrangling," by bringing the parties to issue at once, if not to agreement; and thus saving a waste of ingenuity.

Whately, Richard. *Elements of Logic.* Boston: James Munroe & Co., 1855, http://archive.org/stream/elementslogicco12whatgoog/elementslogicco12whatgoog_djvu.txt

Chapter 12

Hugh Blair

Hugh Blair's (1718–1800) main contribution to the discipline of rhetoric was to offer a teaching manual that stressed the importance of argumentation and virtue for effective persuasion. In addition to being a minister, he was also a teacher and author. One of his goals was to compile a manuscript from his lectures that would teach young men how to facilitate their ascendance in social status. His famous work, *Lectures on Rhetoric and Belles Lettres,* is a proscriptive guide on how to write and speak properly. Heavily influenced by Cicero and Quintilian, Blair admits that his work essentially combines and summarizes the thoughts of writers before him. Nevertheless, it offers an organized and systematic guide for persuasive discourse, including a thorough discussion on the value of virtue. Very little had been written on the value of virtue since Quintilian, so Blair's perspective adds considerable weight to the idea that to be an effective rhetor, one must live a life of integrity. Additionally, his *Lectures* are a significant contribution to the study of rhetoric, particularly during this time, as they highlight some of the most important recommendations for the composition of rhetoric in important social settings. In other words, while many manuscripts on rhetoric discuss the creation of persuasive messages, Blair's *Lectures* is one of the few texts that address the importance of situational context to connect with particular audiences (Walzer 2007).

Lectures on Rhetoric and Belle Lettres

HAVING finished that part of the Course which relates to Language and Style, we are now to ascend a step higher, and to examine the subjects upon which Style is employed. I begin with what is properly called Eloquence, or Public Speaking. In treating of this, I am to consider the different kinds and subjects of Public Speaking; the manner suited to each; the proper distribution and management of all the parts of a discourse; and the proper pronunciation or delivery of it. But before entering on any of these heads, it may be proper to take a view of the nature of Eloquence in general, and of the state in which it has subsisted in different ages and countries. This will lead into some detail; but I hope an useful one; as in every art it is of great consequence to have a just idea of the perfection of the art, of the end at which it aims, and of the progress which it has made among mankind.

OF Eloquence, in particular, it is the more necessary to ascertain the proper notion, because there is not anything concerning which false notions have been more prevalent. Hence, it has been so often, and is still at this day, in disrepute with many. When you speak to a plain man of Eloquence, or in praise of it, he is apt to hear you with very little attention. He conceives Eloquence to signify a certain trick of Speech; the art of varnishing weak arguments plausibly; or of speaking so as to please and tickle the ear.

"Give me good sense,"

says he,

"and keep your Eloquence for boys."

He is in the right, if Eloquence were what he conceives it to be. It would be then a very contemptible art indeed, below the study of any wise or good man. But nothing can be more remote from truth. To be truly eloquent, is to speak to the purpose. For the best definition which, I think, can be given of Eloquence, is, the Art of Speaking in such a manner as to attain the end for which we speak. Whenever a man speaks or writes, he is supposed, as a rational being, to have some end in view; either to inform, or to amuse, or to persuade, or, in some way or other, to act upon his fellow-creatures. He who speaks, or writes, in such a manner as to adapt all his words most effectually to that end, is the most eloquent man. Whatever then the subject be, there is room for Eloquence; in history, or even in philosophy, as well as in orations.

The definition which I have given of Eloquence, comprehends all the different kinds of it; whether calculated to instruct, to persuade, or to please. But, as the most important subject of discourse is Action, or Conduct, the power of Eloquence chiefly appears when it is employed to influence Conduct, and persuade to Action. As it is principally, with reference to this end, that it becomes the object of Art, Eloquence may, under this view of it, be defined, The Art of Persuasion.

THIS being once established, certain consequences immediately follow, which point out the fundamental maxims of the Art. It follows clearly, that, in order to persuade, the most essential requisites are, solid argument, clear method, a character of probity appearing in the Speaker, joined with such graces of Style and utterance, as shall draw our attention to what he says. Good sense is the foundation of all. No man can be truly eloquent without it; for fools can persuade none but fools. In order to persuade a man of sense, you must first convince him; which is only to be done, by satisfying his understanding of the reasonableness of what you propose to him.

THIS leads me to observe, that convincing and persuading, though they are sometimes confounded, import, notwithstanding, different things, which it is necessary for us, at present, to distinguish from each other. Conviction affects the understanding only; persuasion, the will and the practice. It is the business of the philosopher to convince me of truth; it is the business of the orator to persuade me to act agreeably to it, by engaging my affections on its side. Conviction, and persuasion, do not always go together. They ought, indeed, to go together; and would do so, if our inclination regularly followed the dictates of our understanding. But as our nature is constituted, I may be convinced, that virtue, justice, or public spirit, are laudable, while, at the same time, I am not persuaded to act according to them. The inclination may revolt, though the understanding be satisfied: the passions may prevail against the judgment. Conviction is, however, always one avenue to the inclination, or heart; and it is that which an Orator must first bend his strength to gain: for no persuasion is likely to be stable, which is not founded on conviction. But, in order to persuade, the Orator must go farther than merely producing conviction; he must consider man as a creature moved by many different springs, and must act upon them all. He must address himself to the passions; he must paint to the fancy, and touch the heart; and, hence, besides solid argument, and clear method, all the conciliating and interesting arts, both of Composition and Pronunciation, enter into the idea of Eloquence.

AN objection may, perhaps, hence be formed against Eloquence; as an Art which may be employed for persuading to ill, as well as to good. There is no doubt that it may; and so reasoning may also be, and too often is employed, for leading men into error. But who would think of forming an argument from this against the cultivation of our reasoning powers? Reason, Eloquence, and every Art which ever has been studied among mankind, may be abused, and may prove dangerous in the hands of bad men; but it were perfectly childish to contend, that, upon this account, they ought to be abrogated. Give truth and virtue the same arms which you give vice and falsehood, and the former are likely to prevail. Eloquence is no invention of the schools. Nature teaches every man to be eloquent, when he is much in earnest. Place him in some critical situation; let him have some great interest at stake, and you will see him lay hold of the most effectual means of persuasion. The Art of Oratory proposes nothing more than to follow out that track which Nature has first pointed out to men. And the more exactly that this track is pursued, the more that Eloquence is properly studied, the more shall we be guarded against the abuse which bad men make of it, and enabled the better to distinguish between true Eloquence and the tricks of Sophistry.

WE may distinguish three kinds, or degrees of Eloquence. The first, and lowest, is that which aims only at pleasing the hearers. Such, generally, is the Eloquence of panegerials, inaugural orations, addresses to great men, and other harangues of this sort. This ornamental sort of composition is not altogether to be rejected. It may innocently amuse and entertain the mind; and it may be mixed, at the same time, with very useful sentiments. But it must be confessed, that where the Speaker has no farther aim than merely to shine and to please, there is great danger of Art being strained into ostentation, and of the composition becoming tiresome and languid.

A SECOND and a higher degree of eloquence is, when the Speaker aims not merely to please, but also to inform, to instruct, to convince: when his Art is exerted, in removing prejudices against himself and his cause, in chasing the most proper arguments, stating them with the greatest force, arranging them in the best order, expressing and delivering them with propriety and beauty; and thereby disposing us to pass that judgment, or embrace that side of the cause, to which he seeks to bring us. Within this compass, chiefly, is employed the Eloquence of the bar.

BUT there is a third, and still higher degree of Eloquence, wherein a greater power is exerted over the human mind; by which we are not only convinced, but are interested, agitated, and carried along with the Speaker;

our passions are made to rise together with his; we enter into all his emotions; we love, we detest, we resent, according as he inspires us; and are prompted to resolve, or to act, with vigour and warmth. Debate, in popular assemblies, opens the most illustrious field to this species of Eloquence; and the pulpit, also, admits it.

I AM here to observe, and the observation is of consequence, that the high Eloquence which I have last mentioned, is always the offspring of passion. By passion, I mean that state of the mind in which it is agitated, and fired, by some object it has in view. A man may convince, and even persuade others to act, by mere reason and argument. But that degree of Eloquence which gains the admiration of mankind, and properly denominates one an Orator, is never found without warmth or passion. Passion, when in such a degree as to rouse and kindle the mind, without throwing it out of the possession of itself, is universally found to exalt all the human powers. It renders the mind infinitely more enlightened, more penetrating, more vigorous and masterly, than it is in its calm moments. A man, actuated by a strong passion, becomes much greater than he is at other times. He is conscious of more strength and force; he utters greater sentiments, conceives higher designs, and executes them with a boldness and a felicity, of which, on other occasions, he could not think himself capable. But chiefly, with respect to persuasion, is the power of passion felt. Almost every man, in passion, is eloquent. Then, he is at no loss for words and arguments. He transmits to others, by a sort of contagious sympathy, the warm sentiments which he feels; his looks and gestures are all persuasive; and Nature here shows herself infinitely more powerful than all art. This is the foundation of that just and noted rule: "*Si vis me flere, dolendum est primum ipsi tibi.*" THIS principle being once admitted, that all high Eloquence flows from passion, several consequences follow, which deserve to be attended to; and the mention of which will serve to confirm the principle itself. For hence, the universally acknowledged effect of enthusiasm, or warmth of any kind, in public Speakers, for affecting their audience. Hence all laboured declamation, and affected ornaments of Style, which shew the mind to be cool and unmoved, are so inconsistent with persuasive Eloquence. Hence all studied prettinessess, in gesture or pronunciation, detract so greatly from the weight of a Speaker. Hence a discourse that is read, moves us less than one that is spoken, as having less the appearance of coming warm from the heart. Hence, to call a man cold, is the same thing as to say, that he is not eloquent. Hence a sceptical man, who is always in suspense, and feels nothing strongly; or a cunning mercenary man, who is suspected rather to assume the appearance of passion than to feel it; have so little power over men in Public Speaking. Hence, in fine, the necessity of being, and being believed to be, disinterested, and in earnest, in order to persuade.

THESE are some of the capital ideas which have occurred to me, concerning Eloquence in general; and with which I have thought proper to begin, as the foundation of much of what I am afterwards to suggest. From what I have already said, it is evident that Eloquence is a high talent, and of great importance in society; and that it requires both natural genius, and much improvement from Art. Viewed as the Art of Persuasion, it requires, in its lowest state, soundness of understanding, and considerable acquaintance with human nature; and, in its higher degrees, it requires, moreover, strong sensibility of mind, a warm and lively imagination, joined with correctness of judgment, and an extensive command of the power of Language; to which must also be added, the graces of Pronunciation and Delivery.—Let us next proceed, to consider in what state Eloquence has subsisted in different ages and nations.

[...]

THE power of Eloquence having, after the days of Pericles, become an object of greater consequence than ever, this gave birth to a set of men till then unknown, called Rhetoricians, and sometimes Sophists, who arose in multitudes during the Peloponnesian war; such as Protagoras, Prodicas, Thrasymus, and one who was more eminent than all the rest, Gorgias of Leontium. These Sophists joined to their art of rhetoric a subtle logic, and were generally a sort of metaphysical Sceptics. Gorgias, however, was a professed master of Eloquence only. His reputation was prodigious. He was highly venerated in Leontium of Sicily, his native city; and money was coined with his name upon it. In the latter part of his life, he established himself at Athens, and lived till he had attained the age of 105 years. Hermogenes (*de Ideis*, l. ii. cap. 9.) has preserved a fragment of his, from which we see his style and manner. It is extremely quaint and artificial; full of antithesis and pointed expression; and shows how far the Grecian subtlety had already carried the study of language. These Rhetoricians did not content themselves with delivering general instructions concerning Eloquence to their pupils, and endeavouring to form their taste; but they professed the art of giving them receipts for making all sorts of Orations; and of teaching them how to speak for, and against, every cause whatever. Upon this plan, they were the first who treated of common places, and the artificial invention of arguments and topics for every subject. In the hands of such men, we may easily believe that Oratory would degenerate from the masculine strain it had hitherto held, and become a trifling and sophistical art: and we may justly deem them the first corrupters of true Eloquence. To them, the great Socrates opposed himself. By a profound, but simple reasoning peculiar to himself, he exploded their sophistry; and endeavoured to recall men's attention from that abuse of reasoning and discourse which began to be in vogue, to natural language, and sound and useful thought.

IN the same age, though somewhat later than the philosopher above-mentioned, flourished Isocrates, whose writings are still extant. He was a professed Rhetorician, and by teaching Eloquence, he acquired both a great fortune, and higher fame than any of his rivals in that profession. No contemptible Orator he was. His orations are full of morality and good sentiments: they are flowing and smooth; but too destitute of vigour. He never engaged in public affairs, nor pleaded causes; and accordingly his orations are calculated only for the shade: "*Pompae*," Cicero allows, "*magis quam pugnae aptior; ad voluptatem aurium accommodatus potius quam ad judiciorum certamen.*"

[…]

HAVING treated of the rise of Eloquence, and of its state among the Greeks, we now proceed to consider its progress among the Romans, where we shall find one model, at least, of Eloquence, in its most splendid and illustrious form. The Romans were long a martial nation, altogether rude, and unskilled in arts of any kind. Arts were of late introduction among them; they were not known till after the conquest of Greece; and the Romans always acknowledged the Grecians as their masters in every part of learning.

[…]

AS the Romans derived their Eloquence, Poetry, and Learning from the Greeks, so they must be confessed to be far inferior to them in genius for all these accomplishments. They were a more grave and magnificent, but a less acute and sprightly people. They had neither the vivacity nor the sensibility of the Greeks; their passions were not so easily moved, nor their conceptions so lively; in comparison of them, they were a phlegmatic nation. Their language resembled their character; it was regular, firm, and stately; but wanted that simple and expressive naïveté, and, in particular, that flexibility to suit every different mode and species of composition, for which the Greek tongue is distinguished above that of every other country.

[…]

AS the Roman government, during the republic, was of the popular kind, there is no doubt but that, in the hands of the leading men, public speaking became early an engine of government, and was employed for gaining distinction and power. But in the rude unpolished times of the State, their speaking was hardly of that sort that could be called Eloquence. Though Cicero, in his Treatise "de Claris Oratoribus," endeavours to give some reputation to the elder Cato, and those who were his contemporaries, yet he acknowledges it to have been a rude and harsh strain of speech. It was not till a short time preceding Cicero's age, that the Roman Orators rose into any note. Crassus and Antonius, two of the Speakers in the dialogue De Oratore, appear to have been the most eminent, whose different manners Cicero describes with great beauty in that dialogue, and in his other rhetorical works. But as none of their productions are extant, nor any of Hortensius's, who was Cicero's cotemporary and rival at the bar, it is needless to transcribe from Cicero's writings the account which he gives of those great men, and of the character of their Eloquence.

[...]

To account for this difference, without any prejudice to Cicero, it has been said, that we must look to the nature of their different auditories; that the refined Athenians followed with ease the concise and convincing Eloquence of Demosthenes; but that a manner more popular, more flowery, and declamatory, was requisite in speaking to the Romans, a people less acute, and less acquainted with the arts of speech. But this is not satisfactory. For we must observe, that the Greek Orator spoke much oftener before a mixed multitude, than the Roman. Almost all the public business of Athens was transacted in popular Assemblies. The common people were his hearers, and his judges. Whereas Cicero generally addressed himself to the "Patres Conscripti," or in criminal trials to the Praetor, and the Select Judges; and it cannot be imagined, that the persons of highest rank, and best education in Rome, required a more diffuse manner of pleading than the common citizens of Athens, in order to make them understand the cause, or relish the Speaker. Perhaps we shall come nearer the truth, by observing, that to unite together all the qualities, without the least exception, that form a perfect Orator, and to excel equally in each of those qualities, is not to be expected from the limited powers of human genius. The highest degree of strength is, I suspect, never found united with the highest degree of smoothness and ornament; equal attentions to both are incompatible; and the genius that carries ornament to its utmost length, is not of such a kind, as can excel as much in vigour. For there plainly lies the characteristical difference between these two celebrated Orators.

[...]

IN the decline of the Roman Empire, the introduction of Christianity gave rise to a new species of Eloquence, in the apologies, sermons, and pastoral writings of the Fathers of the Church. Among the Latin Fathers, Lactantius and Minutius Felix, are the most remarkable for purity of Style; and, in a later age, the famous St. Augustine possesses a considerable share of sprightliness and strength. But none of the Fathers afford any just models of Eloquence. Their Language, as soon as we descend to the third or fourth century, becomes harsh; and they are, in general, infected with the taste of that age, a love of swollen and strained thoughts, and of the play of words. Among the Greek Fathers, the most distinguished, by far, for his oratorial merit, is St. Chrysostome. His Language is pure; his Style highly figured. He is copious, smooth, and sometimes pathetic. But he retains, at the same time, much of that character which has been always attributed to the Asiatic Eloquence, diffuse and redundant to a great degree, and often overwrought and tumid. He may be read, however, with advantage, for the Eloquence of the pulpit, as being freer of false ornaments than the Latin Fathers. AS there is nothing more that occurs to me, deserving particular attention in the middle age, I pass now to the state of Eloquence in modern times.

[...]

SEVERAL reasons may be given, why modern Eloquence has been so limited, and humble in its efforts. In the first place, I am of opinion, that this change must, in part, be ascribed to that correct turn of thinking, which has been so much studied in modern times. It can hardly be doubted, that, in many efforts of mere genius, the antient Greeks and Romans excelled us; but, on the other hand, that, in accuracy and closeness of reasoning on many subjects, we have some advantage over them, ought, I think, to be admitted also: In proportion as the world has advanced, philosophy has made greater progress. A certain strictness of good sense has, in this island particularly, been cultivated, and introduced into every subject. Hence we are more on our guard against the flowers of Elocution; we are on the watch; we are jealous of being deceived by Oratory. Our Public Speakers are obliged to be more reserved than the antients, in their attempts to elevate the imagination, and warm the passions; and, by the influence of prevailing taste, their own genius is sobered and chastened, perhaps, in too great a degree. It is likely too, I confess, that what we fondly ascribe to our correctness and good sense, is owing, in a great measure, to our phlegm and natural coldness. For the vivacity and sensibility of the Greeks and Romans, more especially of the former, seem to have been much greater than ours, and to have given them a higher relish of all the beauties of Oratory.

[...]

THUS I have given some view of the state of Eloquence in modern times, and endeavoured to account for it. It has, as we have seen, fallen below that splendor which it maintained in antient ages; and from being sublime and vehement, has come down to be temperate and cool. Yet, still in that region which it occupies, it admits great scope; and, to the defect of zeal and application, more than to the want of capacity and genius, we may ascribe its not having hitherto risen higher. It is a field where there is much honour yet to be reaped; it is an instrument which may be employed for purposes of the highest importance. The antient models may still, with much advantage, be set before us for imitation; though, in that imitation, we must, doubtless, have some regard to what modern taste and modern manners will bear; of which I shall afterwards have occasion to say more.

[...]

IN treating of the constituent parts of a regular Discourse or Oration, I have already considered the Introduction, the Division, and the Narration or Explication. I proceed next to treat of the argumentative or reasoning Part of a Discourse. In whatever place, or on whatever subject one speaks, this beyond doubt is of the greatest consequence. For the great end for which men speak on any serious occasion, is to convince their hearers of something being either true, or right, or good; and, by means of this conviction, to influence their practice. Reason and Argument make the foundation, as I have often inculcated, of all manly and persuasive Eloquence.

NOW, with respect to Arguments, three things are requisite. First, the invention of them; secondly, the proper disposition and arrangement of them; and thirdly, the expressing of them in such a style and manner, as to give them their full force.

THE first of these, Invention, is, without doubt, the most material, and the ground-work of the rest. But, with respect to this, I am afraid it is beyond the power of art to give any real assistance. Art cannot go so far, as to supply a Speaker with arguments on every cause, and every subject; though it may be of considerable use in assisting him to arrange, and express those, which his knowledge of the subject has discovered. For it is one thing to discover the reasons that are most proper to convince men, and another, to manage those reasons with most advantage. The latter is all that Rhetoric can pretend to.

[…]

TWO different methods may be used by Orators in the conduct of their reasoning; the terms of art for which are, the Analytic, and the Synthetic method. The Analytic is, when the Orator conceals his intention concerning the point he is to prove, till he has gradually brought his hearers to the designed conclusion. They are led on step by step, from one known truth to another, till the conclusion be stolen upon them, as the natural consequence of a chain of propositions. As, for instance, when one intending to prove the being of a God, sets out with observing that everything which we see in the world has had a beginning; that whatever has a beginning, must have had a prior cause; that in human productions, art shown in the effect necessarily infers design in the cause; and proceeds leading you on from one cause to another, till you arrive at one supreme first cause, from whom is derived all the order and design visible in his works. This is much the same with the Socratic method, by which that Philosopher silenced the Sophists of his age. It is a very artful method of reasoning; may be carried on with much beauty, and is proper to be used when the hearers are much prejudiced against any truth, and by imperceptible steps must be led to conviction.

BUT there are few subjects that will admit this method, and not many occasions on which it is proper to be employed. The mode of reasoning most generally used, and most suited to the train of Popular Speaking, is what is called the Synthetic; when the point to be proved is fairly laid down, and one Argument after another is made to bear upon it, till the hearers be fully convinced.

NOW, in arguing, one of the first things to be attended to is, among the various Arguments which may occur upon a cause, to make a proper selection of such as appear to one's self the most solid; and to employ these as the chief means of persuasion. Every Speaker should place himself in the situation of a hearer, and think how he would be affected by those reasons, which he purposes to employ for persuading others. For he must not expect to impose on mankind by mere arts of Speech. They are not so easily imposed on, as Public Speakers are sometimes apt to think. Shrewdness and sagacity are found among all ranks; and the Speaker may be praised for his fine Discourse, while yet the hearers are not persuaded of the truth of any one thing he has uttered.

SUPPOSING the Arguments properly chosen, it is evident that their effect will, in some measure, depend on the right arrangement of them; so as they shall not justle and embarrass one another, but give mutual aid; and bear with the fairest and fullest direction on the point in view. Concerning this, the following rules may be taken:

IN the first place, avoid blending Arguments confusedly together, that are of a separate nature. All Arguments whatever are directed to prove one or other of these three things; that something is true; that it is morally right or fit; or that it is profitable and good. These make the three great subjects of discussion among mankind; Truth, Duty, and Interest. But the Arguments directed towards either of them are generically distinct; and he who blends them all under one Topic, which he calls his Argument, as, in Sermons, especially, is too often done, will render his reasoning indistinct, and inelegant. Suppose, for instance, that I am recommending to an Audience Benevolence, or the Love of our Neighbour; and that I take my first Argument, from the inward satisfaction which a benevolent temper affords; my second, from the obligation which the example of Christ lays upon us to this duty; and my third, from its tendency to procure us the goodwill of all around us; my arguments are good, but I have arranged them wrong: for my first and third Arguments are taken from considerations of interest, internal peace, and external advantages; and between these, I have introduced one, which rests wholly upon duty. I should have kept those classes of Arguments, which are addressed to different principles in human nature, separate and distinct.

IN the second place, with regard to the different degrees of strength in Arguments, the general rule is, to advance in the way of climax, "*ut augeatur semper, et increscat oratio.*" This especially is to be the course, when the Speaker has a clear cause, and is confident that he can prove it fully. He may then adventure to begin with feebler arguments; rising gradually, and not putting forth his whole strength till the last, when he can trust to his making a successful impression on the minds of hearers, prepared by what has gone before. But this rule is not to be always followed. For, if he distrusts his cause, and has but one material Argument on which to lay the stress, putting less confidence in the rest, in this case, it is often proper for him to place this material Argument in the front; to preoccupy the hearers early, and make the strongest effort at first; that, having removed prejudices, and disposed them to be favourable, the rest of his reasoning may be listened to with more docility. When it happens, that amidst a variety of Arguments, there are one or two which we are sensible are more inconclusive than the rest, and yet proper to be used, Cicero advises to place these in the middle, as a station less conspicuous than either the beginning, or the end, of the train of reasoning.

IN the third place, when our Arguments are strong and satisfactory, the more they are distinguished and treated apart from each other, the better. Each can then bear to be brought out by itself, placed in its full light, amplified and rested upon. But when our Arguments are doubtful, and only of the presumptive kind, it is safer to throw them together in a crowd, and to run them into one another: *"ut quae sunt natura imbecilla,"* as Quintilian speaks, *"mutuo auxilio sustineantur;"* that though infirm of themselves, they may serve mutually to prop each other. He gives a good example, in the case of one who was accused of murdering a relation, to whom he was heir. Direct proof was wanting; but, "you expected a succession, and a great succession; you was in distressed circumstances; you was [sic] pushed to the utmost by your creditors; you had offended your relation, who had made you his heir; you knew that he was just then intending to alter his will; no time was to be lost. Each of these particulars, by itself," says the Author, "is inconclusive; but when they were assembled in one group, they have effect."

[. . .]

AFTER due attention given to the proper arrangement of Arguments, what is next requisite for their success, is to express them in such a style, and to deliver them in such a manner, as shall give them full force. On these heads I must refer the Reader to the directions I have given in treating of Style, in former Lectures; and to the directions I am afterwards to give concerning Pronunciation and Delivery.

[. . .]

To be an Eloquent Speaker, in the proper sense of the word, is far from being either a common or an easy attainment. Indeed, to compose a florid harangue on some popular topic, and to deliver it so as to amuse an Audience, is a matter not very difficult. But though some praise be due to this, yet the idea, which I have endeavoured to give of Eloquence, is much higher. It is a great exertion of the human powers. It is the Art of being persuasive and commanding; the Art, not of pleasing the fancy merely, but of speaking both to the understanding, and to the heart; of interesting the hearers in such a degree, as to seize and carry them along with us; and to leave them with a deep and strong impression of what they have heard. How many talents, natural and acquired, must concur for carrying this to perfection? A strong, lively, and warm imagination; quick sensibility of heart, joined with solid judgment, good sense, and presence of mind; all improved by great and long attention to Style and Composition; and supported also by the exterior, yet important qualifications of a graceful manner, a presence not ungainly, and a full and tuneable voice. How little reason to wonder, that a perfect and accomplished Orator, should be one of the characters that is most rarely to be found?

[...]

NOTHING, therefore, is more necessary for those who would excel in any of the higher kinds of Oratory, than to cultivate habits of the several virtues, and to refine and improve all their moral feelings. Whenever these become dead, or callous, they may be assured, that, on every great occasion, they will speak with less power, and less success. The sentiments and dispositions, particularly requisite for them to cultivate, are the following: The love of justice and order, and indignation at insolence and oppression; the love of honesty and truth, and detestation of fraud, meanness, and corruption; magnanimity of spirit; the love of liberty, of their country and the public; zeal for all great and noble designs, and reverence for all worthy and heroic characters. A cold and sceptical turn of mind is extremely adverse to Eloquence; and no less so, is that cavilling disposition which takes pleasure in depreciating what is great, and ridiculing what is generally admired. Such a disposition bespeaks one not very likely to excel in anything; but least of all in Oratory. A true Orator should be a person of generous sentiments, of warm feelings, and of a mind turned towards the admiration of all those great and high objects, which mankind are [sic] naturally formed to admire. Joined with the manly virtues, he should, at the same time, possess strong and tender sensiblity to all the injuries, distresses, and sorrows of his fellow-creatures; a heart that can easily relent; that can readily enter into the circumstances of others, and can make their case his own. A proper mixture of courage, and of modesty, must also be studied by every Public Speaker. Modesty is essential; it is always, and justly, supposed, to be a concomitant of merit; and every appearance of it is winning and prepossessing. But modesty ought not to run into excessive timidity. Every Public Speaker should be able to rest somewhat on himself; and to assume that air, not of self-complacency, but of firmness, which bespeaks a consciousness of his being thoroughly persuaded of the truth, or justice, of what he delivers; a circumstance of no small consequence for making impression on those who hear.

[...]

Good sense and knowledge, are the foundation of all good speaking. There is no art that can teach one to be eloquent, in any sphere, without a sufficient acquaintance with what belongs to that sphere; or if there were an Art that made such pretensions, it would be mere quackery, like the pretensions of the Sophists of old, to teach their disciples to speak for and against every subject; and would be deservedly exploded by all wise men. Attention to Style, to Composition, and all the Arts of Speech, can only assist an Orator in setting off, to advantage, the stock of materials which he possesses; but the stock, the materials themselves, must be brought from other quarters than from Rhetoric. He who is to plead at the Bar, must make himself thoroughly master of the knowledge of the Law; of all the learning and experience that can be useful in his profession, for supporting a cause, or convincing a Judge. He who is to speak from the Pulpit, must apply himself closely to the study of divinity, of practical religion, of morals, of human nature; that he may be rich in all the topics, both of instruction and of persuasion. He who would fit himself for being a Member of the Supreme Council of the Nation, or of any Public Assembly, must be thoroughly acquainted with the business that belongs to such Assembly; he must study the forms of Court, the course of procedure; and must attend minutely to all the facts that may be the subject of question or deliberation.

BESIDES the knowledge that properly belongs to that profession to which he addicts himself, a Public Speaker, if ever he expects to be eminent, must make himself acquainted, as far as his necessary occupations allow, with the general circle of polite literature. The study of Poetry may be useful to him, on many occasions, for embellishing his Style, for suggesting lively images, or agreeable allusions. The study of History may be still more useful to him; as the knowledge of facts, of eminent characters, and of the course of human affairs, finds place on many occasions. There are few great occasions of Public Speaking, in which one will not derive assistance from cultivated taste, and extensive knowledge. They will often yield him materials for proper ornament; sometimes, for argument and real use. A deficiency of knowledge, even in subjects that belong not directly to his own profession, will expose him to many disadvantages, and give better qualified rivals a great superiority over him.

[…]

I would, therefore, advise all who are Members of such Societies, in the first place, to attend to the choice of their subjects; that they be useful and manly, either formed on the course of their studies, or on something that has relation to morals and taste, to action and life. In the second place, I would advise them to be temperate in the practice of Speaking; not to speak too often, nor on subjects where they are ignorant or unripe; but only, when they have proper materials for a Discourse, and have digested and thought of the subject before-hand. In the third place, When they do speak, they should study always to keep good sense and persuasion in view, rather than an ostentation of Eloquence; and for this end, I would, in the fourth place, repeat the advice which I gave in a former Lecture, that they should always choose that side of the question to which, in their own judgment, they are most inclined, as the right and the true side; and defend it by such arguments as seem to them most solid. By these means, they will take the best method of forming themselves gradually to a manly, correct, and persuasive manner of Speaking.

Blair, Hugh. *Lectures on Rhetoric and Belle Lettres.* New York: James Conner Publishing, 1832, http://archive.org/details/lecturesonrhetoo1millgoog

Chapter 13

George Campbell

Stressing the importance of psychological and emotional appeals when combined with logos, George Campbell (1719–1796) was also an important figure in the rhetorical tradition during the Enlightenment. Like Whately and Blair, Campbell was a minister, and he was very interested in the relationship between theology and rhetoric, especially since ministers had to use persuasion in the course of their profession. Although Campbell respected the scientific tradition, his approach to rhetoric during this time was unique compared with his contemporaries. While stressing the importance of inductive and deductive reasoning, Campbell also emphasized the proper role of pathos—or emotional appeals—in rhetorical discourse. In his *Philosophy of Rhetoric*, Campbell provides a detailed account of the importance of understanding one's audience, the presentation of different types of reasoning, and the incorporation of expressive and emotional language when using emotional appeals to support arguments (Walzer 2003).

Philosophy of Rhetoric

Eloquence in the largest acceptation defined, its more general forms exhibited, with their different objects, ends, and characters.

IN speaking, there is always some end proposed, or some effect which the speaker intends to produce in the hearer. The word eloquence, in its greatest latitude, denotes "that art or talent by which the discourse is adapted to its end."

All the ends of speaking are reducible to four; every speech being intended to enlighten the understanding, to please the imagination, to move the passions, or to influence the will. Any one discourse admits only one of these ends as the principal. Nevertheless, in discoursing on a subject, many things may be introduced which are more immediately and apparently directed to some of the other ends of speaking, and not to that which is the chief intent of the whole. But then these other and immediate ends are in effect but means, and must be rendered conducive to that which is the primary intention. Accordingly, the propriety or the impropriety of the introduction of such secondary ends will always be inferred from their subserviency or want of subserviency to that end which is, in respect of them, the ultimate. For example, a discourse addressed to the understanding, and calculated to illustrate or evince some point purely speculative, may borrow aid from the imagination, and admit metaphor and comparison, but not the bolder and more striking figures, as that called vision or fiction, prosopopoeia, and the like, which are not so much intended to elucidate a subject as to excite admiration. Still less will it admit an address to the passions, which, as it never fails to disturb the operation of the intellectual faculty, must be regarded by every intelligent hearer as foreign at least, if not insidious. It is obvious that either of these, far from being subservient to the main design, would distract the attention from it.

[...]

In general, it may be asserted that each preceding species, in the order above exhibited, is preparatory to the subsequent; that each subsequent species is founded on the preceding; and that thus they ascend in a regular progression. Knowledge, the object of the intellect, furnish the materials for the fancy; the fancy culls, compounds, and, by her mimic art, disposes these materials so as to affect the passions; the passions are the natural spurs to volition or action, and so only to be rightly directed.

[...]

When a speaker addresses himself to the understanding, he proposes the instruction of his hearers, and that, either by explaining some doctrine unknown, or not distinctly comprehended by them, or by proving some position disbelieved doubted by them. In other words, he proposes either to dispel ignorance or to vanquish error. In the one, his aim is their information; in the other, their conviction. Accordingly, the predominant quality of the former is perspicuity; of the latter, argument. By that we are made to know, by this to believe.

The imagination is addressed by exhibiting to it a lively and beautiful representation of a suitable object. As in this exhibition the task of the orator may, in some sort, be said, like that of the painter, to consist in imitation, the merit of the work results entirely from these two sources: dignity, as well in the subject or thing imitated as in the manner of imitation, and resemblance in the portrait or performance. Now the principal scope for this class being in narration and description, poetry, which is one mode of oratory, especially poetry, must be ranked under it. The effect of the dramatic, at least of tragedy, being upon the passions, the drama falls under another species, to be explained afterward. But that kind of address of which I am now treating attains the summit of perfection in the sublime, or those great noble images which, when in suitable colouring presented to the mind, do, as it were, distend the imagination with some vast conception, and quite ravish the soul.

The sublime, it may be urged, as it raiseth admiration, should be considered as one species of address to the passions. But this objection, when examined, will appear superficial. There are few words in any language (particularly such as relate to the operations and feelings of the mind) which are strictly univocal. Thus, admiration, when persons are the object, is commonly used for a high degree of esteem; but, when otherwise applied, it denotes solely an internal taste. It is that pleasurable sensation which instantly arises on the perception of magnitude, or of whatever is great and stupendous in its kind; for there is a greatness in the degrees of quality in spiritual subjects analogous to that which subsists in the degrees of quantity in material things. Accordingly, in all tongues, perhaps without exception, the ordinary terms which are considered literally expressive of the latter, are also used promiscuously to denote the former. Now admiration, when thus applied, doth not require to its production, as the passions generally do, any reflex view of motives or tendencies, or of any relation either to private interest or to the good of others; and ought, therefore, to be numbered among those original feelings of the mind, which are denominated by some the reflex senses, being of the same class with a taste of beauty, an ear for music, or our moral sentiments. Now the immediate view of whatever is directed to the imagination (whether the subject be things inanimate or animal forms, whether characters, actions, incidents, or manners) terminates in the gratification of some internal taste; as a taste for the wonderful, the fair, the good; for elegance, for novelty, or for grandeur.

But it is evident that this creative faculty, the fancy, frequently lends her aid in promoting still nobler ends. From her exuberant stores most of those tropes and figures are extracted which, when properly employed, have such a marvellous efficacy in rousing the passions, and by some secret, sudden, and inexplicable association, awakening all the tenderest emotions of the heart. In this case, the address of the orator is not ultimately intended to astonish by the loftiness of his images, or to delight by the beauteous resemblance which his painting bears to nature; nay, it will not permit the hearers even a moment's leisure for making the comparison, but, as it were, by some magical spell, hurries them. They are aware, into love, pity, grief, terror, desire, aversion, fury, or hatred. It therefore assumes the denomination of pathetic, which is the characteristic of the third species of discourse, that addressed to the passions.

Finally, is that kind, the most complex of all, which is calculated to influence the will, and persuade to a certain conduct, is in reality an artful mixture of that which proposes to convince the judgment, and that which interests the passions, its distinguishing excellence results from these two, the argumentative and the pathetic incorporated together. These, acting with united force, and, if I may so express myself, in concert, constitute that passionate eviction, that vehemence of contention, which is admirably fitted for persuasion, and hath always been regarded as the supreme qualification of an orator.

[...]

It is not, however, every kind of pathos which will give the orator so great an ascendency over the minds of his hearers. All passions are not alike capable of producing this effect. Some are naturally inert and torpid; they reject the mind, and indispose it for enterprise. Of this kind are sorrow, fear, humility. Others, on the contrary, elevate the soul, and stimulate to action. Such are hope, patriotism, ambition, emulation, anger. These, with the greatest facility, are made to concur in direction with arguments exciting to resolution and activity; and are, consequently, the fittest for producing what, for want of a better term in our language, I shall henceforth denominate the vehement. There is, besides, an intermediate kind of passions, which do not so congenially and directly either restrain us from acting or incite us to act; but, by the art of the speaker, can, in an oblique manner, be made conducive to either. Such are joy, love, esteem, compassion. Nevertheless, all these kinds may find a place in suasory discourses, or such as are intended to operate on the will. The first is properest for dissuading; the second, as hath been already hinted, for persuading; the third is equally accommodated to both.

Guided by the above reflections, we may easily trace that connexion [sic] in the various forms of eloquence which was remarked on distinguishing them by their several objects. The imagination is charmed by a finished picture, wherein even drapery and ornament are not neglected; for here the end is pleasure. Would we penetrate farther, and agitate the soul, we must exhibit only some vivid strokes, some expressive features, not decorated as for show (all ostentation being both despicable and hurtful here), but such as appear the natural exposition of those bright and deep impressions made by the subject upon the speaker's mind; for here the end is not pleasure, but emotion. Would we not only touch the heart, but win it entirely to co-operate with our views, those affecting lineaments must be so interwoven with our argument, as that, from the passion excited, our reasoning may derive importance, and so be fitted for commanding attention; and by the justness of the reasoning, the passion may be more deeply rooted and enforced; and that thus both may be made to conspire in effectuating that persuasion which is the end proposed. For here, if I may adopt the school-men's language, we do not argue to gain barely the assent of the understanding, but, which is infinitely more important, the consent of the will.

[…]

IN contemplating a human creature, the most natural division of the subject is the common division into soul and body, or into the living principle of perception and of action, and that system of material organs by which the other receives information from without, and is enabled to exert its powers, both for its own benefit and for that of the species. Analogous to this there are two things in every discourse which principally claim our attention, the sense and the expression; or, in other words, the thought, and the symbol by which it is communicated. These may be said to constitute the soul and the body of an oration, or, indeed, of whatever is signified to another by language. For as, in man, each of these constituent parts hath its distinctive attributes, and as the perfection of the latter consisteth in its fitness for serving the purposes of the former, so it is precisely with those two essential parts of every speech, the sense and the expression Now it is by the sense that rhetoric holds of logic, and by the expression that she holds of grammar.

The sole and ultimate end of logic is the eviction of truth; one important end of eloquence, though, as appears from the first chapter, neither the sole, nor always the ultimate, is the conviction of the hearers. Pure logic regards only the Subject, which is examined solely for the sake of information. Truth, as such, is the proper aim of the examiner. Eloquence not only considers the subject, but also the speaker and the hearers, and both the subject and the speaker for the sake of the hearers, or, rather, for the sake of the effect intended to be produced in them. Now to convince the hearers is always either proposed by the orator as his end in addressing them, or supposed to accompany the accomplishment of his end. Of the five sorts of discourses above mentioned, there are only two wherein conviction is the avowed purpose. One is that addressed to the understanding, in which the speaker proposeth to prove some position disbelieved or doubted by the hearers; the other is that which is calculated to influence the will, and persuade to a certain conduct; for it is by convincing the judgment that he proposeth to interest the passions and fix the resolution. As to the three other kinds of discourses enumerated, which address the understanding, the imagination, and the passions, conviction, though not the end, ought ever to accompany the accomplishment of the end. It is never formally proposed as an end where there are not supposed to be previous doubts or errors to conquer. But when due attention is not paid to it by a proper management of the subject, doubts, disbelief, and mistake will be raised by the discourse itself, where there were none before, and these will not fail to obstruct the speaker's end, whatever it be. In explanatory discourses, which are of all kinds the simplest, there is a certain precision of manner which ought to pervade the whole, and which, though not in the form of argument, is not the less satisfactory, since it carries internal evidence along with it.

[...]

If, then, it is the business of logic to evince the truth, to convince an auditory, which is the province of eloquence, is but a particular application of the logician's art. As logic, therefore, forges the arms which eloquence teaches us to wield, we must first have recourse to the former, that, being made acquainted with the materials of which her weapons and armour are severally made, we may know their respective strength and temper, and when and how each is to be used.

Now, if it be by the sense or soul of the discourse that rhetoric holds of logic, or the art of thinking and reasoning, it is by the expression or body of the discourse that she holds of grammar, or the art of conveying our thoughts in the words of a particular language. The observation of one analogy naturally suggests another.

[…]

Campbell, George. *Philosophy of Rhetoric*. New York: Harper & Brothers, 1868, http://archive
.org/details/philosophyofrhetoocampuoft

CONCLUSION

Rhetoric in Our Contemporary World

This anthology has traced the key figures in and ideas about rhetoric from Ancient Greece through the Enlightenment. It necessarily cannot be an exhaustive account of every work that deals with rhetoric since its inception, but we have tried to provide a reasonably thorough snapshot of the important texts and concepts of our rhetorical tradition. As we have seen, much of the writing on rhetoric builds on preceding ideas, and many of the authors of these works reference or credit their predecessors. And, when we look at the historical trajectory of rhetoric from Ancient Greece to Rome through the Middle Ages and then to the Enlightenment, we see almost a full circle of what is considered to be most important by the scholars of the time. For example, in Ancient Greece, we know that ethos, pathos and logos were grouped together as the components necessary for effective rhetoric. The Romans elaborated on ethos. The Middle Ages was characterized by a significant emphasis on style. Then, with the Enlightenment, we see a shift to favoring logos, but George Campbell, the last of the so-called Enlightenment rhetoricians, reminds us not to ignore the importance of pathos. If we look at more contemporary rhetoricians, we see a sort of neo-Greco understanding of rhetoric, with a reliance on ethos, pathos and logos for successful rhetoric, just as we saw in Aristotle. In fact, in the mid-twentieth century, a form of rhetorical criticism, known as neo-Aristotelian rhetorical criticism, was quite popular (Foss 1996; Hendrix 1968).

Another issue in contemporary rhetoric that is heavily influenced by classical—and ancient—ideas about rhetoric is the concept known today as the "rhetorical situation" (Bitzer 1968). Taught in most basic rhetorical criticism and theory courses, the rhetorical situation is the concept that a specific context is either established or exploited by an effective rhetor. Lloyd Bitzer was a scholar of rhetoric who introduced the concept of the rhetorical situation, arguing that every rhetorical situation involves exigencies, constraints, and types of audiences that constitute a context to produce a potentially effective persuasive message. In most instances, an examination of a rhetorical message would benefit greatly from a realization of the rhetorical situation. And, of course, rhetors who understand the nature of rhetorical situations can improve the likelihood that their persuasive messages will be successful.

The rhetorical situation, then, is a crucial concept for rhetorical scholars. The idea itself, however, is nothing new. Bitzer's rhetorical situation is essentially a reworking of the concept of *kairos*, discussed primarily in the work of Isocrates and Plato (Isocrates 1894; Sprague 1972). *Kairos* is the idea that moments can emerge in discursive exchanges that either provide opportunities for or challenges to a rhetor. *Kairos* was central to the Sophists, who stressed a rhetor's ability to adapt to and take advantage of changing, contingent circumstances. In "Panathenaicus," Isocrates (1894) wrote that educated people are those "who manage well the circumstances which they encounter day by day, and who possess a judgment which is accurate in meeting occasions as they arise and rarely misses the expedient course of action." *Kairos* is also very important in Aristotle's concept of rhetoric. *Kairos* is, for Aristotle, the time and space context in which the proof will be delivered.

It should come as no surprise, then, that much of the current thinking about rhetoric incorporates ideas from Ancient Greece, Rome, the Middle Ages, and the Enlightenment. Virtually all modern studies of formal logic utilize the Aristotelian concept of dialectic; contemporary books on argumentation rely on the concepts of proofs, evidence, inductive and deductive reasoning, fallacies, and so on that are all mentioned in this volume. One idea that is not discussed much in contemporary argumentation studies, but probably should be, is the enthymeme. Although syllogisms are still taught, the use and critique of enthymemes are not emphasized. Their value, however, in understanding the relationship between rhetors and their audiences, the likelihood of fallacious reasoning with enthymemes, and their sheer frequency of use in modern discourse cannot be overstated.

Over the centuries, rhetoric has been a domain fought over by various loci of power. In academia, we call these power struggles "disciplinary" battles, turf wars, or territorial disputes over intellectual issues. Even in the selections included in this book, we see some evidence of these conceptual conflicts. Different groups want to claim rhetoric as their own, take ownership of it, and suggest that other groups either have no right to it or are inferior in their understanding and thus have less standing in their attempts to claim it. For example, we historically have seen such different disciplines as philosophy, history, philology, English studies, communication, argumentation studies, psychology, sociology, etc., argue over their "ownership" of rhetoric. Although these disputes have been frustrating, contemporary scholars of rhetoric can benefit from these spats since each disciplinary group offers some unique views and insights into the rhetorical tradition. For instance, psychologists potentially can offer some useful perspectives on the intention of persuasion and the reception of audience members, while, philosophers might provide some interesting perceptions on ethos and the relationship of rhetoric to truth. In the end, we are seeing a much more interdisciplinary approach to rhetoric today, and I believe we all benefit from a more collaborative and cooperative environment when studying rhetoric and persuasion.

Furthermore, an interdisciplinary view of rhetoric enables a variety of perspectives to be used in conjunction with rhetoric. For example, if we take a traditional view of rhetoric (as persuasion) and combine it with Marxist theory from political science/philosophy, then we can begin to have some very interesting possibilities of seeing rhetoric as a tool for both maintaining and resisting hegemonic power relations (McKerrow 1989; Ono and Sloop 1992; Zompetti 1997; Zompetti, 2012). Or, we might combine rhetoric with feminism to see how persuasion can perpetuate patriarchy (Biesecker 1992; Campbell 1973; Dow 1995; Foss and Griffin 1995). Other areas have also been linked with rhetoric to produce fascinating and informative perspectives, for example, cultural studies, post-colonialism, information technology, biology, mathematics, and practically any subject area that incorporates persuasion.

Another important contribution by classical rhetoric to contemporary applications is how rhetoric relates to citizenship. As we have discussed, rhetoric in Ancient Greece and Rome was mainly concerned with persuasive oratory for the benefit of the city-state, the Senate, or the community. Since rhetoric was speech that occurred in the realm of forensics (law), deliberation (policymaking), and ceremonial events, the techniques used to develop and criticize persuasive messages were integral to community building and what we would today call "political engagement" (Welsh, 2002). For example, Cicero in the *Rhetorica ad Herennium* remarks, "The task of the public speaker is to discuss capably those matters which law and custom have fixed for the uses of citizenship, and to secure as far as possible the agreement of his hearers. There are three kinds of causes which the speaker must treat: Epideictic, Deliberative, and Judicial." During the classical period, citizens used rhetoric to advocate for their beliefs, and rhetoric was a sine qua non for components of citizenship. Today, with growing apathy, cynicism, and detached engagement of citizens from politics (Putnam 1995; Rimmerman 2011; Verba et al. 1995), efforts have been made to reemphasize the importance of rhetoric in reengaging citizens in their communities. Rhetorical scholars have recently been exploring this intersection of rhetoric and citizenship/engagement (Del Gandio, 2008; Kahn and Lee, 2010; Zompetti, 2006). With efforts under way in the United States, such as the American Democracy Project, we should see a continuation of this area of scholarship.

Thus, contemporary rhetorical theory is really a multidisciplinary endeavor. Kenneth Burke (1945, 1969), one of the most influential rhetorical theorists of the twentieth century, came from the field of English studies but is often used by rhetoricians in the communication discipline. Argument studies use Chaïm Perelman (1969), who was influenced by philosophy, and Stephen Toulmin (1958), who was influenced by mathematics, in addition to others. Contemporary rhetoricians also borrow from Walter Fisher (1987) to analyze narratives and Joseph Campbell (1949) to examine myths. Therefore, not only do modern views on rhetoric employ a wide range of different perspectives, they also utilize a host of methods—or tools—for criticizing rhetoric. If we pick up a textbook that teaches approaches to rhetorical criticism, we will find methods grounded in mythic studies, dramatism, genre, ideology, feminism, etc. (Brummett, 2011; Lucaites, Condit and Caudill, 1998; Foss, Foss and Trapp, 2002). To be sure, rhetorical studies today are ripe with exciting possibilities, with much of this potential attributable to the hard work and contributions of authors like the ones represented in this book.

In the end, rhetoric is simply about persuasion. The study of rhetoric includes learning how to construct persuasive messages, how to analyze persuasive messages, and how to understand our ethical contributions to rhetorical conversations. When we consider the power that persuasion has in our lives—in our attitudes, beliefs, religious convictions, political ideologies, etc.—we cannot overstate its importance. To learn about rhetoric is to learn about the human condition. It requires us to delve deeply into how we make sense of the world around us. And, it reveals what we deem most important in our affairs. If any of us want to improve our relationships or communities, then we must consider the realm of rhetoric. It is our sincere hope that the material collected in this volume can help all of us in this pursuit.

Bibliography

Andrews, James. "Why Theological Hermeneutics Needs Rhetoric: Augustine's *De doctrina Christiana*." *International Journal of Systematic Theology* 12, no. 2 (2010): 184–200.

Aristotle., *Poetics*, vol. XXIII. Translated by Stephen Halliwell. Cambridge MA: Loeb Classical Library, Harvard University Press, 1995.

_____. *The Rhetoric of Aristotle*. Translated by R. C. Jebb. Cambridge, UK: Cambridge University Press, 1909.

Augustine. *De Doctrina, Nicene and Post-Nicene Fathers*. Series 1, vol. 2. Translated by Philip Schaff. Grand Rapids, MI: Christian Classics Ethereal Library, 1887 & 2004.

Barney, Rachel. "*Gorgia's* Defense: Plato and His Opponents on Rhetoric and the Good." *Southern Journal of Philosophy* 48, no. 1 (2010): 95–121.

Bede. *Libri II De Arte Metrica et De Schematibus et Tropis: The Art of Poetry and Rhetoric*. Translated by Calvin B. Kendall, in *Bibliotheca Germánica*. Nova, vol. 2, edited by Hans Fix. Saarbrücken, Germany: AQ Verlag, 1991.

Benson, Thomas W., and Michael H. Prosser. *Readings in Classical Rhetoric*. Bloomington: Indiana University Press, 1969.

Biesecker, Barbara. "Coming to Terms with Recent Attempts to Write Women into the History of Rhetoric." *Philosophy & Rhetoric* 25 (1992): 140–61.

Bitzer, Lloyd. "The Rhetorical Situation." *Philosophy & Rhetoric* 1 (1968): 1–14.

Blair, Hugh. *Lectures on Rhetoric and Belle Lettres*. New York: James Conner Publishing, 1832.

Brinton, Alan. "Quintilian, Plato, and the *Vir Bonus*." *Philosophy & Rhetoric* 16, no. 3 (1983): 167–184.

Brummett, Barry. *Rhetoric in Popular Culture*. 3rd ed.. Los Angeles: Sage, 2011.

Burke, Kenneth. *A Grammar of Motives*. Berkeley: University of California Press, 1945.

———. *A Rhetoric of Motives*. Berkeley: University of California Press, 1969.

Campbell, George. *Philosophy of Rhetoric*. New York: Harper & Brothers, 1868.

Campbell, Joseph. *The Hero with a Thousand Faces*. Bollingen, Switzerland: Bollingen Foundation Press, 1949.

Campbell, Karlyn K. "The Rhetoric of Women's Liberation: An Oxymoron." *Quarterly Journal of Speech* 59 (1973): 74–86.

Chase, Kenneth R. "Constructing Ethics through Rhetoric: Isocrates and Piety." *Quarterly Journal of Speech* 95, no. 3 (2009): 239–262.

Cicero. *Cicero: Vols. III–IV, De Oratore, Books I–III*. Translated by E. W. Sutton and H. Rackham. Cambridge, MA: Harvard University Press, 1942.

———. *Cicero: De Inventione, De Optimo Genere Oratorum, Topica*. Translated by H. M. Hubbell. Cambridge, MA: Harvard University Press, 1949.

———. *Cicero: Vol. I, Rhetorica ad Herennium*. Translated by Harry Caplan. Cambridge, MA: Harvard University Press, 1954.

Clarke, Martin L. *Rhetoric at Rome*. London: Cohen & West, 1953.

Cole, Thomas. *The Origins of Rhetoric in Ancient Greece*. Baltimore: Johns Hopkins University Press, 1991.

Crowley, Sharon, and Debra Hawhee. *Ancient Rhetorics for Contemporary Students*. 3rd ed. New York: Pearson, 2004.

Dante. *De Vulgari Eloquentia*. Translated by Steven Botterill. London: Cambridge University Press, 1996.

Del Gandio, Jason. *Rhetoric for Radicals: A Handbook for 21st Century Activists*. Gabriola Island, British Columbia: New Society, 2008.

Demetrius. *On Style*. Translated by W. Rhys Roberts. Cambridge, UK: Cambridge University Press, 1902.

Derrida, Jacques. *Of Grammatology.*, Translated by Gayatri C. Spivak. Baltimore: Johns Hopkins University Press, 1967.

Dow, Bonnie. "Feminism, Difference(s), and Rhetorical Studies." *Communication Studies* 46 (1995): 106–117.

Enos, Richard L. *Roman Rhetoric: Revolution and the Greek Influence.* Prospect Heights, IL: Waveland Press, 1995.

Enos, Richard L., and Margaret Kantz. "A Selected Bibliography on Corax and Tisias." *Rhetoric Society Quarterly* 13 (1983): 71–74.

Erasmus, Desiderius. *On Copia of Words and Ideas.* Translated by Donald B. King and H. David Rix. Milwaukee, WI: Marquette University Press, 1963.

Fisher, Walter R. *Human Communication as Narration: Toward a Philosophy of Reason, Value, and Action.* Columbia: University of South Carolina Press, 1987.

Foss, Sonja K. "Neo-Aristotelian Criticism." In *Rhetorical Criticism: Exploration & Practice* 2nd ed., edited by S. K. Foss, 23–59. Prospect Heights, IL: Waveland Press, 1996.

_____, and Cindy L. Griffin. "Beyond Persuasion: A Proposal for Invitational Rhetoric." *Communication Monographs* 62 (1995): 2–18.

_____, Karen A. Foss, and Cindy L. Griffin. *Readings in Feminist Rhetorical Theory.* Prospect Heights, IL: Waveland Press, 2004.

_____, Karen Foss, and Robert Trapp. *Contemporary Perspectives on Rhetoric.* Prospect Heights, IL: Waveland Press, 2002.

Futter, D. "*Gorgias* and the Psychology of Persuasion." *Akroterion* 56 (2011): 3–20.

Garver, Eugene. *Aristotle's Rhetoric: An Art of Character.* Chicago: University of Chicago Press, 1994.

Gilson, Etienne. *Dante and Philosophy.* Translated by David Moore. New York: Sheed & Ward, 1968.

Golden, James L. "Cicero and Quintilian on the Formation of an Orator." *Speech Journal* 6 (1969): 29–34.

_____, and Edward P. J. Corbett. *The Rhetoric of Blair, Campbell, and Whately.* Carbondale: Southern Illinois University, 1990.

Grossberg, Lawrence. "Marxist Dialectics and Rhetorical Criticism." *Quarterly Journal of Speech* 65, no. 3 (1979): 235–249.

Hendrix, J. A. "In Defense of Neo-Aristotelian Criticism." *Western Speech* 32, no. 4 (1968): 246–252.

Horace. *Satires, Epistles, and Ars Poetica.* Translated by John Conington. Cambridge: University of Oxford Press, 1878 & 2004.

Howell, Wilbur S. "Aristotle and Horace on Rhetoric and Poetics." *Quarterly Journal of Speech* 54, no. 4 (1968): 325–340.

Isocrates. "Panegyricus," in *Isocrates' Orations Vol. I.* Translated by J. H. Freese. London: George Bell & Sons, 1894.

––––––. "Against the Sophists," in *Isocrates: On the Peace, Areopagiticus, Against the Sophists, Antidosis, Panathenaicus.* Vol. 229 of Loeb Classical Library. Translated by George Norlin. Cambridge, MA: Harvard University Press, 1929.

––––––. "Panathenaicus," in *Isocrates: On the Peace, Areopagiticus, Against the Sophists, Antidosis, Panathenaicus.* Vol. 229 of Loeb Classical Library. Translated by George Norlin. Cambridge, MA: Harvard University Press, 1929.

Johnson, W. R. "Isocrates Flowering: The Rhetoric of Augustine." *Philosophy & Rhetoric* 9, no. 4 (1976): 217–231.

Kahn, Seth, and JongHwa Lee, eds. *Activism and Rhetoric: Theories and Contexts for Political Engagement.* New York: Routledge, 2010.

Kennedy, George. *The Art of Rhetoric in the Roman World: 300 B.C.–A.D. 300.* Princeton, NJ: Princeton University Press, 1972.

Leathers, Dale G. "Whately's Logically Derived 'Rhetoric': A Stranger in Its Time." *Western Speech* 33, no. 1 (1969): 48–58.

Liebersohn, Yosef Z. "The Problem of Rhetoric's Materia in Plato's *Gorgias.*" *Rhetorica: A Journal of the History of Rhetoric* 29, no. 1 (2011): 1–22.

Lucaites, John L., Celeste M. Condit, and S. Caudill, eds. *Contemporary Rhetorical Theory: A Reader.* New York: Guilford Press, 1998.

McKerrow, Raymie E. "Method of Composition: Whately's Earliest 'Rhetoric.'" *Philosophy & Rhetoric* 11, no. 1 (1978): 43–58.

––––––. "Critical Rhetoric: Theory and Praxis." *Communication Monographs* 56 (1989): 91–111.

Miller, Joseph M., Michael H. Prosser, and Thomas W. Benson. *Readings in Medieval Rhetoric.* Bloomington: Indiana University Press, 1974.

Murphy, James J. "Aristotle's Rhetoric in the Middle Ages." *Quarterly Journal of Speech* 52, no. 2 (1966): 109–116.

––––––. "Cicero's Rhetoric in the Middle Ages." *Quarterly Journal of Speech* 53, no. 4 (1967): 334–342.

O'Donnell, Anne M. "Rhetoric and Style in Erasmus." *Studies in Philology* 77, no. 1 (1980): 26–50.

Oliensis, Ellen. *Horace and the Rhetoric of Authority*. Cambridge, UK: Cambridge University Press, 1998.

Ono, Kent A., and John M. Sloop. "Commitment to Telos—a Sustained Critical Rhetoric." *Communication Monographs* 59 (1992): 48–60.

———. "The Critique of Vernacular Discourse." *Communication Monographs* 62 (1995): 19–46.

Panizza, Letizia. "Literature in the Vernacular." In *The Cambridge History of Italian Literature*, edited by Peter Brand and Lino Pertile, 152–159. Cambridge: Cambridge University Press, 1996.

Perelman, Chaïm, and Lucie Olbrechts-Tyteca. *The New Rhetoric: A Treatise on Argumentation*. South Bend, IN: University of Notre Dame Press, 1969.

Plato. "Gorgias." *The Dialogues of Plato*. 3rd ed. Translated by Ben Jowett. London: Oxford University Press, 1892.

Putnam, Robert D. "Bowling Alone: America's Declining Social Capital." *Journal of Democracy* 6, no.1 (1995): 65–78.

Quintilian. *Quintilian: The Institutio Oratoria of Quintilian, Vol. 1*. Translated by H. E. Butler. Cambridge, MA: Harvard University Press, 1922.

———. *Quintilian: The Institutio Oratoria of Quintilian, Vol. 4*. Translated by H. E. Butler. Cambridge, MA: Harvard University Press, 1922.

Ramsey, Shawn D. "*Consilium*: A System to Address Deliberative Uncertainty in the Rhetoric of the Middle Ages." *Advances in the History of Rhetoric* 15, no. 2 (2012): 204–221.

Ramus, Peter. *Dialectique de Pierre de la Ramée*. Paris, 1555.

Rimmerman, Craig A. *The New Citizenship: Unconventional Politics, Activism, and Service*. 4th ed. Philadelphia: Westview Press, 2011.

Rossini, Egidio. "Introduction to the Edition of Medieval Vernacular Documents." In *Medieval Manuscripts and Textual Criticism*, edited by C. Kleinhenz, 175–210. Chapel Hill: University of North Carolina Press, 1976.

Schenkeveld, Dirk M. "The Intended Public of Demetrius's *On Style*: The Place of the Treatise in the Hellenistic Educational System." *Rhetorica: A Journal of the History of Rhetoric* 18, no. 1 (2000): 29–48.

Sinclair, Patrick. "The Sententia in *Rhetorica ad Herennium*: A Study in the Sociology of Rhetoric." *American Journal of Philology* 114, no. 4 (1993): 561–581.

Sprague, Rosamond Kent. *The Older Sophists*. Columbia: University of South Carolina Press, 1972.

Toulmin, Stephen. *The Uses of Argument*. London: Cambridge University Press, 1958.

Verba, Sidney, Kay L. Schlozman, and Henry Brady. *Voice and Equality: Civic Voluntarism in American Politics*. Cambridge, MA: Harvard University Press, 1995.

Walzer, Arthur E. *George Campbell: Rhetoric in the Age of Enlightenment*. Albany: State University of New York Press, 2003.

_____. "Blair's Ideal Orator: Civic Rhetoric and Christian Politeness in Lectures 25–34." *Rhetorica: A Journal of the History of Rhetoric* 25, no. 3 (2007): 269–295.

Ward, John O. "The Catena Commentaries on the Rhetoric of Cicero and Their Implications for Development of a Teaching Tradition in Rhetoric." *Studies in Medieval and Renaissance Teaching* 6, no. 2 (1998): 79–95.

Welsh, Scott. "Deliberative Democracy and the Rhetorical Production of Political Culture." *Rhetoric & Public Affairs* 5, no. 4 (2002): 679–708.

Whately, Richard. *Elements of Logic*. Boston: James Munroe & Co., 1855.

Wichelns, Herbert A. "The Literary Criticism of Oratory." In *Studies in Rhetoric and Public Speaking in Honor of James Albert Winans*, edited by Alexander Magnus Drummond, 181–216. New York: The Century Company, 1925.

Zompetti, Joseph P. "Toward a Gramscian Critical Rhetoric." *Western Journal of Communication* 61, no. 1 (1997): 66–86.

_____. "The Role of Advocacy in Civil Society." *Argumentation: An International Journal of Reasoning* 20 (2006): 167–183.

_____. "The Cultural and Communicative Dynamics of Capital: Gramsci and the Impetus for Social Action." *Culture, Theory and Critique* 53, no. 3 (2012): 365–382.

SELLING
HIGH
TECH
HIGH
TICKET

Using
Relationship
Management
Techniques To
Sell & Service
Today's Complex
Products

John Katsaros

IRWIN
Professional Publishing®
Burr Ridge, Illinois
New York, New York

This publication is designed to provide accurate and authoritative information in regard to the subject matter covered. It is sold with the understanding that the author and the publisher are not engaged in rendering legal, accounting, or other professional service.

ISBN 1-55738-511-4

Printed in the United States of America

BB

CTV/BJS

2 3 4 5 6 7 8 9 0

Dedication

To my young bride, Robin, and our two boys, Christopher and Matthew.

Contents

Foreword

When I founded Crosspoint Venture Partners over a decade ago, we set out to finance and assist entrepreneurs whose ideas and talents lead to rapid-growth, new companies providing unique products, services, and market opportunities. Since then, Crosspoint has helped build many start-up companies through providing initial seed capital and follow-on rounds of equity financing. Our successful portfolio companies have one factor for success in common—they develop a distinctive selling style tailored to their unique needs.

In an era when new products are constantly streaming into the market, a high-tech company's sales strategy is one of its most important long-term strengths. Unfortunately, too many companies recycle unimaginative sales plans and fail to use their sales investment to establish competitive entry barriers. Their early sales planning mistakes cause them problems later on from which they may never recover. New ideas in high-tech selling are sorely needed to invigorate these companies.

Until now, very little help has been available for people involved with high-tech sales. There are many books preaching the benefits of effective time management for sales, systems selling and solutions selling. And there are many books covering high-tech marketing. Although these subjects are helpful in understanding the sales process, they don't address the core issues, nor do they deal with the demands of selling technology based products.

Selling High-Tech/High-Ticket presents far-reaching ideas on how to go about building high-tech sales. John Katsaros gets to the heart of customer development for people involved with selling high-tech products and services. His explanations of selling distinctive value and market share selling provide valuable insights for anyone involved with sales growth within a high-tech company.

By punctuating his high-tech selling concepts with real-world industry examples, Katsaros presents an exciting new sales vision based upon his Smart Selling process. His model for company-to-company selling applies equally for firms selling high-ticket products directly to mainstream customers as well as for those involved with multi-tier reseller programs selling inexpensive technology products.

Selling High-Tech/High-Ticket is an important contribution to the management of high-tech companies. It proves that in today's constantly changing high-tech markets, it is possible to create a sales plan that both builds customers and creates important competitive distinction. This book will quickly become an important tool for everyone in high-tech business involved with building and keeping customers.

John Mumford
Los Altos, CA

Preface

One weekday afternoon in 1981, I was in Manhattan standing in front of The Associated Press Building in Rockefeller Center. I looked up at this fifty-story skyscraper and felt I was all alone in the world. I ran the sales for Equatorial Communications, a Silicon Valley startup company, and we needed to sell the Associated Press our satellite communications system. Even though I had been working in sales for almost ten years, I felt totally unable to sell them our services. Here was the oldest user of data communications (the first data communications circuit was installed between New York and Washington, D.C. in the mid-1800s to relay news to the Associated Press members). My startup company was just ramping up production of a brand new set of products and services that would bypass terrestrial circuits and provide direct access between the Associated Press and its member newspapers. My competition was awesome; the phone company literally lived in this account—many of the communications executives of the AP had come from AT&T and Western Union, its two principal communications suppliers. We had been locked out of this account since our company started. We didn't have the credibility of the big communications companies. We weren't financed to the extent they were. We didn't have armies of people that gave large users comfort that someone is out there, ready to service their every need. We barely even had our product working and in limited production. And our financials represented mostly the three-year product development investment. Yet closing this one account could do so much for us. We needed it. If we won this sale, we could continue to expand our business. If we were not successful, we might never gain acceptance by other accounts in the same class. I was responsible for making it happen, and even though I had lots of successful sales experience, I didn't have the faintest idea what to do. How do you go about removing an incumbent supplier, and one with such a long working history with the customer?

I needed a new way to sell. The selling methods that had been useful in the past did not apply. We needed more. I began looking for a new selling model that high-tech companies, salespeople, and sales managers could use to improve their ability to gain customers and market share.

If you are involved with selling high-technology products you may have had a similar feeling—that you are in an impossible situation. There's too much to be done and your resources are too limited. You just cannot get there from here. The newer the technology, the smaller the company, the harder the problem seems to be.

There's a need for a new model for going about selling. It's no longer enough to hire sales people, find the right contacts and develop an account. Today's customers need much more. Creating a new selling model means enlisting your entire work force in your account development process.

We did eventually win over the Associated Press and many more customers and continued to expand our company. This book highlights the sorts of strategies and new thinking that will help high-tech sellers to improve their ability to win new customers in today's markets. It describes the smart selling process. Selling smart means forming partnerships between your work force and your customers, your resellers, and your business partners. This book is written for everyone involved in selling products of a technical nature, regardless of how you sell—through direct sales, retail distribution, telesales, or catalogs; and regardless of the price of your product—less than $10 or more than millions of dollars. It is for people looking for new ideas on how to sell to businesses in the 1990s and how to position themselves as business partners to their customers and key channel participants.

John Katsaros

Acknowledgments

During the past two years, many people have contributed and helped turn this project from an idea to reality.

Thanks to John Karakash, Dean Mack, Andy Paul, and Jim Willenborg for their time and input. Jim Kouzes generously gave his time to provide insight into what lay ahead. Raymond Chin, George Korpontinos, and Tom Tisch filled in the missing pieces for some of the cases. Carol Anshaw did a superb job editing. And a special thanks to Marge Mueller for helping to get the manuscript in shape and sticking with the project to the end.

Part I

Selling Market Share and Cost Savings

I magine having a chance meeting with your customer—the president of the company—on an airplane. You've got a whole hour or more to tell him what your company does and how they'll benefit from partnering with your company. You know he's not going anywhere unless you are so boring he decides to lock himself in the bathroom. What would you say? You've got a short time period to get your point across that the best thing in the world for him to do when he deplanes is to establish a long-term partnership with your company.

This sort of chance encounter is unlikely. But thinking through your approach will help you create a message for the members of your customer's team with whom you are in daily contact. They in turn can carry your message to the rest of their team.

After 20 years of selling and marketing high-tech products, I am convinced that there are two—and only two—sales propositions that successful high-technology companies can use to build market share over the long term. Either you are:

1. providing your customers with a significant and substantial competitive advantage, or

2. you are replacing well-known costs with an alternative—persuasive cost savings—that has a short payback period.

The better you establish the selling proposition, the quicker you will receive an order. Your customer either will gain a significant competitive advantage or can cut operating costs dramatically. Anything else may be interesting, but irrelevant. Bigger, faster, better, smaller—all are interesting technical comparisons. But the rubber meets the road with these two selling propositions. To become the market share leader in your area, you must show your version of bigger, faster, better, smaller—or whatever will result in competitive advantage or lower costs for your customer.

Relating your product to your customer's higher level business goals is the most difficult part of high-tech selling. (Throughout this book, I'll be using the term "product" generically to refer to both products and services.) You can base your sales proposition on your ability to improve your customers business or significantly reduce their cost structure.

There are two things to keep in mind as you create your product's selling proposition.

1. Your customer needs and wants to grow his company's customer base

2. Everyone is willing to make a low-risk investment that can save a lot of money in a short time.

Chapter 1

High-Tech Sales, Markets, and Customers

We all share the same goal: To achieve consistent, above-average sales performance for our high-tech companies. Beating quotas month after month, year after year will make you successful and put your company on the path toward long-term success in its field. Whether your company makes semiconductors, medical equipment, biotech products, communications equipment, computers, or software, your goal is to build customers and distribution to leverage your distinctive value, thereby returning premium prices for your company's products. Achieving this goal is not easy. Being an above-average sales performer leads to success. Sales groups that constantly miss this goal put their companies on the road to disaster.

The purpose of this book is to put you on the right road for unequaled success in your business. This book is about selling high-technology products and services. For a variety of reasons, selling at most high-tech companies has become somewhat of a back room operation removed from the rest of the company's work force. That's unfortunate. People at high-tech companies shudder at the thought of being part of a "sales driven" organization, preferring instead "market driven" or "engineering driven" name tags. *Selling High-Tech/High-Ticket* helps people working in the high-tech industry and people in companies selling high-ticket items get and keep customers. Success means being part of a customer driven company where sales, marketing, development, manufacturing, customer service, and engineering are interwoven with business partners and your customer's work force for the common purpose of identifying and fulfilling your customer's needs.

3

Selling is the "person to person" part of every business. Direct marketers sell through their catalogs or phone staffs. Steel producers have outside
sales forces making direct sales calls on their customers. Auto manufacturers sell through their dealer showrooms. All companies have a way to sell
their products and services.

I am often asked how high-technology selling is different than selling
any other type of mainstream business to business product. The answer to
this question has two parts:

1. High-tech selling involves your customer's strategic decision making. Your customer is buying empowerment. When you are involved with your customer's strategic planning, you influence his
   corporate direction. You affect the way he does things and interacts
   with his customers, and the way his company creates value. Commodity products don't impact a buyer's long-term strategic direction. High-tech products can.

2. Technology selling is different from other business to business selling because technology products are adaptive—they can be dramatically altered to suit their environment. This malleable quality
   of technology means that adaptations are possible to ensure a
   match between product and application. It also means that technology sellers can recreate their products to better suit selected market
   subsegments.

Selling high-technology products and services is art and science, but
not mystery. Good selling doesn't happen through sales black magic. It
means setting achievable expectations with your customer and beating your
competition. Today you no longer compete with one or two companies
creating similar products. You are facing global competitors all promising
your customers the latest in high-tech offerings especially suited for their
businesses. New product introductions come at lightning speed. Just as
soon as your company brings out its latest products, two or three competitors appear with similar offerings. As you begin to grow important new
markets for your products, your existing markets splinter, forming new
niche opportunities for smaller, more agile competitors.

To survive and excel in today's technology markets, you've got to
home in on the two most important aspects of selling high-technology:

1. Today's technology customers use technology as a business strategy fundamental to their entire corporate persona, and

2. Successful high-tech selling means finding your differentiated value and positioning this differentiation as your customers' means of improving their long-term business position. Your customers want to be long-term, above-average performers within their industries. They need technology partnerships to do this. They are looking at you as their potential business partner to achieve and maintain leadership in their industry. Finding the right business partners isn't an easy journey for your customers. Nor is it easy for you to position your company as a credible partner in your customer's future success.

Two aspects of high-technology selling dominate today's sales arenas:

➡ People buy technology because it is a fundamental part of their corporate business strategy.

➡ A high-tech company's long-term distinctive value is its key to dominance of its markets.

You are looking for unparalleled success for yourself and your company. Your job isn't just to bring your company's new product to the market and get a few good customers. Your company has probably spent millions on its new product development and may be in a position to capitalize on a new growth market worth hundreds of millions over the long-term. You've got to hit a major home run with your company's new products. You must enter new market segments and quickly gain customer acceptance. If you don't, your company risks becoming an also-ran in its industry. If you are not number one, you'll become a supplier with good products but always just a little out of the market's mainstream. You don't want to come in second or third in today's markets. You've got to lead.

Imagine a scenario where you and your company meet and exceed sales goals every quarter. Wouldn't it be wonderful if you could accurately forecast the potential of each prospective client to know how and when to allocate resources to meet their needs? This level of forecasting success can be tremendously rewarding for you and your company. Your company's business improves tremendously as your ability to accurately project customer situations and forecast events improves. What if each new product your company brought to market lived up to its fullest sales potential? What if each potential customer problem was anticipated and resolved before a crisis occurred? Imagine your product lines growing and gaining customers and new submarkets until you dominate your competitors. And imagine if your product's market share growth continues annually at double-digit rates.

That's a great dream. One that each of us would love to live. Going to work each day would be terrific. Who wouldn't love it?

Unfortunately, few companies experience these achievements. Not many sales forces can accurately forecast their futures. Even when they do predict sales revenues, their product mix and customer mix forecasts may be far off, resulting in tremendous internal gymnastics and misguided resource allocation. Many companies don't even dare dream about meeting or exceeding their numbers. If you are lucky, you may achieve success like this for one or two years out of ten. Achieving even that would make many happy. Sometimes success is only for a quarter or two. When we fail to reach these levels, more often than not we never understand what went wrong, or why.

A high-tech company usually has thinly stretched resources. It certainly doesn't need the diversions that come from inaccurate forecasts. Accurately predicting outcomes from sales investments and finding achievable and affordable scenarios can mean the difference between success and failure in most businesses. What business consultant doesn't recommend setting plans that are achievable? Consistently meeting plans is much more likely to produce a long-term success than constantly missing targets, even if the more accurate planning involves considerably lower financial targets. As sound as this advice is, most sales plans are not met.

So what's wrong here? You wouldn't get in your car to go somewhere if you thought you had less than a 50 percent chance of arriving. But you are willing to spend day after day in a business where you have less than half a chance of meeting your forecast numbers. Most new products fail in the market. Most sales groups fail to meet their targets. Success is defined by how close you come to your target—not by how much you actually exceed it.

The problem is that the way people sell products and services to mainstream customers hasn't changed very much for the past 30 years. Yet today's customers are completely different than they were even a few years ago. Terms like Information Superhighways, Just-in-Time Manufacturing, Global Competition, Enterprise Computing, Sigma 6 Quality Levels, Virtual Corporation, Knowledge Workers, Value Chain, Total Quality Management, ISO 9000 and Electronic Markets are now in our customers' everyday vocabulary, forever changing the nature of their businesses. Despite tremendous changes in the way today's customers structure and process their business, selling to these customers has not changed one bit. (The high-tech companies that have done the most to modernize their internal units— Hewlett Packard and Motorola for example—often are the ones that have done the least to revamp their selling styles.)

In addition, many high-tech companies disenfranchised their sales people over the past ten years by signing up an army of resellers and then passing their customer development responsibilities on to others. With the explosion of the technology markets in the 1980s came a tremendous growth in distribution and reselling channels. New high-tech selling categories include software-only resellers, mail order catalogs, update fulfillment houses, and 800 number direct response centers. High-tech companies using multi-tiered channels confused their resellers' fulfillment role with their own selling responsibilities. These companies mistakenly thought their resellers were going to do the selling for them and lost their own sales ability. Many excellent products died in the marketplace due to sales neglect.

Change is needed in the way today's companies sell their products, but this is difficult to implement. Your company's own management inertia may prevent it from changing to meet today's customer demands. Management wants to repeat the things that worked in the past. Sales roles are defined traditionally. Sales plans are created through a "Cliff Notes" process, recycling the highlights of prior sales experiences into today's markets. If your product category has used direct selling in the past, then a sales force is hired or the existing one is trained on the new product. If the business uses a distribution strategy, the new product line will be brought out through the distributors. If a third-party VAR (value added reseller) channel is needed because the board of directors is trying to keep sales costs down, a VAR channel is assembled. Instead of matching the sales plan to the product's unique selling requirements, people rely on formulas. It worked in the past, it worked in the 1980s, so let's use it again.

There are even a number of high-tech companies that do no strategic sales planning at all. They have an existing way of selling and an existing sales force and, when a new product comes along, it is the product that has to adapt to the existing sales process. High-tech products may be programmable, but they're not able to automatically redesign themselves to meet the idiosyncrasies of a mismatched sales channel. How many times have you seen a high-tech company spend millions on research, development, beta testing, and complex marketing introductions and never spend even a tiny amount of time on sales planning for the product? The product eventually hits the market and the sales force is called in for a few days of training. No sales plan exists. The company's plan is to learn how to sell its new product by the seat of its pants. The sales costs for a $50 million high-tech company are probably $1 million per month. That's a very expensive way to learn how to sell a new product. Sadly, this happens every day.

The central office telephone exchange service marketed by the Bell Operating Companies—Centrex—is a classic example of a product line that lost market share because the sales process to sell it was not in place. Centrex services compete in small business markets with companies selling on-premises customer switching equipment. A customer can either own his own equipment or get the same functions as a monthly service from his local phone company. Centrex is not only affordable, it allows a user to avoid many of the annoying pitfalls associated with having in-house equipment. The phone companies were not prepared as their equipment competitors quickly moved into the market. Even though there were many advantages to using Centrex, the phone companies did not have in place effective sales capability to counter their competitors. As a result, Centrex services languished as private equipment sales soared. Centrex sales finally picked up steam a decade later as the phone companies began to improve their sales issues.

Your Sales Mission

Today's high-technology selling has two primary missions:

1. Sales must take new products into new markets. This doesn't mean just orders for new products. It means finding the right customers in the right submarkets at the right time to build the initial reference accounts for a new product. This first phase of new-product selling is the basis for future market development. Opening up new markets is a sales goal for existing products as well. Years after a product comes out it still may find new submarkets that were not able to adopt the product during its early years. These sorts of markets not only breathe additional life into an aging product, they can be very profitable.

2. The sales group must cultivate and penetrate mainstream markets. Once a new product establishes a beachhead of reference accounts in a submarket, the sales mission is to find more and more customers with similar requirements.

Only when both sales missions are successfully accomplished can a high-tech company receive a return from its new product line.

Most high-tech products are reinvented and reintroduced into the market within the first two years after their initial appearance. So, you've got less than eighteen months to make your new product a sales success. Every month your sales force is "experimenting" in the market can cost millions of dollars subsidizing a less than efficient sales organization. Your opportunity costs in terms of lost initial market development are extremely high. If you stumble for six months you can wipe out your product's sales potential. While your sales group is experimenting with your current customer base, competing alternative solutions may be busily locking you out of your potential customer base (see Figure 1-1).

When a new product is first brought into the marketplace you are in a race against your competition to get innovators and early adopters to begin to use it. There are only a limited number of these early experimenters in any one market. If your competitor is working with one, you probably won't get the opportunity until they've failed. Only after successful experiences with these first users is your product ready for prime time. What invariably happens is that during the year or two it takes to incubate success among these first users, much is learned about what is really needed in the product. Some new ideas come into play. First users focus attention on additional functionality needed in your product. External factors are also introduced into this design iteration. Perhaps your competitor has introduced something new or maybe developments on the supply side will cause some design additions (for instance, a larger cache memory will be considered if the price of memory significantly dropped during the interim). The net result is that some degree of redesign is necessary in most technology products from the date they are first sold to the innovators and early adopters until the time they are brought to the larger market. From the moment your product is brought to the market, you are in a race to get down this early acceptance curve.

Figure 1-1   Anticipating New Product Sales Requirements before Launch Will Lead to Higher Returns, Sooner

The redesigning of the product is also coupled with an overall "relaunching" of the sales plan. The results of the first users helps everyone understand the real value of any new product. In turn, this leads to improvements in the sales and marketing plans as a better understanding of the potential customer base is developed. The sales curve for a new product is made up of two curves, superimposed—sales to early adopters and sales to the general marketplace. The type of product, the length of time to incubate the first users and the complexity of the product's "reinvention," determine the result of the overall sales curve. In some cases, these will come together smoothly to form a continuous growth curve. In most other cases, there can be a huge dip in sales as the product is repackaged for the general market. Today, most technology products fall into the latter category and have sales dips. Companies that don't anticipate these dips view them as real disasters (see Figure 1-2).

Disaster can strike at any moment. A company spends years developing its new product. Eventually the product is introduced and has some initial sales success in its first three to six shipment months (generally, these sales are to existing customers who were involved with the product from the start). Sales for the new product then drop off.

At the same time sales of the company's existing products start falling and the management panics. Sales people are told to get new customers even though the new product clearly is not yet ready for production use by

Figure 1-2   Sales Drops Are Common for New Products

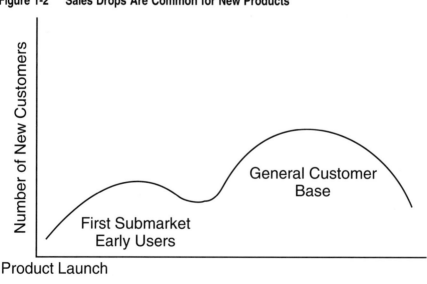

their customers and must undergo extensive engineering modification before it's ready for prime time. Sales quotas are not met and heads start to roll. Some sales people are fired. Eventually the vice president of sales is dumped in favor of someone with more sales leadership. The company is now so embroiled with managing itself through a period of missed expectations that it is unable to focus on the main issue of why its new product is not successful.

This company created its own crisis. Without proper sales planning, it put itself in a position of developing sales strategy in real time, and only immediate and constant new sales growth could prevent disaster. In the 1970s and 1980s, markets were growing fast enough to allow sales teams to do this. Products were less complex. The first set of capabilities was sufficient to satisfy most customer needs. Customers were willing to take "raw" technology products and play with them. Many of these customers had groups whose sole purpose was to experiment and perform prototype integration of new products. Sales groups surrounded themselves with a mystique. Sales were happening because customers were willing to figure out what to do. Ineffective sales practices were left to work themselves out. The argument went, "If sales are high, our current methods are working and our sales planning is just fine." This type of approach doesn't work in today's markets.

Times have changed. Customers can no longer employ "jack of all trades" analysts who magically are "specialists" in every new technology. They no longer have the staffs to be the "proving ground" for new technologies. Today's businesses are increasingly complex and their technical work force focuses on strategic value. Your customers want their specialists concentrating on issues within their own business segment, not solving the last-mile problem for high-tech companies. They don't have the time or patience to experiment with new technologies. They want vendors who will enrich their business and solve problems, not create more unsolved problems. At one time you could dump a new technology on your customer's doorstep and come back in a few months to see if they found a good way to use it. This doesn't work anymore. If you want today's customer to include you in his company's business planning, you will have to part paths with traditional high-technology sales practices and invest more in your ability to improve your customer's business.

Technology-selling principals are also important for people in non-technology type businesses. While the actual product may not be considered high-tech, the customer's value experience from working with your product can significantly differentiate you in the market. When the end product is not high-tech, it's even more important to use the sales process to focus on your differentiated value and to use your differentiation to establish business partnerships with your customers. I first learned this from my uncle, John Damascus, who recently retired as the Vice President of Sales for Artisan Industries, a machine tool shop outside of Boston where he worked for over forty years. He expanded Artisan's welding business by adapting welding processes that improve the stress properties of the final product. By focusing on its nearby aerospace and defense contractors, Artisan built a significant business as a subcontractor of welding services to this industry. He used its welding process as a "technology" that differentiated its business from competitors' in the eyes of defense contractors.

Fixing Your Sales Model

The present approach to most customers is flawed. You are probably selling to your customers just as you've been doing for years, by dividing the world into two parts—your customer with its procurement departments on one side and your company with its sales and distribution channels on the other. You have to replace this dichotomy with a newer, stronger alignment by focusing on your customer's customer to put yourself on your customer's team—a team aimed at creating the highest satisfaction level for their customers. Defining your position from your customer's perspective is your first step toward restructuring your alignment.

Sales groups want to lump target markets together into general categories and often divide potential customers along simplistic lines. Zip code sellers allow the Post Office to do its major market segmentation. Others let the phone company's prefix and area code numbering do their territory divisions for them. Some sales groups divide their prospects up based on temperature—cold leads, warm prospects, and hot customer opportunities. (If the prospect has never heard of your company or your product, it's a pretty good bet that you've got a cold lead. At the other end, if you visit an account and they've got a wad of dollars sitting on the table and they can't run their factory another minute without your product, you've got a hot prospect.)

These simple categorizations are the basis for most of the sales decisions in today's technology businesses. They set the tone for how businesses decide to present their products to customers. They may be suitable for high-level business analysis but have limited value in today's world of strategic selling. In the 1990s, client segmentation is king and segmentation is a grass roots strategy. The way you segment your market opportunities is unique to your business. It begins, with individual relationships with customers and expands to larger submarket audiences. Segmentation creates sales expertise within a specific submarket that can be brought to bear to link high-tech products to unique customer needs.

Segmentation selling forces you to look at the world from your customer's perspective. Customers within a segment have similar values and perceptions toward the use and reuse of a product. Segments may be divided into subsegments, each containing client groups with slightly different perceptions. Differences in perspectives are fascinating. Even the slightest change can mean major differences in the way the prospect views the seller. These differences in market perspectives are like two gas stations, one located on the entrance ramp to a freeway, the other on the same freeway's exit ramp. These gas stations may only be 100 yards apart, yet their business conditions are very different. One would describe its customers as people on the way to work. They would be concerned with opening early and having plenty of help on hand during the morning rush hours. The other would describe itself as serving the commuter on the way home. Late afternoon would be its busiest hours. The general customer segment of gas stations has a subsegment of freeway gas stations with subsegments of morning busy and afternoon busy. Factoring in these differences can alter the sales planning for developing gas stations as customers. It can influence product mix, distribution and service decisions, delivery methods, and selling strategies.

Combining customers into broad categorizations confuses sales decision making. You need to get away from notions which lump all customers together and create generalized sales approaches. Each customer is unique. Buying decisions and fulfillment requirements interrelate. It's time to begin grouping together logical entities of customer segments, addressing the needs of these segments, and allocating sales resources in order to best cultivate these subgroups.

Strategic selling requires analysis. How you decide to organize your account development process, organize your available business partners, and focus the resources of your company's value chain determines the eventual return on your sales investment. Your choices on how to plan and develop vertical sales segments, how to sell your products and services to each segment, how to choose to spend and not spent time, how to cultivate your business partners, how to select your distribution channel as well as your choice for how to organize your customer partnering strategy will determine the success of your sales investments. You must determine how to develop your plans to optimize the yield of your future sales investments. Whether you are a lone sales representative working a territory or a company president, you have to analyze your sales investment possibility.

Selling Smart

This book uses the term "smart sellers" as a shorthand for describing change that can take place to improve your ability to gain and keep customers. Smart technology sellers apply smart selling principles to find new ways to reach out and partner with their customers. Each time they find a new customer opportunity, they understand their future customer's business planning so they may position themselves as the leading value purchase option available. They find out how they can form a relationship with their customer to improve their customer's business. Technology businesses with direct sales groups can afford to practice this on an individual customer basis while sellers with lower cost products and complex reseller networks look to improving the business of a typical customer within each major submarket. How smart sellers propose customer business improvement differs with each customer and with each major submarket. What is common is the general approach smart sellers use for initiating relationships, communicating value, establishing value functionality, and building lasting business partnerships with their customers. While the techniques of high-technology smart selling may differ across various customer bases and among widely differing channel strategies, the fundamentals are constant. Smart sellers build their businesses similarly.

Smart sellers have these characteristics in common:

1. **Smart sellers sell value**

2. **Smart sellers customize**

3. **Smart sellers form quality customer partnerships**

4. **Smart sellers create a business partner network to build a complete fulfillment channel**

5. **Smart sellers sell vertically into well-understood submarkets**

6. **Smart sellers sell to their customer's customer**

7. **Smart sellers train and motivate their entire work force to develop customers**

8. **Smart sellers form electronic links with their customers and business partners**

The sooner you put smart selling to work for you, the sooner you will be on your road to improving your business performance. Table 1-1 illustrates smart selling at a glance.

Table 1-1 Smart Seller Checklist

✓	Sell Value
✓	Customize
✓	Form Quality Partnerships
✓	Create Partnership Networks
✓	Sell into Vertical Submarkets
✓	Sell to Their Customer's Customer
✓	Train Their Work Force to Develop Customers
✓	Use Electronic Links

Getting and keeping new customers in today's economy requires more than traditional selling methods can deliver. If you want to meet and exceed your forecast month after month, you need to change your sales role to reshape the relationships between your customer and your company. You accomplish this by interlocking your company, your business partners, and your customers into an extended value chain with all participants focused on the improvement of your customer's business.

Every person in your company's value chain has the potential to play a role to help in your account development process. Your customers want direct contact with your company's work force. Your sales role, which has traditionally been a funnel for all significant customer communication, must migrate to a relationship management role establishing and maintaining high levels of communication between your company, your corporate business partners, your customer, and your customer's business partners. Direct relationships between your knowledge workers and your customers that were once nonexistent need to come together to help you compete for today's customers.

You've got to blur the lines between you and your customer and insert your organization within your customer's value chain. A few years ago, your customers wanted you at an arm's-length relationship. Now they want you as part of their quality continuum (see Figure 1-3).

For high-tech companies, selling is more important today than ever before. It is the purpose of this book to present a case for reinstating the dream of unparalleled sales success. Through changing your sales role you can revitalize the vision that you can accurately predict and positively impact future sales activity by restructuring your relationships with your cus-

Figure 1-3   Smart Sellers Unite Their Company with Their Customer

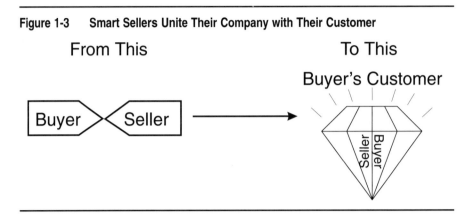

tomer, your business partner, your customer's customer, and your own company. Your customer wants you to fill a role as their business partner. By becoming a member of your customer's business team, you will garner sufficient information ahead of time to allow you to correctly predict the future and better manage your resources to improve your results and those of your company. You can create a new framework for your relationships, a framework based on quality.

I've been fortunate in my career. Twenty years ago I joined a team introducing microprocessor technology to the world of circuit designers. This experience got me hooked on selling technology. Since then, I've been involved with many technology companies building new markets and sustaining existing markets. I've worked with hundreds and hundreds of sales people around the world as their new products entered mainstream ones. As sales and marketing vice president of several high-tech companies and as a sales consultant to many other companies, I've created sales teams and established significant new market opportunities across many different market segments.

I've found that individuals, sales regions, national sales groups, and entire corporate sales teams usually have enough information early enough in their process to accurately predict their future and to anticipate their potential for success. The hard part isn't getting the right information in a timely fashion. It's being able to distill the useful information from the rest. Sales teams often lead themselves into dangerous territories because they don't deal with the future sales implications of their decisions. They don't appreciate their own understanding of their markets. They don't allow themselves to analyze the small fragments of knowledge they have and anticipate the consequences of their actions.

I now spend my time consulting to technology companies that want to improve their sales. Much of my work involves integrating strategies into the early phases of business. By solving sales problems upstream in the planning process, my clients make better decisions and avoid the pitfalls of dealing with sales failures in the field, where solving problems is very expensive. I work with companies to integrate their sales, marketing, product development, technical support, and new product planning into a unified account development process. We combine our client's account development process with his long-term market development goals to target and develop his customer potentials.

Sales people feel separated from corporate decision making in their attempts to expand customer bases and successfully launch new products. They often use this as the basis for explaining away their failures to meet plans. This island mentality inevitably wastes resources. It is the primary cause for failed business planning. This isolation—the feeling of not being able to influence the big picture and of not knowing what is going on at the home office—is the number one reason companies miss their sales plan, why new products fail, why new customer expansion doesn't occur and why existing products fail to penetrate major new markets. The irony is that these are precisely the areas where a sales individual can most influence change. The realignment needed in today's businesses begins at the most fundamental level—with the sales level contacts of a business. The negative impact of this isolation affects the most crucial aspects of the business—the ability of a company to open up new markets and introduce new products. Change to a unified account development process can be initiated most rapidly when it coincides with new product introductions or with the penetration of new markets by an existing product.

During the period of rapid growth for either an emerging new product or the period of sales growth for an existing product, a high-tech company's work force must form a partnership with its customer base. The employees must develop a common purpose with their customers and share a common bond united by the same goals. Their bond extends internally and across company boundaries to customers and to potential business partners. Forging this bond is not solely the responsibility of the sales organization. The employees must form an inter-organizational sense of unity and purpose to achieve success. Somewhere during this process, the employees of a business assume the sales development role to help create new alliances and expand existing ones. Sales responsibilities of one form or another pervade the entire work force during these growth periods. Everyone must find new ways of doing business that make their new products more successful and, in turn, their customers more successful.

This book can serve as a new sales tool for people dealing with the technology customers of the 1990s. As a high-tech supplier you must redefine your structure based on quality principles to enjoy long-term above-average performance levels. By the nature of the situation, businesses selling to today's quality-oriented customers will themselves have to establish quality-selling perspectives if they are to be successful. The new alignment that must take place begins with the way you relate to your customer. This book can serve people in sales as well as people in any role involving frequent customer interactions. Through an understanding of the changing nature of your customer and your need to clearly establish and articulate your value, this book can help you improve the odds that you and your company will achieve a greater level of success.

High-tech companies differ from one another. So too do their sales strategies differ. Two similar products can have two completely different sales strategies. Finding the right road to successful high-tech selling is your number one job. Today's markets are much more complex than the high-tech markets of just a few years ago. Today's customers are even more complex than before. The starting point for putting yourself on the road to success is to understand these changes.

It's Time to Change

You are caught in a world of change. The decade of the 1990s opened with corporate America downsizing its white collar work force. Unlike previous business cycles, this latest downturn was accompanied by huge reductions in middle management and tremendous redefinition of business functions as your customer responded to the realities of competing in a global economy. Your customers are reacting to today's realities stemming from worldwide economic forces. Your customer is undergoing rapid change as is the company for which you work. For the first time in the history of the technology business the industry has reduced the size of its work force. Major technology institutions are undergoing massive reorganizations brought about by today's economy.

Changes are also going on in the way people buy and use high-tech products. Application areas that were taken for granted in the 1980s are in turmoil. In the past, technology usage was isolated from the main business function. Today's businesses define themselves through the technology they deploy. Their customer interaction is shaped by their technology infrastructure. Change is occurring in your customer's technology architecture. Mainframe-based management information systems (MIS) shops are all downsizing or eliminating their host computing investment. Networks are getting more intelligent and creating newly distributed computer paradigms. Biotech companies are starting to unleash their new products and redefining their customers' processes. And more change is on the horizon.

The sales infrastructures change along with each new wave of technology entering the market. A sales infrastructure is, essentially, the life support system of a technology. Host computer markets needed large computer vendors with massive field support personnel that could respond at the drop of a hat. Coupled with field support, these markets relied on a cadre of software vendors, system integrators, and consultants and large internal MIS groups to be successful. Likewise, other technology markets required their own life support system functions. New technologies threaten the underlying financial stability of the entrenched sales structures. Sometimes, these structures can adapt and absorb the new technology. Other times they are swept away as the new technology takes hold.

The lifetime of a sales structure was once measured in decades. The mainframe structure lasted the better part of twenty-five years. Minicomputer sales structures survived for fifteen years. As technologies sweep through today's markets, the life span of a sales infrastructure is much shorter. The computer stores that formed the life support system for personal computers sold to first-time buyers have all but disappeared in less than ten years. In the 1990s, some technology sales infrastructures won't last even that long.

Your customers once bought high-tech products for their ability to improve the operational aspects of their businesses. They would buy a new computer to improve their accounting operations. Or they could invest in manufacturing equipment and make things bigger, better, and faster. Today, their technology purchase decisions are not isolated specific operational business functions. Their technology usage is enterprise-wide and their technology investments are strategic. Technology decision making is part of your customers' boardroom strategic planning process and is fundamental to their success.

Unless you've been under a rock for the past few years, you cannot have missed these changes. Yet, even though you've seen your customer rebuilding his company to compete in today's real-time economy, you may have told yourself that you don't need to change. You may have convinced yourself that your business is immune from these changes. Most high-technology sales people and the sales groups operate as they've done for years. Your customer's structure changes, your products and services change, your customer's buying motivations change, even your own company changes—yet what you do and how you do it doesn't change.

The old saying applies: "Change is great for the other guy." Well, you're now the other guy. Change is great for you.

Selling High-Tech/High-Ticket is about changing the way you sell high-tech products. It presents new ways to go about your business to achieve higher levels of success for yourself, your company, your customer, and your strategic business partners.

Your customers' investment in your high-tech products is similar to any other financial investment they make. They invest their money in your products to get a return. With stocks and bonds they measure their return in terms of percentage yield over time. With your product, they measure their return in terms of the fundamental improvement in their business. In both cases, their investment's return is time-sensitive. When they make their investment with you, their business success takes center stage.

Treating your customers' acquisition of your products like an investment they make in stocks is a good starting point for determining the way you add value to your customers' business. Instead of having stock certificates representing their investment, your customers have your product. Your product must accelerate their business success.

In the end, the analysis is straightforward. Your customer measures his anticipated investment in your products and services against his anticipated satisfaction quantified through its expected business improvement. High-yield/low-risk investments are made ahead of low-yielding/higher-risk projects. Successfully selling high-tech products involves lowering your customer's risk expectation and increasing their potential yield through their investment in your products and services. *Selling High-Tech/High-Ticket* will serve as a guide to help you get these points across to your customers.

Chapter 2

Selling Market Share

High-technology products and services have value when they improve the customer's competitive advantage. One simple underlying motivation sums it up—your customer purchases high-tech products to substantially and significantly improve his company's business position. High-technology products are a success when they improve buyer performance.

High-technology products do not have intrinsic value of their own. They are a means to an end. Many industry participants are so fascinated with their products that they don't focus on the buying motivations of their mainstream customers. Product features are interesting to people within the industry. Your customer wants business benefits, not features. Users have a much different metric for features. It is easy to confuse the buying motivations for customers of high-technology products with consumer electronic products like stereo equipment. A stereo delivers value through listening pleasure. High-technology products do not usually have such direct or immediate value. Their value is measured in business opportunities for the buyer.

What do your customers want most from your high-tech products? They want an unfair competitive advantage. The best sellers of high-tech products have driven this point home to their buyers:

"Buy from me and you will gain a set of advantages that will put your competitor at a significant disadvantage."

"Using the competitive advantage offered by my product will help you keep existing customers and get new ones."

Many people resist the notion that successful high-tech products translate to unfair competitive advantages for users. But your customer would love to have as many unfair competitive advantages as possible. These are not illegal competitive advantages. The better you can show your customer's management team that they can get a significant and sustainable competitive advantage from deploying your products, the faster you will increase your sales.

The two "S" words are key—sustainable and substantial. They directly affect the value your customer places on your products. You must be successful in showing your customer how your products provide substantial and sustainable competitive advantages. If you are successful at doing this, your customers will place an extremely high value on what you sell. They will want you closely tied to their organizations. Your product offerings do not have to be technically better than your competitors'. The key is your ability to differentiate your organization by projecting sustainable and substantial user advantages.

Success for your customer can have many definitions. Probably the most general long-term objective statement for commercial enterprises is to have long-term, above-average performance. I look at success for a company defined in terms of its ability to get and keep customers, and its ability to increase market share. Your key to success is to define your products in terms of helping your customer reach his long-term business goals.

Selling Perceptions

Your high-technology company is in the business of selling increased market share. What's more, your customer generally purchases your products well before any measurable business improvement results. It is the anticipation of business improvement that is important. Your customer must develop a set of indicators for predicting business improvement. Through your sales process you actually help your customer select relevant indicators. You first must sell the perception of increased market share and then deliver the reality. Your customer's perceived value increase determines your product's price.

Market share is an important measure of your customer's success. In an ideal world, you sit across from your customer and start your discussion with "Using my technowidgets in your business will increase your market share and result in more substantial and sustainable competitive advantage than any other business strategy available to you."

High-technology producers must show value creation through deployment of their products. Measuring the value of high-technology products is complex. The process involves using potential deployment scenarios to measure the value of the anticipated results of using a product. You create the perception of value before your customers get hands-on experience. Price premiums directly relate to your ability to establish the link between product use and your customer's business success.

Often it is difficult to view buying a product in this light. It is hard for your customer to make the connection between technology purchase decisions and business success. This is the case even with basic computer purchase decisions. For example, a field scientist for a midwest seed supplier will purchase Persuasion, a desktop presentation software product from Aldus Corp., to convey to farm managers the potential yield expectations that can result from different seed planting combinations. This $600 software investment, with the necessary PC hardware and printer support, will improve the field scientist's customer communications capability. The farm prospect may act on the information and benefit from a larger, more profitable harvest. Assuming the farmer improves productivity, the field scientist's company will benefit through increased purchases during the next growing season.

Taking this example one level further, the seed company, after seeing this successful change in their selling technique, may set up desktop presentation facilities for all their field scientists. This larger investment could result in many more improved sales situations, better seed selection decisions among customers, and a general business segment improvement. Given some estimates on how much improvement the company can expect from deploying these systems, it can weigh the cost of the technology investment with its expected increase in business.

Making the leap from a $600 software package to large dollar increases in market share may sound esoteric, but it can and should be real to the sellers of these products. When it is not done, these sellers are hoping that enough random customer events eventually lead to purchase decisions. While this may eventually happen, their products may not be among those selected and they may not be rewarded price premiums due to their product's uniqueness.

Your customers are willing to pay for the significant value increases achievable through using your product. Higher price premiums will be paid when they have the most to gain. As a high-tech supplier, you must recognize this. Too many suppliers think customers just want low prices. They target their sales strategy toward the lowest common denominator. Many suppliers fail to realize that many customers—especially those with the most to gain—are willing to pay more for high-tech offerings that maximize the positive impact on the users' goals. All too often high-tech companies are pursuing a pricing parity with their competitors instead of understanding and amplifying their value contribution.

Pricing Perceptions

Suppliers that win the perception game can get the highest prices. Your customers are willing to pay a premium for the products they think will have the greatest impact. Your customers will pay more for products that they perceive—when coupled with the supplier's organization—can add more value (as measured by their perceived performance improvements). Your customers will also pay a premium for image-enhancing nontangibles associated with their supplier. To have value, these image enhancements must be transferable to your customer's own image projection. Years ago, customers of IBM would flaunt their IBM computer centers to their own customers, using IBM's prestigious image to enhance their own. Today, many high-tech companies in many business areas can take advantage of image enhancement to differentiate their products. Your entire organization can be useful for differentiating your offering. Your core product has only to meet functional sufficiency. It is much harder for your competitors to leapfrog a superior organization than a superior product.

The ugly truth about selling high-technology products is that it is a lot like dealing in the futures market. You pay now to lock in future exchange rates. Nothing can guarantee your success with this investment. Likewise, when your customers buy your product, they are purchasing a type of future. They are successful when your product combines with their organizations and results in significant business improvements. In the futures market, any individual buyer or seller plays a small role in the outcome of the investment. In the high-tech market, buyers and sellers play a substantial role in the risk equation.

Your customers do not buy technical elegance. They buy potential competitive advantages. Competitive advantages can run the gamut from market share increases to faster product development cycles. Your customers are not looking for the lowest prices; they want the best value. The eventual price is directly related to their perceptions of their achievable market share improvements. You play a big role in establishing this. Table 2-1 provides a checklist to help determine if you're offering your customers competitive advantage.

You will get the greatest returns from your products when you maximize your impact on your customer's potential to increase market share. You don't have to be the technology leader in your field to accomplish this. More often than not, a pragmatic vendor can do more to increase the customer's market share than the vendor who relies on leading edge technologies to impress its customers.

It is hard for any company to keep this in mind when setting its product pricing. It is much easier to develop pricing models based on tech-

Table 2-1   Competitive Advantage Checklist

✓	Market Share Increase
✓	Faster Time to Market
✓	Reduced R&D Cycle
✓	Flexible Manufacturing
✓	Greater Communications with Customers
✓	More Responsive Customer Service
✓	Quality Improvements

nology price performance criteria, competitive alternatives, and even plain old manufacturing costs. Have you ever sat in on a new product announcement and heard the product manager say, "Knowing that our sales force will be able to convince prospective customers that our products will increase their sales by 30 percent resulting in a net profit margin of five percent, we've decided to price our product at 20 percent of our customer's improvement?" Not only have you never heard this before, it's unlikely that you ever will. Nevertheless, just as your customers are basing their purchase decisions on anticipated future business improvement, you need to gear your pricing information to this level of decision making. It is not unrealistic to sum up your product pricing by saying; "As you know, the projected 30 percent sales improvement will result in a 5 percent increase in your profits, or the equivalent of $1 million annually. Since the price of our product is $200,000 during the same time period, its deployment can have substantial value even over such a short period of time." It's not hard to approximate your customer's anticipated business improvement. You can then relate that amount to your product's price.

Strategic Technology Planning

Technology is a strategic resource for your customer. Somewhere, somehow your customer decided which technologies he thought were important to his company's future and which were not. In your customer's eyes, you are only as valuable as your ability to improve his business. The art of high-tech selling is overlaying your product and services on your customer's existing belief system. Sometimes, when things don't fit, you've got to change their belief system.

If you were IBM and the year was 1980, you were in technology sales heaven. The current belief for computer buyers was that one computer vendor could span the entire needs of even the most complex enterprise. Whether the selected computer company was IBM, DEC, or HP, no one really challenged this belief system. No one except companies like Apple and SUN. For long-term success, they promoted the idea that there are infinite ways to solve any business problem and any one computer company is finite. What is more valuable—one company doing the majority of the computer research and development for its customers, or a cluster of companies working around a common architecture as a means of exploring the infinite possibilities? Apple promoted this cluster approach. SUN promoted the idea of standards-based computing.

Your customer faces technology decisions throughout his company's value chain. Your customer's management has an instinctive sense of timing of when and where to invest in a strategy. Companies operate in any one of three modes when they assesses the potential of a technology. They are either

1. Actively considering using a product,

2. Waiting for others to act first, or

3. Completely ignoring the decision.

Large businesses with complex value chains are in multiple modes simultaneously with multiple technology decisions. Smaller companies may be investigating technology alternatives sequentially.

In any case, you must help chart for your customer the strategic possibilities and implications involved with using your product. Time is scarce. You can waste your sales time in front of customers with little to gain from your products, or you can sit across from customers who can gain the most from dealing with you. Often, the people with the most to gain may not be aware that you even exist. You've got to translate the language of your technology into the language of your customer so they can better understand all that you offer. It is not unusual to find that the people with the most to gain from a technology deployment are often not even involved with its acquisitions. You must recognize how pervasive your technology is on your customer's business and seek out the people inside the company who may gain the most from using your product. Selling to the wrong people at the right customer isn't only inefficient, it can be a disaster. Even if you succeed at signing up customers, the wrong buyers will undervalue your offerings, leading to prices that are much lower than they could have been. You'll be left wide open for a competitor to come along, redefine the customer opportunity, and walk away with your entire customer base.

Not only can your product reshape your customers, your customers can use it to reshape their industry structure. Their strategic deployment of your technology can change the nature of their relationship to their own customers. This is pretty powerful stuff. Think of the long-term advantage to your customer when use of your products puts them in the position of redefining buyer/seller relationships within their industry.

Sometimes the advantage of a technology is straightforward. In the early 1970s the airline industry understood the importance of on-line reservation systems. At the same time, the idea of a nonstop computer was mostly an academic pursuit. Commercial customers put their capital dollars into performance and let their service dollars address availability. Along came Tandem Computers. Instead of merely focusing on the nonstop nature of their computers, Tandem looked at the importance of their products in a transaction processing environment. Tandem swept through the reservations market by positioning its nonstop computers as transaction processors helping airlines deploy continuously available reservation networks. Tandem's sales development cycle in those early days involved creating a known value for every minute of outage of the reservation network. For instance, a major airline could estimate the dollar cost of lost reservations and lost ticket-writing opportunities resulting from a 15-minute outage. This figure, plus a recent history of the outage frequency, would then be used to put a value on the notion of 100 percent availability. Tandem salespeople developed customers based on the financial value of nonstop computing.

Your Customer's Goal Is Business Improvement

Your customer is in business to make a profit. (Government agencies chartered to deliver a service have service improvement goals that parallel these business improvement goals.) The decisions are consistent with this goal. Within their industries, your customers are trying to be long-term, above-average industry performers. Their strategic direction will encompass a wide range of plans. Some companies set out to be the lowest cost provider. Most others go after differentiation-based strategies. No matter which plan they develop, they want to lead their industries in overall business performance. Businesses use these strategies to create unique barriers, improve cost advantages, provide multiple avenues of differentiation, and increase switching costs. The target of their differentiation strategy may be their ultimate customer, their distribution channel, their suppliers, or another related group. The bottom line is that your customers are trying to increase their value in the eyes of their customers.

Long-term success in selling high-technology products depends on your ability to link what you do to your customer's long-term business goals, especially when you have many customers in many industries. Your day-to-day contacts with your customers are not likely to be their key corporate strategists. Therefore, figuring out their strategies can be a time-consuming process.

The process of moving from their unique market vision to an effective strategic plan is complex. Only a few people excel at it. Fortunately, your job isn't to develop your customer's strategic plan. It's to adapt your products to your customer's existing plan. Once you find out what the plan is, you can establish the linkage between your products and your customer's long-term business strategy.

Federal Express redefined the package shipment industry by using technology to provide instant access to package delivery status. In the mid-1980s Federal Express deployed a transaction processing network with a new generation of hand-held data entry systems. This system allowed Federal Express to use shipping status information as an important service differentiation. At the time, the package shipping industry offered a crude tracking service supplying little information on the shipment until well after the packages arrived. Since most packages arrived within 24 hours, timely information meant a customer would wait until the package did not arrive before the shipper would trace it. Federal Express combined a computer and communications strategy to provide immediate information on the package status within its own system—a brand new notion for shippers. The company made this information instantly available to its customers via a toll-free number. This service earned Federal Express many long-term customers.

In the early 1980s, Federal Express also had an expensive technology failure named Zap Mail. Concerned over the potential impact of facsimile equipment on their business. Federal Express embarked on a major technology investment in a satellite-based facsimile network to provide document transmission services direct from one location to another, bypassing the telephone network. After spending millions developing and field testing this service, the entire project was abandoned. Federal Express' strategic planners did not anticipate the ubiquitous deployment of fax machines within businesses and the ability of the public phone network to adapt itself to fax. Their strategy was dependent on fax equipment being expensive to own and operate.

Strategic End Users Are
Either Differentiators or Lowest Cost Suppliers

As a high-technology supplier, your job is to increase your customers' value by being part of their overall business plan. Your customers' strategy will fall into one of two very broad classes—establishing long-term differentiation or maintaining a long-term, low-cost position. There will also be a strategy relating to when their differentiation plans are implemented. Some companies try to be first-movers and are innovators at differentiation. Others are more inclined to avoid short-term fads and invest in longer term differentiators. The most effective way to create long-term value for a customer is to link what you do to your customers' primary differentiation plan. The more you participate in their differentiation, the more valuable you can be to your customers.

Everyone must differentiate. Even cost leaders are differentiators. Cost leaders pursue differentiation strategies to prevent price erosion. Highly differentiated products command price premiums through their uniqueness. Connecting your products to your customer's differentiation strategy will, in turn, help you focus on the true value customers will receive from your product. If a company is not basing its sale on firm cost savings, the sale must be based on the supplier's ability to help customers differentiate.

You'll be amazed at all the places where you can help improve your customer's business. There are as many areas as there are facets to your customer. Your product probably doesn't affect just one department. It can have secondary benefits on others in the business. The same product that improves manufacturing quality can impact marketing, distribution relationships, employee compensation—even community relations. You've got to convert the general word "impact" into specific improvements in your customer's business position.

Individualize Your Business Improvement Message

Technology end users are sophisticated. Linking your high-technology products to your customer's long-term success is fundamental to your success. Every high-level, strategic plan contains significant technological implications. It's your job to establish these relationships regardless of the distribution and product delivery strategy. Even if you depend on third party resellers, it is still up to you to relate what your company does to your customer's business strategy. You cannot rely on third-party sellers to communicate these ideas for you. While you may not be able to personally deliver this message to each and every customer contact, you are still responsible to see that your message is delivered. Talking about your vision, architecture, and internal technology are all ways of conveying your high-tech persona on a large scale. Articulating these statements of direction is essential because your customers must comprehend their ability to incorporate what you do into their decision-making process. Of course, your vision is much more useful once you link it to your customer's overall strategic direction.

How you communicate your vision is as important as what you communicate. After you come up with your business improvement message, you must devise a way to deliver it to each and every individual with influence within your customer's organization. You must find the proper vehicle for evangelizing your mission. Some companies benefit the most by using a broad-based marketing campaign to communicate their vision. Others may use a direct person-to-person strategy.

Apple Computer did a great job delivering a sales mission message when it wanted to increase its penetration in business sectors with the marketing theme "The Power To Be Your Best." This was really a terrific positioning statement. It can be interpreted by many buyers in many markets. Potential users can define "being their best" in their own personal ways. For a company like Apple Computer and their Macintosh products, a large marketing campaign was the best way to deliver this sales message across many complex markets.

When Is Technology Most Welcome?

There are times when you feel you cannot get a customer to talk with you even if you paid him. It just seems no one is interested in what you are selling. There are also times when this situation can change overnight. The first question you must deal with is whether anyone in your customer's vertical market has made a similar technology move. There are three probable answers to this question:

1. No one else has done it.

2. Others have done something similar.

3. There is a history of failure of trying to use the technology.

Sometimes customers are anxious to be the first in their industry to move ahead with a new technology. In the banking industry, the first banks to install ATM machines in a town saw an increase in new accounts. In other cases, though, a customer's own organization may be a major inhibi-tor from its making the first move. Sometimes, a technology may result in the potential restructuring of an industry and the dominant industry partici-pants will resist it.

Independent producers of microwave communications equipment ran into this problem in this industry's early days. Everything in their market was dominated by AT&T. When MCI started deploying microwave equip-ment to install its own private network for resale to commercial customers, AT&T used its influence with the FCC to create massive legal obstacles. Clearly, MCI had much more to gain by deploying commercially available private microwave equipment than did AT&T. An outside private micro-wave supplier would have encountered little success at AT&T, and it would have been wasting its time making sales calls there. After all, when AT&T needed microwave equipment, it would mostly use its own. Unlike MCI, AT&T placed little value on the offerings of the private microwave equip-ment producers. AT&T did not want to lose its customer stronghold so it fought MCI's move all the way. After lengthy court battles, MCI secured its rights to compete in the long-distance business against AT&T. By estab-lishing its own bypass private network, MCI restructured the U.S. telephone industry. This proved to be a windfall for microwave communications manufacturers.

Technology may be more welcome in some market segments than in others. Markets familiar with technology's impact will be more aggressive than those that have little experience with industry-wide technology initia-tives. These experiences also may help determine what value customers will place on offerings and what price premium they will offer either for the base products or for specialized differentiation of a product.

Understanding your customer's market segment's experiences with similar technologies will help you decide on your best sales cultivation strategy. If the industry experiences have been dismal, it may be fair to assume your customer may not readily accept products on technology's cutting edge. On the other hand, companies in industries that have aggres-sively pursued technology as part of their core strategies are more willing to be early adopters of immature products.

First-Mover Strategies

The long-term results of your customer's early deployment strategies may be tremendous performance benefits. First movers often gain new long-term customers immediately. For instance, the first banks to deploy statewide ATM network often got immediate, long-term market share improvement.

These banks gained new customers that stayed with them for years. They also forced their competitors to play catch up. The first-mover bank could open in second-tier cities while the laggards were trying to keep up in the primary markets. These first-mover advantages stayed in place well after the immediate competitive advantages were gone.

First movers often gain by raising the barriers to entry within their business. A well-financed company can invest in a technology that others in their industry segment cannot afford. First movers successful in getting their customers to adopt new services can raise their customer's switching costs. The more painful it is to switch, the more stable their customer base will be.

Marriott led the way with a widely available on-line system providing a high-quality reservation network, central reservation services, and on-line services available at each property. Marriott recognized the positive impact this technology investment would have, especially in the key business traveler market. Marriott adopted a strategy embracing its reservation network as key to its differentiation. And it paid off—Marriott led the pack in growth of the business market segment.

Hyatt hotels has a different technological approach to reducing guest registration delays. By electronically inter-networking all Hyatt's properties to a central reservation service in Omaha, a guest (or the guest's travel agent) can register by phone and pick up the room key upon arrival. Hyatt intends to use this network to facilitate other services as well, including the consolidation of many locally performed accounting services.

Hyatt's strategy is interesting. Its approach involves a considerably higher level of technology integration; to create this capability Hyatt is using the same reservation software at each property and in its Omaha center. This central reservation service will have an accurate system-wide picture of the room assignments, unlike systems in which each property allocates a portion of their available rooms for assignment by a central service. Customers who frequent Hyatt properties and change their travel plans often will be able to distinguish this electronic reservation system from services offered by other hotels. Hyatt's central reservation phone service is more informative as to the availability of rooms and can make room assignments on the spot.

Just as some industries readily accept the use of high-technology, others may reject a technology because they fear the results. The technology may lower the entry costs to outside competition. Or it may lead to an industry's customers having more influence and lowering the differentiation capability. Today's biggest industry rejecting high-technology usage is the government. As government agencies start using technology, a smaller staff can provide higher service levels. However, the resulting decrease in agency size will lead to an overall decrease in an agency's status level.

Some companies are able to afford substantial investments in high-tech strategies while their competition cannot. These companies have the ability to squeeze out their competition, or restructure their industry by rolling out large ticket programs. They are willing to invest substantial amounts to differentiate themselves through their technology offering and they place a high-value on products that increase their differentiation.

Linking Technology to Strategy May Not Be Easy

Converting the general qualities of your high-tech product into an increase in your customers' performance is not easy. First, you have to come up with a way to measure your customers' business performance as it relates to their before-and-after experiences with your products. You must establish the relationship between your product and your customer's business performance, and continuously improve your product and organization to increase your impact on performance.

High-technology product managers often fail to establish the linkage between use of their product and increased market share for their customers. They deal with the general qualities of a product at a technical level. They leave the question of the resulting impact on buyer performance for sales people to figure out. That's probably because the sales person focuses on the one-to-one relationships between customer and product offerings. By zeroing in at the customer-by-customer level, you're able to relate your company's products to your customer's performance. Marketing groups dealing with customer segments cannot as easily come to terms with any one customer's business model.

For years I watched a company torture itself taking a good idea into the wrong business situation. This company's office was across the parking lot from mine. They had an infra-red technology for replacing wiring used in Local Area Networks. From a technology standpoint, their product was nifty. It reminded me of the AT&T pavilion at the New York World's Fair in the 1960s—talking through light beams. The product thrilled everyone involved with the company—engineers, marketing, sales, and investors. At last you could replace office wiring with light beams! The trouble came when they could not get customers excited by these products. Customers couldn't care less about using light beams instead of wires. The company never really established the link between their products and their customers' business improvements.

After several rounds of financing and almost giving up, a reorganized version of the company did find a market opportunity for the technology, but in a different form. Instead of channel marketing, shrink-wrapped, end user product, they developed a chip version of the product to provide a wireless printer connection for laptop manufacturers. Their product added value to laptop users by eliminating an inconvenience. Embedded inside portables, their product eliminates the need to plug portables into local area networks (LANs), thereby creating a value differentiation for laptop manufacturers. The technology was fine. It worked well. When packaged as an end-user product it was technically interesting but had little business value. When packaged as an original equipment manufacturer (OEM) product, it could provide a strong differentiation for portable applications. The first market they chased had glamour and excitement, but they never found a way to make a significant business improvement case for the buyer. As an imbedded product things began to work out.

Amplifying Your Strategic Business Improvement Position

First, you've got to understand where you fit within your customer's value chain. Next you should amplify your ability to improve your customer's performance. Amplifying your business improvement position will help you to distance yourself from what your competition can do. There are an infinite number of ways to create product and service extensions for what you sell. Some are complex, while others are simple. Remember, what is simple for you may be impossible for your customer. You need to design extensions to improve your customer's business while improving your own competitive differentiation.

I ran into an interesting version of this while doing a sales consulting project for a PC word processor software company. WordPerfect had entered the market and quickly grew to be my client's largest competitor. WordPerfect's strategy of providing wonderful customer service won long-term customer loyalty, and the company's success had devastated my client.

I was on the team called in to improve the company's sales situation by working with its field force. While doing that, we started looking at ways of making its customers successful. One thing kept coming across. This company had a very good product with lots of capability. But most users didn't use these features either because they couldn't be bothered with the complete installation process, or didn't know that the feature even existed.

This situation happens often with high-tech products. A newcomer enters a high-growth market and quickly captures market share by focusing on great customer service. An existing market leader with a better product is knocked out because its customer service infrastructure is broken.

We developed an installation strategy that could help the company's sales problem. Installing PC word processor software on DOS PCs took about an hour. Installation instructions accounted for almost half the documentation—believe it or not. There was about two inches of installation material. Getting the basic word processor up and running was where most end users stopped. They didn't bother with the rest of the features. Furthermore, users often got it wrong and had to call into the hotline with relatively simple questions. The complications arose because PC users have so many different configurations of video boards, screens, LANs, and printers. Installing the right combination was a big problem. Some features of the product required extended configurations. (If you wanted to imbed signatures in your document you could do that but, unless you had an optical scanner, you had no way of creating a computer image of your signature.) We found customers loved these features when they had them working. Most never got to that point. A large percentage of the new users would call the company's hot line at least once during the installation process, increasing the congestion of the company's already overburdened support center.

These installation difficulties translated into two major business problems for this software company. Overall customer satisfaction was low and customers were not getting much benefit from the product's extended features. In a test lab the product was well ahead of the competition on a feature-by-feature comparison. On the customer's desktop, it wasn't. Users were not experiencing full functionality. By not significantly improving its user effectiveness the company was not improving its customers' business positions. What's more, it was making matters worse by tying up users with installation difficulties. Computer dealers were not recommending the product. Users were not recommending the product to co-workers. By the time we arrived, this company was using heavy price discounting to move its word processor through its channel.

We developed a program whereby this company could provide free, on-site installation services for new customers. The company would continue to sell the product through existing sales channels. Any new purchase would be installed at the customer's site at no charge. We enlisted the help of third-party training companies who loved the idea of getting new sales leads and earning a fee. (As a side benefit, this sales program would rebuild the third-party loyalty that had migrated to WordPerfect. The installation fee to the training companies turned out to be half of what their discounting program was costing.) This program would have produced an extended product offering aimed at improving its customers' overall business effectiveness. It could have produced a much higher customer satisfaction level than even WordPerfect Corporation was delivering. It required no product changes. Its impact went right to the heart of its sales development process.

Sadly, this sales campaign never started. The software company's board of directors removed the president from his job shortly before the program's start. WordPerfect had really beaten them. (The notion of extending the product through an installation program is a great idea in the PC software business; I've successfully used it since. It is unfortunate that the company that originally paid for the planning could not take advantage of it!)

Applying Market Share Increases to Your Business

There are three planning steps for selling business improvement to your customer:

➡ **Step One—Identify Industry Trends**
Look at the overall trends in your customer's industry. Find where the competitive pressures are being applied across the industry and determine the positive and negative factors influencing long-term industry growth. The best places to look for ideas are in business publications covering these subjects and by asking your customer.

➡ **Step Two—Understand Your Customer's Mission Statement**
With the industry trends serving as a background, formulate an understanding of the specific position your customer has within its industry. Is the company on top of the trends or is it catching up? What does the company view as its role within its industry? Is it the low-cost producer? If there is a strategy based on differentiation, is the differentiation unique to this company?

➡ **Step Three—Improve Your Customer's Business Position**
Understanding the industry and your customer's business goals within his industry provides the background for developing the most important aspect of your sale. It gives you some reference points on understanding your customer's decision-making preferences. What role does your company play in accelerating your customer's movement toward achieving his major goal of insuring his company's long-term leadership position within its industry? The linkage that you are looking for connects the things you do to the things your customer wants to do.

Figure 2-1 reviews these important steps.

Figure 2-1   Three Steps to Selling Business Improvement

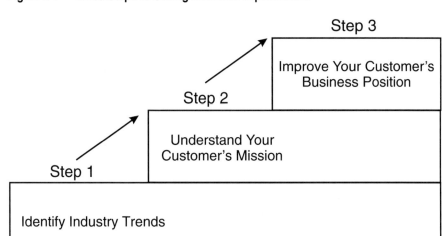

Building credible connections between what you do and your customer's most important strategic goals is not easy, but it is essential if you want to dominate your market. A lot of high-tech people hear this and say, "That kind of sales proposition is made in other markets segments but not mine—I don't deal with situations like that." That doesn't have to be true, but operating at this level with your customer requires participation from your reseller channel and your customer. It takes time to develop these connections. Companies with direct sales forces can do this on a customer-by-customer basis. Companies that sell indirectly may need to create general cases that cover customer groups. This three-step method works for every type of high-tech product being sold. It provides a way for you to be certain that your products continue to improve the business position of your customer. In fact, everyone involved with business-to-business selling—not just high-tech sales forces—should operate at this level. When you do, you are selling fundamental business improvement to your customer.

The following section offers two examples of using this process to relate what your company sells to your customer's business. At one extreme is the computer superstore, at the other is a software company in the electronic mail business.

People in retail computer sales often say they cannot be bothered with selling business improvement to their customers. The common wisdom is that it's the retailer's job to explain the characteristics and working requirements of the product and let the customer figure out if it will do the job. There are hundreds of customers coming and going all day long. There is not enough time to form this sort of business-improvement connection with each customer.

While it is time-consuming to work out a business-improvement connection with each and every customer, it probably is worthwhile to understand the links between products and business performance on some sort of submarket basis. It's also worth doing this to form a basis as to which products are worth carrying and which are not.

The computer superstore can break down its markets by certain criteria. Perhaps it sees a high concentration of certain types of businesses. For instance, it may be a major hospital and can attract lots of doctors. Maybe it would look at last year's store traffic and see that from May through June many accountants came through their store after tax season looking to improving their business methods. Maybe the superstore is located near some aerospace customers and would like to penetrate the buying channels of these companies as they downsize. The store's sales department can take just one of these submarkets and go through the three steps to understand its ability to improve its customer's business. This may lead them to position some of its offerings in a business context that would appeal to a select segment of customers.

Based on the findings the store may find that a trend in the medical profession is to come out from under the tons of paperwork that accumulates in private practice. In addition, the store may have heard from several doctors (call them power computer users) of new methods of using standard packages to create basic computer-based forms. The store might then decide to assemble a collection of its products that improve doctor office procedures, combined with a short sales message on how this collection combines to reduce paper flow within an office and provide better document tracking.

For the accountants, a recent industry trend may have been reducing the amount of end-to-end processing time with tax preparation clients. Realizing that the majority of its local accountants already own computers, the superstore management decides to position electronic connectivity products to accountants, starting with fax add-on products to speed delivery of completed tax information and continuing with electronic link products. This way the accountants can take electronic data from clients' computers all through the year in order to provide additional tax forecasting services to their clients. This could even lead to selling these same accountants laptops so they can enter the data directly when they are on-site.

Finally, for its aerospace neighbors, the management of the superstore may focus on industry downsizing and start to build up its opportunity to pre-configure systems for these companies. This would eliminate the need for these companies to do this work on their own as part of their downsizing efforts. The store may even try to become certified as a systems integrator for these accounts.

Making the connection between product functionality and business improvement is never easy. Companies in the electronic mail business are very familiar with this problem. When an electronic mail prospective customer does not see the business linkage between E-Mail and his mainstream business, he'll use E-mail only if it costs next to nothing. The electronic mail seller must link his selling position to his customer's business success early in the sales cycle or else he'll be laughed out of the room when they start to discuss price. A customer that sees the business value in E-mail will budget large sums of money for it. Once the customer agrees on the business value of electronic mail, then the seller can get on with the sale. Changing the basis of the sale from product functionality (the customer's comparison matrix) to business improvement can be done by linking the seller's differentiated features of a product to the customer's fundamental business improvement. The seller must make the case for the buyer to use electronic mail and must establish the seller's unique position.

If the potential electronic mail buyer is an industrial manufacturer, the industry trend may be toward improvement in manufacturing quality. A seller can show how its E-mail package empowers this trend by finding the names of the businesses that are key in this manufacturer's supply chain and determining the best way to use the electronic mail package to set up connections between these suppliers. The seller can even show specific references of companies using its products in a similar way. The customer would see that it not only gains enterprise-wide use of E-mail but also gains overall value chain improvements by having electronic links with its suppliers. This method allows the E-mail supplier to apply its unique value capability to this specific customer's quality improvement program and overall industry business improvement.

Identifying with Your Customer's Mission

Your customers want to gain competitive advantage and increase market share. They are on a mission. You've got to relate your product to their mission.

Buyers have just as much difficulty as sellers forming the link between use of a product and the resulting performance improvements. The transition from overall corporate missions to daily activities is often not well understood by your customer's personnel in the trenches. It's hard for many people to connect technology purchases to corporate missions. You've got to become an expert at doing this. Most times, your customer cannot do it for you.

A buyer that does not fully understand its own corporate mission can never put an accurate value on the merits of a high-technology product. The fallback is to focus on general qualities of several products, not the specific business improvements of just a few. Often, one side of your customer's company doesn't immediately see the impact of its decision on other parts of its operation. It's your job to seek out other members of your customer's management team that will appreciate the business improvement your product offers.

The need to shift decision makers comes up quite often during high-technology product selling. A different audience may have more to gain or may more rapidly receive your product's benefits. Sometimes, it is necessary to go even one step beyond your customer—to its customer or business partner—and deliver your sales message.

My favorite example of a company delivering its message to its buyer's customers is Raychem, a high-technology company specializing in high-end electronic connectors and wiring. In the aerospace market, Raychem provides connector solutions for use within commercial aircraft. The company differentiates its product through a very simple technique—weighing the plane. An aircraft using Raychem's components will weigh less than one using its competitors' products. Raychem delivers that message not just to the aircraft manufacturers, but directly to the airlines. It probably takes United Airlines only about two seconds to figure out the business advantage it gains from lighter aircraft. You can bet United consider this when they are developing their aircraft procurement specifications.

Smart Sellers understand their customers' business well enough to show how their products will improve it. You are selling smart when you cross the bridge between the qualities of your product and measurable improvements in your customers' business.

One of the two selling propositions for a high-technology sale is selling market share improvement. To the degree that you can build a case whereby your customer will receive long-term market share improvement exclusively by buying your product, you will determine your ability to accelerate your success and that of your company. The other buying premise is to help significantly improve your customer's balance sheet by saving them a lot of money in a short time period. We'll look at this premise more closely in Chapter 3.

Chapter 3

Selling Cost Savings

S elling cost savings is the most difficult way for a high-tech company to gain long-term market share. Achieving success via cost substitution-based sales requires the right product, the existence of many repeatable substitution opportunities, vulnerable competitive alternatives, and great timing. A good substitution rationale is difficult to establish and maintain over an extended period. Cost substitution opportunities eventually run their course. The number of customers with costs high enough to justify substitution is limited. Successful products saturate the available replacement opportunities. Newer full-featured products enter the market offering cost savings plus functionality enhancements. You must get your sales strategy flowing before your market runs dry.

Most high-technology companies design their products to improve functionality, not to improve cost substitution factors. These products generally increase functionality, improve performance, and offer new features. Using high-tech products involves worker retraining, technicians with special skills and significant work-flow redesign. Both successful high-technology deployment and building a successful sales campaign based on cost savings take time and money. You first must provide the rock solid financial justification to convince risk-conscious prospective users of positive investment return. You do this by clearly establishing payback—the financial justification that, over time, the cost savings from using a product will more than pay for the product.

Many companies fail when they base their value proposition on savings. Inexperienced marketing groups confuse low prices with cost reduction selling. A cost reduction sales premise justifies the investment through the replacement of real existing costs. For a cost substitution strategy to work, a sales team must identify market segments that clearly are using the

41

higher cost alternative and demonstrate specific financial benefits gained by deploying their product in each sales opportunity.

Quantifying Cost Savings

In order to carry out high-tech product cost reduction sales properly, you must quantify your customer's savings potential and get his agreement. High-tech companies win these markets when the payback fundamentals of the sale are very clear. The payback fundamentals consist of developing two financial justifications for your customer:

1. The Payback Period

2. The Net Present Value

Your customer will consider at least two options when looking at a potential technology investment. The company can continue unchanged, or migrate to a new method involving your product. There may be other options as well. Remaining unchanged has well-known, predictable costs and risks. Changing involves a new investment, switching costs, new risks, and some transition period of concurrent expenses while the new method is operating simultaneously with the old. Once the change is complete, there will be a new set of ongoing operational costs. Sooner or later during the sales cycle, someone within your customer's organization will analyze these financial issues to determine if your product is a favorable investment.

Establishing Payback

The payback period is the amount of time it takes for your customer to pay for your product from the savings gained from using it. You can go crazy with graphs and charts showing the monthly savings curve crossing the initial investment line. You can net it out in terms of months. How many months does it take your customer to recover the costs associated with your product?

Calculating payback requires some work. Generally, the payback period can be computed by capturing the capital costs and the monthly operating costs associated with each path—the continuation of business as usual and the new method under consideration. The payback period is the difference in investment costs divided by the difference in monthly savings.

$$\text{Payback Period} = \frac{\text{Incremental Captial Cost of New Investment}}{\text{Incremental Monthly Savings of New Investment}} =$$

$$\frac{\Delta \text{ Capital Cost}}{\Delta \text{ Monthly Savings}}$$

Present Value Measures the Size of the Return

While the payback period helps your customer understand how long it takes for an investment to be financially rewarding, it does not provide a dollar amount of the absolute savings over the life of the investment. Present value is a way to quantify this. The present value is a comparison of the cash streams involved for each alternative. Future cash equates to the present-day dollar equivalent using anticipated interest rates. The investment's present value represents the total value of the savings over the expected life of the investment in today's terms.

Fundamental to the development of the present value is agreement with your customer on the time period over which the investment is relevant. When you sell technology substitution you want long investment windows (five to ten years). When you are fighting a substitution you want shorter periods. The reason is that the so called "out" years, the ones with continual savings payback after the initial investment is paid off, add substantially to the return. Furthermore, your customer's present methods are most expensive during the out years.

The 20/10 rule for a high-tech company entering a market with a cost savings sales mission works well as a high level sales qualifier. Will the investment pay for itself in less than 20 months and will the present value of the savings be greater than 10 percent of the customer's anticipated profits? If so, you are off to a good start. If not, you need to rethink your sales strategy, rework your approach, and adjust your pricing to improve the payback period and present value. Or, maybe you should not pursue a cost savings strategy and look instead at business improvement impact as your primary sales mission.

ROI Calculation—The Awkward Approach

The net present value, the payback period, and the return on investment calculation are mathematical cousins. Business schools once relied heavily on ROI (return on investment) analysis as part of the corporate capital investment decision strategy. Their reasoning was that ROI methods level the playing field for all investment decisions and by measuring these decisions against the anticipated cost of money.

ROI analysis provides financial managers with a good tool for comparing lots of decisions. It's a great tool for netting out the entire world in terms of dollars and cents. But ROI decision making is too abstract for 99 percent of the decision makers you are likely to meet. Your customer is dealing with empowering his business through technology and not with the inner workings of financial wheeling and dealing. Focusing your customer on a decision that has a 15 percent ROI is not as graphic as discussing an investment that pays off in 18 months and can increase his company's profits by millions of dollars.

The whole idea of ROI decision making is to group all of the capital investments a company can make. In an ROI analysis mode, your customer will weigh making a strategic technology investment against repainting the company's factory. No thanks. I try to avoid presenting high-technology decisions on this level whenever possible.

Selecting Relevant Costs

To reach customer acceptance on a present value or a payback period, it is necessary to agree on which costs factor into the analysis. The possible costs range from well established "hard" business costs for which your customer has historical billing information to abstract "soft" costs.

Hard costs are any your customer presently has that results in direct invoice such as monthly equipment maintenance. All other costs, such as reduced application creation costs through efficient software development tools, are soft costs. Hard costs directly enter the present value and payback period analysis. Establishing this baseline brings your substitution opportunity into focus.

You can only count on reaching customer acceptance on replacement of hard costs. While you may be able to make a strong case for the importance of the removal of soft costs, you'll have difficulty convincing your customer of this. Soft cost replacement presents several problems. Many soft cost replacements result in the elimination of certain job functions and the possible creation of new functions involving a new set of job skills. Measuring these costs not only is difficult, it may be a political bombshell within a customer's organization. Other soft cost reductions are subject to a wide range of arguments on the actual dollar value of the savings. For instance, using a new computer with a new state-of-the-art, object-oriented language may not only save hard dollars in a specific situation, it makes new application development a snap. But the real question is whether or not reduced application development costs are part of the payback period. The longer training costs and the lag time until the development team is effective may mitigate much of the savings. Your customer may even wonder whether its present programmers are capable of learning the new object-oriented language. In that case the company would have to consider a layoff, new hiring costs, and higher salary positions. You may reach the point where you wish you had not brought up this soft cost savings in the first place.

Hard costs, on the other hand, present a straightforward picture for the buyer. You will say to your customer; "I am going to replace this set of existing invoices with this new set of expenses and you will save a great deal of money."

Bringing Soft Costs into the Picture

It is to your advantage to include soft cost benefits to make your cost substitute case. Even though you may not be able to directly include soft costs in your payback analysis, you can bundle the benefits of your technology into the long-term advantages of making the substitution.

For instance, job elimination may not be measurable from a short-run single application analysis basis but, over the long-term, your customer doesn't want a competitive disadvantage due to a bloated work force. Sometimes, the hard-to-quantify soft benefits of using a high-tech product are image enhancements in the eyes of the user's customers that may have great long-term value for your customer. (Putting glass walls around IBM computers allowed IBM customers to show off their status symbols.) Even though these soft costs do not affect the investment's payback period or the present value, you can build these influencing factors into your sale.

Agreeing that soft costs have real dollar implications is often a function of your customer's industry. One industry may put little value on benefits that another industry considers paramount.

For instance, a scientific research assistant connecting a remote workstation to a computer might consider high-circuit availability to be an abstract soft cost. A seller guaranteeing 99.9 percent circuit availability (44 outage minutes per month) may be indistinguishable from a seller with 99.999 percent availability (26 outage seconds per month). This outage difference has little impact on the researcher's ability to perform a task. Yet, for a travel agency there is a well known hard cost difference between the two availability levels. Each outage hour costs them money. The scientific application workstation connection will view both circuit sellers equally, though one provides 100 times greater availability. The higher availability vendor will not be awarded any price premium for the improved availability. On the other hand, the improved reliability for the travel agent directly translates to increased revenue. The fewer number of outage hours will result in increased ticket sales. For this market, the increase in revenue can be factored into the present value and payback calculations.

The bad news about soft costs not entering the cost savings formulas is that your product's sales price may not rise as you increase functionality over the existing solution. Unlike selling business improvement, the cost substitution sale is extremely price sensitive. The present value and payback financial fundamentals establish the price of the high-tech product. Soft costs not included in this calculation cannot translate to increased vendor revenue. Technology cost savings substitutes are credited only with their hard-dollar replacement value.

Sell Either Market Share Increases or Cost Savings—Not Both

The two selling positions—selling business performance improvements and cost reductions sales—are at opposite ends of the sales spectrum. At one extreme, the product's sales premise is based solely on improving the business of the user. At the other extreme, the sales premise is solely based on providing significant cost savings. Technology vendors are successful when they operate at the extremes. Going down the middle creates fuzzy sales situations that lead to failure. This middle road dilutes your business improvement sales premise by building in cost savings benefits that may limit the functionality (and price!) of your product. Or, your cost savings sale will get cloudy when you try to show new functionality that also increases cost. You've got to avoid the middle course. If your sales premise is cost savings, you need to prove it. And when you prove it, you need to hit a home run by showing lots of cost savings and early investment payback. If you are selling long-term business improvements, stick to the topic. Don't dilute the strength of your message by introducing a weak cost reduction analysis. (See Figure 3-1.)

Another problem with mixing cost reduction sales strategies with business improvement strategies is the value limitation you establish in your customer's eyes. A cost reducer cannot sell his product for more than the costs that are being replaced. The maximum money a cost reducer can eliminate occurs when the substitute product costs absolutely nothing and has no recurring fees. The price of their replacement product can never exceed the amount saved. A business improvement seller does not have a similar built-in upper limit. The more it can improve its customer's business, the more the customer will value the product and the more the cus-

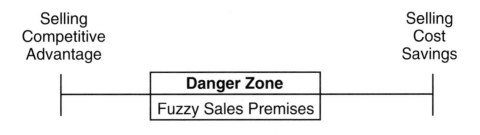

Figure 3-1   Don't Get Caught in the Middle. Base Your Sales Proposition Either on Cost Savings or Competitive Advantage—Not Both

tomer will spend. What's more, the cost reducer will have problems using an increase in functionality as a way to increase price. The company has already established the maximum value of its product in its customer's eyes. When you are a provider of cost reduction technology you cannot increase your price based on extended functionality.

Shifting the Present Value and Payback Period to your Advantage

The financial underpinnings of your cost savings sale are not stagnant. There are eight basic ways in which you can significantly impact the present value and payback period of your products:

1. Lower prices

2. Reduce your total substitution costs

3. Lower the investment threshold

4. Lower your customer's costs to switch

5. Reduce the risk factors assigned to the investment

6. Redefine the service strategy

7. Address work force retraining requirements

8. Change the acquisition strategy of the investment from an initial capital procurement to a monthly service fee (or vice versa).

Table 3-1 quick-references these points.

Table 3-1

✓	Lower Your Price
✓	Reduce Your Total Substitution Costs
✓	Lower the Capital Investment Threshold
✓	Lower the Switching Costs
✓	Reduce the Risk Factor
✓	Redefine the Service Strategy
✓	Address Work Force Retraining
✓	Change the Acquisition Strategy of the Capital Investment

Lowering prices seems straightforward. Most sellers have the notion that they can enter the market with high prices and lower these over time. This approach has the early adopters paying the highest prices. For cost reduction sellers, this strategy can ruin a product before it has even had a chance in the market. Unnecessarily high prices are amplified when factored into the payback period and present value calculations. They result in your customer viewing an investment as undesirable and may prevent you from winning over the early adopters.

During the early days of microprocessors, Fairchild Semiconductor brought to market a two-chip microprocessor as a cost replacement device. Marketing felt it would sell well since, unlike other new microprocessors, it did not require 15 or so auxiliary circuits. Two circuits did the entire job. Fairchild priced this product at a level that was competitive with high-performance microprocessors brought to market by Intel—about $150 per circuit. Marketing thought the cost advantage argument of their product could be seen through the elimination of the auxiliary circuits and associated costs (between $15–$35 savings per system). The product line met with limited success after a year on the market. Even though the savings were there, customers chose to use the higher performance Intel circuits and pay the 20 percent premium. They were building a new generation of applications and opted for performance. The trouble was that Fairchild was halfheartedly pushing the device as a cost replacement to the wrong type of buyer. The company priced the product to be the lower cost alternative—cost avoidance, instead of pricing to eliminate cost—cost substitution.

A year after the introduction, I was on a team set up to fix the sales problem associated with this microprocessor. We found that a substantial cost substitution opportunity existed in the marketplace that Fairchild was not addressing. Back then, microprocessor technology was very new. The installed base of applications was slim. The original premise of the product was correct—there was a substitution cost savings market. What they got wrong was the target customer and the price point. Since microprocessors were still very new, there were virtually no high-volume applications in productions that could benefit from a cost reduction sale. The customers that could benefit most from the Fairchild microprocessor were not using microprocessors in volume. They were using mechanical devices to control consumer appliances—ovens, refrigerators, washing machines, televisions, and microwave ovens. We decided to set our sights on this replacement opportunity and forget about competing against other microprocessors. We targeted on replacing mechanical control devices in high end consumer products. The cost replacement model was based on the cost of building a mechanical product. We reduced the product price to $10 for the very high-volume consumer appliance market and started design of a new, single-chip version of the product—the 3870. This lowered the entry cost even more and resulted in designs costing one tenth as much as competitive alternatives. The 3870 was not nearly as expandable as Intel's high-end products but it had substantially lower costs. Within 12 months, the 3870 was the largest volume microprocessor in the business. It had a narrow customer base—manufacturers of high-volume consumer appliances. But these customers consumed a lot of units.

When you successfully sell using a cost-based substitution strategy, your product and services must have immediate financial impact. It is not enough to show a successful set of numbers. Significant financial savings must be immediate. Your customer is looking for cost savings and wants that savings up front.

You can influence the immediacy and the size of your customer's savings. Your customer will trade longer term cost savings for immediate savings but not the other way around. Your customer wants as much savings as he can get as soon as possible.

Lowering price is not the only way to raise the present value and shorten the payback period of a substitute technology. Changing the texture of your customer's investment can influence decisions. Reshaping the acquisition strategy can significantly improve the financial picture. If your customer replaces a monthly recurring service with a capital equipment purchase, the payback period can be very short. Many high-tech companies in the network equipment business have successfully based their strategies on cost replacement of telephone company fees. The telephone companies charge for installation, equipment rental and monthly services. New products entering the market allowed large communications users to consolidate activities and lower long distance private line costs. The procurement decision involved a capital purchase for the equipment. In addition, vendors of these products offered installation, maintenance, and even network services to lower end user switching costs and eliminate any specialized skill requirements by their customer. The successful vendors addressed a complete spectrum of end user switching needs and revamped the acquisition strategy associated with these services. They changed the purchase strategy from high installation and high monthly costs to initial capital investment and low monthly fees.

Gathering a consortium of users together is another way to help reduce the initial investment and reduce the payback period for the substitute product. This is easier than you may think. Most industries have consortiums to deal with industry common problems. Some of these are formal groups and others are informal user groups. The larger cooperative organizations are well-known institutions. The New York Stock Exchange and The American Stock Exchange are member-owned institutions. The Associated Press serves the independent news industry. The farming communities have established large cooperatives like Farmland and Ocean Spray. In the aerospace industry, the Aerospace Industry Association is a member-run organization. The American Petroleum Industry services the energy companies. A cost substitution strategy not affordable by an individual customer may become viable when introduced through an industry consortium.

Substitution Roadblocks

Having the greatest substitute in the world does not readily convert into a long line of customers waiting at your door. You must motivate your customers to switch. They need more than a compelling set of cost replacement issues. Your customer has established his present patterns and techniques and may not want to deal with the risks involved in switching. The company's management may have a negative bias. Their work force can play a substantial role in the ultimate decision. Or the company might simply have better things to do.

I was once involved in a wide-area communications connection replacement sale with United Airlines as the prospective user. The vendor sales team had worked with their counterparts at United to find the possible cost savings involved. After a month or so of discussions, we set up a meeting with the top decision-maker at United. He agreed that the replacement opportunity was a good one. In fact, it was the best he had ever seen.

He agreed that the savings would be significant and that the risks were manageable. Then he told us that his group was also responsible for turning on the computer network for their new airport terminal in Chicago—their future crown jewel. This terminal was due to open in 18 months and he wanted every aspect of the computer network to be production worthy on opening day. His program management staff was devoted to this project. Failing to meet that date for any reason was unacceptable. All the other activity under his control would be run in a status quo mode until opening day. So, though there was a substantial cost savings involved, they would not consider initiating a project for fear of delaying their more important mission.

Various vertical markets will view the same substitution opportunity differently. In some markets, potential customers are looking for every opportunity to leapfrog one another. Other markets may be interested in modifying the functionality of a service instead of saving money. This all affects the willingness of a market segment to initiate substitution. In each vertical market, there is always a lead user that stands to gain the most by moving first. For cost savings sales this user is probably the one with the most precarious financial position. Using a high-tech cost savings substitute that can deliver immediate improvement and turn around marginal performance may be just what the doctor ordered. Establishing the lead user in a vertical market will serve as a model for future customer penetration. The good news here is that it is easy to identify the first user. The bad news is the first mover is probably in the worst financial shape.

In high-tech product cost reduction situations, your customer's substitution decision revolves around three questions:

1. What does the dollar investment look like?
2. How does the functionality compare?
3. What is the customer's willingness to act?

Product Life Cycle

High-tech replacement products have unique product life cycles. For your cost-based substitute to succeed in a market, it will go through four phases:

1. Functional Trials
2. Acceptance Period

3. Full-Scale Deployment

4. Ongoing Operation

The length of time for each of these phases is dependent on the situation. If your customer can buy just one copy of your product, or if your product involves multiple units, your significant sales windows will generally come during the second and third phases. Usually you subsidize the first phase when your customer is determining if your product functions at all. During the last phase—ongoing operation—your service and operational revenue may be substantial, though your sales revenue is low. So, the usage curve for your customer may look like Figure 3-2.

For your product to succeed in a vertical market, many users must buy it. The saturation point for your product equals the sum of the usage decisions available in the market. If all prospective customers use the product in all possible situations your product will hit its saturation point. The adoption curve within a vertical market may look something like Figure 3-3.

The product life cycle curve then becomes the sum of the product's potential vertical markets. Depending on the size and timing of these markets, the anticipated product life cycle may have a dip during which customers are still deciding on their potential to use your product in volume.

After a cost savings technology product has reached the saturation point in a market, its major sales opportunities are gone. If you cannot find new markets for this product, its sales will drop to a maintenance level supporting the installation base. Reaching this saturation point can be a traumatic experience. Suddenly, new usage opportunities have vanished.

Figure 3-2   Usage Curve for a Specific Customer

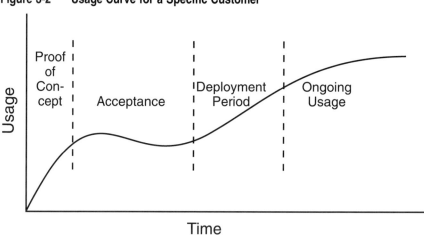

Figure 3-3   Adoption Curve of a Product within a Vertical Market

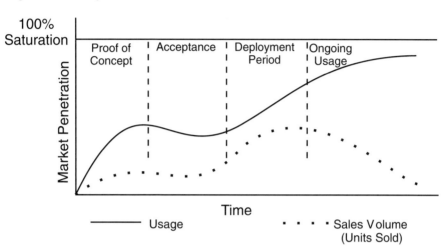

One year, the product is a rising star and everyone is scrambling to meet demand. The next year, the new installation rate crumbles and management is being forced out the door. Reaching saturation for a product sold as a cost replacement should be very predictable to the vendor. When you're selling a cost savings product, you have a limit on the maximum worth of your product and a limit on the replacement opportunities.

Proving the Actual Savings of a Cost Substitute

Selling cost substitution is a risky business. It's easy to end up spending an enormous amount of time in a sales situation and suddenly finding your entire cost savings disappear right before your eyes. This happens because there are so many factors that can eliminate the costs substitution model. To use your substitute, your customer may have to make broad operational changes. Workers must be retrained. Other parts of your customer's value chain may change. To realize the eventual cost savings from using your product, your customer must complete these changes within budget and time constraints. This increases the substitution risk. The greater the risk, the less likely the customer is to go ahead with the project.

Your prospective customer will ask the questions: "Can we really get the proposed cost savings? What is the real cost to cut over to the substitute?" You may be asking your customer to spend millions over long time periods to eventually save tens of millions over longer time frames. You must establish your company's track record for your products and services and your ability to eventually save your customer money. The two most effective ways for proving the reality of your cost savings are using industry-specific reference accounts and establishing well-defined acceptance test periods. Successful reference accounts within your customer's industry go a long way toward reducing risk assessment. Once you've successfully built a customer within a market segment, that customer can help energize others. The down side is that the existing reference customer is likely to be a competitor of your prospective customer.

Acceptance periods are important when there are risks that can only be quantified by on-site usage of your product. However, trial periods are often a two-edged sword. A field trial can be disastrous when a customer creates a testing environment that is more science fair than reality check. Trials without clear expectations and goals often end with uncertain results. It's depressing to spend months working in a trial situation and end up with the evaluator being more concerned about performance improvements than risk reduction evaluation or proving cost savings.

Trials can help you prove the potential savings offered by the cost substitute and accurately predict the risk factors as part of your replacement sale. This takes time—time that impacts your ability to penetrate a replacement market.

Putting Cost Reduction Strategies to Work

Your ability to build a cost reduction sale depends largely on your timing. When you are the first to sell a new technology you can skim the most lucrative opportunities. Of course, you must first plow the ground and develop the market. You must select the customer situations where your products offer the greatest savings and establish these opportunities as your reference base. When additional suppliers enter your market, they not only must prove cost substitution, but offer greater savings. If they can't do this, they will try to change the sale from cost reduction to functional competition combined with cost savings. Your competitors will be telling your customer that they can get tremendous cost savings and wonderful new functionality. All of your account development logic will get thrown out the window. Competitors are now pulling your customer toward business improvement considerations that may or may not be relevant. Nevertheless, it will eat your success rate. You'll wish you had never begun selling cost savings in the first place and start circulating your resume.

One of the largest recent markets for cost replacement selling has been the T1 Multiplexor market. (A T1 Multiplexor can pack a lot of low-speed telephone connection services onto a long distance, high-speed line—a T1 trunk—and unpack these services at the other end.) When they first came out, T1 Multiplexors were cost replacements for services the telephone companies provided. For a business that required large volumes of voice and data over long distances, customers were presented an alternative. They could continue buying phone company services on a monthly basis or make a substantial capital investment, build their own mini–long distance, high-capacity telephone network backbone switch, reroute traffic onto this new network, retrain network management employees, and operate their own private network. The cost reduction sales case was created from four basic pieces of information:

1. Existing Monthly Costs—The present costs of providing the services needed to be compiled. This was found by going through the monthly phone bills and identifying long-term trends.

2. Purchase Cost of New Equipment—The equipment costs involved were mostly the purchase of the T1 Multiplexors. Along with this, the way these costs were handled by the buyer's accountants affected the savings model. Cost of money and length of depreciation schedules also influenced the customer's savings projection.

3. Other Ownership Costs—Other costs involving training, service, and monthly maintenance added to the ownership costs and needed to be included in the savings model.

4. Ongoing Monthly Operational Costs—The new monthly telephone service costs resulting from using the T1 Multiplexors were estimated and added to the proposed cost savings model.

Once this information was understood, the T1 Multiplexor sale could be established on its financial merits. When the monthly savings from the costs reduction was one-eighteenth of the capital investment, this became a very attractive purchase for the customer. The first sellers of T1 Multiplexor equipment put these cost reduction sales strategies to work.

Time's Impact on the Cost Substitution Sale

The present value and payback period for your product are not static. They constantly change. Your customer will change his opinion about your product as he receives new information. External factors most often influence significant changes in the payback model. There are three dominant external factors that affect your customer's view of his company's present value and payback period model:

1. Changes initiated by the supplier of the product being replaced

2. The appearance of competing substitution technologies

3. The experiences of other customers

The vendor of the product being replaced can do a lot to damage your substitute technology's cost benefits. At first, the entrenched suppliers may not feel any real threat from an untried alternative, especially if the alternative is relevant to only a portion of their market. After you draw blood by developing significant usage, your entrenched competitor will start to fight back by improving its end of the cost equation. It may reconfigure the user's system, reprice its product, adopt different service methods, or announce future plans. All of these are tactics aimed at preventing its users from jumping ship. Remember, this product may be the cash cow generating huge amounts of profits in proportion to even modest sales. Your substitution success can cause them to respond in a big way.

Another impact on your present value and payback period model can come from a newer substitute technology. As time passes and you increase your market share, other high-technology vendors will enter your submarket. You'll be most concerned with those products that offer similar cost savings capability and will need to develop a strategy to deal with these competitors.

As your existing customers continue to use your product, their satisfaction levels will change. This new data will enter their present value and payback period models and may change their risk assessment of your product. New customer prospects will learn about these changes as they talk with your existing users. Buyer consortiums may form to help users better deal with the costs of the technology and improve the cost savings for more and more users. All of these real-world experiences eventually affect your ability to develop new customers.

Even the best present value and payback period models come under competitive pressure and eventually erode. Like products, present value and payback periods have shelf lives. Sooner or later the benefits dwindle. Either the entrenched suppliers improve their end of the equation or new substitutes develop. The irony of having a successful high-tech cost substitute is that your success becomes a magnet attracting competitors. This will eventually change the financial fundamentals that made your product a success in the first place. One way or the other, a product yielding very attractive financial returns will find itself a victim of its own success. It is necessary for the supplier to use its initial success to build entry barriers and gain economies of scale and leverage this initial success into longer term opportunities. Successful cost-based sales strategies have limited life spans.

The Three Rules of Cost Substitution

Cost substitution selling is not for the faint-hearted. You shouldn't try to sell a high-technology product as a cost substitute unless you are absolutely certain your product and company can survive the process. The three fundamentals of selling technology as a cost substitute are:

1. You will never be worth more to your customer than the costs you replace.

2. Your sales volume and the rate of growth of your market is determined by the market of the product you intend to replace. The replacement's present installed base and the rate of growth of this base determine your substitution opportunity.

3. Successful cost-based sales strategies have limited life spans.

Cost-Based Strategies That Fail

Some high-tech products and services are just not meant to be positioned as cost saving substitutes. These typically are products with lots of white collar productivity savings that customers cannot measure in terms of hard dollar substitution. Object-oriented software development tools are an example. They make programmers more productive and can be a great benefit to a programmer. But you do not want to be selling these products based on cost savings fundamentals. The indirect savings advantages for software productivity tools are hard to assess and do not readily translate to dollars and cents. What's more, the entire cost of switching to an object-oriented software development environment can be enormous when you factor in all the computer upgrades, retraining of personnel, and rewriting of existing applications.

Another cost-based sale that leads to problems occurs when savings come late in the program. Today's world changes very fast. People have little faith that things will be the same for long time periods. The worst type of sale to chase after is one in which cost savings are postponed. Cost savings sales have a sense of urgency. Your customer wants to save money now, not later. Time erodes the savings benefits, and it erodes your customer's enthusiasm for achieving them. Customers chasing after savings want real dollar savings immediately.

Products with a huge impact on your buyer's behavior are generally not good to position as cost savings. Customers are willing to save money but only up to a point. Restructuring a business for cost savings reasons is tricky. Companies restructure for strategic reasons, not for tactical cost reductions. The goals of the restructuring need to go well beyond a present value/payback period analysis. Your customer's middle management carries out product substitution. High-level management performs large organization restructuring for other purposes. Middle management decision makers will shy away from things that involve organizational restructuring.

If the benefit analysis for your product or service does not lend itself to dollars-and-cents savings, then do not try to position its sale as a cost substitute alternative. For rhetorical purposes it may be okay to say, as part of the total product benefits, that there is a savings to be had. But don't get carried away with this idea. The translation of soft cost benefits, delayed savings, or large organization changes into cost savings is too hard to make. Products with these characteristics need to be positioned as providing significant competitive advantage if they are to be successful.

IBM's Substitution Business

Poor IBM has gone from being the Big Blue to having the big blues in just a few years. The 1990s will be remarkable for IBM. They started the decade as a huge company with a slight blemish. In just a few years they became a "troubled" company reaching to outsiders for corporate leadership. Who knows how or if they'll come out. For the first time IBM's mainframe business is declining, and rapidly. The company is feeling the financial impact of this decline in a big way. The decline is worse than it looks because IBM's high-end computer business has a short-term growth opportunity keeping sales numbers higher than they normally would be. This growth business is the replacement of their own installed mainframes with IBM's newest models for cost substitution reasons.

The economics of this substitution are straightforward. The risk factors are extremely low. The conversion costs are small. The consolidation of several old processors into a newer, bigger model lowers the customer's total net operating costs and reduces operating personnel and costs. Furthermore, the new system will have greater availability and reliability.

That facilitates a great cost substitution-based sale. IBM has a huge, installed base that meets the required ownership profile. Whether it wants to or not, IBM will be very successful at replacing its own products. The down side of this, of course, is that IBM will be replacing its own products at its existing accounts. These substitutions are decreasing its customer's usage of IBM products and services. Distributed processing and network computing has brought any growth in their mainframe market to a halt. In the short run, IBM will sell big boxes. Not long after that, it will lose mainframe revenue and ongoing service revenue as this no-growth market struggles along. It's as though the company doesn't know whether to cheer or boo each new mainframe order. Every time a customer buys a new box to consolidate the functions of several older units, IBM's mainframe business moves one step closer to its own demise.

Fighting a Substitute

As a high-technology provider you may find yourself on the other end of the substitution equation. A new product may enter the market as a cost substitute for your product. Your new competitor will be replacing your installed base by offering a significant cost savings. If this is the case, you will have to reassess your sales strategy and focus on fighting off this new competitor.

The first thing to do is understand the market segment the competitor is attacking. Most successful cost replacement strategies focus on a specific usage situation. A potential cost saving rival is probably attacking a segment of your customer base, not your entire installed market. Once you understand this segmentation and your competitor's cost savings perspective, then your mission is to adapt your strategies to fight off the attack within this segment.

After you understand your competitor's segmentation strategy, you can look within this segment and develop the present value and payback period fundamentals for your competitor's product. Most likely, you can uncover improvement areas in the maintenance, replacement overhead, warranty, or value added engineering associated with your offering. By lengthening warranty and service agreements you can stretch out financial payback periods to your benefit or postpone your customers' opportunities to switch. Perhaps, by performing this grouping, you can lower the ongoing costs of using your product.

If you are still having difficulty developing a defensive strategy, you may find it helpful to divide this collection of customers into two groups—one group of customers least vulnerable to switch and one most likely to. Then, develop a strategy for dealing with each group. Depending on the size and characteristics of these groupings, you may find it to your benefit to develop even higher barriers for your least vulnerable group and strategically abandon the customers most receptive to your competitor's products.

One strategy that works well for fighting off a cost-focused competitor is to announce future plans. As previously discussed, the present value and payback period financial figures are time sensitive. Announcing your long-term product plans can put your customers in a wait-and-see situation. This is devastating to your competitor—time is the biggest enemy for the cost-based sale.

Know When to Harvest and Know When to Join

Sometimes, when you are the incumbent supplier and a new technology cost replacement threatens to take away your customers, your best course of action is to harvest. You may decide that it is no longer worth defending your position. Offering price concessions to prevent switching may not make sense. Technology is a leapfrog business. What was a leading technology product five years ago is old hat today. During the life of your product, you may find a new competitor cost replacing your product. You also may find that, no matter what you do, you cannot avoid the replacement of your product.

In this situation, the best course of action may be to go into harvest mode. Instead of lowering prices to ward off the competition, you may want to find a price level that will maximize your return while your customers go through the conversion to another product. A high-tech provider faced with a cost replacement strategy that will ultimately prove to be unstoppable may, at some point, choose to join. The entrenched marketer is in the best position to provide the substitute technology since this supplier has access to the customers and the distribution channel. As the current provider you should have the best present value and payback period equation in the business. The difficulty is knowing when to join.

The use of satellites for long distance voice applications went through two major cost replacement cycles. In the 1970s, the first geosynchronous satellites provided significant cost savings for long distance connections. It was hard for AT&T to ward off this use of technology since telco rates apply to such broad classes of users. It could not just lower the tariffs for the customers most vulnerable to substitution. It had to sit and watch operators like RCA rifle-shoot these large users and switch them to satellite connections for their long distance trunk lines. AT&T had little choice but to keep prices where they were and harvest the larger markets while it used legislative action to delay their competitors' tactics. AT&T eventually entered this business itself.

In the 1990s, the situation reversed. High-capacity fiber has cost-replaced satellite voice links. Plus, the quality levels fiber offered and the noticeable lack of transmission delay put fiber in a much better position than satellite links for point-to-point communications. This market is once again in the hands of the terrestrial providers. Over 20 years, technology spun this business in a complete circle.

First to Market Rings the Bell

High-technology cost substitution is a funny business. In any single vertical market the window of opportunity stays open for just a short period. The first high-tech product positioned in a market as a clear-cut cost savings can sign up the most significant opportunities. This seller can select the best situations and build substantial market share and entry barriers. Not only does this market leader start with important entry barriers such as marketing, sales, and service coverage, but the leader is in the best position to lower risk and provide customer savings.

Any supplier entering the market after the first cost reduction seller has been successful will find rough going. Besides establishing the present value and payback period criteria for moving to a substitute, this new provider also must show financial benefits when compared to the first entry.

The high-speed packet switch marketplace provides a good example of this situation. Network Equipment Technologies entered this market with a new technology providing an alternative for end users employing telephone lines to interconnect different offices forming high-capacity corporate backbone networks. NET offered end users an opportunity to purchase capital equipment that could lower monthly telephone costs for years to come. The present value for the investment was high and the payback of the investment was immediate. NET signed up an impressive list of large end users for their T1 network equipment.

When companies like Stratacom and Timplex entered the market, not only did they have to show the cost savings their products offered for monthly phone services, they had to distinguish themselves from NET. Since the cost structures of these products were similar, Timplex and Stratacom looked to improve functionality and capacity to develop market segments. Stratacom based its sale on the superior technology behind its products—better voice and data line utilization, natural integration with on premise equipment, and superior infrastructure management. The company was competing for consolidation of the customer's phone services on the one hand and with NET's competitive pressure on the other. By that time, NET had already established economies of scale in the manufacturing, marketing, customer service, and installation portions of the business. Plus, NET had the most reference accounts spread out over different industries. So a customer's risk of using NET was lower than with new market entrants. For the new entrants, selling to an installed NET account was almost impossible. They needed to find submarkets that NET had not yet penetrated. They did, of course, succeed in establishing usage, but never really had the wide field of opportunities NET had. Years later this market migrated from a cost replacement purchase to a business improvement decision. As customers became more experienced with running their own wide area networks, they began to see the competitive advantages available through extensions of their data networks across their enterprises. This drove the business from a cost substitute to a deployment based on achieving competitive advantages.

Timing is everything. Being the second entrant with a high-technology cost savings sales mission is a difficult business problem. A high-tech provider must look for undeveloped market segments.

Smart sellers involved with cost substitution follow these guidelines:

1. Get to market fast.

2. Demonstrate great cost savings in short time periods.

3. Lock up the customers that have the most to gain early.

4. Migrate to a competitive advantage strategy as your cost advantage position erodes.

Part II

Changing Markets and Changing Customers

Change is good. Without change you cannot ride the bus, do your laundry, or pitch pennies.

Five years ago no one would have dreamed of the changes that are taken for granted today. Big companies are being downsized at lightning speed. Self employment, growing at the fastest rate in this century, is now up to 13 percent. The massive corporations that dominated the post–World War II era—the structure that we've all grown up under—may just have been an abnormality. Now such huge corporate structures are out. Industrial giants are forming partnerships with smaller, more adaptable businesses. Modest-sized companies will become dominant.

No matter what type of product that you sell, these changes will impact you. Selling to a small- to modest-sized business that is integrated into its market is a lot different from selling to a huge, vertically integrated entity.

The Fortune 500 companies are changing, as are the small- and mid-sized businesses that dominate the landscape. Your own company is also undergoing change. By understanding these changes and priorities, you can better position yourself and your company.

Chapter 4

Changing Markets

This is an exciting decade for people involved with high-tech companies. At last, customers are incorporating technology into their core business planning. After spending the past three decades using technology for application-specific problems, your customers have embarked on wide-scale technology deployments, positioning themselves to compete in the twenty-first century. Their technology programs now span enterprises and unite their entire industries. Technology is your customers' catalyst for change—change in their business scope, change in their organizational fabric, change in their business processes, and realignment in their business partnering strategies. Whether your customers are large end users, original equipment manufacturers, or small businesses, their use of technology is essential to their success.

Changes are going on all around you (see Figure 4-1). Even though you may have been selling to the same customer for ten years, everything around you has changed. Your customers' markets are changing. Their competitors are putting more pressure on their businesses than ever before. Your sales channels are changing. Your competitors are not just companies with similar products; they may include alternate methodologies. The 1990s seem to have brought nothing but change.

There are seven major changes impacting your marketplace:

1. Global Competition—Your customer is operating in a worldwide, real-time, on-time, right-the-first-time economy.

2. Technology-Based Business Strategies—Technology decisions are interwoven with your customer's strategic plan.

Figure 4-1   Changes Are Going on Everywhere

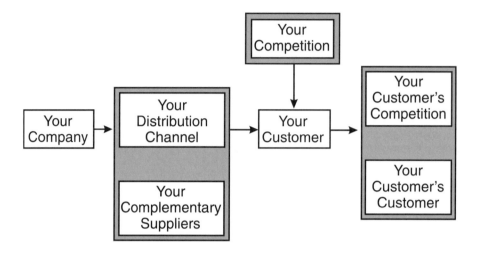

3. Information-Based Economy—Your customer relies on electronic information for both running the business and as part of his products line. Information access is crucial to its future success.

4. Quality Relationships—Your customer has become quality conscious. Quality conscious customers want their suppliers to become their business partners. The relationship between you and your customer must change from buyer/seller to business partner as the bar on quality rises.

5. Sales Partnerships—One company selling to one buyer is becoming a community of sellers selling to a community of buyers. Your sales role is expanding to include the management of selling and customer-partnering relationships.

6. Competing Solutions—The nature of your competition is changing from competing products to competing alternatives.

7. Standards-Based Decisions—Your customer's reliance on a single vendor solution has diminished through technology standards. This reduces your customer's switching costs.

Table 4-1 summarizes these trends.

Table 4-1   Seven Major Trends Influence Your Business

Global Competition	Your customer's markets are more competitive than ever before
Technology-Based Business Strategy	Technology investments are made at the board room level
Information-Based Economy	Your customer uses electronic information to run his business and as part of his company's products
Quality Relationships	Quality processes are imbedded throughout today's businesses. Customers want suppliers to be part of their quality chain.
Sales Partnerships	You must form partnerships that are beneficial to your customer
Competing Solutions	Your biggest competitor is an alternate method, not a competing product
Standardization	Your customer is aware of the advantages of plug-and-play equipment

Your Changing Environment

The post-industrial era of the 1990s is putting new pressures on your customer. Today's information-driven markets are open to global competition. Your customer is not just competing with the firm across the street or across town. He is competing with businesses halfway across the world. Your customer's customer is demanding 100 percent quality coupled with on demand, instantaneous service levels. OK is not good enough. Perfect is expected. He is also competing in "my time, my place" marketplaces.

Information technology is not just part of an interesting tactic to improve some operational aspect of a business. It is strategic. Your customer, no matter how big or small, will fail if she does not incorporate information technology as a fundamental part of her strategic plan. This change in your customer's technology usage in turn becomes a change in her relationship with you, her technology provider. Your customer doesn't want you as her vendor, she needs you to become her business partner.

Your customer relies on information access. Information keeps her business running. Information is built into her product and delivered to her customers. She must combine product, buying experience, delivery location, customization, and more to gain and keep clients. Your customer turns to the high-tech industry to provide her with the raw material needed to integrate information into her business.

Your sales environment is changing. Buyer/seller relationships that once limited communications by funneling information flow through "proper" channels are being replaced by high-fidelity communications directly between the value providers of your company and your customers. Your role as supplier has changed from "What do you want to buy?" to "How can my company and our business partners work together with you and your business partners to increase your ability to get and keep customers?"

In turn, the sales role within your own company changes. The salesperson, who was once the information provider between you and your customer must evolve into a value-oriented knowledge provider across business partnerships. Your company has probably already begun to change its customer communications flow. More and more people in your company are in contact with more and more people within your customer base. This trend will grow until customer contact will be a daily occurrence throughout your work force.

Your competitor is changing. In the good old days, you competed with companies providing similar products to similar customers. Not anymore. Now you're competing with alternate solution sets. Your customer's platform deployment can make or break your market share and affect you more than your worst competitor ever could. Decisions to use your products may never be made if technology alternatives preclude your solution set. You may lose the sale to a competitor's way of doing things before you've even made your first sales call.

Going into the 1980s, "standards" was a word hardly mentioned by technology companies. Today, words like "open" appear within product names. A not-so-funny joke in the industry is "standards must be great because we've got so many of them." On one hand, standardization removes certain product differentiation. On the other hand, it presents the opportunity to use industry standards as a distinct selling feature.

Finally, the reliance your customer had on a single vendor has greatly diminished. Just look at what's happened in the phone industry. Once upon a time in the distant past (the early 1980s) if you wanted any external communications you called AT&T. Your communications department was one person taking extremely long lunches in between phone calls to AT&T. Expediting meant getting telephone service installed in less than two months. AT&T took care of everything. Costs weren't an issue because all rates were set in cooperation with the government. (Cooperation may be too loose a term; collusion may have been more accurate.) The notion of interconnecting anything else other than AT&T-certified equipment in the telephone network was considered to be something of a federal crime until the Carterfone decision. AT&T was definitely in a single-vendor position. That has all changed today. Almost all phone customers are reliant upon multiple vendors.

After decades of high growth and comfortable profit margins, high-technology businesses are undergoing massive changes. While the markets for high-tech products continue to grow, day-to-day life for technology companies gets more difficult. Increased global competition, lower entry barriers, standardization of technology and lower customer switching costs are taking their toll on the high profit margins our industry enjoyed during the 1970s and 1980s.

The simple sales channels of the past are gone. Simultaneously conflicting needs are present throughout our markets. In order to increase sales, we've got to deliver custom technology-based business solutions on a mass market scale. Yet, to meet customers' quality demands, each deliverable must be perfect and unique. Technology customers don't want suppliers—they want business partners. Each customer must have an individual buying experience, yet we must organize business-partnering strategies to leverage third-party reseller channels. Succeeding in today's technology markets requires new selling methods. The individual sales and sales management styles of the 80s need to adapt to the business needs of today.

Eventually your sales role will change as well. The old saying—"Change is good as long as I don't have to do anything different"—has become obsolete. There's a whole new marketplace going on out there. When you visit your customer, you may not notice the difference in their bricks and mortar. Don't be fooled because things look the same. Their building may not have changed much, but their ideas have. You've got to respond to these changes. Stepping up to meet these changing sales environments is difficult. Your own management inertia wants to keep your company operating in a status quo. Your company's sales organizations may be tactically centric but strategically isolated from your corporate core. Your internal power players—one step removed from customers—don't want to hear that anything's different. Your sales function may be treated like a separate, independent entity—even to the extent of having a separate identity. While it may once have made sense to isolate sales teams from the rest of the business, continuing to do so is a formula for disaster. In today's high-tech company, responding to today's new customer initiatives is everyone's job.

Dell Computers' meteoric rise is an excellent example of a company responding to a changing customer profile. Going against the conventional wisdom, Dell went directly to the customer with its PC-compatible products. At the same time, customers were willing to buy direct to get price savings. Dell built its reputation by providing consistent quality and service through its direct marketing sales channels.

High-tech selling is rarely treated as the core component of a high-tech company. Technology companies have been successfully operating in this mode for years. Startup companies initially are usually very sensitive to what's important to their customers because there aren't enough people to go around. Everyone in a startup gets involved with customers. Unfortunately, once a high-tech company achieves critical mass and structures its sales group, people in the core of the company often become isolated from the customer base. The function of going out and getting any significant information from customers is delegated to marketing. As the sales group grows, its own weight isolates it more and more from the own company's strategic direction. The reverse is also true. The rest of the company gets more and more isolated from the cutting edge of its account development.

Through the 1960s and early 1970s, high-tech companies had a product and manufacturing focus. Engineering produced a product, sales produced customers for the products. In the early 1980s high-tech markets exploded. High-tech companies became technology marketers. Technology markets were flooded with first-time customers. Companies began to sort the available customers into market segments and then focused on building their success through market development. They built complex product families and associated services to meet the defined needs of their customers. Through this process these companies increased functionality, built greater customer loyalty, established entry barriers, and forestalled competitive product leapfrogging. High-tech companies began spending a much greater percentage of their revenue on marketing. Their marketing influence moved into the early phases of their product development cycle to the point where marketing became the buffer between a company's value organization and its customers (see Figure 4-2).

The shift to a marketing-centric organization was important for technology companies in trying to meet the explosive growth in the markets of the 1980s. It wasn't enough to have a good idea and a good product. Technology companies had to back their product investment with substantial marketing investments to solidify customer bases. All new technology under development required a corresponding market development process to ensure success. If your company didn't do that, your competitors did—and beat you in the market.

This focus shift toward marketing helped high-tech companies deal with their strategic issues at the macro level. But this is no longer enough. Everyone does this today. Every high-tech company calls itself marketing driven. Today, a shift toward more customer involvement throughout your company is needed.

Figure 4-2   Marketing Placed Itself as the Enterprise Traffic Cop

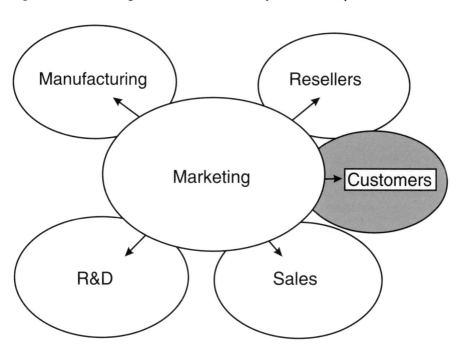

But just because a company calls itself market driven does not mean that the company is close to its customer base. It may, in fact, be quite far removed from its customers' directions because the marketing group has inserted itself between the company's knowledge workers and its customers. A high-tech company's marketing focus may create a separate reality removed from the heartbeat of the customer.

Without diminishing the importance of marketing, it's time to break the lock that marketing and sales had on customer communications and significantly ratchet up the interaction between your company's work force and that of your customer. The competitive markets of the 1990s facing today's technology end users require that all groups in your company interact with your customer. You must compete on your ability to relate to individual customer needs while still solving your mass market needs. This means meeting general market requirements side by side with specialized requirements. To do this, your organization must have direct unfiltered involvement with your customer. That means your key value providers (design, manufacturing, service, repair, support) need to be directly accessible to your customer. Stop defining your sales role as being in the middle.

Your selling role has now shifted to the more important role of managing communications (see Figure 4-3).

When you think about it, it's pretty funny that a book on selling advocates that salespeople get out of the way. But that is just the point. Your customer needs the value your company's work force provides. He needs you to manage the relationship, not be in the middle of it.

Communications flow to and from your customer base and your work force is essential whether your company sells through third parties, or sells direct. Third-party sales channels are important resources for developing many high-tech markets. But, just because you use a channel for customer fulfillment, don't be fooled into believing that your organization cannot

Figure 4-3   Some High-Tech Companies Have Begun to Form Direct Partnerships between Their Value Functions and Their Customers

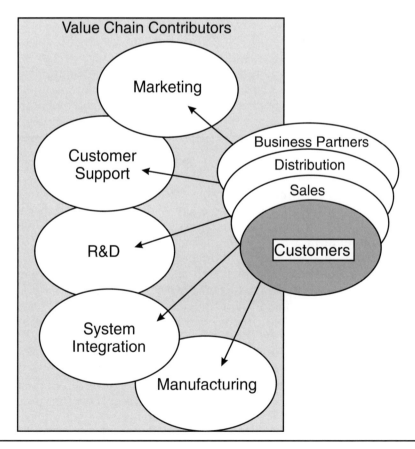

have direct customer involvement. It's even more important for companies relying on distribution channels to foster direct customer communications to establish their customer bases and to maintain continuing customer development. Accomplishing this may mean using new communications techniques that fit your channels and markets. It's not appropriate to use your channel as an excuse for eliminating your customer contact.

The notion that direct customer involvement is a primary factor for long-term success in high-technology companies runs counter to the prevailing wisdom. Direct customer involvement means people working with people about specific issues. It means your people, not your products are the key to your future. It also means that it's your job to get and keep customers even if you have a complex sales channel. Top management wants to achieve "shrink-wrapped products" that they can make in high volume and sell through leveraged, low-cost channels. They'll point to Lotus' success in the early 1980s and say, "All we have to do is build a great product, shrink wrap it, and sell it through channels." It's easy to make the mistake of thinking that standard products sold through layered channels conflict with the notion of direct customer involvement. It's easy for management to incorrectly assume that a third-party sales channel is, in fact, the customer. A management team trying to increase the use of distribution channels, reduce the amount of customer hand holding, and reduce the cost of sales will laugh you out of the room if you tell them that the way to do all that is to get more people in your company into direct daily communications with your customers. They'll throw you out and get someone with "channel experience." If that management team instead focuses its goals on increasing the size of its customer base while leveraging its distribution partnerships to operate more efficiently, it is more likely to accept the notion of restructuring customer communications flow as a way of accomplishing these goals.

You shouldn't feel caught in the middle between your company's organization and your customer's demands. You're living in the real world. It's natural that your company is reluctant to change its ways and wants to keep doing things the way they did in the 1980s. Your customer is saying to you, "I need more contact." While your company may be slow to improve its organization, you can still create an environment satisfactory to your customer. Your company will eventually face the organizational implications of the quality partnerships demanded by today's customers. In the meantime, you can begin training your company at the micro—customer by customer—level. While organizational changes take time to pan out, technology professionals can be very responsive to individual customer demands.

If you think your company won't eventually respond to these changing customer demands, think again. The industry is changing. Right now, high-tech selling is just beginning to feel the effects of IBM's leadership withdrawal and the sharp reduction of in-field organizations supporting the myriad of computer companies. These changes are creating opportunities for other technology companies to do things differently. The new direction is away from keeping the mainframe computer at the center of the universe and toward helping the customer compete in the marketplace.

Your company will eventually discover new ways of expanding communications with your customer, either because of enlightened management or a pragmatic work force. Let's face it—it's difficult for any organization to respond to events that threaten its internal structure. People in power positions are often so far removed from customer contact it's almost impossible to see when and if they'll ever know enough to change. When you examine companies with third-party distribution channels you'll often find their executives far removed from customer buying decisions. This, of course, is the complete opposite of what they need. At Microsoft, for example, members of the Excel marketing group may not meet an actual customer who has made a recent Excel buying decision for long periods of time. Certainly, their involvement with the market through conversations with editors, channel participants, salespeople, and even some corporate buyers may give them the impression that they are close to their customers, even though they are actually buffered from valuable customer input. It's easy for home office management to have the impression that they are on the cutting edge of customer involvement when, in fact, they are far removed from today's buyers.

Changing Your Third-Party Relationships

Technology companies put too much emphasis on what they expect from their third-party channels. Technology providers eventually find that their distribution channels—the ones they have been counting on to gain sales leverage—may have little to do with forming their customers' selection decisions. The value of resellers remains centered on fulfillment activities. A reseller will not invest the time and money to meet end users' growing specialization demands unless it can sustain a long-term profitable presence through fulfilling these specialty demands. The supplier may think the reseller will do something extra, when in fact the something extra costs money the reseller does not care to spend. Suppliers often discover this truth too late. If they're lucky, they may still have enough capital left to rework their channels.

NeXT provided an example of this situation. In 1988, when NeXT started marketing their products, it appointed Businessland as its sole distribution source for U.S. sales. Both companies acted as if they just pulled off the marketing coup of the century. Within two years, this strategy failed at both ends. It was not consistent with the market development needs at NeXT. Businessland could not perform the sales development needed to build the NeXT customer base. It had other problems on its hands. From a financial perspective, NeXT was saddled with the cost of sales development, with revenues lowered by dealer margins. Businessland's attempts at getting new customers for NeXT computers were ineffective. Both companies were operating with good intentions. Businessland wanted to extend its value role to market development. NeXT wanted to establish its ability to build channel loyalty. Both companies were operating inefficiently in this relationship. The NeXT target customers did not care about this relationship as it didn't add much net value to their mission. This program diverted both the supplier and the distributor from focusing on their main business.

Today's markets are different because today's customers are different. Yesterday's neophyte is today's hacker. As the personal computer market boomed in the 1980s we experienced a decade of unprecedented growth. Technology products broke out of their isolated applications arenas and affected everyone's workflow. First-time computer users outnumbered all other markets. Fifteen years ago few people had direct access to MIPs (computer cycles). Today, most people have idle MIPs on their desktops. Everyone has many access points to computers. The majority of customers are experienced buyers.

In the 1980s, the explosion of first-time business computer owners turned everyone's focus away from dependency on customized solutions toward shrink-wrapped products. Before 1980, almost all high-tech products sold required customization by someone before they were usable. That's not so anymore. The tremendous inflow of customers turned everyone's attention to mass-produced solutions sold in standard configurations through multiple layers of distribution. These first-time customers were not sure of what these products were, or why they were buying them, let alone how they were buying them. High-tech companies turned from engineers to marketers in order to create differentiation in these exploding markets. During these high-growth years, the big problem was gaining acceptance among first-time users. If you were selling networks, telephone bypass, or biotech products, your largest customer bases were first-time users. These customers were just learning how to connect what you sold to their business goals. Times have changed. To sell to today's experienced users, it is necessary to relearn customer interactions.

The difference in today's market is the shift in customer focus. The computer-illiterate business manager of the 1980s is now an experienced user out to solve a specific business problem. Today, your customer assimilates technology understanding and usage into her business planning. Your customer's demands are more complex than ever. Her purchases are mission critical. What's more, she has opinions about technology and ways to purchase technology. Even the smallest computer user has come to value systems integration. Just ask anyone who has tried to install a printer driver on a PC.

Changing Your Sales Model

These changes in your marketplace are significant. The important questions to ask are the going forward considerations:

1. What do these overall market changes mean for the way I sell?

2. How can I restructure my relationship with my customer and improve the overall quality of our relationship?

3. What are my significant value contributions to my customer and how can I amplify this value?

The key to successfully building your business in the 1990s is to reset the relationship you have with your customer so that you can simultaneously satisfy individual customer needs while leveraging market level resources. If you're waiting for your corporate home office rearrangements to create improved customer partnering relationships you must also like watching the grass grow in Scottsdale. Fortunately, you don't have to wait for an organizational edict to turn your customer relationship into a business partnership. You can recognize what's needed in the partnership and act accordingly. For instance, your company may not yet realize it needs to institute a quality process program with its top accounts. That shouldn't stop you from establishing an ongoing process management relationship with your customer. You can organize people within your company to participate with your customer in a quality improvement program without waiting for an official edict from above. Eventually, your customer will see the light and generalize what you've started.

At the heart of the relationship between you and your customer is your value contribution to your customer's business. Continuously demonstrating the many facets of your value to your customer is your number one tool for getting and building customers. From an organizational vantage point, increasing contact initiates this process. Strengthening existing lines of communications and building new ones increases your chances for long-term success.

There are three types of customer communicators among today's technology companies:

1. Those that have a strong sales and market organizations and funnel all customer activity through intermediaries

2. Visionary companies whose sales function coordinates the overall account relationship between its work force and its customer.

3. Companies caught in the middle, organized to act through their intermediary sales and marketing function while many of their customers have broken the code and built a back door channel directly to the internal organizations

Your company operates in one of these three modes. Moving away from a sales-centric communications structure takes time. The good news is that change will come and communications will increase through customer demand. When customers want change, it eventually will come.

Success in today's high-technology companies depends on understanding your company's key value contribution and fostering direct involvement between elements of your value chain and your customer. Smart sellers link each value organization within the account development process.

You are selling smart when your managers see the need for enterprise-wide customer participation and communicate their desire to see things change. Account development and customer advocacy are not activities monopolized by sales groups. Everyone can get involved. Your job is to foster these lines of communication where they can be of most value. After all, your company's work force is its most valuable and rare resource.

Many resources are available to extend your work force on a large scale. For instance, if you are a software company selling shrink-wrapped, low-cost software through Egghead, you're probably thinking that the idea of extending your value expertise directly to your customers is nonsense. At $30 per package, you can't even answer the phone call of a customer without losing money on the sale. Plus, you've put a distribution channel in place to handle this. This sort of thinking can lead to trouble. There are many things that you can do no matter what your level within this company. First, you can open up a Compuserve Forum where customers can access information about your products and where they can exchange product usage ideas. Of course, you've already thought about putting together a newsletter. Well, why not extend this idea and assemble user conferences (or maybe even geographic user luncheons)? You can also identify clusters of users to leverage your time. This idea list can go on and on.

Have you ever thought of just when you learned how to deal with customers? Some of what you do you may consider to be instinctive. But for the most part, the overall framework forming your customer interactions is something acquired during your professional lifetime. In a sense, the tools that you use have been passed on from others who went before you in business. It's difficult to substitute your traditional framework with one that's so drastically different.

Most of the models for forming sales groups within the high-tech arena stem from one variation or another of the very successful IBM sales structure of the 1960s and 1970s. The basic form is salespeople supported in the field by very technical applications specialists. The sales divisions are formed regionally with some form of secondary split along general vertical business lines—manufacturing, banking, insurance, public sector, federal government. The field sales group acts as the funnel for all information flowing back and forth to the customer. On top of this are various levels of infrastructure tasked with managing the people, people managing the managers managing the people, and some people representing different operating units of the home office. Throw in a few lawyers for contract work and human resource personnel to hire and review everyone, and you've got your basic high-tech selling model. If you are a large company you've got a lot of these people. If you are small, you have fewer but your structure may be similar.

While that model once worked well, it's time to find a better way. Look at the other end of the spectrum to find it. Think of yourself as the lone representative for your company with thousands of miles between you and your home office. How would you operate? You're all alone—no one else in the office, just you, your desk, and your customer down the street. Also imagine that your own company's products are so complex that you only know enough to articulate the reasons why prospects should buy it.

Since you're imagining all of this, why not throw in a new financial arrangement for yourself? Imagine that as the independent sales representative you earn your living entirely through sales commissions. No base. No draw. Just commissions paid after your customer realizes value from your product.

How different are the worlds of the lone sales representative versus that of the IBM rep in a huge office tower? For one thing, as the lone sales rep you would have a lot more time for selling. A tremendous amount of time-consuming, bureaucratic details erode the schedule of the IBM representative. More importantly, the lone sales rep has to be a lot closer to the customer. You live and die through each customer decision. Without the customer, you quickly realize there is no money in the equation for anyone.

As a lone rep you quickly become a pragmatist. You are not trying to be the funnel for all customer contact. You begin trying to manage information flow. You move from participation in information flow to relationship management. You've got to pick up the relationships where your company leaves off. Over time you care less and less about your own corporate structure and more and more about fulfilling the customer's business mission through a high-quality relationship. Your company begins to look more like a resource which, if properly stimulated, can respond in a known and consistent manner. You begin to define your sales job as being one of pragmatic management of the remote home office. That's a lot different than the IBM model, in which the sales force is in the middle of the value delivery chain of the organization.

The IBM model and the lone sales representative are two opposite ends of the sales spectrum. You are probably operating somewhere in between. You can take the best from both worlds by coupling the high training level of the IBM salesperson with the customer advocacy of the lone sales agent to produce the Telecommuter Sales Model. This is a value-oriented sales representative electronically coupled to the internal infrastructure, whose job it is to manage the value contribution that the supplier, in conjunction with its business partners, can make on the customers. In this model, your selling moves into its next phase, relationship management.

Your Telecommuting Sales Role is a microcosm of your company. Embodied in you are the values and culture consistent with your company. You set up the relationships through which value flows between organizations. What's different is that you can establish the bridge between your company's values and those of your customer. Your value providers are knowledge workers. By definition, this remote individual's financial dependence is in the hands of the customer.

Selling Smart

Smart sellers are able to respond to the changes going on around them. Maybe you've never thought of yourself as implementing the partnering relationship between your company and your customer (or, if you sell products through resellers, using these partnership concepts for your major resellers). But that is today's sales role. It is as though your company has initiated a joint development project with your customer and you are the sole individual selected by both organizations to manage the relationships between your company, your company's business partners, and your customer. Of chief concern in this relationship is the health and welfare of your customer. Your goal setting starts with the things that your company can do to improve your customer's business. Your customer's long-term mission sets the stage for the entire relationship. You'll set up this partnership to foster the long-term success of your customer in getting and keeping its customers.

Resource management is nothing new to the sales role. What is new is the restructuring of the current buyer/seller relationship into a business partnering relationship. What's also new is the need to identify important third parties and bring them into the partnership.

Smart sellers are relationship managers. They build long-lasting customer partnerships. Smart sellers immediately view themselves as being part of their customer's team, as a part of their customer's internal resources. They act in the best interest of amplifying the strengths of their customer's business.

Smart sellers do things differently:

1. Smart sellers empower their work force to participate in customer development.

2. Smart sellers form customer partnerships and mutually establish performance goals.

3. Smart sellers share their customer performance goals with their distribution chain and their business partners, thereby broadening their customer's partnerships.

4. Smart sellers pass their customer performance goals throughout their work force to gain everyone's participation.

5. Smart sellers make account development everyone's job.

6. Smart sellers constantly communicate.

In essence, smart sellers are quality sellers. They use quality processes to define and maintain close inter-workings between themselves and their customers. The smart seller's primary sales mission is to initiate and manage the partnering relationship between his company and his customers. (See Figure 4-4.)

While your company may not yet be operating as a smart seller, it soon can be. Smart selling will become pervasive within the technology industry of the 1990s just as systems selling took hold in the 1970s. All high-technology companies call themselves system sellers. Like a "market

**Figure 4-4	Smart Selling Is Everyone's Job**

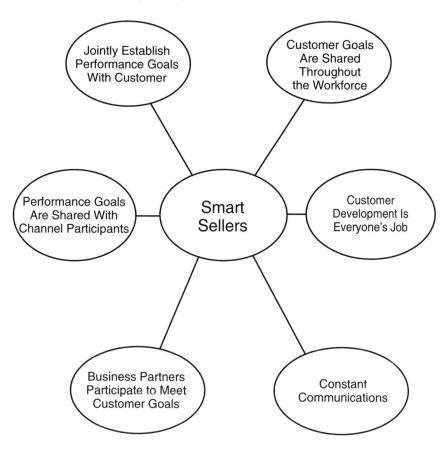

driven" company, system selling stopped being a differentiation when everyone started doing it. Smart sellers go well beyond system selling by throwing out the buyer/seller mentality and replacing it with business partnerships. Whether or not your company is yet operating as a smart seller, this shouldn't stop you from being one and establishing a partnership relationship between your company and your customer.

Staying ahead of the changes in your external market boils down to creating real-time relationships between your work force and that of your customer. How you go about doing this is dependent on the situation. Here are some ideas that can be adopted to your environment:

1. Jointly set account development goals with your customer. These goals should start from ways you and your customer can improve your customer's business and help him get and keep more customers.

2. Include members of your company's work groups in this customer goal setting process.

3. Include your resellers in your account development activity by sharing these goals with them.

4. Develop electronic links interconnecting your customer, your business partners, your distribution channel, and your work force.

5. Create feedback periods during which you can jointly discuss goal achievement and come up with ways to improve your processes.

6. Reward performance whenever possible.

You've got a difficult job ahead. External market conditions are pressuring your customer, making your job harder than ever. The good news here is that your customer needs technology more than ever before. Meeting the customer demands with the right products and services delivered in the right manner in the proper time frame is your job. Your success is dependent on increasing the communications between your company and your customer.

Chapter 5

Changing Customers

Your customer is in business to make a profit. He wants to generate long-term, above average performance on his investment of time and capital. He is coming face to face with today's information-based economy. Ubiquitous information access and limitless processing capability is forcing your customer to come to terms with high-tech's impact on his industry and causing him to rethink every aspect of his enterprise.

Your customer's customer, in turn, is relentless in her demands. Quality, once a differentiation in your customer's business, now pervades his industry and is expected by his customers. Your customer's customer wants things on her doorstep at the exact instant she needs them. If your customer misses this "Magic Moment," his competition may not. All businesses today, large and small, face these pressures.

Your customer is restructuring his value chain to eliminate pipeline delay and to emphasize his company's unique contribution. He is eliminating internal operations that add little or no unique value and replacing these with partnership strategies. He wants to be in a position where he adds the most value with the least amount of delay. Your customer wants your technology to amplify his company's value.

In his own unique way, your customer must deal with incorporating technology into his value chain. To meet the needs of today's competitive environment, your customer's success is dependent on his technology plan. While the manner in which a business decides how to deal with these changes differs among firms, the underlying tendencies are similar. Ten basic trends influence your customer's restructuring as he prepares for the future. It is not a coincidence that each trend is, in turn, influenced by your customer's technology deployment.

Ten Trends Affecting Your Customer's Business

1. Flattening of the organization

2. Cycle time reduction

3. Reduction of product development cycles

4. Mass customization

5. Shift toward electronic markets

6. 100 percent quality norm

7. Increase in direct customer involvement

8. New work force compensation methods

9. Work group domination

10. Empowerment to the knowledge worker

These top ten trends influence your customer. Technology provides the underlying current supercharging the jolt of these trends. Your customer's use of technology is fundamental in strategic planning. During the 1980s only a few businesses used technology as part of their core business plan. In the 1990s, all businesses—small and large—include technology planning in their strategic decision making. Managers can no longer get by with a "hands off" attitude on technology. This type of management will disappear forever.

From Tool to Strategy

Selling high-technology products and services has always been a lot of fun. It's even more exciting today because technology usage is fundamental to the success of most businesses around the world. The first business applications carved out by technology products were all stand alone. Your customer had to manipulate both the input to get it in the right format for the technology to process and the output to use it. Technology products of the past were specialized tools requiring experts. Today that has all changed. Your customer can deploy technology products throughout his work force and incorporate these products into his products and services. Technology products, not brick and mortar, form the load-bearing walls of tomorrow's successful enterprises.

What's more, applications across an industry interrelate (or can be made to interrelate) worldwide. Your customer's supplier in Hong Kong and his sales outlet in New York City will be dynamically sharing critical information. Today's complex enterprise wide applications will become the primary nodes in tomorrow's industry wide, high-tech power grid.

While some of your customers may be grappling with how to come to terms with today's technology, there are still companies that have not yet begun asking themselves these questions. It is as though they want the world to slow down and not change at all. Even though you may not be able to sell them anything, you may consider saying a little prayer for them. A business that does not consider the implications of technology is letting its competition prepare its long-term strategic plan. Obviously, this is a formula for failure.

Your customers' desire to use technology within their business goals presents you with a new type of customer and many new opportunities. While just a few years ago you would frequently hear your customer say that top management doesn't want him dealing with technology, it's relatively rare to hear that today. American business is killing off its technology ostriches that hide their heads from their companies' inevitable use of technology. The only first-generation computer users left today are either religious isolationists or kids under the age of five. No one in business can escape using high-tech products. Today's technology customers are nth generation users—a computer-literate group that expects big returns on their technology investments.

Single application solutions gave way to enterprise wide platforms. These in turn evolved to industry wide technology integration. Once upon a time, computers were called upon to improve isolated functions within an organization. Today, high-technology can change the nature of an entire industry. Your customers have buildings made of brick and mortar. Their industry is housed in a virtual building, constructed of silicon and biotech, though, not steel. Your customers compete for industry market share in a real-time global economy. Technology can supercharge their growth.

Why has technology pervaded industry? There are several reasons for this. First and foremost, today's economy is information-based. And today, most forms of information may be converted to an electronic representation. This same information may then be manipulated and massaged into representations that have special value to others.

If, for instance, you are in a car and you don't know how to reach your destination, a map is a handy device. But, to get the most from your map you must be able to first locate your present position. Today you do all of this yourself. Products are already available to let you electronically determine your position to within a few feet, automatically feed this into an electronic mapping system, and use your computer to suggest alternative directions to your destination. Although this function may be only somewhat useful in your own day-to-day life, this technology can open new competitive frontiers in the package delivery industry.

Your customer cannot ignore how pervasive technology is. While he may argue the degree to which technology affects his business sector, he still must deal with the importance of dealing with technology at the strategic level. He cannot get away from it. Everyone, everywhere in American business is influenced by technology. From the small to large. Legal to illegal. Production to service.

Furthermore, technology has spread throughout the education system. If you are currently the proud parent of a high school student, you probably bought or soon will buy a computer, FAX, and a copier. Students who don't learn to express their ideas electronically will be at a disadvantage in the twenty-first century.

The baby boomers taking over the management reins of today's major corporations are all to some degree computer literate. Given that top management will "speak the language" of technology, business will be pervaded by technology.

A not-so-subtle shift happens when technology literates enter the management ranks of American businesses. Technology stops being an add-on and becomes intertwined within the business itself. The question stops being "How can this stuff save us money?" and becomes "What technology investments are consistent with our long-term business plans?" Technology usage within these top business trends produces a new type of customer opportunity.

TREND #1: Flattening of the Organization

For a few hundred thousand dollars your customer can get one of the big eight consulting firms to come in and suggest structural changes. These suggestions follow similar patterns—reduce middle management, eliminate information workers (jobs that either change the medium of information or jobs that apply rule-based logic to information), invest in knowledge workers (jobs that add value to information), and eliminate routine operations.

Electronic links will empower managers by increasing their communications capability. If eight people reported to yesterday's manager, tomorrow's manager will have twenty. The biggest challenge a manager must face is communicating to employees. In yesterday's world, strategic advantage meant physical things. Land, coal, oil shipping routes all added up to industrial strengths. Bureaucracies grew to protect, manage, and leverage these strengths. In tomorrow's world, ideas are your customer's natural resource. Information-empowered workers are public enemy number one to a bureaucracy. Your customer excels when his workers' ideas are empowered through information technology.

TREND #2: *Cycle Time Reduction*

As John Madden, the football commentator, might say about running a business, "It's pretty simple—stuff comes in and stuff goes out. You've got to collect more money for the stuff that goes out than the stuff that comes in." The process that your customer goes through to take the "stuff" he gets in and convert it to the "stuff" his eventual customers pay for is his value chain. The time period it takes to convert input "stuff" into output "stuff" is the time length of his value chain—his cycle time. Your customer's industry has well-known averages for these time periods. For instance, in the paper industry, the time from when the tree gets cut until the customer is writing on the paper (or perhaps the time from when the seedling is planted until the reader is reading the book) is the cycle time for a paper manufacturer. Your customer wants to reduce the amount of time it takes to perform its value contribution for its customers. Reducing cycle time is big business today. Everything improves when industries reduce their value chain time periods. Quality improves. Time to market improves. Product development plans are more accurate. Customer satisfaction goes up. Value chain accelerations maximize your customer's ability to leverage his company's unique value contribution.

Your customer will turn to technology to find innovative ways to leverage his company's value and reduce its value chain. Doctor's offices will electronically connect with medical labs to get test results quickly. Auto manufacturers will use EDI (Electronic Data Interchange) to create electronic links to their suppliers. Your customer can eliminate major chunks of time from his value chain by integrating electronic links within his value process. For instance, a customer trying to redo his company's computer systems has a choice. He can continue to use his existing methods (otherwise known as paving the cowpaths), or he can rework the systems. Vendors selling to this customer must be part high-tech sales and part business consultant.

TREND #3: *Reduction of Product Development Cycles*

Imagine two identical companies in the same market with just one difference—one can bring to market five new products over a 10-year period while the other can bring out only three. Which company will be more successful? Most likely, the company introducing a new product every two years will have a much greater chance of succeeding. Its designers will be more experienced. Its manufacturing groups will be more adaptive. The company will be taking fewer risks in product planning since it doesn't have to be as accurate in its long-range trend forecasts. Its market research will not have to predict customer needs as far into the future. With more product introductions and more adaptive manufacturing, the company will be able to focus special products on special needs. Whether the product is a physical entity or a financial service, businesses have a lot to gain by significantly reducing their product to market time frame.

Have you ever thought about positioning your sale in terms of your customer's reduced time to market? Why not? If your customer currently takes 30 months to go from product idea to introduction, can you take 90 days out of this process? If you can, you are helping them get to market in 10 percent less time. This alone can be more important than anything else your product may have to offer. Technology reduces the turnaround time associated with bringing new products to market. Technology investments impacting new product creation cycles may result in significant market share increases.

TREND #4: Mass Customization

Your customer's customers are unique. They want goods and services on their terms. They want products that are perfectly suited to their needs. They want the "custom" put back in customer. Business customers demand specialization. Even if the actual product is somewhat standard, the service surrounding that product must be customized.

This presents a dilemma for your customer. On the one hand, standardization helps achieve economies of scale. On the other hand, customers crave uniqueness. Your customer is trying to figure out how to marry these two opposing viewpoints. Technology may be the answer. Oldsmobile offers an interesting example of how specialization can be added after a product is produced. The company's customer care program provides an 800 service number to any customer with a problem. You simply call and they'll take care of the rest. What's interesting about this is the way Oldsmobile is using the phone system and its computer network to repackage a standard automobile into a custom appliance.

We haven't even begun to see the differences high-tech changes will make to standard, mass-produced products. Laser cutters coupled with computer design terminals have the ability to let a shirt manufacturer create custom-fitted shirts right on its mass-production line. It is possible for the clothing retailer to have a full history of the sizes and previous purchases of the client to provide better advice on his next purchase. (It is not hard to imagine a clothing retailer with a computer terminal that visually displays a closet with all the customer's past purchases as a way to assist the salesperson in making suggestions and preparing custom orders.) So the shirt manufacturer can electronically receive orders directly to its production line from its retailer for custom tailored shirts and ship them the same day.

TREND #5: Shift toward Electronic Markets

An array of buying and selling events naturally interrelate. The original purchase of an auto relates to the customer's future service requirements. Travel purchases for airlines, hotel, and rental cars are naturally clustered. The health care industry is filled with transactions that are linked together. Furthermore, the buying and selling clusters in consumer and commercial markets are increasing daily.

As buying and selling clusters form, they may be electronically integrated throughout an industry's value chain. Imagine an industry whose use of technology is so pervasive that information entering the system at any one point is forever accessible! Today's best example is the travel industry where buyers and sellers of travel services meet in an electronic marketplace. These sorts of electronic markets will become the norm throughout the economy. Your customers may soon be in a position where electronic markets are fundamental to their success. This opens them up to an entirely new world of technology-based business strategies.

TREND # 6: 100 Percent Quality Norm

Quality is no longer a differentiation. It is an expectation. Your customer cannot participate in today's markets without providing quality at every level. While the details of quality are unique to each business, the general tendencies are similar. First, your customers will reduce the number of suppliers, allowing them to spend more time with their remaining suppliers. The next step is to open up their value chains to enable suppliers to participate on an equal level with their own work forces. Finally, they will forge electronic links with their suppliers to enrich their partnerships. Table 5-1 gives a capsule view of these steps.

The shift toward quality occurred in U.S. businesses in the 1980s. While the individual actions of each producer differed, the general tendency toward higher quality meant raising management's expectations, reducing the number of suppliers, reducing and eliminating work in process inventories, and forming closer partnerships with the remaining suppliers. Busi-

Table 5-1   Your Customer's Four Steps to Quality

Step 1	Reduce the number of suppliers
Step 2	Build partnerships with the remaining suppliers
Step 3	Open up value chain activity to suppliers
Step 4	Forge electronic links with suppliers and work force

nesses became more tightly coupled as they strove to increase their quality levels. Before these shifts, your customers acted independently of their vendors. They dealt with one another through separate and distinct channels. After the move to quality, your customers begin partnering with their important suppliers, and information technology provides the infrastructure for empowering these partnerships (see Figure 5.3).

TREND #7: Increase in Direct Customer Involvement

Companies have been eliminating their "back offices." A greater percentage of your customer's work force is directly involved with its customers than just a few years ago. Your customer's employees who have direct contact with customers must have access to the information necessary to properly interpret their customers' requests. Each "transaction" must be available at their fingertips. What's more, this must be an enterprise wide resource.

There is an interesting conflict that comes up as greater percentages of people get involved with customer interaction. Satisfaction is inversely related to the number of different people with whom a customer must deal—the fewer, the better. So, on the one hand, your customer is competing by increasing customer contacts. On the other, the company must take care to put a knowledgeable person in front of its customer.

TREND #8: New Work Force Compensation Methods

Your customer is revamping the way he compensates his work force. A decade ago, annual reviews with merit increases were widespread. A decade from now they will be extinct. Taking their place will be a comprehensive set of rewards that link your customer's work groups to their corporate mission. The net effects will be a lowering of the base salary as a total percentage of earnings and a corresponding increase in incentives for individual and work group contribution to the value of the business. These incentives will be computed and paid weekly, monthly, quarterly, and annually.

To enable performance-oriented compensation packages, your customer wants to reward and increase his work force's value contribution. Their information technology structure will be called upon to become the scorekeeper as these new incentive programs come on-line.

TREND #9: Work Group Domination

Work groups began taking over the factory floor when manufacturers moved to quality processes. This worked so well that work groups already form the dominant power base in many of today's companies. Work group orientation is moving from its manufacturing origins throughout your customer's entire enterprise. Even your customer's technology management team will use work group methods to create its next generation systems.

Work group management is the 1990s version of the management grid of the 1970s. (If you were working in the 1970s, you've probably learned not to mention grid management in public.) The difference is the availability of information technology to allow work groups to function across an enterprise. The management grid system didn't succeed because the electronic information resources in the 1970s and 1980s were unable to support it. Work groups work and they work well. They can only be widespread if information technology is enterprise wide.

TREND #10: Empowerment to the Knowledge Worker

Your customer is coming to terms with his company's unique value and is investing in workers who add value—today's knowledge workers. Knowledge workers are your customer's keys for applying his company's unique value. To be effective, knowledge workers need access to information across the enterprise. New communications platforms are beginning to facilitate knowledge worker participation within enterprise wide and even industry wide information exchange. In store for the knowledge worker is access to more information, increased processing power and greater communications capacity to manipulate this information.

Figure 5-1 illustrates these trends.

These top ten trends influence every business in today's economy. The degree to which individual trends are absorbed differs by industry and company. Within an industry, various firms incorporate these trends differently. The question is not whether or not your customers are responding to

Figure 5-1   Top Ten Customer Trends

the pressures of today's economy, but *how* they are responding. The net effect is that today your customers are changing and modifying their role within their industry's economy.

Your customer is under considerable competitive pressures. These ten business trends encourage use of technology in a new role. This will change the nature of technology supplier relationships. This, in turn, will change your sales role.

Whatever Happened to Good Old-fashioned Cost Cutting?

A recent news account about the ongoing restructuring and massive cutbacks at General Motors suggested that General Motors' primary motivation was cost cutting. It's not that simple anymore. Today's corporate restructuring is centered on eliminating operations inconsistent with adding value. Cost cutting—at least the cost cutting we have come to know over the past twenty years—is not the reason your customer and your customer's industry are restructuring. Your customer is looking at his own entire value chain and his company's relationship to its industry. Your customer wants to restructure in order to best leverage his company's value contribution. This, in turn, leads to more efficient resource allocation and improved long-term industry position. Lower operating costs result after your customer focuses on today's real issues of adding value.

As your customer's role changes, you must change your own role. How you sell is as important as what you sell. Your customer wants much more from information technology today than 10 and 20 years ago. Back then, it was an application-specific world. Multiple applications were rarely linked. Today, your customer is dealing on an enterprise wide and industry wide scale.

Quality Is Pervasive

Your customer is using quality practices throughout his organization. Quality processes that started in manufacturing are taking hold of other parts of your customer's business practices. It's not unusual to walk into any conference room in any of your customer's buildings and see posters on quality reminding employees of their pledge of allegiance to quality. Companies have sent their entire work force to quality process courses. Your customer wants to extend the ideas that worked so well in manufacturing to his company's entire value chain.

The factor that will affect you most in your customer's move toward quality will be new work group processes. Your customer is decreasing the number of suppliers to allow more time to work with the suppliers that remain. Quality "out" goes up when quality "in" goes up. Now, he may want you as his business partner making you part of the extended work group. Becoming part of the work group puts you in the position of sharing the same performance goals. You become your customer's business partner. Your customer's drive to quality has changed your role from "selling" to "partnership."

Before and After Picture

Your customer's decreasing number of suppliers has other long-term implications. You may already be a value added supplier and have the ability to transfer this relationship and become a member of your customer's quality team. If you are currently a second- or third-tier supplier, you run the risk of being left out. You may need to develop an alternate way to remain part of your customer's value chain, or drop out of the picture completely by developing a supply position where you are a subcontractor with a supplier your customer has chosen. This may actually be the best of all worlds for you and your customer. Higher quality suppliers may find it necessary to consolidate customers. You can expand your business channel to include third parties that perform direct customer integration functions. These third parties may act in a similar capacity for multiple vendors, thereby completing the customer fulfillment processes across a variety of requirements. For instance, in the semiconductor industry, industrial distributors have always played an important role with second- and third-tier semiconductor customers. They now have an opportunity to play an extensive role within the supply chains of the largest semiconductor customers.

It's Not Just a Systems Sell Anymore

Sometime during the 1970s, system selling ideas became the strategy "du jour" in high-tech selling. We gave it many names including solutions selling, applications selling, consultative selling, and the system sale. Systems selling continues to be the strategy that high-tech sellers believe gives them a competitive differentiation. While systems selling may be useful, it does not make you unique.

Almost everyone in high-tech considers himself a systems seller (and considers his competitors component sellers). Have you ever asked "What is a systems seller?" People tell you they are systems sellers because they sell their product and services from an "in situ" perspective. They'll build features and services for improving the customer's experience. They may also be hoping their customers don't notice some of the uglier aspects of their product, like high prices or missing features. You're a systems seller when you tell your customer that the systems aspect of your product mitigates the fact that you've got a high-priced/low-performance product and that you really are the lowest cost vendor. That's pretty slick. You're a systems seller when you can spin that yarn without visiting a priest before your next sales call.

If you think systems selling is special, you should ask "Who isn't a systems seller?" Most non-systems sellers are technology startup companies fresh out of their R & D labs with a hot new product. They haven't been around long enough to learn to spell systems selling. But look at some of the results. Dell Computers, one of the fastest growing Fortune companies, is the best example of a component seller taking advantage of the systems-sellers in its market. While its competitors spin their system selling webs, Dell sells lots of computers. So perhaps being a "non-systems seller" isn't so bad.

In the real world, the truth about systems selling depends mostly on what your customer wants. If you're selling resistors to IBM, a systems sale probably won't be too believable. Selling turn key, multi-user computer systems to dentists often is a systems sale. You can probably divide your own customer base into two categories—those that want you to operate in a systems selling mode, and those that don't. The difference is in your customer's own perspective for completing the "last mile" effort.

The point is that systems selling is important to many companies in high-technology. Being a systems seller can be the way toward building an important high-tech company. Not being a systems seller can also be the right path to building an important high-tech company. Today's technology markets are open to both approaches. This isn't a right way versus wrong way situation.

Systems sellers brag about the benefits their holistic thinking has on customers. Systems sellers want to move their customer's buying criteria from feature-by-feature comparisons to "in use" owner benefits. Even if your product is not the fastest in the world, does it get the application done within the appropriate amount of time? When sales are up, management declares its "system selling" approach to be working. If sales are not up to expectation, the sales force needs to find a rock to hide under. The sales department blames its lost sales on product deficiencies. Sales managers, convinced that these lost orders are due to their salespeople's lack of system selling skills, start sending their salesforce back to solutions selling courses. However, the reason for these lost orders may be that your customer is not sharing the same "systems" definition of his company's problem.

Systems selling works best when buyer and seller agree on the things that they need surrounding the product. When you don't have this agreement, the seller is selling things the buyer isn't buying. Too often, sellers use system selling as a way to cover up the less than perfect nature of their product lines. In some cases systems sellers have built too much infrastructure into their definition of a system and their new products are shackled by the deficiencies of their legacy products. DEC's new Alpha Series processor family is a good example. These new computers may be excellent products. They are easier to use and much more reliable than DEC's older computers. DEC customers will need just a fraction of the installation and on-site service than they once needed. One of the strongest selling propositions of DEC, their cradle-to-grave support, deteriorates now that they have a product that will probably need only one on-site service call over five years. Meanwhile, as customers retire DEC's older products, the economies of scale supporting DEC's field service group diminish, further stressing DEC's profitability. DEC needs to devise ways to prevent their infrastructure from burdening potential Alpha customers.

There's nothing wrong with systems selling. If it works for you, keep doing it. If you are successful without it, you probably don't need it. Systems selling, once a sales strategy, is today merely a tactic. However, you do need to have a strategy for dealing with modern customers that goes well beyond the solutions selling techniques of yesteryear.

Sales 2000

Your customer's movement from application-specific thinking to enterprise wide strategies and the eventual move toward industry wide use of technology changes your selling role. You can continue to treat each selling opportunity as a set of isolated activities, or you can directly participate in your customer's value chains and that of the industry. In the short term, either path will produce success. Your long-term success depends on your ability to contribute to your customer's long-term, above average performance.

Your high-technology sales role needs to expand from locating sales situations to creating the framework for the promotion of enterprise wide and industry wide opportunity development. Finding and closing new customers will always be key sales roles. What has also become crucial is your ability to penetrate your customer's entire enterprise and entire industry. Your selling co-participants expand to include key members of your value work force, your distribution channels, your business partners, as well as other participants in your customer's value chain.

As your customer is assembling his strategy for competing in the twenty-first century, you should consider how you will adapt your selling methods for the year 2000. Your customer is past thinking in application-specific terms and is well on his way toward treating technology across his company's enterprise. Technology and strategy commingle in his vocabulary. Next will come dealing with industry wide technological issues in an attempt to gain competitive advantages through expansion of technology strategy. Developing an enterprise wide focus will put you on equal footing with today's customer. Expanding your thinking one step further to encompass your customer's entire industry will make you eligible to participate in your customer's business model for survival in the twenty-first century.

Changing the Way You Sell

The first step for restructuring your customer relationship is to familiarize yourself with his current business model. Look at what's going on around you. Your customer is in the midst of a major structural change. The company needs its key suppliers to follow in step with the changes it has initiated. The opportunity is there for you to change your role from supplier to business partner. To do this, you'll need to reorient yourself around your customer's business goals.

Your customer is rebuilding to leverage value contribution. His changes involve replacing areas in which his work force adds little substantial value with long-term business partnerships with suppliers, distributors, and complementary market providers which are in a better position to provide important services. Your customer's new strategies depend on the alignment of a mutually cooperative cluster of associations. Long-term success depends on these business partnering strategies.

These changes in your customer's business strategy can open up terrific opportunities for you and your company. You can utilize these changes to become partners with your customer. Furthermore, the changes your customer wants to make depend entirely on successful use of technology. Your customer will become even more dependent on technology than he is today. To successfully participate with your customer you must adopt his framework for cooperation. You must work as if you were part of his business.

Selling Across All Dimensions

During the past two decades, selling high-technology was done on an application basis. Purchase decisions were done on a case-by-case basis. Justification frameworks were considered comprehensive when they compared long-term ownership costs for alternate solutions. Individual, stand alone applications formed the majority of the end user market. There was very little integration of these applications within a department and almost none across the enterprise. Communications networks were more useful for providing access to an application across a wide area than for sharing information across an enterprise. OEM high-tech sales considered only the costs and manufacturing complexity of the potential product.

High-technology companies developed efficient sales capability for purchases of single applications. Successful sales groups excelled at isolating applications within their accounts and converting these to orders. Independent third-party sales groups that specialized in particular customer usage became important leverage devices for high-tech companies.

On the buying side, technology customers learned to buy technology on an application-specific basis. Their procurement teams isolated the application so that it could reasonably be solved. In fact, one of the most important jobs of a data-processing department was to purchase and manage these applications.

Thus both buyer and seller separated their technology applications specialties from their core business units. The high-tech sales departments consisted of sales, application technical support, and service. The buyer's side consisted of systems designers and MIS production management. Seller and buyer met in just one dimension. The application design and production requirements formed the framework for this relationship. (See Figure 5-2.)

This model worked well for over two decades. It was very efficient for you and your customer. Sellers could profitably manage the care and feeding of the sales requirement and buyers could afford internal support staffs. This process worked so long as seller and buyer operated around well-defined applications.

In one-dimensional selling, seller and buyer interacted across a single dimension. This model led to problems because the relationships did not scale well when the user's needs became more complex. Complex applica-

Figure 5-2   One-Dimensional Selling Limits Communications between Buyers and Sellers

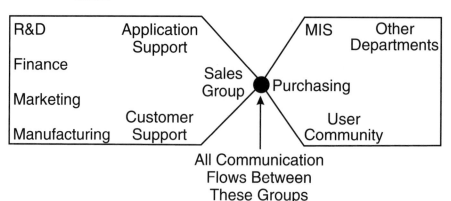

tions, problems that span multiple departments, enterprise wide electronic infrastructures, and industry wide computing all contributed to the eventual breakdown of single-dimensional selling. Just stating these problems is complex. Solving them is even harder.

These one-dimensional sales relationships did not scale well on the seller's side either. Bigger, more widely dispersed applications required high degrees of cooperation among the supplier's own staff. Often, your internal organization was the biggest barrier you faced when selling across an enterprise.

The reason single-dimensional selling was so popular is that it didn't take rocket scientists to make it work. You could hire a horde of salespeople and fire the ones who didn't come back with a briefcase full of orders after a few months. Managing these organizations was also simple since the seller was not dealing with complex buying problems.

In one-dimensional selling, excellent individual contribution leads to success. Group efforts take time and hardly improve the seller's overall business position.

The failure of the single dimensional framework occurs when your customer begins to realize that use of technology is an enterprise wide issue. Application planning is done in the context of an overall enterprise wide technology use plan. Your customer's usage needs now are no longer just business improvement tactics. Enterprise planning forces your customer to drive technology adaptation throughout his company's value chain. Once your customer starts operating in this mode, he will begin to encourage you to change your selling approach. He will seek to form quality partnerships dedicated to mutually agreed business goals with all of his vendors.

Some technology markets have reached the point where single-dimensional relationships are no longer effective and both buyer and seller create new frameworks for success. Other markets are just beginning to deal with these issues.

When one-dimensional relationships run out of steam, buyers and sellers begin to extend the scope of their relationship to include other parts of their organization. Your customer forms a work group consortium among his suppliers. The selected vendors participate firsthand with the planning of technology deployment strategies. As the seller on such a team, you may begin to expose your customer to more knowledegable workers in your organization, thereby making your experts more available to your customer.

Reshaping the relationship between you and your customer results in more direct access on both sides. Your customer's technology planning now gets its leadership from the work group level. The MIS people who once operated in the middle now become the catalysts in the technology process.

**Figure 5-3   Two-Dimensional Selling Involves the Supplier's Entire Organization
Interacting with the Buyer's Organization**

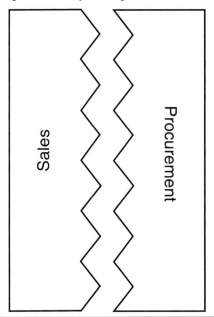

By reshaping your relationships, your customer's work group can be in direct contact with your work force (see Figure 5-3).

On the selling side, you must start operating at a different level. As a seller, you become aware of your customers' long-term enterprise technology planning so that you can relate your solutions to this model. You also can play an active role at developing these plans. Within the work group planning process, a partnering atmosphere is established providing technology vendors the option of long-term participation. Both sides benefit from this relationship. Buyers get long-term technology platforms tailored for their needs. Sellers get long-term relationships.

The next level of involvement comes about as buyers begin extending their technology usage to incorporate their important business partners, including their key suppliers and their customers. Your customer's focus shifts from enterprise wide to industry wide planning. In this phase, the business partners are now included in the definition of the enterprise. Along with this, the technology platforms of the business partners have become part of your customer's platform. Sellers also can have their significant business partners participate in their customer partnerships.

Figure 5-4   Selling in Three Dimensions

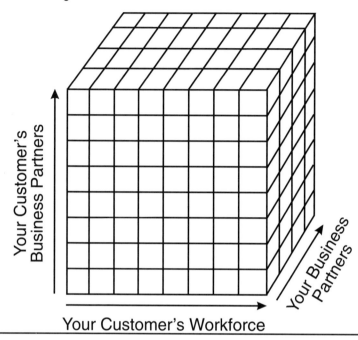

Your Customer's Business Partners

Your Business Partners

Your Customer's Workforce

The one-dimensional buyer/seller relationship now changes to a three-dimensional model (see Figure 5-4). You, along with your business partners, provide enabling enterprise technology to your customer and your customer's business partners.

You are rapidly heading toward three-dimensional selling. Vertical markets, the backbone for high-technology sales, are being subdivided along technology platforms. For instance, tens of thousands of suppliers to General Motors will have unique technology requirements based on their participation within General Motors' technology framework. If you are selling to a General Motors supplier, you will soon have to interrelate your technology platform to your customer's daily interaction with General Motors. If you are selling to law firms, your customers will want your products to eventually interact with their clients over extensive, wide-area networks. Your future success is dependent on successfully combining your business partners with your customer's business partners. What once was "my company selling to your company" has become "my company and my company's partners enabling your business and your business partners" to meet and exceed your business goals. Your customer's work group is the vehicle ensuring success.

Intel, which makes the processors that drive many personal computers, does an enviable job when it comes to three-dimensional selling. The company began 1993 by reclaiming the title of the world's largest semiconductor company for the United States. While Intel ships products directly to PC manufacturers, it includes PC users in its marketing campaigns. Intel does this by promoting the benefits of i86-based systems. It promotes the fact that using products with Intel processors will extend your laptop's battery life and its instant on/off feature eliminates boot-up and shut down sequences. It also sells a family of performance add-in chips directly to PC owners to dramatically improve overall system performance. Plus, Intel works closely with i86-based applications developers to increase the value of i86-based personal computers through the availability of tens of thousands of compatible software applications. Their message to end users is that an i86-based computer is the best value around. Intel sends a very clear message to end users. (See Figure 5-5.)

In one dimension, Intel is selling directly to PC manufacturers and competing with other makers of i86-based processor chips. In another, Intel is working to keep application developers assured of efficient development environments and financially rich markets. In still another dimension, Intel

Figure 5-5   Intel Directly Markets the Benefits of Intel Processors to Consumers and Software Designers

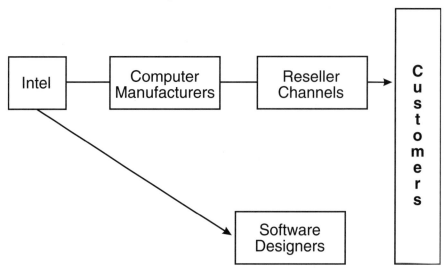

We're putting i486™ technology in a whole new light.

Now that we've introduced our i486™ SL processor to the world of mobile computing, you'll never look at notebooks the same. That's because, for the first time, you can have the performance of a true 32-bit i486 DX chip to go, with added features to help you garner maximum power from your mobile computer.

One unique feature, our Intel SL technology, actually conserves precious battery life by routing power only to where it's needed. Battery life is further extended through the i486 SL processor's low 3.3-volt operation—which gives you up to an extra hour of computing. Plus, a unique power management feature retains data and instructions even when power is off.

Perhaps more important, however, is the fact that the i486 SL processor is just the latest step in Intel's long-term strategy to provide mobile computer users with uncompromised desktop performance. Together with our ExCA™ cards such as faxmodems and LAN adapters, Intel's mobile processors will give your notebook more versatility. It's no surprise that leading notebook manufacturers are putting Intel SL technology in the spotlight.

To learn more about the new i486 SL processor, call us at 1-800-228-4549, and let us shed some light on the latest in mobile computing.

©1993 Intel Corporation. Reprinted with permission from Intel.

is selling performance enhancements for its products to improve user satisfaction.

Technology Sales Investments Are Changing

The cost of selling high-technology products has steadily increased over the
past ten years. Each year, you need to increase your company's direct involvement with your customers. Your initial customer contacts are made
through direct sales contacts or through your third-party selling assistants.
Your follow-on customer contacts come from within your own organization. These include support, planning, engineering, production contacts, as
well as building links between your customers and your business partners.

This increased customer involvement seems to run contrary to the
prevailing wisdom. Your management may be reluctant to involve its non-
sales work force directly with customers. They immediately relate direct
customer contact to higher business costs. They fear the high sales costs at
companies like IBM and DEC. But don't confuse the problems of these big
companies with yours. The IBMs of the world face incredibly high sales
costs because they have tremendous bureaucracies and use ancient field
sales organization models. Unless you are part of one of these giants, you
don't have the same situation. Their rules and constraints don't apply to
you. You're able to promote direct customer involvement using state-of-the-
art techniques. Electronic access tools such as automatic call processing,
voice mail, on-line information services, bulletin boards, and electronic mail
can increase your ability to provide direct customer access while lowering
your overall cost structure. Today, the lowest cost provider can simultaneously have the greatest degree of contact between its work force and that of
its customer.

Creating a capable account development team for your company requires a unique set of choices. Your account development team is not a
replacement of your fulfillment channel. If you use a third-party VAR channel to sell your product, your work force still needs to participate in account
development. The idea isn't to replace what you've got, but to enrich it with
a new organizational model. You must establish the capability for members
of your organization to improve your customer's business. This requires an
investment in training, equipment, and building your infrastructure, all in
the interests of supporting your work force's ability to directly increase
your total market share.

Account Development Is Job #1

Identifying these changes in technology customers and, in turn, identifying the need to change high-technology account development does not mean your company needs a direct sales force. What is needed is to create direct customer involvement strategies across your work force promoting account development. Sales groups must move aside from participating in the main-stream of value fulfillment to managing the interactions between your work force and that of your customer. Sales groups with their channel partners, in turn, can begin selling at the enterprise level.

Your customer spends money on technology and expects something in return. He wants to gain something from his investment. Your customer is trying to improve his company's fundamental business position through its technology acquisition. Understanding your customer's long-term strategic technology investment decision is your key to understanding what role your organization can play.

Part III

Adding Value

Explaining your company's value is the most important part of high-tech selling. Smart sellers understand that customers will pay price premiums for value they understand. You are not just trying to explain any value. The value that means the most to you is the one that distinguishes you from your competitors—your distinctive value (also known as your differentiated value). Distinctive value is where you can add value to your customer, while your competitors cannot. It's not enough to explain how your customer will benefit from your product. You've got to show why your company's version of the product is substantially better for use within your customer's target application arena than any other offering. This is how you become unique in your customer's eyes.

Understanding your company's value in the eyes of your customer is important to selling high-tech products. You first must be able to communicate your distinctive value to your customers. Then, over time, you'll want to find ways to extend your differentiated value so that you further increase your competitive advantage. Specialization often becomes the avenue high-tech sellers use to gain the greatest degree of differentiation from their competition.

You offer distinctive value to your customer. However, your competitor also offers distinctive value. From your customer's perspective, you are each unique. Your customer must choose the supplier he believes presents the value proposition most suited for his company's needs.

Both You and Your Competitor Offer Distinctive Value

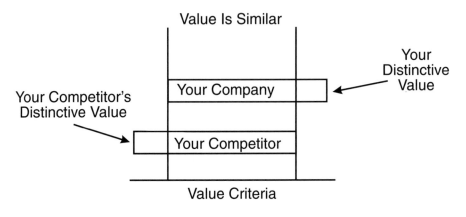

Chapter 6

Establishing
Distinctive Value

High-tech products create value for users. The more your products and services improve your customer's long-term profit position, the greater your value contribution. Your customer's potential for improving his company's business position determines his investment level. Too often, technology sales and marketing people avoid the issue of value. It's easier to understand tangibles such as product price, performance, and competitive comparisons than to deal with the abstract areas such as a product's impact on long-term profit improvements across a variety of customers. Smart sellers deal with value head on. They confront all of the issues that surround value. Selling smart means clearly establishing the value of what your company does in your customer's eyes. But simply determining your value contribution is not enough. It's your job to compete using your differentiated (distinctive) value. Your differentiated value is what you do to contribute to your customer's success. When your customer compares you and a competitor, you are measured by your distinctive value. Your pricing premiums are largely determined by your differentiated value.

Value is an enigma. Although establishing value is paramount for your long-term sales success, the concept is not definable. You cannot see it, touch it, or feel it. When you establish value, you distinguish yourself as part of your customer's successes and get compensated based on your contribution. When you do not establish value, your cost structure and your competitors determine your price.

According to the dictionary, value is "An amount considered to be a suitable equivalent for something else." That's not very helpful for selling high-tech products and services. As a high-tech supplier you must express value in terms of how much your differentiated product contributes to improving your customer's business.

Value is an abstraction. You can talk about value in general terms all day long and never get to the specifics of value in your customer's situation. This abstract nature of value makes it difficult to understand and even more difficult to articulate. Establishing value for a new high-tech product is even harder than for existing products. With an existing product class, your existing customers have told you how much value they derive from your products and you can repeat their success stories to your new prospects. But with a new product, everyone may be asking the sixty-four-dollar question "Why should I buy it? I know what it does but why do I need it?" With a new product class the answers may not readily be apparent.

You've got to begin to establish your value in your customer's mind from the very beginning of a sales cycle. To determine value, you must know what your customer does and why. You must understand your customer's goals, objectives, and values and relate the technical specifics of your products and your company's differentiation strategy to your customer's ability to make money and gain competitive distinction. This is a process of converting your bits and bytes to dollars and cents in your customer's pocket. What is important to making your customer a success? Where does your customer want to be in five years? Place your product and services into your customer's business model, project the company's business improvement and net it out in terms of cash, profit, and market share. This is easy to say and hard to do.

Marketing and salespeople often describe products and services in intricate technical detail and leave it up to the customer to extrapolate from tech talk to value. If this eventually results in a sale, it reinforces the jargon. In the next sales situation, the technical discussion gets even more intense. After a short while, the idea of establishing value is completely forgotten. If the customer doesn't figure out the value by himself, it's time to lower the price. If that doesn't work, find another prospect who wants to hear about the technical details. Changing from a features-based sale to value selling is essential for communicating the important role you can play in your customer's success.

It's easy to pay too much attention to the technical qualities of a product and not relate these to your customer's value potential. Companies plan and build products without ever relating their investments to the potential value customers will derive. They build things because they think the technology is cool. High-tech companies price their product without considering value. They set prices based on costs, or relative to competitive alterna-tives. This is backwards. Your product's distinctive value determines the incremental price your customer should be willing to spend compared to alternative solutions. Costs set the limits on when your business is unable to make a profit. Competitive pricing sets the baseline for undifferentiated functionality.

Value is like quality. You can quantify it. You can compare it. Both describe higher states that can be reached. Neither can be defined but both can be described.

Characterizing Value

Each customer measures your product's value differently. Value is applica-tion-specific. Given two similar customers in the same industry, one may place a very high value on your offerings while the other may not. The reasons for this may have little to do with any difference at your end and a lot to do with your customer's specific situation. Even though you cannot define value, you can characterize it. There are five different characteristics of the value your customer can place on your high-technology product (see Table 6-1).

Value Characteristic # 1—Value Can Be Quantified in Dollars and Cents

Corporate management loves to count things. They'll count anything—time, dollars, defects, response—you name it, they'll count it. Management's motto goes, "If you can't measure it, you can't manage it." Measuring and counting are part of our business fabric.

Table 6-1   Characteristics of Value

1	Value can be quantified
2	Value is time dependent
3	Value is usage specific
4	Value has components
5	Value is constrained by external factors

Measurements useful for managing the operational and tactical part of a business may be inadequate for strategic decision making. There are aspects of your sale that can readily be quantified in hard currency terms. As a high-technology product seller you provide your customer with empowerment. The result of this empowerment may not readily convert to a dollars-and-cents measurement. It is not real to assume that you can quantify in accounting terms many of the benefits you offer. Nevertheless, to best describe your value to a customer, you've got to create a way to measure it.

Looking at this another way, you must communicate the value that you bring to your customer. Dollars and cents, profit increases, and market share improvement are the most effective ways to communicate value benefits to your business customer. You can talk paradigm shifts till you are blue in the face and your customer may still go to your competitor. Netting out your value in dollars communicates your message quickly and precisely. A dollar measurement gives meaning to your value proposition and delivers your message to the widest possible audience. The good news is that you can relax the accounting rules a bit when you quantify your value. In fact, you ought to throw out the rules.

Quantifying value lets you describe it. Percentage increases in market share, projected sales growth, improved quality measurement, and lower cost structure are all good ways to measure value. Your customer understands these terms.

Unmeasured value is unrealized value. It means that you may leave out some of your differentiated value. Unmeasured value eventually puts you at a competitive disadvantage. People will not pay extra for value they don't know about, even though they will benefit from it. While your customer may still buy what you sell, he won't pay as much for it. This reduces not only your profit but also your ability to fund your business functions that increase value. This situation—providing unmeasured value—puts your company at a long-term competitive disadvantage.

When microcomptuers entered the market, Digital Equipment was poised to become a significant vendor by adopting its minicomputer successes into this emerging market. DEC had the technology, the market position, and the financial strength to win market share as this new market developed. It unfortunately mistook its installed software base as one of the value propositions for this emerging market. It underestimated the importance of its other value components clearly in its favor—its marketing presence, technical direct sales coverage, and excellent software development tools. The result was that Intel received little opposition from DEC on its way to market domination.

It is also possible to express value too soon. Osborne Computers provided a world-class example of what can happen when you get your value proposition timing wrong. The company's early product announcement of a new portable computer convinced potential buyers to wait until Osborne's newest product became available. This tactic worked too well. Osborne's own potential customers decided to wait as well, causing the company to go into a financial tailspin as orders failed to come in the door for products that were already built. The company never recovered and entered high-technology selling folklore.

Sometimes it is easy to place a specific value on your customer's deployment of your product. A value measurement your customer will accept. In fact, customers may do it for you. Consumer electronics retailer Circuit City boasts about its new computerized inventory and distribution system. They claim this investment added 1 percent to its 1991 pretax margin over and above the amortized cost of this system's deployment! Circuit City claims that its system eliminated excess inventory across its 229 stores, increased sales by reducing out-of-stock situations, increased customer satisfaction, and allowed Circuit City to operate a super automated distribution center with an operations staff of just 13 people. Which consumer electronics retailer would not want to meet with Circuit City's technology suppliers? Adding 1 percent to any company's pretax margin gets people's attention. That magnitude of performance improvement can pay for a lot of hardware, software, communications, and systems integration work to custom create a unique solution for any major electronics retailer.

Value Characteristic #2—Value Is Time Dependent

The same technology acquisition will yield different results at different points in time. Your customer is operating in a very competitive world. He can win and lose market share by acting at the wrong time. If the company pictures itself as a first mover, it may try to use your product in an innovative manner to capture market share and consolidate its market position. Plus, the first mover sets the stage for structuring the actions of its competitors. In the prescription drug business the first drug to market is likely to dominate a segment. Pharmaceutical manufacturers will invest large sums of money in technology to speed up the government drug approval process in order to get to the market first.

First movers have a lot to gain by successfully rolling out new capability. Their products will be valued more than others in the same market. The first mover generally measures value in terms of increased market share.

Followers of the first mover measure value in terms of preventing further market share erosion.

There are time periods when your customer establishes leadership (product, performance, service, information, pricing, or marketing leadership) and the company's competitors have not yet figured out how to neutralize this leadership. These situations fuel your customer's market growth. Your customer will place a higher value on your product when it allows his company to clearly establish leadership. They can turn this leadership position into growth. This growth relates to your value.

Characteristic #3—Value Is Usage Specific

A desktop publishing system and a client information system supporting an insurance agent cost about the same amount of money. An ad agency places more value on the desktop publishing system than does the insurance agent. The insurance agent places more value on an on-line transaction network than does an advertising agency. Now, invert the situation. When would an insurance agent value a desktop publishing system and when would an advertising agency value an office management system?

The point is that customers place value on a technology acquisition from the perspective of their specific need. This is easy to understand when looking at extremely different cases such as advertising agencies and insurance agents. But how do you determine value when your technology spans many different markets and each market places varying degrees of importance on the acquisition? Do you price your product for the high-value market and lose customers in other market segments? Or do you appeal to the lowest value market, leaving money on the table when you're selling into the high value markets?

It's not unusual for two competitors in the same industry to place substantially different value levels on your products. If you are selling semiconductor diffusion tubes to IBM and Apple, you'll find that IBM is very interested in producing its own semiconductors while Apple is not. At IBM you'll have lots of potential buying situations. At Apple, they wouldn't have the foggiest idea what your products do.

Your market is a collection of independent vertical applications, each with its own underlying value set. Customers within each vertical market make their own independent value assessment. You can build a value model from the top down by estimating the likely value level each submarket will place on your product. You can build value models from the bottom up taking one customer at a time and working through the specific value each would likely place on your product. Working through either of these methods takes time. But doing it puts you in a position to understand your customer's perspective on your product line.

Characteristic # 4—Value Has Components

There are many ways your product contributes value to your customer. The total value offered by your product accumulates from a set of components, each representing a subvalue. The resulting value determination is a function of the relative weight your customer places on each of these subvalues. You need to understand how your customer's submarket in general determines value and how they specifically go about setting value. What is important to them? How do they factor the subvalue into the total acquisition decision? And, of course, how well can your offerings influence each value factor?

Coming to terms with the major value categories increases your understanding of your customer's technology acquisition. Potential customers who are striving to be the lowest cost supplier will likely place great emphasis on the value components that decrease their cost structure and improve quality. A customer viewing itself as a high-value differentiated supplier will be more interested in how your product can improve his company's customer service capability than in reducing manufacturing cost. Whatever the case, two different entities in apparently similar businesses may place substantially different values on the same acquisition. Their value differences relate to their different viewpoints.

Characteristic #5—Value Is Constrained by External Factors

There are limits to your product's value in every sales situation. If your product could double your customer's sales in the next twelve months and if the incremental profit contribution on this sales increase is $2 million, does that mean your customer will pay you up to that amount to get it? Maybe. And maybe not. First, a lot of the answer to this question lies in your own product's differentiation. Can your customer acquire similar capability from another source? If so, this alternative's cost enters your customer's value equation. Or maybe your customer has a completely different way to double sales during this same time period. These alternatives limit the prices you can charge.

You know that high-technology is a very competitive business. The logic of your customer having other ways to solve his business problem may not involve you at all. Customers have an assortment of ways to reach the same business goal. And all solutions have a price that, in turn can be compared to value (see Figure 6-1).

The alternate solution paths form the boundaries for value comparisons. Using these your customer can compare what the company spends to solve a problem with the value it places on expected return. These alternatives form limits to the price your customer will pay for your products and service offerings. On the one hand, they determine your customer's switching point when your acquisition costs are too high. On the other hand, low price alternatives set the minimum entry threshold available to your customer

These five value components allow you to begin chipping away at the abstract concept of value and create some broad measurement tools for determining your product's value to a specific customer. When taken as a whole, the key characteristics of value help you firm up in your customers' eyes the price they should expect to pay for your product. Though value cannot be defined, these characteristics give it meaning in your customers' eyes.

Figure 6-1   There Are Always Several Ways to Solve the Same Problem

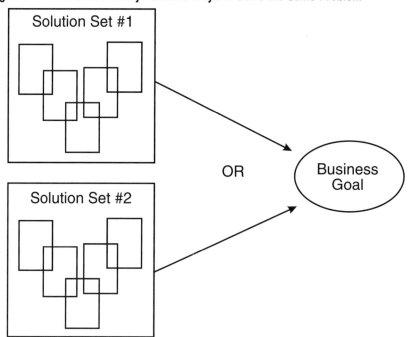

Differentiated Value

Differentiated value is your key to successfully winning market share. Your customer can compare two products by looking at price/performance criteria. Comparing value moves the discussion from features versus cost to the overall impact of your product, your services, your company, and your business perspective on your customer's success. Value is an assessment of the total impact you can have on your customer's business plan over the projected lifetime of the project. The criteria for determining value can extend through multiple technology refreshment cycles within the time frame of the purchase.

Selling point-of-sale equipment to the retail industry quickly comes to mind when discussing a customer's concern about multiple technology refreshment cycles. This industry has the worst of all possible worlds. It uses every type of computing device over all types of networks, has terrible seasonal peaks, stressful peak loads, and a relatively unskilled work force running most of the equipment. Technology products bought by a retailer are constantly being swapped in and out. A technology seller to this industry can distinguish itself by proving to be highly adaptable to changes throughout the retailer's system.

From the selling side, looking at value makes the actual product less important and the depth and the breadth of you as the supplier more important. It focuses value assessment away from the product and toward your customer's "big picture." It flattens out product differences and relates the decision criteria to the company's overall commitment to the market. Selling in this way helps technology vendors that have established themselves beyond a product/price perspective.

You want to clearly establish in your customer's eyes your distinctive value. That's a crisp categorization of your unique contribution unmatched by your competitors. Your distinctive value lists out each and every factor that is unique to your company and your product line. You want to establish the business impact your differentiation will have on your customers' ability to meet and exceed their goals (see Figure 6-2).

Your distinctive value is the answer to the question, "Why should I buy your product versus solving my problem another way?" The differentiated value takes into account the impact your solution can have on your customer's overall business performance. Of course, your goal is to create a substantial and sustainable business case for distinguishing your product offerings from competing alternatives.

Figure 6-2   Your Distinctive Value Separates You from Your Competition

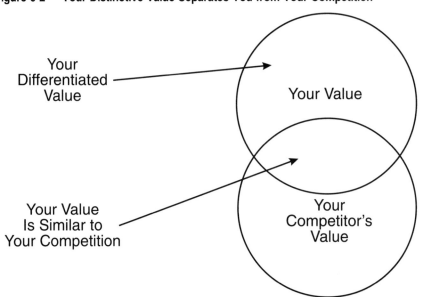

Your differentiated value is a comparison of your solution versus that of a single competitor. Your customer can choose only one solution. Your distinctive value may be different for one competitor than it is for another. It's important to establish that, compared to each competing alternative, you offer important added value.

Value versus Price

Price is related to value. Value determines price over the long haul. In the short term, your customers compute value based on future expectations. New technologies are sold on anticipated returns. If a product fails to deliver value, its price will drop. Firms that establish their product's value clearly in their customer's mind will yield the highest prices for their products. Unrealized value deflates the sales price.

The ideas of value and price have become confused over the years. At one time high prices equated to high value. In systems selling, IBM cornered the market on high-value/high-priced products by concentrating on their customers' long-term MIS requirements and supplying products and services enabling these customers to maximize their computing investment and build reliable computing infrastructures.

The relationship between high value and high price is not so direct anymore. The highest price vendors may not necessarily be the ones supplying the greatest value to their marketplaces. Instead, they may just be the aging dinosaurs with large cost structures and an installed base that has to overcome a considerable amount of inertia before they can switch. Short term, they can command high prices. In this case, prices do not equate to high value. Wang computer systems were very expensive the day Wang entered Chapter 11 bankruptcy, even though very few of them were sold. They were expensive because the maintenance fees for their existing customers were based on the products' list prices, so they kept their prices high to keep their maintenance revenues high long after their product line had lost its luster. It cost a lot to keep your Wang computer in operation. To many customers using Wang computers at the time it cost even more to throw the whole thing out. If you weren't prepared to junk them, then you had to pay dearly to keep them running.

Many high-tech sellers use costs and competitive prices to price their products. This doesn't make sense. Cost and competitive pricing do provide interesting information, but the real price decision should relate to value. Your production cost is not a measure of the value you add to your customer. Production costs tell you only what your product cost to build and get to market. Your competitor's pricing does not tell you what your customer will gain from your differentiated product. Competitive pricing tells you how customers value your competition's unique differentiation. (This assumes your competition has been successfully selling something. Competitive pricing charts often show lots of products and lots of prices, but fail to tell you whether or not anything is actually being sold.) Buyers and sellers confuse production costs and competitive pricing with the real question: What is the value of your product in a specific customer application? Competitive pricing and cost may each play a role in limiting the overall range of your product's value. The value that your customer is willing to place on your offering determines your pricing.

Your product's value may be contained deep within a multi-step process associated with application functionality. To a large-end user, what is the value of an intelligent Ethernet card? On one hand, you could say it is very little since the customer really wants the applications running over the network using the Ethernet card. On the other hand, the supplier of Ethernet cards can make a pretty good case for the empowering capability afforded to an end user deploying thousands of their Ethernet cards across an enterprise because its Ethernet cards were certified and pretested for use by hundreds of applications developers. This vendor could argue that the time spent certifying its product with large numbers of applications vendors significantly differentiates it for end users with lots of diverse network requirements. The product's value translates to rapid deployment of new applications, greater application portability, and common applications development interfaces. The dollar value of these items in terms of business improvement can be estimated and substantiated.

Channel participants often place greater value on a product than does the end user. In the preceding example of the Ethernet card manufacturer, a small user with only a half dozen workstations may not place the same weight on the above value criteria as does the large-end user. Yet, the value added reseller selling to this small-end user probably will place high value on many of the same criteria. The value added reseller will place substantial value on a vendor who will help improve the business position of the VAR. If this Ethernet card will lower the VAR's own cost of installation and reduce technician training complexity, then this vendor is likely to get designed into more of this VAR's customer solutions. Of course, the VAR's appreciation of this supplier's Ethernet card increases and so will their willingness to pay a premium for the differentiated product offering.

You need to be a magician to set a price for a new product in a new field. Determining the right value components isn't easy when there is little information available from similar applications. Before your new product's introduction, you must estimate the major value contributions your product offers your potential submarkets, and the effects of competing alternatives limiting the upper end of your value. Finally, you've got to guess what people will pay to receive the value you anticipate delivering.

You Can Become the Value Leader

Lowest price doesn't guarantee you'll become the market share leader. Long-term market leaders are the value leaders in their arenas. People mistakenly convert short-term price reductions into their long-term tool for capturing market share. It's easy to understand how this can happen. During the normal course of business transactions everyone focuses on the purchase transaction. When you are in the final stages of a sale, if your company has not created successful differentiated value in the eyes of your customer, the only tool you have left is price reduction. If you are about to lose an important sale, your customer may be saying; "All things considered, your competitor is offering more value per dollar than you are." You've essentially failed to prove that your company provides the best value either because it is not true or because you've been unsuccessful at communicating it. Since there's not enough time to create new value differentiation, people lower their price to turn the value-per-dollar-spent ratio in their favor. Whether this works out or not, sales reports that product pricing is too high (instead of saying that perceived customer value per dollar was too low). This sort of interaction takes its toll and companies end up competing on price reductions instead of value creation.

How much does your customer pay and what did he get for it? Many competing high-tech products appear indistinguishable from each other when it comes to delivering value. It's not surprising that marketers get distracted and begin to focus solely on price and feature comparisons, leaving it up to the customer to translate functionality into value. Value is an abstract idea, so why even bring it up? Why not just become the price leader and concentrate on getting manufacturing costs down?

Your company wants to be the value leader because this should be the most lucrative position to occupy. A value leader isn't just the supplier who can provide the greatest value; it's the supplier with the greatest value per dollar spent by the customer. When you are the value leader, your customer will get the most business improvement per dollar spent with you. You are the supplier whose customers appreciate your distinctive value highly. In the process of becoming the value leader you have the opportunity to build up competitive barriers to entry that extend well beyond your product. Your customer will pay a premium to get your unique value. With each year that passes your competition will find it harder and harder to enter your business arena. It is easier to go down the path of becoming the price leader. It is more lucrative to become the value leader in your business. Being the value leader puts you in the best position to capitalize on long-term market growth.

Your customer wants value. He appreciates value today more than ever before. Customers of all sizes understand the nonprice issues associated with technology ownership. The more experience your customer has with technology products, the more receptive he is to understanding value. Today, low price does not automatically translate to the best deal.

To become the value leader means that you offer your customers the greatest amount of business improvement per dollar spent. When they assess your value versus your direct competitors and when your solution is juxtaposed with alternate methods of solving their problems, your solution will show the greatest potential return even after risk factors are taken into account. This is the industry position you can occupy. It offers your firm the ability to form close knit partnerships with your customers. You and your customers are able to share in supporting and expanding each other's business. As the value leader you differentiate your product and your company in ways that improve your customer's business position. You do this by successfully linking your goods and services to your customer's business problem.

Inmac, the computer accessory catalog company, does a terrific job of linking their products to their customers' business problems. Their product headlines always convert product qualities to owner benefits. "Why sit and wait?" for preformatted data cartridges, and "Send data error free" for its modems are typical Inmac product headlines that project the usage benefits of the company's products. Reading through the catalog is always an enjoyable sales experience.

The industry value leader doesn't use price as its sole competitive weapon. The value leader's prices are often at the highest end of the competitive spectrum. That's because the value leader is receiving revenue for nonproduct associated goods and services. It then uses this extra revenue to finance the growth of auxiliary differentiation to further increase its competitive barriers to entry.

Figure 6-3 delineates value/price relationships. In very broad terms you can operate in one of four positions with respect to price and value. The ideal position to occupy is in the upper right hand corner—high price/high value. When you are the high price/high value market leader, your customers reward your differentiation strategy through their purchases. You will be attracting premium prices that you can reinvest in your business. If your customers are willing to pay the highest prices to obtain your unique differentiation, your competitors will find it hard to win over your prospective customers.

Figure 6-3   Value versus Price Leadership

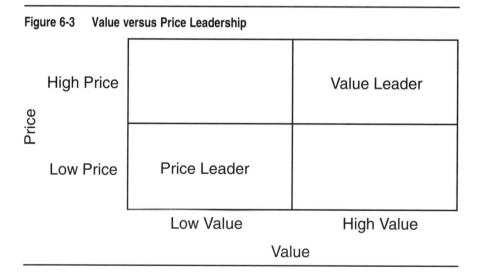

When you operate in the lower left hand corner of the price/value matrix, you use price to get and keep market share. You have determined that, even with your differentiated product, your customer's price concerns are significant. This is often the case in markets where no vendor has established significant differentiation. Your success as the low-price leader heavily depends on getting and keeping a cost advantage. In markets like this you're in for a never-ending cycle of price cuts and competitor shake out. When your unique differentiation has little customer value, your market share is always at risk to competitive price-cutting technology replacement strategies.

High-tech companies operating in the lower right hand quadrant provide high differentiated value to their customers at a low price and are often in a transition mode. Products fall in this category when the technology is very new or very old. New product categories may start here when customers get tremendous value from a new product or when a new product allows them better use of other technology products they are already using. An older product line may still have high customer value but with lowered prices to ward off newer competing technologies. Products may fall in this quadrant because a vendor simply does not realize the large value customers place on their product. A supplier in this section can probably raise its prices without sacrificing many customers.

Ignoring Value

You can deal with value or ignore it. Not coming to terms with your differentiated value is a formula for disaster. It's easy to ignore value as too abstract and concentrate on performance and functional descriptors like MIPs, bps, baud rates, and dollars and cents. Your customer also has problems specifying value. Your customer's project staff is interested in specification-related information—price and performance issues. As you move higher up in your customer's management, the issues involve converting technological actions into tangible business improvements. This results in people within your company receiving conflicting signals from your customer. Buyers often send out conflicting messages making it even harder to understand their value goals. Often, the loud signals from the lower ranks overshadow the more important messages from the top. A buyer who is always asking for price concessions makes you forget your customer's president wants to develop a mutually profitable partnership (see Figure 6-4).

The value of your product is not greater than the amount your customer is willing to place on it. Value is unseen if the customer is not aware of it. Unrealized value lowers your prices and reduces your ability to fi-

Figure 6-4   Senior Management Places Greater Emphasis on Business Improvement

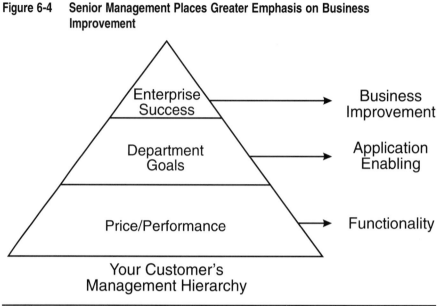

nance future products and services that may help your customer even more. Your customer can easily overlook value, and focus on price and performance. He may have trouble relating things like installation and maintenance ease to his business' eventual goal of having a more strategic work force. It's your job to communicate the specific value of your product and teach your customer how to relate product functionality to fundamental improvements in their business. If you don't do this, your value capability may be ignored.

Establishing Value

You must find out where you help improve your customer's business plan and what the relative level of improvement is. It's up to you to understand your customer's business well enough to know what's important to him and what's important to the industry. Your value is customer and industry-specific. (See Figure 6-5.)

First, it's necessary to look at your customer's overall position in their industry. This is the 10,000 foot view of their market's fundamental direction and their relative position. At a high level, this perspective can tell you what your customer wants to achieve and how fast they'd like to move.

The second place to look at is your customers' value chain. What goes into their enterprise? What major value functions do they perform? What

Figure 6-5   Four Steps to Value

Step 1	Step 2	Step 3
Understand Your Customer's Industry	Look at Your Customer's Value Chain	Review Your Company's Value Success

Step 4
Putting the Value Puzzle Together

goes out? You've got to look at the structure of their businesses. How do competitors interrelate? Who are their partners? Are there any significant trade associations? Like the TV detective Columbo, you must collect lots of details to formulate the big picture.

The third thing to do is find where you fit in. Selling to manufacturers may mean you should help control costs or improve product quality. You may help reduce their time to develop and introduce new products. For a service-oriented company, you may be its way to reduce customer response time.

Finally, the fourth way to link your products and services into your customers' value equation is to look at their big picture—concentrate on the areas that make up the majority of their business. Go to the heart of their numbers. Research their business areas that have the fastest growth rate and the greatest profit potential. Find out what is important to your customers' management.

Here are some of the best starting points to start measuring your value (see Figure 6-6).

1. Manufacturing costs and output quality—This is the most common route for everyone selling to your customer. You can be certain your competition and your customer are going to look at cost savings and quality improvement. So you will spend time here as well. Don't spend all of your time in these areas. Even if you identify

Figure 6-6   Eight Areas That Establish Value

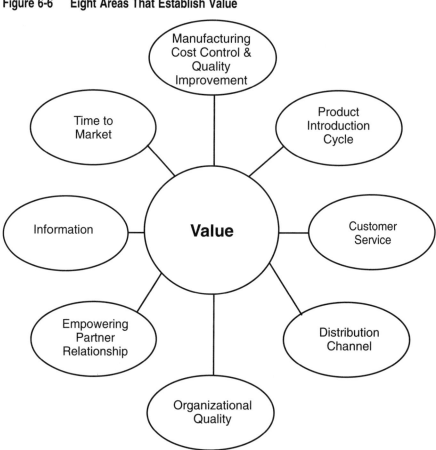

some important value opportunities, you must keep looking for value differentiation in other arenas to distance your company from your competition.

2. Reduced cycle time (reduced time to market)—How many days does it take from the time your customer receives raw input to the time customers are getting value from their purchases? Companies in all industries want to drastically reduce their cycle time. (This is valid for manufacturers and service companies alike. For example, a bank values a product that cuts the time from when they receive funds to when these funds are in productive use.) Find out the norm for your customer's industry, measure your potential cus-

tomers against the norm and then project how much you can improve this. Saving even a small percentage of time to market can be vital and can give your customer a significant competitive advantage.

3. Reduced product introduction cycle—A 10 percent reduction in time from concept to product can translate to huge increases in market share for your customer. Bringing new products to markets takes vast amounts of your customer's energy and permeates the entire organization. Things that you can do to reduce your customer's product cycle are valued highly. This is a great topic to discuss with your customer. I've often uncovered great ideas when customers relate the importance of a product to reducing their product introduction cycle.

4. Changes in your customer's information flow—Your customer today may be entering the same data many times into the same computer system. If you don't believe that, just look at how often your company types your customer's name into your computer systems—once for forecasting, once for order entry, maybe again for invoices, yet again for the financial reports, probably again for commission reporting and again for service monitoring. And your company is a high-tech company! Imagine what goes on at companies that are not as adept at technology as you are. Changing your customer's information flow eliminates valueless redundant information entry while broadening information access and availability. This converts to value through an improved business model and a much better utilization of your customer's work force. When you are selling your product, always keep an eye out for ways your product can improve your customer's information flow.

5. Improvements in your customer's distribution and delivery channel—This is a never ending concern. How does your customer get its products to its customers in a timely fashion? Again, within an industry, well-known norms exist and you can develop the idea of (1) how your customer compares to the norm and (2) how you can improve this area. Your customer's customer demands when and where she wants things. Your customer must keep up with his customer's demands. Look for ways in which your product improves your customer's ability to get his product to market.

6. Enterprise quality improvements—Your customer wants to deliver 100 percent quality products and services 100 percent of the time. His customers expect it. Maintaining high quality is an ongoing

process. You can establish the relationships between your offerings and your customer's quality. Your products and services can be linked across many or all of these major areas. Each linkage establishes greater value to your offering.

7. Improving business partnerships—Your customer cares about the relationship he has with key business associates. Most companies are trying to expand their web of business partnerships. How do your products and services contribute to improving your customer's partnerships, and establishing a seamless association throughout his company's activities?

8. Improvements in your customer's customer service—Service is king in today's business world. It is important to see how and where you can improve your customer's ability to provide enhanced services to his customers. Can you also improve the access that your customer has with his customers by moving the availability of information from your customer's facility to his customer's location? How does that translate into improved market share?

Building a Value Matrix

After looking at each of these eight areas of value contribution, your next step is straightforward. You can build a value matrix to tell how well your product increases your customer's value in each of these categories (see Table 6-2). If you don't know the actual amount of value impact, you can still apply an overall rating to the category. If your product reduces network administration by one person, you can put the company's fully loaded annual cost of this job function in this cell of the matrix. If you don't know exactly how much personnel savings is involved, but you do know there is some, you can at least check off this cell and record in your matrix that there are some additional administrative savings from your product. This matrix can give you a better ideal of the value you provide to your customer.

Table 6-2   A Value Matrix Lets You Zero in on Your Distinctive Value

Vendor	Function 1	Function 2	Function 3	Function 4
You				
Competitor A				
Competitor B				

Selling smart means looking at value through your customer's eyes. Smart sellers not only know the value of their product, they know the value of their competitors' products. After you build this value matrix for your product, you can do the same for each major competitive alternative available to your customer. Putting these checklists side by side will tell you how you think your customer is likely to value your solution and allow you to compare your value proposition with your competitors'. What you find when you look at your value proposition from your customer's perspective may surprise you. You may realize that your offering is not as strong as you thought. It may be time for you to do more than just acknowledge your own value. You may want to start taking steps to improve your value proposition to your customer.

Chapter 7

Increasing Your Value

D istinctive value establishes the differences between you and your competitors. It tells why your customer should buy from you and not from someone else. Your distinctive value is constantly changing. Your job is to make sure that your company's distinctive value improves and that your customers understand your value.

A sales team's most important role is to articulate and improve the value your customer places on your company, products, and services. The first thing you must do in a high-tech sales situation is to make value the center of the discussion. You want people to stop talking about price and start thinking in terms of value return per investment dollar. Would you rather have a customer say, "Your price is $50 too high," or, "For the extra $50 in price, where is the additional benefit?" The former leaves you with a pricing problem on your hands. The latter gives you the freedom to discuss additional value you may offer.

Your customer will appreciate your concerns with the value impact that your company can have on his business. He too, has a problem quantifying value. What's more, in today's economy, it is essential that your customer relate technology infrastructure investments to the corporate business plan. Your customer will be more than happy to get your ideas on surfacing the value components of his potential investment. He knows that you see many customers in similar business environments and that you can share with them some of the ways others have been effective using your products.

Once you and your customer begin understanding where you add value, you also can understand additional value opportunities open to you. Where is it that you can add value? Which vertical markets get the most value from your products? How can you transform these successes into your other markets?

131

Value is not static. Value is constantly changing. It is up to you to insert yourself into this equation and favorably impact your relationship into their value equation. The best way to take control of your value is to select a vertical market and figure out how you can positively project your value across prospective opportunities. What major nonproduct specific investments can you make to the benefit of this collection of customers?

Value can increase. After you establish the value your customers place on you as a supplier and how they compare your value to alternate solutions, you must put in place the strategy to increase this value. In the final analysis, you are trying to become your customer's business partner. Analyze your value from this perspective. Learn how to set yourself up as if you were a part of your customer's organization. Selling high-technology involves increasing your customer's value for products as long as your company continues to sell these products.

It helps to look at value as a process and not as a fixed object. This gives value a time component, allowing you and your customer to prepare a plan to constantly improve your value over time. This will also help you and your customer to agree on the real value you're expected to deliver and ways for you both to measure this value. Creating a value improvement process and a value measurement mechanism will benefit your customer relationship.

After you and your customer start dealing with the process issues relating to value, you can begin working day by day to increase the value your customer receives. If you are working with large-ticket items that require many repeat purchases, you can set up this value enhancement process through frequent direct contacts with your customer. (You may even set up weekly or monthly discussions on value improvements.) A salesperson covering a remote territory can set up a monthly luncheon for customers to get together in roundtable fashion and discuss ways to help make their investment in your products more valuable to them. If your company sells lower-cost products to many different customers, you may want to do it for a sample of your customers much like a Nielson family provides TV rating information. You may want to employ a user group forum or a focus group format to stimulate customer participation as you generate a long-term plan for value enhancement.

Whether you engage just one customer or many in your value enhancement process, the benefits to you are phenomenal. What you learn from one you can apply to all existing and future customers. When you do this you put yourself on the cutting edge of new ideas that can accelerate your company past your competition and make you more valuable to your customer. Not only will your customers love to participate with you in this process (after all, they are helping themselves when they show you more ways to increase their value), they'll offer some amazing ideas. They'll even show you ways that you can use their own net of video/voice/data communications to help your team support their team. New doors, and new ideas will open up to you.

A good starting point for establishing value is to ask your customers what they think are the most important value aspects relating to this purchase. What do they consider to be the criteria for success. Often, customers have prepared weighted evaluation lists containing a potpourri of information they have collected in the months leading up to their consideration of the problem. Even if they have not prepared extensive evaluation criteria, they ought to be able to tell you what they consider the most important factors in their product selection.

Microsoft implements user conferences as a powerful tool for constantly pursuing value enhancement for its software products. The company seems to have a steady stream of conference topics—Microsoft Mail, Windows, multimedia, data bases. Since Microsoft's products are relatively inexpensive and are sold through a multi-tiered distribution channel, these user conferences provide excellent opportunities to go directly to customers and gain feedback concerning the benefits of its products.

Asking your customer to tell you what's important can help him as much as it may help you. It is a common occurrence for customers to get so wrapped up with feature comparisons and checklists that they forget to put these items into perspective. If they are looking at the speed of a product, do they want the fastest product available, or do they really want to make certain that their product is fast enough to get the job done? It leads to the age-old sales problem where your prospect keeps you responding to difficult technical questions while she loses sight of the fact that the answers to these questions have little or no bearing on the worth of your product in her company's application.

Value Selling

Value underlies every high-technology sale. Somewhere during the sales process your customers decide how much value you provide and make their business decisions. When they buy from you, they equate the price they are willing to pay to the relative value level they think you will provide.

Value is a measurement of the entire anticipated buying experience. It takes into account the actual products, services, tangibles, and intangibles.

Establishing value is the most important function of a high-technology sales force. Each and every aspect of your business contributes to your value. All members of your company should be performing roles in adding value to your customer's business. If they are not adding value, maybe you need to reevaluate their roles. If your people are not aware of their part in this value process, now is the time to get them to understand their importance to your customer's business function.

Sometimes you are not sure which value component is the most important or where it may come from. When Read Only Memories (ROMs) first became popular, semiconductor designers were inclined to focus on circuit designs that could produce the lowest cost chips. Manufacturing these devices required one of the many photo wafer masks to be customized to the bit patterns required by the customer. At the design stage for the semiconductor ROM chip the designer had a choice—make the custom mask the first mask of the process, or make it the last mask. The first mask programmable device would produce the smallest chip, result in the highest yield/lowest cost circuits and require eight weeks to create the first working prototypes from a customer's data input pattern. The last mask programmable devices would result in larger, more expensive chips requiring only one week to produce prototypes. The question was which product to build. On the one hand, the higher cost device could save the customer seven weeks and reduce his volume manufacturing lead time. On the other hand, the lower cost device would pay off in volume situations and could provide more manufacturing capacity to quickly meet high volume demands.

What would you have done? What value do you place on the benefits to the customers of getting their prototype circuits back in less time and having considerably more flexibility throughout their product's manufacturing life? The time to decide whether the device would be last or first mask programmable was before the chip circuit design began—at least twelve months before the first marketing of the product started. In many companies, the ROM design strategy was set before the sales and marketing groups were even aware of the value consequences of the tradeoff. The winners in this market were the last mask programmable manufacturers. The shorter prototype turnaround time resulted in many design wins and new customers.

Value has limits. Customers always have other places to turn. There are competing products, solution alternatives, and the decision to take no action at all. Your cost structure serves as the lower limit establishing the minimum return you need. Unrealized value results in benefits to the buyer without any compensation to the seller. It's up to you, the seller, to establish as much value as you can throughout your customer base.

Who Owns This Responsibility?

Sales and marketing groups play the major role in the process of establishing value. But a company's entire work force can play a role. One of the biggest differences between sales and marketing groups is when the issue of value is considered. Marketing worries about establishing value for products that are not yet in the market. Sales worries about establishing value for products already in production. For semiconductor companies making read-only memories, their circuit designers had the first opportunity to see the value trade-off in their design decision. It's not uncommon for marketers and sales to be unaware of value choice decisions being made. It's up to everyone in an organization to participate in creating value.

Delivering a value message is a constant process for sales groups. Direct sales groups can do this when they meet with customers. Sales teams involved with channel sales can pass on to their indirect sales agents the understanding and the tools they need to establish value with customers. Marketing groups can develop communications messages targeted at new and existing customers promoting the many facets of their value.

Delivering your value message is a continuous process. Value is dynamic. External factors are always changing the value your customer places on you and your products. You have to find, measure, and communicate your value continuously.

Estimating Value through Norms

You must link what your customer does to the value you provide. Then you must quantify the future value of your product and begin proving it to your customer. You usually do not have nearly enough data, time, or expertise to perform a detailed financial analysis. You can develop a set of comparisons based on more easily obtained information to compare with your business case. In mathematics, this process of gathering a collection of data points into the right range is called normalization. You can develop "norms" for your customer's business case, then show how you can improve his company's situation compared to these norms.

First, though, you need to find the right norms. You can then find historical data from your customer or collect data from similar customers for comparison. We all buy products by looking at industry norms. When you buy your car you look at miles per gallon and miles between major tune-ups to get a range of the operating costs. You can also look further at historical repair costs of the car model over several years, and Blue Book valuation of trade-in. When you make a stock investment, you look at the company's price/earnings ratio and other financial norms. In a similar way, you can create norms for technical procurements like computer hotel reservation systems. Some comparative norms are cost per reservation, communications cost per transaction, software development hours, installation/training time per property and the average time it takes for a guest to make a reservation.

These comparisons can then be applied across three dimensions:

1. Your customer's historical estimate of his company's past and present systems

2. Your customer's industry's estimate of this same information

3. Your estimate of the impact your product can have on these norms

Using References to Increase Your Value

In the short run, reference accounts can increase your prospective customer's perception of value more than anything else. This is one of the best ways to turn around a sales situation that isn't going well. The best references are existing customers who have a nearly identical situation that they can describe to your prospect.

A good reference shares a business perspective with your customer. She can talk in your customer's terms about what her company did, why it did it, and whether it would do it again. This sort of reference situation will actually do much of the value selling for you. She can say to your customer, "Here is what we were planning. These are the reasons we went with this vendor, and this is what actually happened."

The result of a good referral will be that your prospective customer will increase his valuation of your proposal. He will have a better idea of the rewards and a clearer understanding of the risks involved. If the reference went well, your proposal's valuation will go way up and the associated risk assessment will go way down.

In order to select which reference to use for a particular prospect, create a matrix to compare the choices. The rows of the matrix contain the value components important to your prospect, followed by the identified risk areas. The companies from which you are choosing form the columns. In the cells of the matrix, you can rate from one to five the possible impact each customer can have on each value and risk component. Ideally, you are looking for a reference site that has a balance of relevant experience in the important areas with first-hand experiences in the high-risk areas.

Watch Out for Value Gulfs

The most dangerous pitfall is ignoring the difference that occurs between people in your own company anticipating value and your customer realizing that value. Items that your marketing people think will be of tremendous value often don't have the slightest correlation with what your customer sees as value improvement. Other things that go unnoticed by your marketers may be tremendously important from your customer's perspective.

You cross this value gulf by adopting your customer's perspective. He knows what he wants and why he wants it. Think in your customer's terms and you will see real value from his perspective. Using this perspective will also improve your ability to communicate your own company's value ideas to your customer. Sometimes customers don't see all of the value that you provide simply because the idea wasn't communicated in their reference frame. For instance, an equipment lease usually doesn't mean much to a large company with lots of financing alternatives. However, if your lease can include upgrades to other related systems, the retirement costs of the system being replaced, and other services not normally financed, it can substantially change the budget impact of this decision, and you may begin to generate an order more quickly than you think.

Increase Value by Lowering Risk

Customers expect a certain amount of risk in any purchase. Some risk is high and some is trivial. When you buy a car you run the risk of getting a lemon. When you dial a phone, you run the risk of getting a wrong number. Technology purchases also have risks that run the gamut from low to high. Low- to medium-risk situations generally don't affect how your customer values your products. What should concern you the most are the high-risk items. These can destroy the best value proposals you have.

Your customer's risk of not getting value for your products factors into his consideration in two ways. High-risk situations can lower your entire value proposition—increasing your customer's costs by creating backup alternatives to cover the possibility that your solution won't deliver as planned. Or, the high risk can be associated with assumptions in your value components which cause your overall value to deteriorate.

If your customer perceives certain parts of your solution as high-risk items, you must reduce or eliminate them. The risk areas most common in high-technology selling are meeting budgets and schedules for installation, support, and creating/programming auxiliary application functionality. There are a million and one war stories about companies with the best paper solutions, yet unable to deliver production worthy solutions.

Risk elimination is a powerful high-technology selling tool. It's a great way to create substantial differentiation from your competitors. You can win over new customers by eliminating risks in their project planning. Risk reduction can include installation guarantees, in-service operation availability, and cost control of future upgrades.

The most common tools used to reduce and eliminate risk are on the service side of the equation. Changing contract terms and conditions to cover acceptance periods, guarantee installation, and cap maintenance expenses are all familiar ground to high-technology sellers. It's actually possible to go beyond such service guarantees to provide contractual assurance that you will meet and exceed certain norms.

My Software, Inc. produces a popular line of highly functional software products targeted at mainstream America's small businesses, and sold through a multi-tiered distribution channel. Most of My Software products sell for less than $50. As part of its distinctive value, the company provides a lifetime money-back guarantee—something you don't get for software products costing ten times this company's prices. Satisfaction guarantees can be used to eliminate risks throughout many high-tech markets.

Imagine that you are with a company selling computers for a reservation system and you decide to create a value-oriented sales focus with contractual guarantees that your customer's cost per reservation will be less than a certain amount. Imagine what happens to your sales situation when you do that. Customers wouldn't have to worry about the component price of your equipment. They'd be paying for your product as they received your value contribution. You and your customer need to establish the criteria to allow you to make this sort of proposal. Your company might want certain conditions specified such as, "If you use our computer with a certain type of reservation application; if your volume of reservations is no less than a preset amount with preset peak traffic rates; if you use a certain type of wide-area network; and if the other elements of the reservation network have predetermined ranges of cost; then we guarantee your cost per transaction using our computer system will not exceed a certain amount or we will refund your money." While that statement is a mouthful, it can be a milestone in your attempt to reduce a risk factor in a sale. It helps you better understand your customer's operating environment. It may also help your company to better understand the application of your product in your customer's situation. Selling this way lets you increase your value by reducing your customer's risk. Your proposal transfers the financial implications of your customer's risk from him to you.

Value Creation as the Differentiator

There are an infinite number of ways for you to increase the value of your company and your products in your customer's eyes. You cannot take all the available paths. First, you've got to discover which ones are feasible. Next, you must decide what you can do to put your company in the most favorable value position. You must choose the best time to make a move to increase your value.

From time to time within a technology submarket, companies can make value itself THE ISSUE. They can turn the entire sale from a buy/sell situation to a "pay only when you receive value" situation. There are many ways of doing this. Dialog, a leading producer of information, does it by providing customers with a profile matching service that automatically compares its data base additions to its subscribers' prestored profiles. When category matches are detected, the customer is notified. This eliminates the need for Dialog's customers to frequently search for new data base additions and, instead, informs the customer that value additions have been made.

Selling only when you provide your customer a value improvement is like a stock broker charging only when his customer has made money on the trade. Imagine the number of new clients your neighborhood broker would get if they stopped charging when customers bought stocks and received a commission only when their customers sold for a profit. Imagine how frightening this prospect would be to the competition. Of course, your broker's business would also need a very different financial base to accommodate the initiation stage in which lots of buys and few profitable sales are generated. Plus, he would need a substantial kitty in place to protect him from long periods of unprofitable trades caused by bear markets. Selling on value is a powerful tool if you can afford to use it.

In the middle of its battle with Microsoft for the hearts and minds of software authors, Apple Computer focused on the emerging multimedia market. Apple wanted to have its Macintosh be the platform of choice for multimedia developers. By winning this community, Apple could extend its channel success by making available the best line of multimedia software.

Retail Macintosh multimedia products would increase Apple's percentage of its retailers' total sales and would widen the Macintosh channel.

To gain a significant lead in this market, Apple created a robust multimedia tool, QuickTime, and included it within its base operating system. Next, Apple made QuickTime compatible with Microsoft Windows so that it could be used for cross-platform applications. Apple then built high-capacity CD-ROM drives into several of its computers and made these drives available at its manufacturing cost to insure the broadest customer acceptance. The results were tremendous. In one year, the Macintosh computer had about the same population of CD-ROM drives installed as did Microsoft Windows computers. A year later, Apple was selling nearly one million CD-ROMs for Macintosh computers. An incredible early base was built on which Apple could extend its value.

The Canadian digital communications systems developer, Newbridge Networks Corp., extended its distinctive value by focusing on a well-identified submarket, telephone companies (telcos) around the world. Newbridge targeted the telcos with a specialized product brought to market with a specialized field force. The Newbridge founding team recognized that, although telcos represented a huge opportunity for data communications equipment, their large mass prevented rapid technology deployment into the phone systems. Plus, the Newbridge founders realized the unique network requirements of the phone companies—strict industry standards compliance, feature-rich products, large capacity, and centralized management. The company identified this large potential market for high-speed multiplexor equipment and created a family of differentiated products to fill these future needs, then brought these products to market with a field force dedicated to service the needs of these specialized buyers. Selling and servicing the phone companies are significantly different enterprises than selling and servicing large-end users. While their competitors were trying to sell the same product family to a mix of end users and to the telcos, Newbridge concentrated on being the best at meeting the needs of the telcos. After several years of working with telcos as they designed their first products, the company began to develop its base. By combining a specialized communications product with a specialized field force they expanded their company's sales to over $250 million in just a few years.

There are many opportunities for a supplier to price and collect specifically on value enhancement. In the software business, a supplier can create value-based differentiation based on this type of pricing strategy. Software companies selling complex and expensive products to large-end users often fall into a "Sell and Abandon" mode. They create professional, highly charged sales forces narrowly focused on prospecting and closing. After the order is in, the software company's product installation and delivery team is often understaffed and over-committed, resulting in long delays from purchase to production installation. The wonderful attention the customer received during the courtship turns into total abandonment. The customer must then use much more of his own resources than he expected to get the product up and running and, eventually, to get value from his purchase.

A software supplier in a submarket where "selling and abandoning" is rampant may want to turn the tables on its competitors by making its customer's entire purchase a value purchase. The supplier with the most interest in doing this is probably the second, third, or fourth market share supplier. These have the most to gain by changing the nature of their customers' purchase from buying before they receive value to buying after. It would require only a policy change from payment on shipment to payment on successful installation. This one change could throw their competitors into complete chaos, which may be exactly what's needed by a company in fourth market share position. New customers will readily accept the logic that they shouldn't part with their money until the product is up and running. This would also serve as a way for this supplier to get customers to focus on the seller's value differentiation by expanding the pre-sales discussion to include the installation and support requirements as well as the level of customer expectation for a production system. This strategy is a fast way for a lagging company to leapfrog its competitors. It's an example of how you can create differentiated value to put some distance between your company and your competition.

Smart sellers sell value. Selling on value works, and it works well. Finding and keeping your value distinctions is difficult. Sales people who think creating distinctive value is out of their control need to expand their perspective. Certainly, their home offices play a big role in value creation. But forming distinctive value doesn't stop there. It's up to the sales person to translate her company's value criteria into terms her customers can relate to. Through the understanding of customers' value perspective smart sellers find new ways to extend their companies' value to their customers. Selling smart means constantly finding and communicating your distinctive value to your customers.

Chapter 8

Increasing Value through Specialization

Customers are willing to pay premiums for differentiated value that improves their business. It's your job to identify and create real differences that are unique to your company and have value to your customer. Once you successfully capture market share through your differentiation, your competitors will be all over you in a heartbeat. They'll analyze every aspect of your product to try to beat you at your own game. They won't just match what you do, they'll try to do it better. You will try to build entry barriers to keep your distinctive value unique. The best entry barriers are unique ones that can be protected by patents and trademarks. (Intel is a legend at using its extensive patents to keep its competition at a disadvantage.) Most others have to do with your singular customer perspective and vision. In all cases, your competitors will try to figure out ways to deliver similar functionality and customer satisfaction. So you can see, finding and sustaining differentiated value is not easy.

One of the most important and frequently ignored means of establishing differentiation and building additional barriers to entry is through specialization. Your customer's wants and needs are unique and cannot always be fulfilled with standard products. Specialization means that you are able to identify and service unique customer requirements. It also means putting your company in a position to extend your value to a specific customer. You become the only vendor able to stand up and meet a particular customer requirement. Specialization also means you are willing to react to your customer's problem to encompass both his standard product requirements as well as his use of your product. Specialization enables you not

143

only to solve individual customer requirements but also to create important value differences between your company and competing alternatives at individual customers.

There are two important aspects of specialization:

1. Deciding how and when to specialize

2. Coming up with a standard approach to specialization so that you can repeat it.

Determining how and when to specialize is unique to your product arena. Your customer will want you to do things that you do well and that he doesn't have the time or patience to learn. Today more than ever, your customer wants to stay away from doing things that do not directly add to his value. He'd rather hire you as a specialist to do this for him.

Once you find the specialization area that makes sense to you and your customer, you may find that many customers have similar requirements. You'll want to improve your tools and techniques for producing custom solutions. Today, extended specialized product offerings may look difficult and complex to complete. Yet, there may be ways to redefine your delivery path to accommodate tremendous specialization and customization in a consistent and easy to deliver manner. It's up to you to come up with a way to "mass customize" your products so that you can extend a unique product offering to each and every customer. Mass customization is the dream of every high-tech seller. It means that you have the ability to uniquely adapt your product to the specific needs of each and every customer. When you mass customize you are extending differentiated value on an account-by-account basis. Custom solutions are part of your standard offering.

Fortunately for you, most high-tech companies do not and will not engage in custom work. I have trouble understanding why some companies don't use customization to gain market share. There must be a high-tech rule book stating that the only way for a technology company to become a success is through standard products. For many companies, the reasoning is that custom work doesn't fit into the formula. Advocating custom work is an unpopular position to take in today's high-tech world. High-tech companies don't want to view their customer situations as if each one is unique and requires customization.

For the most part, though, high-tech companies don't want to get involved with these type of customizing situations. They want to be in the "standard" product business. For these competitors, customization causes a dilemma. Their loss can become your gain. You can build important new customers and enter valuable new submarkets because of your willingness to provide specialized solutions.

This presents an opportunity for differentiation. If you're going to step into this gap, you need to detail how to accomplish it. What work will you engage in? What channel development is necessary to deliver unique solutions in the channel? If you do it internally, your company needs to figure out how to finance a business unit that customizes. If your company doesn't want to perform customization, it is possible for you to form third-party relationships that foster customization.

Just as the technology customers must rebuild themselves toward real time markets with mass customization, technology suppliers must take customization seriously. As customers extend their electronic enterprise web out to their business partners, technology systems integration becomes important on an industry level. Buying patterns throughout entire submarkets may be influenced by catalyst systems integration programs solving the initial requirements within a submarket. If you find yourself in a market where your competitors won't customize, you will have a chance of winning important new accounts by taking an adaptive approach to your customer's requirements through customization.

Market share is at stake. A high-tech company can gain significant market share by putting a sign on its door that says "custom work available here." Foregoing any custom work puts a company at risk when developing its most important vertical markets. Even though long-term financial success may rest with a company's standard product line, system integration should be viewed as an important way to get there.

As today's major industries redefine themselves in terms of mass customizing and anytime/anyplace marketing, they turn to technology for the foundation upon which they can rebuild themselves. They are not coming to technology companies for the same solutions as they did in the past. You are not being asked just to help improve their processes, lower their costs, or make their workers more productive. They are looking to you to build the infrastructure for their new age enterprises as they come to terms with how they will go about designing and building the necessary technology resources to achieve their goals. How will their potential customers get there? And how will you as a seller of high-technology be responsive to the needs of these companies?

Differentiation through Specialization

Technology differentiation comes in many shapes and forms. These days, with the numbers of new high-tech products introduced each week, product feature differentiation is relevant over the short term and elusive in the long term. Creating tailor-made systems to meet your customer's specific needs can create significant long-term differentiation.

Just as differentiation is hard for you to achieve, your customer has even greater difficulty sorting through technology selection decisions. There are many competing alternatives for each problem involving complex computing, and communications applications. The way your customer uses technology to win market share is very complex. He must invest more, sooner, to test and deploy these new services.

At the same time your customer is creating a new generation of competitive technology infrastructure, he is learning not to spend time on the mundane aspects of technology usage. He does not want to employ people to create applications from scratch as he may have done in the past. Your customer's technology management wants their people to be the experts on the use of technology within their business, not the creators of the technology. They are more than happy to leave this job to you.

Your customers do not want to do everything themselves. They know the value of leverage. They want partnerships. This is great news. You can pick up the "how to use" problems with which your customer doesn't want to bother. You can create specialized versions of your product, increase your customer's satisfaction and create added differentiation. Plus, your customers will pay you to do this.

Participating in customization allows you to improve your customer partnerships and simultaneously build competitive entry barriers. Opportunities that require specialization also lead to increases in your differentiation and extensions to your core product's functionality. In other words, customization allows you to build greater and greater entry barriers. When you customize, you increase your differentiation which, in turn, increases your ability to succeed. Through differentiation comes increased value, higher competitive barriers, and greater exploitation of the underlying technology. The successful pursuit of custom extensions leads to new differentiation opportunities.

Customization also can help you discover important new product functionality. Leading edge applications in new vertical markets require features not included in your core product. Properly supporting these new usage situations requires functionality expansion. Your early adopters in these markets want extended functionality and are willing to pay you to create these extensions. Later, you can generalize these custom requirements to reach a broader class of users as the standard product.

High-tech companies that do not offer customized services turn a blind eye toward these business opportunities. In high-tech companies there is a tremendous resistance to engaging in custom work because of fears that custom work decreases operating leverage. High-tech companies want profitable, easy to manage cookie-cutter standard products which can return the most on their human and capital investment. For venture capital investors on the boards of directors of high-tech companies, customization is a nasty business. High-tech companies engaging in significant customization require more human specialists and a greater degree of involvement with individual customers. Customization complicates the business planning cycle and increases the investment required for revenue production. Customization opportunities move a company's financial leverage numbers in the opposite direction from the "ideal" investment. Investors wanting instant successes don't like this.

Almost all the objections to customization within high-tech companies stem from financial and management perspectives. People who advocate customization point to the incremental profits and differentiation. People arguing against customization look at the decreased leverage and increased management complexities. It's not uncommon for smaller, venture capital-backed, high-tech companies to steer away from customization and miss out on important opportunities to stabilize their market position. Larger high-tech companies less reliant on outside funding sources are in a better position to realize the long-term advantages available through customization and systems integration. These companies are not scared off by the financial arguments and often have a greater depth of available management to engage in specialized services. They are also not looking for a quick success and view specialization as another way to invest in long-term market development. Their desire to gain competitive entry barriers and increase their differentiation leads them toward tailoring services to their customers.

As a result of the different feelings about customization, we are seeing the largest high-tech companies taking the boldest customization moves. IBM, Microsoft, and Oracle, for example, all have significant investments in building systems integration business units not matched by their smaller competitors. The larger companies participating in customer specific integration will reshape the landscape of the high-technology business within major submarkets. The systems integration businesses of the large, high-tech suppliers can create additional entry barriers for the smaller firms. Today, the amount of high-tech product sold through special programs in which the product manufacturer performs the specialization represents a small percentage of high-technology sales. By the end of the decade, over 25 percent of all high-tech products sold to end users will be bundled within systems integration contracts. An even greater percentage of market share will be influenced by these customized sales. If today's larger providers dominate the customization arena, they will be in the driver's seat influencing product selection and significantly increasing the market share of their products and those of their business partners.

There are important reasons for and against including systems integration into your company's business plan. Picking the right time to start this business unit is as important as selecting the right opportunities to pursue. Custom development groups are very difficult to manage and may increase the complexity of your business at a time when you cannot afford to do so. Successfully finding and executing systems integration efforts is not a trivial business. Knowing when to start this activity is important.

In the 1980s, technology markets grew so quickly it may have made much sense not to engage in customer-specific extensions and integration work. In the 1990s, customization is much too important to ignore. Dealing with systems integration does not mean you have to do this work yourself. That's not necessarily what your customers want most. It does mean creating the delivery vehicle for customization to take place. If you do not or cannot perform custom work around your product, you can still solve your customer's problem by creating an opportunity for your channel participants or other business partners to perform this work. End users need systems integration support to prepare themselves for competing in the twenty-first century.

Technology customization is a business. It requires investment resources and personnel. It has risks, rewards, and limitations. Even though your company makes a profit doing the work, you cannot do everything every customer requests. Reality sets in. Resource constraints of time, money, and expertise mean you can engage in only a certain amount of custom work. You must select custom situations carefully, always looking for the best combination of leverage, risk, and reward.

It's difficult to manage a custom effort within a standard product company. Selecting the right projects and business partners and structuring your customization business channel involve complex strategic choices. The executives in charge of this process must be in step with their enterprise's long-term vision. It is easy to be opportunistic. It's essential to be strategic.

As companies pare down their mainframe computer systems, outsourcing has become a fad. Outsourcing is a unique type of systems integration business whereby a company moves its mainframe computer applications onto the mainframe of its outsourcing supplier (in many cases, this supplier actually takes ownership of the customer's existing mainframe and hires its customer's information support staff). Companies like IBM and EDS have built large outsourcing-based business units in the past few years. In addition, end users themselves are becoming outsourcing experts. In 1990, Mellon Bank in Pittsburgh began outsourcing services for other banks, supplying not only computer support for its bank customers' existing applications, but also providing use of Mellon's own in-house applications.

High-tech suppliers now take on integration responsibilities as full-fledged businesses. During the past few years, almost all of the largest high-tech companies opened at least one system integration unit. Over the next few years multiple, specialized systems integration units will be commonplace. Added to that will be specialized joint ventures spanning industries.

When it comes to systems integration, suppliers are in a key position to control large opportunities. Their strengths range from design expertise to entrenched support channels. What they lack in application perspective they make up in fundamental technology manipulation skills. A large, established supplier positioning itself as a systems integrator comes to the table with lots of credibility, even if it is not warranted.

Financing Custom Work

Financing custom work takes money and management. Participating in systems integration work is complex. Finding, quoting, and successfully completing a systems integration job is a lengthy and time-consuming process. To increase your chances of success, you will want to reduce the technical uncertainties by better understanding the scope of the effort before you commit to the work. This means using valuable engineering and development resources as part of non-funded proposal efforts. Doing this is expensive and takes cash.

The processes involved to seek out, quote, win, and deliver systems integration work adds to your financial risks. This sort of business develops over time. And there is tension between having the proper human services in place to execute business and having the business agreements in place to pay for the staffing. Unlike the product side of high-tech business, specialization puts very little value in inventory. Human capital is the bulk of the investment. The cost of building up systems integration staff is high. Financial success in this business requires management skills that prevent over-staffing or over-committing.

The financial aspects of systems intergration make it difficult for many smaller high-tech companies. Start-up businesses want avoid these expensive high risk quoting activities with unknown return. Why shouldn't a start up put the incremental efforts directly into product development instead?

It's difficult to separate the long term strategic systems integration business opportunity from the short term financial strain. Within the context of an existing financial model, the question of financial dilution of limited development resources is a big concern. Many startup companies cannot afford to be in the systems integration business because custom work was not considered in their original business plan. While this certainly is a problem, the problem is with their funding plan being inadequate, not with the fact that specialization is not strategic. More thought should be given to the financial requirements of a system integration strategy during the funding phase of a startup.

Many small high-tech companies find systems integration pleasant oases on their journey to success. This is especially true for companies dealing with technologies whose markets take time to incubate. They enjoy having a profitable long term systems integration income stream to help wait out their standard product market development period.

Securing the capital base to finance the early cash flow requirements of systems integration is difficult for smaller high-tech companies. Venture capital available for high-tech product companies is not as available for the systems integration ventures of these same companies. As important as it is for all high-tech companies to develop their major markets through customization, it may just be the larger firms, those capable of underwriting their activities, that can move fast enough to develop these market opportunities.

Customized Standard Becomes Standardized Custom

The long-term goal of customization is to enhance your chances for success. In the short term, customization extends your ability to participate in your customer's business. It can also extend your product offerings and generate a consistent and reliable cash flow during the incubation period of your new products. In the long run, customization can also contribute to important new product features. These features can be rolled into your standard product long before your competition can anticipate them. Leading the list of new features are the tool set additions to your product line that let technical people perform customization work. Although in the short run custom work can only be performed by your organization, over the long haul you can build into your product the capability to facilitate customization by anyone.

High-tech customization goes through two phases. First, the sales force identifies applications in which the standard products do not cover all the requirements. Additional technical product manipulation is required that can be made only by a handful of experts familiar with the product. Next, the process of customization becomes a standard as designers create manipulation languages and add these to the standard product so that a wider audience can customize the product. Eventually end users can perform their own modifications. Spreadsheets provide a simple example of this. Before spreadsheets, general ledger programs were pretty rigid. Getting the right output from a general ledger program often involved lots of custom coding. For mainframe and minicomputer solutions, custom adaptations to general ledgers moved to field level experts. After spreadsheets on personal computers became commonplace, users soon learned how to customize their financial figures through the language of the spreadsheet.

Building Channels That Customize

Your company doesn't have to do all of the custom work itself. In fact, it doesn't have to do any. What's important is that your company thinks through the general problem of customization and systems integration activity across your customer base and facilitates the process by which your products can be tailored to meet the needs of each customer. Your goal is to see that your customer has easy access to customized versions of your product.

One of the best examples of this is Apple's Macintosh product line. The biggest difference between Macintosh systems and Windows systems is the degree to which Macintosh presents an array of seamlessly integrated products. Apple has done much prethinking of the system integration issues for their customers, dealers, and Macintosh third-party developers. Performing functions such as adding new applications and installing a new printer are presented in a seamless fashion across Apple's entire development community, as if one vendor did the whole thing. Meanwhile, under the covers is a whole raft of multi-vendor products integrated together in a framework prepared through Apple's integration perspective. Apple's Macintosh is a great example of how a company in the standard-products business can use a systems integration perspective to team up with its business partners and create a significant market differentiation.

High-tech companies can strategically design their distribution channels to support their customer's system integration needs. In the 1980s, distribution channels grew to extend the reach of high-tech companies to broad groups of businesses and consumers. In the 1990s, distribution channels now differentiate themselves through customization services and systems integration facilities. The primary issue of providing access to inventory becomes part of the baseline for all distributions. Providing unique custom services will now be their differentiation.

The last five years clearly took a toll on computer retailing. A one-mile stretch near where I live once had five computer stores. Now it has none. The corner computer store has almost disappeared. The obvious reasons have been the emergence of computer super stores, specialty software re-tailers, and value added resellers. Underlying these changes has been an even stronger force—the need for specialization. Think about it. Today's personal computer customers have been using PCs for years. Which is needed more by an experienced customer—store inventory or knowledge? Is having a limited retail stocking location with generalist salespeople more important than application specialists backed by a substantial inventory base? Do you want a retailer with an investment in limited inventory trying to steer your needs to match its inventory or a VAR with application spe-cialists understanding your problem and configuring a system to meet your needs? (This VAR probably uses the super store as a supplier.) The larger part of the market wants specialization. On-site solutions are more impor-tant than generalized retail inventory. Figure 8-1 shows how high-tech sup-pliers use customization.

Today, you need to establish your distribution channels along vertical market lines. This means expanding the role of your third-party distribution channel participants. These third parties can be active participants in cus-tomization efforts. This may involve source code arrangements, access to development and test methods, joint customizing participation, and special installation and support agreements. A key to designing these new channel arrangements is to align your partnering agreements with the customiza-tion requirements of a specific vertical market. That means that today's

Figure 8-1   High-Tech Suppliers Leverage Their Customization Strengths

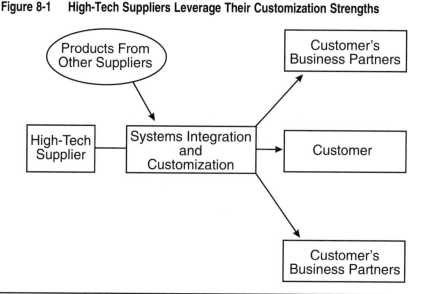

third-party distributor relationships can spawn tomorrow's joint ventures for consolidating a specific vertical market.

Companies need to create product features that promote external tailoring. First, they must add manipulation languages and development environments to their products. Once these are added customers and business partners can then perform the necessary customization. These partners are able to customize a product to meet unique customer requirements.

This has been happening for years in the data base market. Competitors are constantly trying to win advantage by having flexible programming languages that make it easy for value added resellers to create applications. Indigo Software has taken this idea one step further, bringing to market a user interface so simple to use that end users can easily put complex queries into large data bases. Indigo's products allow users information access that was previously available only with extensive customization. In effect, it has standardized customization of data base queries.

New technology platforms require new distribution channels. The new client/server computer architectures are inspiring brand new distribution strategies. These new distribution methods will have customization and integration capabilities to service their customers' enterprise needs worldwide. The move toward customization will put more leverage into channel participants than ever before. There may soon be new third-party arrangements between suppliers and resellers such as franchising strategies to provide source code and design information for third-party participants.

Customized Distribution

High-tech distributors should not view themselves as caught in the middle between suppliers wanting to customize and customers demanding customization. Instead of being squeezed out of the picture, the distribution channel can invert the problem and become the catalyst from which high-tech vertical market opportunities develop.

High-tech vertical markets are collections of sellers working with groups of customers with similar values and requirements. The customization needed by users spans multiple vendors, and high degrees of application/product specialty are required. (See Figure 8-2.)

There is little that prevents distribution companies from moving in the direction of increased specialization. The very notion of specialized market development is the domain of the distribution channel. To become a specialist in just a few markets means you are not going to be a generalist in many. It means paring your supplier list to suit the needs of your key vertical markets and adding specialty lines with vertical market focus. Building ver-

Figure 8-2   High-Tech Distributors Can Capture Vertical Markets through Integration

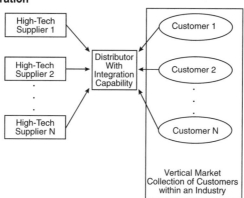

tical market expertise also means having the right experts in place to assist customers. There is also the question of which vertical markets to pursue. Where will your company be most successful? While high-tech distributors can move in this direction, it is not clear that the management of their businesses will put their present market position at risk as they try to move out as vertical market specialists, or that their startup vertical market distribution strategies will take advantage of these market opportunities. The computer retailer Businessland has been one of the most visible examples of being caught in the middle. It failed to move from a computing retail generalist to a successful specialist. Would its outcome have been different if it had moved from being a generalist to a vertical market force?

Standard to Custom and Back

Customized standardization is just the next stop on a multi-year cycle, or maybe spiral is a more accurate portrayal. The high-tech business has been going through its standard and custom phases for years. Each time it changes phase, the texture of the process changes with the cumulative efforts of the previous phases.

In the 1960s and 1970s, almost all high-tech markets involved significant customization. During the 1980s, the general high-tech business moved into the standard product phase with the personal computer dominating the landscape. The words "shrink wrap" entered the vocabulary of every high-tech marketer. Today's customers are drawing high-tech markets to the customization phase. High-tech companies will become immersed in specialization. The new philosophy will be that no two users are identical. Every sale will be custom in one way or another. Over time, the cycle will continue with a new twist—customers will be able to use standardized products that can be easily customized. The new PCMCIA cards appearing in the marketplace provide a good example. Hand-held devices can be given new personalities. When a PCMCIA card is inserted, this new capability puts customization directly into the user's hands. In this way, going through the present customization phase will deliver custom enhancements in a standard fashion.

Customers are pulling high-technology companies in different and conflicting directions. Customers want standardization. They also want specialization. They want unique complex functionality tailored for their needs and delivered in a plug-and-play fashion. They want easy-to-use applications totally transparent across dissimilar systems. They want it all. And they want it now. Many high-tech companies use an outdated model for dealing with these customer situations. Their assimilation of a customer's wants and needs lacks proper perspective. These companies want to sell standard products and are not willing to make product modifications. Without the ability to tailor a product to suit specific needs, it is hard to listen closely to a customer's wants and needs, and the customer's unique desires go unanswered.

Much of this conflicting demand stems from customers having to cope with their own conflicting market directions. Banks, for example, are tugged by tremendous polarizing forces. Government regulation is superimposing a major watchdog function on their loan practices because of the banking fiascoes of the 1980s. Meanwhile, bank customers are demanding higher loan service levels and instant loan approval. Market research shows that banking service levels decline as the number of people interacting with a bank's customers increases. Customers want to deal with one person knowing a lot about their needs rather than with lots of people who know little. The fewer contacts, the higher the satisfaction level. Market forecasters predict that the number of bank branches will decline, yet banks are developing ways to get even closer to the consumer. It is no longer enough to have widespread ATM access available at point-of-sale locations. All banks have that. Branch banking kiosks are opening inside grocery stores providing even more customer access. Twenty-four-hour banking service lines have become common throughout the consumer banking business. How do the bank's business strategists make any sense out of this?

These market forces are pulling banks in many directions at once. It's no wonder high-tech companies in turn receive conflicting customer directions from their banking customers. A bank's technology management must deal with a very dynamic and confusing competitive and legislative environment. Yet banking people must figure out a way to cope. These aren't simple transition problems—many of these conflicts are permanent and will always generate tension. Some can never be resolved. The hard reality of those in banking is managing mutually, simultaneously present conflicting demands.

The banking market is just one of many markets undergoing tremendous stress. Customers of high-technology are coming to terms with today's real-time world. Past business structures are not suitable for the future. Businesses are flattening out their organizations, putting aside their hierarchical infrastructures, and focusing on their value added aspects. These companies are empowering their knowledge workers with enterprise wide information access. They are eliminating information worker roles that simply change the format or media through which information is conveyed. High-tech suppliers must, in turn, provide these customers with the tools they need to build their new order, information-based corporations. These solutions will start off as specialized adaptations of standard products.

The Business of Business Redefinition

Companies of all sizes are restructuring themselves to meet the challenges of the 1990s. Your customer is operating in an anytime/anyplace market. Their consumers want goods and services on demand delivered to their doorstep, if necessary. Your customer must deliver products and services at the exact moment and location where customers need them. Your customers are using "mass customization" as a driving force behind the need to restructure, and relying on technology more than ever to meet customer demand. The technology they will need must precisely fit into their business. Their technology solutions will not be available "off the shelf."

There is an old story in the telephone business about a technology study that AT&T carried out during the early part of the century. The demand for telephone connections was increasing so rapidly the study predicted that—using the then-current operator assisted exchange—every working woman in America would be needed as an operator to switch calls. Something had to be done to meet this challenge.

AT&T did the next best thing. Instead of increasing its work force to create an army of operators, the company simply turned to technology. They created electronic switching networks and turned everyone, from age five on up, into fully-trained telephone operators. From the comfort of our 12-key pad we can dial anyone, anywhere and handle several levels of billing redirection. Service has increased, operator intervention has decreased.

While the phone companies were among the first to use information-processing technology to convert their customers into their work force, they are by no means the last. Over the past five years most of us have become bank tellers and gas station attendants. The more daring of us already have become our own stockbrokers and travel agents. And this is just the beginning.

Citicorp is a good example of a company that began to change the way it carried out its business early in the 1980s. The way Citicorp customers interact today with its services is incredible. For example, using Citicorp's vast networks, clients can get credit card services anytime, instantly. Car buyers get on-the-spot loan approvals in the showrooms. Mortgage loan approval is electronic though not yet out of the bank branch and into the real estate office.

Citicorp's use of technology to deliver distance-insensitive financial services was unprecedented. Looking at them today it is hard to tell whether they are a financial services company that used technology to differentiate itself or a networking company using financial transactions to generate value added functionality for its information packets. Either model can be used to describe Citicorp.

Customers want goods and services on their terms—where and when they want them. We have a world of "my time, my place" consumers. Banking and telephones are good examples of meeting this need. Many more are soon to come. These are examples of an overall economic trend. Businesses are reshaping themselves to respond to customer demand 24 hours a day and deliver their product on their customers' terms. To meet their needs, they will turn to very specialized solution sets spanning their enterprise.

Smart sellers recognize these pressures on their customers. They respond by finding ways to customize their products to meet their customers' needs. You are selling smart when you use customization to open up new markets and win important new customers.

Part IV

Partnerships

I f tomorrow you woke up and were responsible for sales of a high-tech company that was having problems in the market and if you could afford to select only one sales strategy, what would you do? Probably the best thing you could do is form sales partnerships with companies with similar customer targets. You are not looking for just any partner. You want someone who is trying to win (or maybe already has) customers with a profile that closely resembles the profile that you are looking for.

These next two chapters are about forming linkages—combining with your customers and your business partners. It's your job to make a break

Your Sales Model

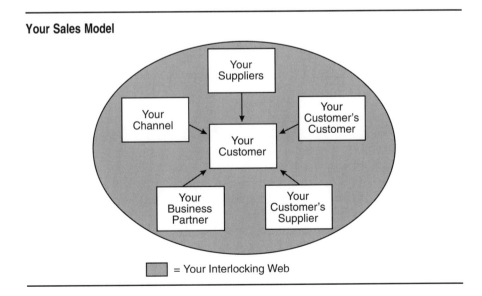

= Your Interlocking Web

with the old way of independence, and instead create a web interlocking you, your business partners, your customer, your customer's value chain, and your value chain. The better your web, the better will be your ability to gain market share.

Chapter 9

Forming Customer Partnerships

The best technology companies of the future will be the ones that interweave their selling into their organizations' fabric. Account development comes naturally to these companies. These are the companies that recognize the importance of customer involvement throughout their organizations. In your customer contacts you already know how much they are coming to depend on individuals throughout your organization—from your customer service experts to your accountants. You put your company in a partnership mode when you weave your company's work force with your customer's staff. Your personal sales role can influence these changes when you step aside and become the program manager of the many relationships your customer needs with your company instead of being the go-between in your company's relationship to its customers.

Smart selling means organizing high-technology companies around a sales mission. Some people don't like the idea of selling. They think it is enough to be a marketing-driven or an engineering-driven technology company. To be a sales-driven organization is simply out of the question. Management will not even consider the thought! From World War II until the 1980s, America ruled the technology markets. American management could play by its set of rules and limit its sales battles. It created sales organizations as appendices to the rest of its companies, not bothering to build a sales mission throughout the entire work force. Such luxuries have disappeared in today's technology marketplaces. Selling is no longer a gentleman's game—it's a fight to the end. Selling does not begin and end with the salesforce. High-technology companies will either teach their entire organization to sell, or die.

Selling is a creative process. Selecting the strategic mix for prospect engagement, product distribution, sales channel development, and ongoing customer support is key to the long-term success of your company. Your entire value chain must be positioned to engage your customer. And it does not stop there. You've got to design your products, installation, and support plans to fit your selling methods. Even the financial plans of a high-technology company must embrace its sales planning. These questions are not an afterthought to a company's business plan. They are an integral part of the entire corporate definition.

Technology companies involved with shrink-wrapped products sold through layered distribution channels hear this and say "That's good advice for people with direct sales groups, but that's not for me." These people have missed the point. Just because your product is shrink-wrapped doesn't mean your company should be shrink-wrapped and kept from inter-working with your customers. This is not to advocate bypassing your distribution channel. It's your job to empower your distribution channel through your abilities and your knowledge of your business sector. You are ultimately responsible for your company's successful account development even if distribution strategies are an important part of your customer fulfillment strategy. It's still up to you to leverage your reseller network in order to set and achieve your customer development goals.

Losing Your Way

Companies get lost and confused. It happens to all companies somewhere along the way. Sales drop. Customers in key vertical markets have major cutbacks. Product sales don't increase as expected. Competitors leapfrog your technology. These events are not the end of the world, but they do confuse people. With the dynamics of high-technology and the high rate of investment in competitive technologies, bad things happen to even the best positioned products. It is unfortunate but multiple negative outside factors often confuse an organization and distract it from its basic mission.

The major reason your company might lose its way is due to a lack of understanding of the overall sales mission throughout your organization. The difference between good and great organizations usually boils down to how well they weather these storms. Can you ride out negative events and still maintain your mission-critical course? Can you create opportunity from near disasters? Can you use your strategic sales mission to chart a successful course of action?

The degree to which your company has organized itself along the lines of its sales mission is a predictor of how well you can rebound from downturns. Does your entire organization get stuck in the mud when problems come up, or are you able to make a mid-course adjustment to your basic mission and persevere through unplanned events?

Prehistoric Selling

High-technology companies with sales groups organized in the same manner as their predecessors of the 1970s and 1980s are setting themselves up for disaster. In today's global economy, these ancient organizational models will not do. Today's high-technology companies must be completely sales conscious.

It is remarkable in this world of global economies that the largest technology companies do not deal with their sales forces globally. For example, a company's sales team selling to General Motors in Detroit may not even be in contact with their counterparts in other parts of the U.S., let alone in Europe and Asia. Yet, General Motors is a worldwide consumer. In today's high-technology sales, most companies have this sort of sales organization team communication problem.

This is a road map for disaster. Given any two competitors with similar market positions, the one that is selling globally to an enterprise will be the long-term victor. By selling on a global level a vendor can develop a broader perspective to improvise and improve on its product offerings. Table 9-1 illustrates the new competition with which vendors must deal.

Table 9.1   Today's New Competition

	Selling Then	**Selling Now**
Competition	U.S.-Centric	Global
Product Time to Market	2-3 Years	6 to 18 Months
Strength of Competition	Emerging	Entrenched
Types of Competition	Single Companies	Partners/Consortiums
Customer Type	First-time Buyers	Experienced Technology Buyers
Market Growth	Explosive	Vertical Market Dominant

Today's sales process is not like it was 20 years ago. In the 1970s, selling high-technology products was a top-down affair. You sold to your customer's highest-level people—presidents and senior vice-presidents. They would then tell their staffs what to do. Technology companies set up salesforces acting as separate entities to carry out this mission. Customers were often purchasing the technology for the first time. They were not sure of why, how, or what to purchase.

Times have changed. Today's end users have experience using and managing technology. Quite often the internal technology resources of a large-end user far outweigh what is available from most vendor organizations. End user technology acquisitions today are much more of a group process within companies. Their acquisition decisions involve many people and departments. These groups have lots of experience buying technology-based products. They know what they want to get out of their investments. They can extensively evaluate alternatives. And they know how to measure the results. Their decisions have a strong sense of business purpose.

What's more, this experienced customer model is equally valid for customers of all sizes. During the 1980s, small businesses gained experience buying technology-based products. Small businesses are now owners of computers, copiers, fax machines, and phone switches. Small businesses buying high-technology products have valuable buying experience. In the 1990s they are incorporating this learning into their plans and will demand more from their future investments.

Today you are selling to experienced buyers. Technology users are not neophytes. Your customer has been using high-tech products for years. Large and small companies have extremely complex needs. To remain competitive, technology companies must be responsive to all the needs of their customers. Sellers have got to get out of the boardroom and start meeting with today's technology decision makers. The process is no longer me selling to you—it has become my organization teaming with your organization.

The Changing Sale

The high-technology industry is on the verge of a huge and unprecedented shakeup. The age of the client/server computer architecture is here. Slowly but surely, end users of all sizes are revamping their technology innards to make way for client/server-based computing platforms. In the early 1990s, the client/server computer market was almost nonexistent. By the turn of the century, it will be the single largest computer market, consuming tremendous amounts of hardware, software, network devices, and services. Its growth curve will be fast and furious. Everyone involved with selling information-based technology products will be affected by it.

Through the 1980s, information technology selling was composed mainly of three types of organizations (see Figure 9-1).

1. Very large companies like IBM, DEC, and HP with tremendous field organizations performing systems engineering, service, and support around single vendor product lines

2. Mid-size organizations with relatively thin direct field staffs

3. Channel-based sales organizations with shrink-wrapped products sold and supported by third parties of various natures

The client/server market will rip apart this entire structure. The big platform vendors will no longer define a market's structure. Customers are moving to standardized, plug-and-play products. The selling model of the past has changed forever. Sales, system engineering, service, and support manpower must span multiple vendors. Technology usage requires multi-vendor integration. Third-party resellers and value added sellers must service enterprise needs. National and global forces will replace today's regional strategies. Each customer will have different service needs. Technology sales staffs will be needed for their application knowledge. They will be more involved with looking at how a business uses products rather than how the product works.

Figure 9-1 Information Technology Sales Structure in the 1980s

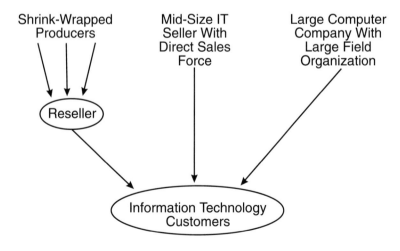

Coinciding with these changes is the migration of the large field staffs of the top computer companies from huge organizations selling closed vendor solutions to a more sustainable vendor-independent systems integration team. This will leave a tremendous void in the market for customers that rely on these staffs as an essential part of their MIS management process. The question remains unanswered—What will replace the customer specific systems integration services that were once the exclusive domain of large computer companies? Which sellers will dominate the client/server markets?

These changes will not just affect the largest computer sellers. Many of the value added resellers that were in these markets at the beginning of the 1990s depended on the existence of the large computer companies to set the competitive playing field. These VARs performed the "last mile" additions to the computing infrastructure. They performed the work that was left undone by the big guys. Without the big guys around to provide a stable selling environment, many of these VARs will soon be caught selling low-margin commodity products in the face of new enterprise-oriented systems integration market specialists.

How You Sell Is Part of Your Product

How you sell is as important today as what you sell. Your sales organization is as much a part of your total offering as is any of your product's vital characteristics. It also significantly differentiates one offering from another. Two product lines with identical technical characteristics and different sales channels (one direct selling and the other using retailers) offer two completely different solutions in the end user's eyes.

For instance, Hewlett Packard produces and sells 486 PCs. You can buy these computers directly from HP through its salesforce. Of course, you could also purchase a functionally identical 486 clone from any one of CompUSA's retail stores. While there are few hard technical differences between these two products, there are substantial soft differences from a buyer's standpoint. A large business may perceive Hewlett Packard's service, discounting practices, and integrated software as a strong differentiation. A small business may find this same differentiation irrelevant or maybe even an inconvenience, and would prefer the clone maker's version of the product teamed with CompUSA's services and discount program. The result is that HP's 486 offering is a very different product offering from the nearly identical clone hardware. The sales channel of each company accounts for very strong differences in buyer perception.

The real question is why is there so little differentiation here? Why doesn't HP expand its differentiation exclusively for the customer base where they are strongest? Why doesn't the clone maker do the same for its customer base? Is it because these companies are trying to cover too much ground and want both market opportunities? Or, even worse, is it because the management of these companies does not really believe in the sales power of their distinctive value? It could be they do not appreciate their sales channel's ability to create a strongly differentiated product.

A good example of a company using its sales structure to create distinctive value is Air Products, a large producer of industrial gases. Some of these products are basic ingredients in the production of semiconductors. For years several suppliers servicing the semiconductor industry had been supplying industrial gases as basic commodity products either through underground pipelines or cryogenic delivery trucks.

Air Products saw the battle in the semiconductor industry to create much higher density circuits. Producing extremely high-density semiconductors requires extremely pure raw materials. In the past, Air Products delivered its gases by truck to its tanks located at its semiconductor customers. As their customers' demand for gas purity increased, Air Products redefined the delivery point for its products from its truck deliveries outside their customers' buildings to the actual semiconductor diffusion tubes on manufacturing floors. Not only did the company capture market share, but Air Products also defined a new "services"-oriented business. It now designs, sells, services, and operates on-site gas purification systems, and partners with its customers to help create the next generation of semiconductor manufacturing plants.

Sales-Enabled Organization

Partnership selling is not just the salesperson's role. The job only begins there. It is up to your entire organization to sell to your customer's entire organization. The degree to which your company can do this rests within its organizational definition. Does everyone view their role, in some way, as part of the company's total sales mission? Do they even know the company's sales mission? Are they able and willing to link and form partnerships with your customers? They have to, and you must help them build a sales-enabled organization.

The sales-enabled organization has a strong sense of sales purpose throughout all departments. The employees relate what they do to what their customers want. The organization does not draw a boundary around its own employees. Rather, it uses its distribution channels, third-party service companies, independent training groups, and outside complementary product vendors as part of its total customer response program. A sales enabled organization builds itself and its partnerships in terms of creating and fulfilling your customer demand.

A sales-enabled organization creates distinctive value through its ability to form customer partnerships. The partnering strategy of a sales-enabled organization can even go so far as to become the reason people select its products. Because a sales-enabled organization operates as a partner, it can see opportunities before outsiders do. These sellers can determine new and interesting requirements and build them into their products before the requirements ever become generally known in the marketplace.

A sales-enabled organization knows how to form customer partnerships. Everyone in its organization is aware of the benefits that accrue when they become part of their customer's problem-solving work force. These sellers extend their relationships to their customer's customers, their customer's suppliers, and their customer's business partners to help integrate their products into their customer's value chain. The sales-enabled organization views the world from its customer's perspective. The sales-enabled organization understands the competitive business environment and attempts to bring about business improvement and competitive differentiation for its customer.

Organizational Disregard for Sales

Many high-technology companies do not take their sales mission seriously. High-tech people are uncomfortable with sales. It is almost a cultural thing—selling is dirty. Somewhere during the past 500 years Western culture developed a negative attitude toward merchants—the agrarian-based community looked on anyone not tilling their fields as doing less than a full day's work. Over the years high-tech sales departments have inherited this negative bias. Today's business schools have zillions of classes on marketing and finance, but none on selling.

The lack of sales experience, knowledge, and the lack of understanding of the sales process in the management of today's high-technology firms is dangerous. It can result in management with little understanding of the selling process. Many people have the attitude that selling is something that just happens. Sales does it. "It's not my job." I've been at companies where the president tells customers that he only views a salesperson's role as bringing in revenue each month. That's not a good stupid way for anyone to feel, let alone to tell the customer. It really wipes out any chances for that customer to use the company's sales team in a business partnership. Nevertheless, that sentiment is held throughout the high-tech community.

This attitude can sow the seeds for failure. Marketing organizations get filled with people without sales experience. Service organizations don't train their people to be sensitive to their customer's perspective. New product definitions lack vital field input. Manufacturing does not understand what the customer will do with the product. Pricing strategies stop being value-oriented and become cost-centric. An organization's distaste for sales will show up everywhere and in many ways throughout a company.

Converting a company to a sales-enabled organization is not easy. Management prejudices run deep. Individuals cannot change this on their own. Change requires cooperation across group boundaries. The management of these groups must want to create a sales-enabled environment and must manage this change—change may not happen by itself. The top management of your company must share in this goal.

The first question to ask yourself is what is the message management sends to the troops? Do your employees really feel part of the overall sales mission of the organization? Are they encouraged to participate in this mission? Do they even know what the mission is?

Reward Performance

To integrate your marketing and sales activity with the rest of your company, your entire work force must measure success along the same lines as you do. Do your company's present motivation schemes tie your work force to your corporate sales mission? Employee reward systems in high-technology companies need revamping from the top down. Companies begin their measurement systems from the balance sheet. Income statement motivation is a straightforward scheme—profits and sales increases are good; losses and sales decreases are bad. This is how the board of directors rates the president, how the president rates the vice-presidents, and so on through the ranks. But balance sheet motivations that may be useful tools for rating the long-term performance of a board of directors do not work for rating everyone else. To most employees, corporate profits are an abstraction that they are unable to affect one way or the other. The average employee doesn't see the direct relationship between her daily activity and corporate profits. It's even hard for many senior people to see this relationship. Nevertheless, balance sheet motivation incentives form the backbone for the performance reviews at high-technology companies.

It is very tempting to use financial information directly from the balance sheet to motivate people. First, this information is readily available—all companies must produce quarterly results in one form or another. In many companies this is the only reliable accounting information available regularly. Second, balance sheet numbers are easy to understand by outsiders on the board of directors even though they are confusing to the internal work force.

What's missing from balance sheet numbers is a sense of business reality. These numbers follow accounting standards that have little to do with managing a high-technology business and a lot to do with measurements useful for industry comparison and tax purposes. Balance sheet numbers rarely relate useful performance information at the proper time. Often your total company sales and profits can be highest at the same time a major new product is failing to win customer acceptance. In this case, balance sheet-based motivation may be rewarding the highest bonus rates at the same time the product acceptance rates are below expectation. These numbers are a poor tool to use in managing and rewarding a high-technology company work force.

The good news is that reward systems are changing. Incentive reward systems are replacing annual reviews. Incentive pay can extend throughout your work force and can become the largest portion of a person's annual compensation. Incentive rewards for sales successes can be specific to individuals, relate to work group and division performance, and will have enterprise success components. Incentives based on successful account development issues should not be limited to sales groups. Incentive systems can be created that can motivate an entire work force to help develop accounts.

Relate Performance Rewards to the High-Technology Use Cycle

All high-technology products and services go through three fundamental usage modes. Your customers will decide:

1. To adopt

2. To expand deployment

3. To continue the use of your offerings.

The sales volume and profit from your operation in each mode will vary widely, as shown in Figure 9-2.

Figure 9-2   Three Phases of the Technology Use Cycle

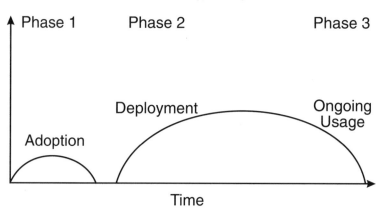

During your customer's adoption mode, your sales volume is the lowest and your non-recoverable costs are the highest. You will be making large investments, courting interest in your products by prospective customers, complementary partners, and potential participants in your sales channel. The start-up costs of working with new customers and new channel members can be high. For products with long sales cycles the sales costs per customer can be astronomical. Your return, if any, is little. When your organization is accomplishing its mission, your sales volume will be low, and your costs high.

When you are in the deployment expansion mode, your organization is working with your customer to increase the usage of your products and services. During this period installations and usage of your offerings grow and result in high purchase patterns and high support requirements within your company.

During the continued use phase your customer may not be expanding its usage of your offerings, but probably will be in a high service mode. Eventually they will become a replacement opportunity. They will want to reduce their long-term ownership costs. This may not be a period of high sales rates but can be highly profitable. Your customer may be willing to invest big dollars with you to help better manage and reconfigure his company's usage of your offerings.

Your customers will go through each of these phases with each of your products, and their support requirements will differ in each phase. These modes are continuous. On the East Coast some customers may be in the deployment mode while in Europe other customers will be in the evaluation mode with the same product.

Creating an organization performance reward system in this environment is difficult but necessary. You need to reward the teams involved with gaining customer acceptance for your products—though these teams generally will be costly to fund and will produce little sales volume during the early phases of a new product's life. You must create a different metric for your teams that are concerned with usage and service expansion.

Something must be done to keep your rewards system in line with your business problems. Today's use of balance sheet-based motivation goals does not work. Management may end up motivating its organization to load up distributor's shelves while not concerning itself with gaining customer usage. Another management system may reward customer shipments but not successful customer installations. Aligning your employee motivation system with your sales mission is a first step toward gaining your employee's participation in solving your customer's problems, and toward creating customer partnerships.

The best way to gain your employees' cooperation is to get their intellectual participation. Smart people will get involved when they can see a purpose in what they are doing. Your business partners also will become actively involved when they too can be part of your sales mission. If you can effectively define and articulate your company's mission, your customer base will sign on as well. Creating the sales mission and motivating your work force consistently within this framework is your first step toward moving to a sales-enabled organization.

Quality Sales Relationships

Two factors have brought about a dramatic shift in the American economy:

1. The service content of the economy has grown tremendously.

2. Businesses in all industries have redefined themselves in terms of quality.

Throughout all aspects of the economy companies have focused on quality and service.

This move toward quality and service has changed your customer landscape. The nature of your sale is much more complex than before. Customer expectations from you—their supplier—have changed. Your customers expect you to be tuned in to their business needs.

Starting with the semiconductor industry, high-tech companies have improved the quality of their products and services. After seeing their Japanese competitors take away major market segments, American semiconductor companies rose to the task to become high-quality producers. Quality consciousness has spread throughout the technology industry. American high-tech companies have also begun to deliver greater service content than in years past. When it comes to manufacturing and, to some extent, service, high-tech companies have addressed their quality processes.

It is almost unbelievable that, in spite of their emphasis on improved quality and higher customer service levels, American high-tech companies have not altered their basic sales approach to customers. The high-tech company sales flow still looks the same as it did over 20 years ago. It is as if IBM's Buck Rogers wrote out the script on how to sell computers in the 1960s and everyone in the industry mindlessly followed it forever. Sales organization structure, job descriptions, interdepartmental relationships, sales training, and incentive systems have stayed much the same despite massive changes in the way customers approach their business problems. Your quality-conscious customers want and need you to increase your participation within their business. To meet today's customer demands, you must rework the way your company designs and carries out its sales processes.

The Impact of Quality on the Way Your Customer Buys Technology

To reach competitive quality levels, your customer has reshaped his company using quality as the starting point. During the first phase of their move toward quality, people first thought of quality as some widget that gets added to the product or service. As time progressed, individuals began to realize that quality is a process and not an added component. Quality is a value concern of every individual during every task. Each event needs to be defined and examined from a quality perspective. Quality values must permeate everything; quality must be a part of every activity.

As your customer moves toward quality, the company's fundamental organizational structures change. Hierarchical organization charts are thrown out. Workgroups consisting of individuals from different parts of their company are formed to concentrate their combined efforts on a specific activity. Today's workgroup emphasis replaces traditional organization charts. Figure 9-3 shows how these changes are often implemented.

Your customer's focus on quality drew with it the company's need to establish multiple teams of people dedicated to doing a job from beginning to end. The workgroup has become the successful organization model for quality-conscious companies. While hierarchical frameworks still exist and

Figure 9-3   Three Steps toward Quality

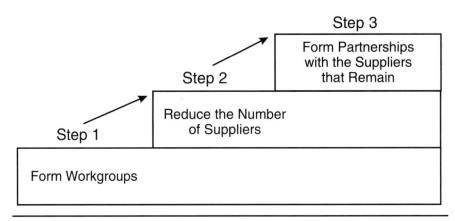

are useful for defining classical corporate structure, real control and authority have shifted to the workgroup.

The drive toward quality has restructured the way your customer uses his suppliers. To move toward higher quality, the company needed to improve the quality of its raw materials. The rationale is simple. If it is going to produce a higher-quality output, it must start with a higher-quality input.

Your customer has found that the drive to quality was forcing suppliers into "lowest bidder wins" relationships. High-quality input is essential for high-quality output. When your customer directed suppliers to reduce component costs, he was creating long-term quality problems. Manufacturers battled their suppliers over prices and ignored the relationship between their raw material input and the rest of their value added processes. Naturally, suppliers told to focus on price alone cut corners to keep prices down, and overall quality deteriorated.

Quality-driven customers realized they had far too many suppliers. Many more than they could handle. It takes time and effort to work with a supplier to improve overall quality. They had so many suppliers, they were unable to spend sufficient time with any one to improve quality. As part of your customers' drive toward quality, they dramatically cut down the total number of suppliers and extended their workgroups to include their most important remaining suppliers. By establishing long-term partnering relationships with suppliers, your customers saw they could drive up their raw material quality and, in turn, improve the quality of their output. Building supplier partnerships has become essential to long-term success in a high-quality world.

Wal-Mart used technology to help it form tighter partnerships with its suppliers. In the 1980s, Sears' and Kmart's larger volume put Wal-Mart at a competitive disadvantage when negotiating wholesale prices. To counter this disadvantage, Wal-Mart created a system whereby its suppliers receive daily sales reports from each Wal-Mart store. In some cases, vendors were provided access to the same decision and analysis software used by Wal-Mart. A promotion run across a sales region could be immediately monitored and analyzed by Wal-Mart and its supplier. The result of this special service is a closer, more productive partnership with vendors than Wal-Mart's competitors could offer. Not only does this capability improve Wal-Mart's own performance, but its vendors are able to improve their performance relative to their Wal-Mart relationship. In the past ten years, ideas like this have helped Wal-Mart become the largest and most profitable retailer—at the expense of Sears and Kmart.

The move to quality has occurred in waves. Manufacturers were the first to move. Service organizations are now just beginning to change. The quality process is infectious. Over time, the quality drive permeates every aspect of an organization, not just manufacturing departments. It's now coming right to your doorstep. Today, information services organizations within your customer's organization are beginning their move toward quality in a big way.

Your customer's information services groups will follow the path of the manufacturing organizations in their drive toward quality. Information services organizations are coming to the realization that they must apply quality values to every aspect of their processes. They will reduce their reliance on their hierarchical organization structure and long supplier lists. They will start to adopt the workgroup process as their basic way to set up new systems. And they will find that they too must reduce the number of suppliers they have in order to work more closely with those remaining in their drive to higher quality.

Selling to Quality-Oriented Customers

Your customers' move to higher quality and a focus on service will have the same influence on the information technology side of business as it did on the manufacturing side. Their logic will be the same. To improve the quality level of their output, information services groups will form focused workgroups and will reduce the number of suppliers with which they deal. Some of these new workgroups will focus strictly within the information services organization on internal projects and processes. Others will extend outside information services departments and form teams with the operational side of a company (otherwise known as their internal customers). The net effect will be a shift in information services decision-making toward the work-group.

Reducing the quantity of technology suppliers will be an important issue for your customer's information services groups. The people at the top of these organizations will care the most about cutting down their supplier lists. Major end users are already experiencing sizable white-collar down sizing. They are aggressively looking to reduce their organization's size and increase its effectiveness. When your customers focused on the lowest price vendor, they were encouraging any new seller to come into the business with their latest and greatest gadget. Using a new product also means spending time and money learning how to use it. End users accepted low-cost products without anticipating the hidden costs involved in working with yet another company. Most end users had the ability to receive tech-nology "raw material" and perform their own systems integration.

If it hasn't already happened, your customers will change their focus. They will become quality pragmatists. Their primary goal will not be to get the latest and greatest widget at the lowest price. Instead, they'll want very practical solutions that leverage their companies' value. Their information services groups will no longer have armies of people standing by to do systems integration. They'll call on outsiders to do this work. Their work-groups are focusing on solving more complicated business issues. They do not have time to get caught up managing unfocused technology excursions.

Personal computer procurements provide simplistic examples of why your customers want to leverage the value skills of outsiders. Should an organization buy the pieces it needs for a 486 PC from the lowest price sellers and use its own organization to configure the complete system, or should it outsource systems integration to a third-party expert knowing it may not get the lowest prices in all cases? The first method should result in the lowest hardware prices. But a focus on the lowest cost hardware will result in companies doing systems integration themselves. The second method may not yield the lowest hardware costs, but better utilizes its work force. Why should an organization want to do its own integration? Why not leverage their experts to get on with the business and use outside experts to do the computer systems integration? Outsourcing this function should re-sult in a higher quality level and allow a company to better use its profes-sional talents.

Some end-user information services groups are already well on their way up the quality path. The first to change were the information services organizations supporting high-quality manufacturers. This is a natural evolution for a manufacturer. After the production area redefines itself through quality, eventually every other group will be influenced and will change. Ultimately, quality processes will spread throughout the information processing industry.

Information services organizations will have the same difficulties dealing with quality as manufacturers once did. They first will try to look at it as an added on feature. When that does not really seem to work, they will eventually come to see quality as an integral part of their processes. They will redefine the way they approach problem solving and form workgroups. They will set up higher quality vendor relationships.

The move to quality and workgroups will have a tremendous impact on high-technology sellers. The focus of technology purchases will move away from price issues and toward value empowerment. Greater percentages of the technology business will shift toward purchase decisions that consider the entire value orientation of the customer—not just the individual component purchases. As a supplier, you will be judged in terms of your total value to your customer's business, not just the raw material you provide.

Is This a Sales Dream Come True?

This shift toward value purchasing is a dream for high-tech salespeople. For decades, the industry wanted to focus end-user purchases on total ownership costs. Sellers emphasized systems selling. In the 1970s and 1980s end users resisted accepting these ideas. Only the large procurements reliably measured vendors in terms of total acquisition and ownership costs.

Today, your customer will listen to your value proposition. His quality initiatives have sensitized him to the benefits of forming partnerships. He will reduce staff to leverage value, not to internally perform integration that can be better performed by knowledgeable vendors acting as business partners. Most customer organizations today have lost their ability to manage every technology acquisition. They are making fewer procurements with each purchase covering a broader set of issues. Today's end users are trying to get more done each time they make an acquisition.

In turn, suppliers are no longer competing on price-only issues. Today's customers are asking vendors to provide much more than just technology. Large- and small-end users are judging vendors in terms of their total value and how well their technology deployment interrelates to their fundamental business strategy. Your customer wants leverage.

Maybe It's a Nightmare

The dream, of course, is that your customer has become absolutely convinced of the true value of products and services that can come from a partnership with a supplier. The nightmare is that today your company may not provide full value services, but will continue to define itself as being only a supplier of products. Your company's organizational structure may prevent it from taking part in your user's quality process. It has set up an imaginary line that it will not cross. On one side of the line is your product, your warranty, and your service organization. On the other side of the line is your customer—left to figure out everything else for himself.

Many high-technology companies selling to quality-conscious information services organizations are uncertain about their customers' metamorphosis. Sadly, these sellers don't want to change from the way they've been doing business in the past. Reinforcement of this attitude comes from within their organizations. They may have elaborate quality and service rating systems that give them high scores on service response time, but these rating systems miss the point. The real issues involve coupling an organization to their customers' internal processes.

Information technology companies are too complacent. Despite rapid changes going on around them, they won't change themselves. They believe that their focus on quality and service stops at their shipping dock. But stopping there is not enough. They've got to reach out into their customer's workgroups and find ways to extend their value contribution into their customer's business stream.

What an irony! For years high-tech sellers have been using the rhetoric of value to differentiate their products. Through the years competitive pressures and buyer apathy pushed these suppliers toward a commodity orientation. Now buyers want more than shrink-wrapped solutions. Finally, end users are preparing to purchase at much higher value levels. Unfortunately, many high-tech sellers are not set up to respond.

Competing through Extended Workgroups

It is fair to assume that each major competitor you face in high-tech sales situations will have high-quality levels. They'll produce products and services that work and meet specifications. Plus, most of your competitors will come up with a service strategy that meets the needs of most of their customers. Since this is the case, you must figure out other ways to create service and quality level differentiation. To achieve differentiation, you must present your company as part of your customer's extended workgroup. You must enable your customer to gain leverage through your resources in order to empower his organization.

When you integrate your service organization into your customer's value stream you shift the quality focus from what you put on his receiving dock to the output resulting from your customer's use of your products and services. Your customer has to meet quality delivery levels of his own. Businesses of all sizes are, or soon will be, using a workgroup approach to run their major operations and expand their technology use. Your job is to form customer partnerships by placing your organization within your customer's workgroups. You want your team to participate with your customer as if they are an extension of your customer's organization. This workgroup extension may be your direct employees, your value added resellers, your telephone/trouble service support team or your third-party support team. Your actual partnering mechanism is dependent on your specific business conditions. It is your job to make this partnering relationship come together. The extension of your customer's workgroup to include your team member participation will increase your long-term success and your customer's satisfaction level.

When you compete on this level you can identify unique things that your company does that add value to your customer. Your customers are willing to pay a premium when you marry your company to their internal needs. They want leverage. They want vendors that add value to allow more effective operations. The relationship between you and your customers changes from buyer/seller to team member. The quality levels of your users' application increase. Their entire business model benefits. Price is no longer the major issue. Your customers want you to be financially successful since their destinies become intertwined with yours, they will benefit when you make a profit. And so they will negotiate for mutual satisfaction.

A major benefit that will accrue when you operate as part of your customer's team is the creation of additional barriers to entry. You are now part of your customer's extended workgroup. It is harder for your competitor to beat you. Your customer's switching costs increase. Changing to a new vendor becomes much more complicated once you get up to speed with your customer's internal processes. Your satisfied customer will work hard to keep the partnership your customer has established with you. He will not want to go through the learning curve with a new vendor.

The desire to form extended workgroups is as important to your customer as it is to you. As industry reduces the total numbers of vendors and expects more from those that remain, your customer needs your involvement at the workgroup level to gain more from each partnership.

Step back and look at what is happening within your customer. His organizational structures are turning inside out as the company redefines itself to compete in the high-quality, high-service global economy of the 1990s. Massive numbers of white collar workers have been furloughed. Managers must expand their business with fewer human resources. Your customer is streamlining his organization to reduce cycle time. He must do more, faster by using less people and more technology. His use of high-tech products and services is growing out of sight.

To achieve closer knit organizations, you can put your employees into your customer's workgroups. Today's customer wants your company's unique perspective. If you are in a business that must commit to delivery dates, product adaptations, or prepare special training material, your customer wants you to understand the uniqueness of his company's requirements and the urgency behind his requests. People responsible for program management and implementation must be available and assigned to your customer's workgroup to focus your company on meeting your customer's needs. The process of getting to the goal is as important as achieving it.

High-tech vendors that have been around for a number of years often have trouble handling these ideas. They have trouble working with their customer's internal process on a day-by-day basis. They aren't sensitive to the uniqueness of each customer. Nor can they commit to the fine-tuning end users require. They want to return to the good old days when there were well-known walls separating their operations from those of their customer.

Time to Rethink Partnering Relationships

Customers want their high-tech vendors to be their business partners. It is fairly common to hear the sales and marketing side of high-tech companies talk a lot about their willingness to partner, only to then see their operating side unable to change. Good intentions are not enough. Customer partnering requires an enlightened management team leading the work force. It also requires a work force trained and ready to respond to new customer teamwork concepts. Business agreements defining relationships may need restructuring to better define the framework for teaming. When companies begin to partner, barriers between organizations disappear.

Even a notion as simple as the shipping dock being the demarcation between a buyer and seller became obsolete when manufacturers formed extended workgroups with their suppliers. Just in time manufacturing brought out entirely new ways to link raw material providers into the manufacturer's value chain, removing the whole notion of a shipping dock.

Suppliers began delivering raw material right into the production stations. That meant suppliers were given time and date production schedules and took over the shipping and delivery function.

Forming extended workgroups goes beyond fielding a sales team or a reseller network. Teaming with a customer requires a company to organize itself in a completely different manner with direct customer involvement throughout its organization.

Don't confuse your need to provide responsive service levels with your customer's need to extend its enterprise. Customers want both. If a customer using a software product has a problem, nine out of 10 suppliers have some form of hotline support. They say "There, I'll give immediate service response to this customer. I will answer their question in nanoseconds." They categorize problems from fatal flaws to inconveniences and develop elaborate rating systems showing how fast they solve customers' problems. Hotlines may be adequate for providing a safety net and can provide a responsive communications vehicle for identifying and patching shortcomings of products already in the field. Unfortunately, many software companies think that staffing a hotline is the beginning and end of their customer service requirements. A customer's use of a software product is only partially serviced through a phone trouble desk. Just think of all of the ways a customer is involved with a piece of software—installation, hardware platform changes, operating system changes, education of users and even electronic interaction of input and output with outside groups. Hotlines don't even begin to address these issues. Other tools must be brought to bear.

Customer service is not the issue here. Customers expect high service levels from their technology suppliers. What concerns customers more is a high-tech company's ability to reach out and link with its customers to find new relationships that go beyond product usage. Today, the questions are: "How can you deliver your technology in a substantially new manner to make my business more successful? Here, this is what my company does well. How can you, my high-tech supplier, couple your value to mine?"

Create Ways to Extend Your Value into Your Customer's Workgroup

New ways of relating are needed—not more hot lines. Let's call these "resource extenders." You must sit down and develop a cadre of resource extenders that uniquely let your company project and imbed your organization into your customer's workgroups. Some resource extenders are humans. Some are processes. Some may be structural changes. Some involve additional training. Your sales, marketing, and operations teams can create a list of possible resource extenders that initiate a partnering process with your customer and are consistent with your sales channel. It's best to start this process for a specific customer and then try to generalize the idea for a subsegment of customers. The most powerful resource extenders are the ones that improve your customer's business (see Table 9-2).

Table 9-2   Resource Extenders Can Benefit Your Customer

	Resource Extenders	**Customer Benefit**
✓	Service Program Managers	Home office-based coordination of fulfillment services
✓	Install Services	Eliminates all customer involvement with installations
✓	Electronic Mail Access	Connects you to your customer's desktop
✓	Electronic Billing	Eliminates an extra step in your customer's operation
✓	Bulletin Boards	Allows idea sharing between your customers and your staff
✓	Video Conferencing	Puts your experts on-site more often
✓	Portable Computing	Gives your field force on site information access
✓	Compuserve Forums	Creates an information source tailored to customer segments
✓	Private Forum	Creates an information network for your third-party resellers
✓	Custom Services	Adapts your products to your customer's exact needs
✓	Weekly Conference Calls	Keeps your experts in touch with ongoing project progress
✓	Quarterly Progress Reviews	Quality tool for managing multiple processes
✓	Trouble Report Newsletter	Low-cost status communicator
✓	Partnering Agreement	Sets management framework for workgroup participation
✓	Contracts	Structures the partnering relationship
✓	Partnering Discussions	Open forum with customers to stimulate partnering ideas

The first resource extender that surfaces is the program manager. This position is probably one you can immediately create and one that can do the most, soonest, to extend your organization's reach to your customer. The program manager helps manage multi-dimensional relationships between your company and your customer. It's the program manager's responsibility to handle all of the detail planning questions that arise around your product. Ninety-nine percent of today's high-tech companies leave it to their sales group to field these questions. That worked in the 1970s and even to some extent in the 1980s, but it doesn't anymore. Customer relationships—like products—are immensely complex. Each customer has a vast array of needs that must be individually handled by discrete parts of the supplier's organization. Plus, selling strategies relying on third parties just cannot count on their reseller's complete participation in managing the details.

The program manager is a home office-based role that assembles the ongoing commitments between your company and your customer. Within your company, the program manager is the customer advocate—shaping and prioritizing issue resolution from the customer's viewpoint. To the customer, the program manager is the organizer of your response team—not the actual delivery source.

Many people still think program management is the role of the sales person, and in many companies it probably is. And it is probably costing them a lot to handle it this way. Salespeople are inefficient in this role and most often lower the priority of their program management activity when it conflicts with their account development role. (It's great to compete against another company whose salespeople also act like program managers. When they're out selling, they're taking away from their company's customer fulfillment processes. When they're program managing they're not out selling. They can't do both well.) Management teams should not confuse the sales development role with the program management role. As far as ultimate reporting authority, program managers can be defined as part of the sales organization. A program management team can work side by side with a reseller network just as well as it can work with a direct sales team. What's clear is that the program manager's role is not a field assignment and not that of the front line sales people. It is a senior level function that can cut across your internal organizational boundaries to identify and deliver you customer's requirements.

Another method of extending your company's resources is by interconnecting your computer networks with those of your customers. Your customers are all computer-enabled. Typically there are many computer systems on which they rely. You have the tools at your disposal to reach out to these companies and inter-work with them right at their customers' desktops. You have heard some terms that form the currency of these inter-corporate transactions—electronic mail, electronic data interchange, public networks. Large-end users are already well down the path of using technology to expand their reach. The infrastructure is in place. What is missing is the willpower to structure these tools in an aggressive business partnering manner. High-tech companies can create information utilities centered on their products and services that allow them to create closely coupled partnering strategies with their customers.

The contract and licensing agreements between a high-tech vendor and its customers form the basis of another resource extender. The relationship framework between you and your customer starts here. High-tech companies today use contracts that rigorously delineate legalistic details about the vendor/supplier relationship. Lawyers and accountants love them because they clearly limit the vendor's responsibility. They are written to make the goal the purchase of the product and not the improvement of the customer's business. These contracts list the responsibilities of the vendor to cure the deficiency in the event the product exhibits certain irregularities. Some vendors write contracts as if the customer's business environment is non-existent. These contracts do not structure a partnering relationship. Today's relationships require more understanding of the way products are actually used. Contracts can be the basis of the partnering agreement. A partnering contract treats the product's shipment as the first milestone in an ongoing relationship to improve your customer's business position.

Some high-tech companies are beginning to catch on. In 1992, Borland entered into an agreement with Price Waterhouse that was a unique step toward partnering. First of all, it provided for unlimited use and copy privileges of certain Borland products for all Price Waterhouse workstation users including use on their at home systems (it's pretty unusual for a large software company to give an end user this sort of reproduction authority). The agreement licensed all 35,000 Price Waterhouse workstations in existence at the time of the agreement, plus it provided for immediate copy privileges for any new systems. At the end of each year, Price Waterhouse accounts for any additional systems it purchases and pays for incremental per-unit license fees. So, in effect, they pay for the software after it has been in use. Price Waterhouse can significantly reduce the administration of its software ownership. They don't have to hassle with software requisitions nor do they have to worry about inadvertent copyright infringements by their employees. This allows them to operate much more efficiently.

Customers want partnerships. They do not care about the average system availability as much as they care about your overall responsiveness to their needs. They want to know that if a suspected problem with your product interrupts their business, you will drop everything and immediately begin helping them work out the problem. Customers want to see these ideas reflected in their business agreements. They want high-tech vendors to realize that they have a business to run, that their business comes first, and that the product is there to serve the business. They want their technology vendors to be part of a team focused on the smooth running of their business.

Selling smart means forming partnerships with your customers. Smart sellers are always on the lookout for new ways to team up with their customers and jointly focus on a common set of goals.

Chapter 10

Organizing Your Business Partners into a Differentiated Distribution Channel

uccessful channel strategies are the hallmark of successful high-tech companies. The simplest form of channel is the direct sales group where everyone selling to your customer works for your company. Only a few companies have the luxury of being in a direct selling situation worldwide. Companies primarily dependent on direct sales in major markets generally use channel selling for reaching foreign and specialty markets. All high-tech products sold are affected by the distribution environment enveloping their product class. You must recognize the nature of the channels within which you operate and take steps to maximize the opportunities these channels present.

Before you even begin to think about what to do with your sales channels, you first must divide your markets into submarkets. This means segmenting your customer base into groups with common characteristics. You are looking for similarities across different businesses. You want to get a better idea of how well your distinctive value plays within a market subsegment. You are also looking for market subsegments that have enough sales potential to be worth pursuing, while you maintain your competitive differentiation.

The characteristics of high-tech channels have become more complex. They influence you, your customer, and your business partners. By understanding their influence on the sale and use of your products, you take the first step toward organizing your business partners toward a competitive advantage (Figure 10-1).

Your channel consists of the market participants required to produce a satisfied customer. Center stage are the products that your company builds along with the services you provide. Then come the associated products and services that allow your customer to create an operating platform. Surrounding this platform are the consultants (internal and external to your customer) and advisors who recommend short- and long-term platform architecture. Next are the market participants that alter, program, or otherwise manipulate this platform to make it perform. Then there are the companies that complement your product and work together to satisfy your customer's needs. Finally, there are the installation and service suppliers required to get things working. Some of these participants may be very

Figure 10-1   Your Complex Sales Channel Relationships

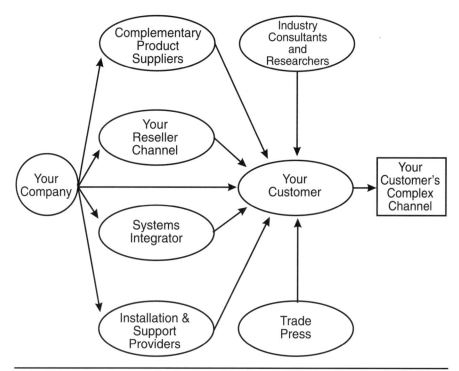

important to your sales strategy, others insignificant. It's up to you to combine all of the relevant participants into a competitive, differentiated entity that can accelerate your company's market share growth.

Most likely, the reseller market surrounding your customer base is pretty complex. Today's high-tech products have multiple paths to your customer. While you may prefer one channel, your competition may be involved with another. Often, the same product can find its way to your customer through a handful of completely different channels.

Table 10-1 summarizes the types of participants in your channel.

Your customer is subject to many environmental influences surrounding purchase decisions. You'd like your channels to be a seamless sales and support team for your customers. Sometimes you are lucky and all of these factors work in your favor. Most of the time you are the one who has to create the channel leading up to your customer's doorstep.

Analyze Your Competition

Just like you, your competitors will have their own business channels. Understanding your competitor's channel strategy is important for several reasons:

1. Your customer's perception of you versus your competition is heavily influenced by the way your products are sold. Your potential customers see you through your sales channel, and see your competition through their sales channel.

2. Your competitors may dominate certain distribution channels, leaving you with a choice. You can try to beat them where they are already strong, or develop potential channels where they do not have an advantage.

Table 10-1   There Are Many Types of Channel Participants

Channel Participant	Role
Distributor	Sells to resellers
Reseller	Sells to customers
Value Added Reseller	Sells direct to customers
System Integrators	Packages solution sets for customers
Direct Sales	Outside sales direct to customer
800 Sales	Telesales

3. Certain channels can be cluttered by too many competitors selling too many products. You may get lost trying to develop this sort of market.

4. Your competition cannot do it all. If they are strong using resellers, they probably do not do much in direct sales. If they provide turn-key functionality, they may not have much loyalty among third-party developers.

Large and successful competitors can be beaten in the market by identifying changes that are happening within their distribution channel which they are unable to cultivate. Technology sales channels, like the products they sell, are always evolving. You can use the channels' inevitable changes to your advantage by anticipating them and putting your company in a position to capitalize on them.

The measure of power in a sales channel is dollars and cents. Sellers generating the largest reseller profits are in a better position to get their resellers to do more for them. Sellers who account for only a tiny amount of reseller profits are along for the ride. If you sell an add-on to Novell's Netware products to installed Netware customers, you'll probably want to go after the Novell resellers. That seems like a good a good decision. Unfortunately, you'll be disappointed that these resellers may not be willing to learn very much about your product, may not care about making any special sales calls for your company, and may not even want to bother to learn how to install a demonstration copy of your product.

This position may seem unreasonable until you put yourself in their shoes. They've got to make a living. They cannot go around selling every Netware add-on in existence (there are thousands). Assuming they are successful, they've made a profit by participating in the Netware "food chain." They make their biggest profits selling new systems. They can go on doing something they know will work and sell more Netware, or they can take a risk and spend time trying to sell your product. This is an opportunity cost on their part. Do they spend their time on a known, or on an unknown? What's their risk and what's their reward? If their potential reward is large, they may be willing to spend a lot of time with you. If their potential reward is marginal, you're probably not going to get much support from them.

Begin by Selecting the Right Business Partners

The best business channels are the ones in which everyone involved wins. Customers, product suppliers, third-party participants, and the resellers themselves all can come out ahead when a channel strategy works well. The starting point is to select channel members that win when you do. Resellers come in all sorts of sizes and shapes. Your selection process is the equivalent of picking business partners who are vital to the long-term success of your operation. You want them to be just as much a part of your business as are your own internal employees. Look at your sales channel participants as if you worked in their companies. Focus on where their income originates. A profit analysis is the quickest way to understand the type of time allotment your sales partner is likely to provide.

Third-party semiconductor sales representatives provide a good example for this discussion. Semiconductor firms often assign independent sales representatives an exclusive territory. The typical representative may have a half dozen salespeople and one technical support person, and can represent about ten separate component companies (principals). Each of

Table 10-2   Revenue Production for a "Typical" Electronic Component Rep Organization

Product Line	Annual Sales	Rep's Commission	Net to Rep	Percentage of Total
Principal # 1	$20,000,000	3 percent	$600,000	45 percent
Principal # 2	$10,000,000	3 percent	$300,000	23 percent
Principal # 3	$5,000,000	3 percent	$150,000	12 percent
Principal # 4	$1,000,000	5 percent	$50,000	4 percent
Principal # 5	$1,000,000	5 percent	$50,000	4 percent
Principal # 6	$1,000,000	5 percent	$50,000	4 percent
Principal # 7	$500,000	8 percent	$40,000	3 percent
Principal # 8	$500,000	8 percent	$40,000	3 percent
Principal # 9	$100,000	8 percent	$8,000	1 percent
Principal #10	$100,000	8 percent	$8,000	1 percent
Total	$39,200,000		$1,296,000	100 percent

Note: These totals are spread out over the rep's entire salesforce and represent income before expenses.

these companies may have one or more component distributors in the same territory which must be serviced by this representative. Each distributor may have about 20 different salespeople each handling many accounts. Some of the principals have house accounts which the independent representative is excluded from servicing. Some of this rep's lines are broad-based while others are niche product-oriented. Table 10-2 illustrates how revenue production breaks out in a typical rep organization.

In Figure 10-2, see how an independent sales rep's income is distributed.

The most obvious thing is that the only real money in this for the representative comes from the top three lines. The product lines in the middle may make sense if their sales come from accounts at which the sales people already have business. The lines at the bottom of the list probably do not make any real sense for this firm unless they represent product lines that might eventually become important.

Another way to look at this sales environment is to count the number of separate relationships that must be occurring (see Figure 10-3).

Figure 10-2   Independent Sales Representative's Income Distribution

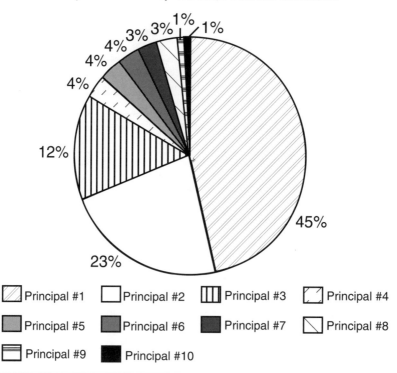

Figure 10-3   An Independent Representative Maintains Many Relationships

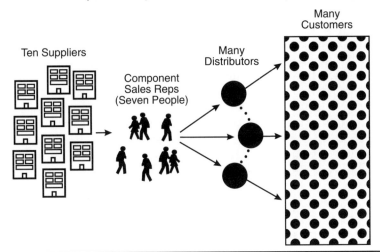

As you can start to see, this situation can get crazy pretty fast. Just start counting the relationships that an individual sales representative must maintain. If each supplier has at least five key individuals in sales and marketing and if each of the top five distributors has five sales representatives with overlapping territory, that's 75 contacts per sales representative before any customer contact is made. If each principal wants each sales representative to develop only one new design win per quarter, and if there is typically a 25 percent hit rate, then that sales representative must find and prospect four design opportunities per principal, or a total of 40 per quarter. This means that he or she must average almost one new design win per week. Given all of these contacts and all of the work winning new designs, this poor sales representative still has not had a chance to spend any time capturing orders for production users.

In the real world, component sales representatives do not spread their time evenly over all of the lines they represent. They take the path of least resistance—the one that will get them the most orders. They must also perfect the art of making each principal believe they are giving him the majority of their time. In the electronic component representative's business, the principal comes first and the customer comes second. The top lines get the greatest amount of sales time while the bottom ones get almost none. In an effort to get and keep as many lines as possible, there is little sales time left over for prospect development. Design wins must be done by the principal through its marketing efforts. The independent sales reps may do some prospecting within existing customers' organizations, but little else.

The hot products are the ones their customers have heard about and called about for information and samples. Anything else is left in the back of the rep's trunk.

The situation is not all that different in the computer reseller network with today's value added resellers. Computer VARs can range in size from one-person organizations to large national resellers. Within a regional area, a typical VAR may concentrate on a few vertical markets and, again, it's profits from short-range sales that drive these organizations.

Each VAR has a different perspective on the computer business that comes from its past experience, present opportunity pipeline, and vision of what the future holds. Below, is an income stream for a vertical market VAR summarizing revenues for a typical month and expanding these on an annual basis. This VAR's income stream is determined by how many new systems it sells, how much add-on business is generated from existing customers, and service revenue from technical support. So this VAR needs to be doing two things—selling things and keeping technical support people on the street, generating revenue. (See Table 10-3.)

As you can see, this VAR's income is driven by selling new systems. New system sales generate well over half of the profit contribution and probably account for much of the service revenue (through installation services). To generate more income over the short term, this VAR is most likely to put all its energy into selling more new systems. If you have a product line that is sold as an add-on component to existing systems, what will this VAR do for you? Probably nothing. The company is out to sell new systems. To the degree that your products help it do this, you are an asset. If you are

Table 10-3   Revenue Sources for a Regional Vertical Market Computer VAR

	Monthly	Annual	Margin	Percent
System Sales				
New Systems	$200,000	$2,400,000	$720,000	59 percent
Add On Sales	$100,000	$1,200,000	$360,000	29 percent
Services				
Technical Support	$20,000	$240,000	$72,000	6 percent
Training	$10,000	$120,000	$36,000	3 percent
Maintenance	$10,000	$120,000	$36,000	3 percent
Total Revenue	$340,000	$4,080,000	$1,224,000	

asking the company to go back into its installed base and develop opportunities for your product, it may not be a very productive use of time.

This income chart (Figure 10-4) tells the whole story. Selling new systems drives this company's business. If you help it do that, your products will be welcome and your time well spent. If you don't help it do this, your time and the VAR's can be spent better elsewhere. If your products are involved in its new system sales, you'll need to look further into the components that make up its new system revenue to make sure that what you are selling will actually increase its projected income stream.

You need to understand your resellers' financial incentives long before you sign them up. You'll want to do this analysis to make sure you and your potential business partners have the same interests. You'll want to select business partners that consider you in their mainstream business and not on the cusp. These are the business relationships where each partner is operating in its mutual best interest and focusing on the most important part of its own profit contribution. It's not enough for your products to generate profits to your business partners. You must contribute profits in areas where they are already focusing.

Figure 10-4   Income Contribution for a Regional Vertical Market Computer VAR

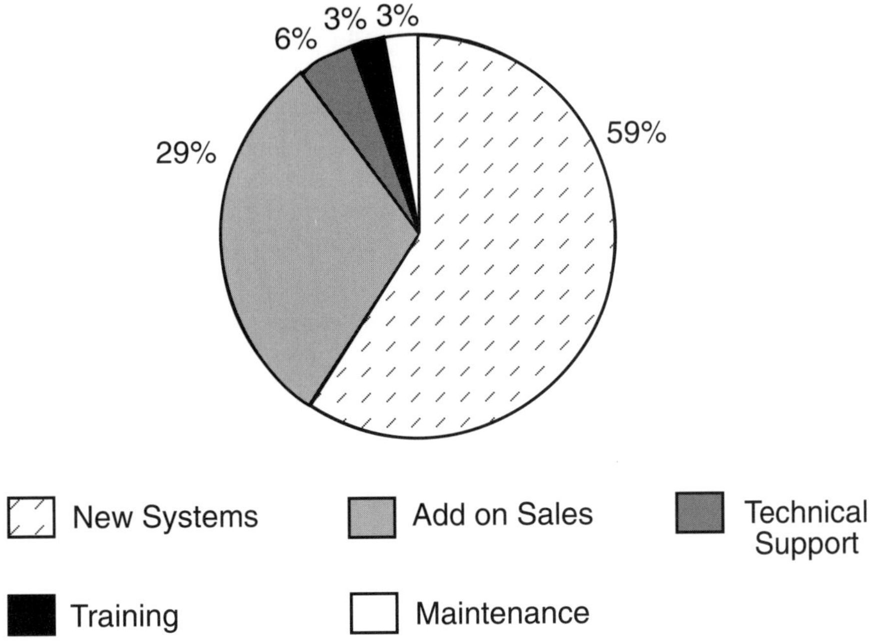

3% 3%
6%
29%
59%

New Systems   Add on Sales   Technical Support

Training   Maintenance

Channel Misconceptions

Channels are like politics. To paraphrase the retired Speaker of the House, Tip O'Neill, "All channels are local." The daily buying and selling events that take place in each of your significant sales regions contribute to your company's success. Setting up the right channels in each market and refining and developing your channel strategy are continuing processes.

Sales channels that look good on a national basis may have strong and weak regional components. Success in one or two sales areas may be hiding problems in other locations. The things that are making your company a success in Chicago may not be going on in New York. Exporting the successes your company is having in its hottest regions may help win market share in other areas. (This also applies for your competitors' channels. They may be having great success in some regions while others are falling apart.)

One of the biggest problems a technology company has with selling is understanding the dynamics of its own sales channel. There are five misconceptions of technology sales channels that often occur:

1. Somebody "owns" the customer. This is the biggest problem you'll likely to run into. Technology salespeople seem to kill themselves over a vague notion of account control. Everyone wants to be in control and have ownership of account situation. The truth here is that the customer "owns" the supplier, not the other way around.

2. Your company employees feel it's not their job to call your customers. This happens all of the time to high-tech companies working with resellers. Workers in your own company often feel that if your reseller sells to the account then its the reseller's job to conduct any and all follow up. This reasoning is not correct.

3. Channels are static. People in your company want stability. They want to believe that a sales channel is a static entity and that it will be there forever. This kind of thinking is certain to doom even the best channel.

4. Sales success is someone else's problem. When you have a sales channel, its easy to get complacent and not worry about the basics of sales. How does value get established for your products? How many customer contacts per week do you and your sales channel have? What can you do to make your overall contact rate go up? What works and what doesn't work for your selling? Sales success is your problem. Don't pass the buck.

5. The sale is complete when our products ship. This is a great way to get your company into trouble. It's easy to trap yourself into thinking that your job is done when your products arrive on your channel's receiving dock. That's when your company's real selling just begins. Your sale is never complete until your customer has the value they expected from putting your product to work.

Integrate Your Selling Efforts

As often happens in the business world, the best intentions get in the way of success. Technology companies stumble badly when they try to merge their existing direct sales forces with their emerging distribution channels. You are probably very familiar with this chain of events. A new technology is brought out to the market. The new products are complex to sell and install, so direct company employees are put in place to do the selling. After a few years, the product line is a success. New competitors have come into the market as well as complementary product offerings. Resellers are better equipped to participate in the sales process. The company is about to bring out its new generation of products which are less expensive and which involve much less technical complexity for customers to use them. This company's new product is introduced using its existing salesforce as well as a new set of distributors serving the market. During the early months of these new relationships, the company's salespeople are not sure how to work with third-party resellers. The resellers don't know which customers to call on. A year later, everyone is confused. The company is holding emergency meetings to figure out what's gone wrong and why sales are way off-plan.

The specific reasons things do not work out in these situations differs from case to case. What's common across all of them, though, is problems stemming from the lack of integration between the different sales groups. The problem that occurs most often is that the sales management tries to divide the customers along unnatural boundaries, telling the direct sales people to call on one group and leave the rest to the resellers. At the end of the day, there is only one set of customers out there and management should solve the problem by integrating the salesforces, not by dividing the customers in unnatural ways.

The problems of getting salesforces to work together isn't limited to direct salesforces cooperating with resellers. Within sales teams there is often a tremendous lack of cooperation across geographic areas and between different market segments. Large global accounts have sales teams in one location disengaged from their counterparts in other regions. Federal sales is removed from one sales team and given to a group of people in Washington even though less than half of the technology procurements originate there. Vertical market successes in one area are not repeated on a larger scale due to poor internal cooperation. Industry associations capable of being catalysts for submarket standardization are not properly cultivated because the associations themselves are not large enough users.

You've probably seen the results of this lack of integration across your company's sales infrastructure. People give it many names—channel conflict, commission splitting, or just plain old office politics. The results of this lack of cooperation are disastrous. Not only do they decrease sales, they cause your company to operate inefficiently. You can sit around and wait for the day that these problems magically go away (with an increasingly sinking feeling that this may never happen), or you can begin to fix the problem yourself. Cooperation is contagious. Salespeople and sales management want to cooperate. Often, though, they don't know how. They'll wait to follow someone else's lead.

The Virtual Sales Company

The best sales cooperation models get people from several co-sellers working and thinking as if they are all part of the same business. Each individual must temporarily forget her employer's goals to create a business from a group of businesses—the virtual sales company—that has as its objective satisfying the needs of a targeted customer base. The "employees" of this virtual sales company are the sales participants. The virtual sales company sets its sales objectives, identifies the available resources, then allocates these resources in the way most likely to achieve success.

There are two important consequences resulting from the virtual sales company:

1. The participants identify and prioritize their sales goals with respect to their sales targets.

2. The ongoing process of setting goals, evaluating results, recognizing successes, and understanding failure points will not only improve the immediate sales situations, it will also feed back process improvements to the parent organizations whose salespeople are part of the virtual entity. Figures 10-5 and 10-6 show how a virtual sales company is formed, and how it sets a goal-achieving agenda.

Figure 10-5   The Virtual Sales Company Is Formed from Interested Market Participants

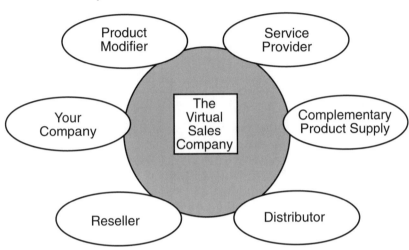

For example, suppose for a minute that you are a sales representative with a UNIX computer company that sells through VARs, and that your territory is Southern California. Suppose also that your company has just had a success on the East Coast selling a system as an inventory management tool for a small parts distributor. You know that there are hundreds of these types of prospects within your territory and you'd like to begin pros-

Figure 10-6   The Virtual Sales Company Sets Its Agenda to Meet Its Goals

pecting these customers. Instead of going it alone, you decide to form a virtual sales company. You call together your co-seller counterparts from:

1. A software firm whose inventory management products work on your platform

2. A local software integrator that specializes in installation and conversion of existing methods

3. The local sales manager for a communications firm that provides the local area connectivity required to support your system

4. A systems VAR that has been successful within this market

This group becomes your virtual sales company, selling to the inventory management market. At your first meeting, you provide relevant market-sizing information to help scope out the opportunity. Then the group discusses and selects its goals and budgets the sales resources they are able to muster.

Once formed, the virtual sales company has three ongoing responsibilities:

1. Execute the sales plan

2. Regularly meet to analyze successes and reset goals

3. Try to understand the barriers preventing its further success

The idea of forming virtual sales organizations makes sense for everyone involved. Technology markets are intertwined and your success relates to the success of your business partners. Making this virtual organization a success is dependent on the degree to which the management of a technology company encourages this sort of business participation. Unfortunately, many companies are still living in the Dark Ages and are unable to form these relationships.

IBM's Cooperative Sales Partner (CSP) program is an example of a partnering program that doesn't work. When you are an IBM CSP your company pays IBM a portion of your sales (above 10 percent) for IBM's sales help whether or not the IBM sales team was of any real value. What's worse, this is a corporate-run marketing program and IBM cannot even guarantee that the regional sales teams will participate with your sales development program. In theory, the IBM salesperson sees an opportunity, runs back to his office and looks in his on-line CSP database to find the appropriate business partner, then calls you up and involves you with the sale. IBM's CSP program would be great if the world really worked that way and if your competitors were kind enough to wait around until IBM found out about the sales opportunity.

IBM's CSP program isn't just a bad partnering idea, it's also a long-term disaster for IBM. Imagine two computer companies that compete. One has a partnering program where it jointly develops and cultivates customers. The other doesn't partner very well and charges its business partners large fees for sales references. In the long run, the company that partners well will end up with healthier business partners while the one that charges its partners fees will be stripping them of the margins they need to reinvest in their products and remain competitive.

Information Networks Can Interconnect Your Business Partners

The old story about the cobbler's children without shoes applies to high-technology sales groups and their use of technology tools. Many companies sell computers and networks to end users and never think about making a similar investment in their own salesforces. Just as bad are the companies that buy their sales group computers but fail to network them to form appropriate information webs. Information networks can be the load-bearing walls framing your business relationships in the 1990s. The ubiquitous availability of information technology creates an opportunity for businesses worldwide to use technology to enhance their competitive positions. You can use today's communications networks to link your business partners and to extend your reach to your customer base (see Figure 10-7).

The first question you ask when forming your electronic business alliance is "What information do we need to share and how do we empower our available resources to significantly improve our customers' business performance?" These networks usually start with electronic mail access and expand to bulletin boards, news feeds, and workgroup communications. Some information sources already exist, but new information collection and distribution strategies may be needed to further enhance electronic business partnering.

You can empower your virtual sales company by using electronic partnering tools. The electronic links within your group form a collaborative framework to exchange information and ideas among the members of your virtual sales company and with your potential customers. This network can also facilitate the account development and ongoing service relationships you will have within your sales group.

Large companies can initiate their own networks that will serve as the framework for their virtual sales teams. Apple Computer's AppleLink Serv-

Figure 10-7   Electronic Networks Can Be Your Information Pipeline

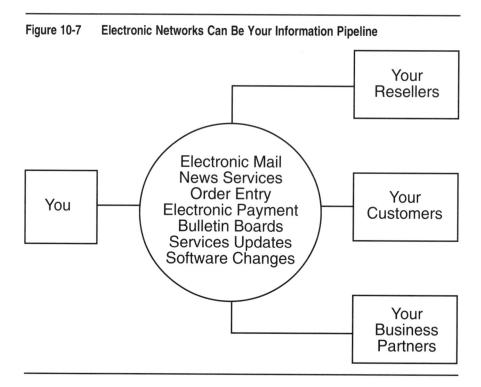

ice and IBM's Information Network are two examples of widespread collaborative networks that foster market development. Networks like Compuserve and America On-line offer private and public forums that also allow collaborative nets to form easily. Using a Compuserve Forum, your virtual sales company participants can access private electronic bulletin boards containing your price information and data sheets. You can also post information databases for them to search containing possible sales leads in their sales territory. Plus, you can set up interactive access for specific questions, information exchange, and electronic mail.

The Internet has grown to become the largest collaborative network in the world. You'll find that many of your customers and your business partners already use the Internet in one way or another. You may find this to be the best starting point for your electronic partnering links.

The techniques which will work best for you are highly dependent upon your sales situation. It's up to you to begin empowering your sales partnerships with electronic access tools.

Information-Based Electronic Markets

Using electronic links to interconnect your business partners is just the beginning. You can create distinctive value for your company through electronic, information-based network strategies. Until recently, information-based business strategies were in the hands of people who could invest in large-scale projects. Successful information-based strategies required lots of computers, vast magnetic storage facilities, expensive, wide-area networks, specialized-user terminals, and armies of programmer and information workers to prepare the raw material. To pay for these investments, large, financially solvent information foundries were needed. Stock exchange quotations (Quotron), legal briefs (Lexis), news research (Nexis), and travel reservations (Saber) are some examples of successful information-based businesses that grew up in the 1980s. Today's technology lets even small organizations band together to form networks and realize the benefits of information sharing without requiring large up-front investments. By projecting the future impact these information-based electronic markets will have on your key customers, you can align your future product strategies in these directions.

100 Percent by 100 Percent by 100 Percent

Once upon a time, only a few people had computer terminals on their desks. All that has changed. We are now moving to 100 percent of the employees in a business having personal workstations. Many businesses (usually the smallest ones!) already have workstations for all of their employees. No matter what the market or job, every worker will have one, although there will be differences among them. The quick-service gas attendant's personal workstation (already in place) will look a lot different from the workstation on the desk of the president of the oil company (not yet in place). Just when your customer is getting used to a 100 percent networked workstation availability across his company's work force, he will have yet another new capability—100 percent of his customer's employees will have workstations. Throw in the fact that 100 percent of the company's suppliers' work force will have network connected workstations and you have a brand new business world. As workstations become ubiquitous, the communications industry is driving toward high-capacity, low-cost interconnection. That's something that a TV set has had for years. In the 1990s, personal workstations are going to achieve an equivalent communications link.

You can harness this information technology and build a competitive edge into your sales strategy.

Along with all of these new corporate information structures comes a new set of strategic choices for your business. This technology offers exciting new business opportunities for reshaping your sales relationships. These systems will dramatically change information access. Entire work forces, customers, and competitors can have access to endless amounts of information relative to their business situation.

Take car repair as an example. With respect to information access, the auto repair market has not changed very much in the last ten years. Cars have become much more complicated and the degree of repair specialization has increased. Retailers specializing in oil changing, engine tune-ups, brake repair, and muffler repair have taken hold of the high-volume, routine maintenance operations. The biggest infusion of technology has come from the diagnostic equipment makers to repair the high-tech engines. But electronic information access in the industry is not very different today than a decade ago.

Imagine, though, how the auto repair market could change if all service providers were electronically connected to a real-time information network. Customers would also have access to consumer services available from these networks. Many new changes in auto repair would result. Accurate repair history over the life of the car could be compiled across all service providers. Customers could compare their repair costs to norms for their vehicles and driving conditions. Information about anticipated repair requirements could be developed from statistical databases for each car model—both what preventive maintenance would be worthwhile and what the most likely cause of a problem could be. Such an information service could then be used to establish several electronic markets—one for the consumer shopping for price, location, and scheduling of repairs, another for the repair shop that uses outside jobbers to locate, price, and order parts required for repairs. What might begin as an information requirement could then move to an electronic market.

When such an electronic auto repair market reaches critical mass, more and more market players will want to be part of it. Towing services, used car purchasers (looking for repair history on a car), and auto parts retailers will connect to the network. Car owners will want to register their cars as part of lowering their ownership costs and increasing the resale value. Auto clubs will join. Insurance companies will participate. Even the government will use this for managing its own fleet of cars, locating stolen cars and to facilitate registration. Finally, the auto makers themselves will join.

As this information-based marketplace takes hold, the dynamics of the market will change. Market share will shift dramatically. But who will take the initiative and make this sort of market happen? Auto makers are in the best position, but probably see this sort of open market as a threat to their retail channels. While they are in the best position to act first, they may actually be the last to move.

If an auto maker does not move first to create this information market, who will? Credit card companies may be in a good position. They are already involved with many of the transactions and can expand their information collection capability. Or maybe one of the retail point-of-sale systems companies specializing in the auto after-market (like TRIAD) will make the move. Maybe it will be a wide-area access information service with strong ties to the consumer (Compuserve or Prodigy). Perhaps one of the phone companies will expand its yellow pages business and form this information marketplace. Or maybe none of the established players will move, and it will take a brand new startup company.

Will this information-based electronic marketplace change the auto repair industry? Yes. And the change will be big time. Repair shops will be competing on their past successes—information on how long and how much previous repairs cost will be available for consumers. Invoicing and payment procedures will become instant and paperless. The role of the auto parts distributor and retailer will become more specialized as electronic access changes parts locating methods. New types of competitors can enter the market with ready access to customers.

This electronic market can also change the way new cars are sold. Some auto sellers could change their service structure if they could electronically form a nationwide group of authorized service shops, complete with access to all vital maintenance manuals, training guides, and warranty practices. This may not mean much for the high-volume auto maker, but can put specialty auto makers on a factory direct basis.

This auto repair information-based market is an example of what can happen over the next few years in every market. Ten years ago, it would not have been believable. Today, it's possible. To succeed, this type of network must reach a critical mass which will take years. A major market participant may serve as a catalyst for building market momentum. Major market participants may even do the reverse and try to prevent this sort of information-based market from happening for fear of losing market share.

If your company is involved with technology selling to companies in this industry, you can adopt their electronic commerce model. Selling from this perspective lets you position your company as a catalyst of change. These companies will begin to view you as a way to move themselves into these electronic markets. The only thing that inhibits these markets from forming is the limited imagination of the companies in the marketplace. High-tech companies must reach into their markets and ignite the forces that can bring about new information-based electronic facilities. The question is no longer whether or not these sort of networks are possible. The question in front of your customers is how and when to use information to change their business.

Collecting and Using Information

Your customer has an opportunity to collect information about his customer each time he comes in contact with her. Take something as simple as a bathroom scale. It is easy with today's technology to imagine a scale that can take your weight, store it for days or weeks, print it out along with some useful charting information, or even dial a database to connect to your medical files. Tied to a weight reduction program it can differentiate a weight counseling program with in-home feedback. Or this scale can be used in a medical program where weight monitoring is helpful toward outpatient care. Maybe an infant version of this product would be popular among new parents.

The point of this example is that your customers probably have frequent interaction points with their customers. They may not be aware of how frequent these are, or can be. For instance, would the bathroom scale manufacturer say he had indirect contact with his customers through their retailers once every few years when the product is purchased? Would he say he had daily direct contact with the customers every time the scale was used? Do the people who manage the Weight Watchers program know they can get client follow-up multiple times per day through this scale? Today's technology allows your customers to collect valuable information whenever they come in contact with their customer. They can then use this information to differentiate themselves from their competitors and improve their business. It's up to you to show them how. What can be collected and how to make use of the information provides the unique business choice for your customers. The technology does not set the limitations as before. Today's limitations are mostly due to our own imagination.

Sometimes your customers don't have to go very far to find information that can boost their market share. It may already be on their doorstep. Such was the case for AMP Inc., the largest producers of electrical connectors in the world. AMP's $3 billion sales comes from over 70,000 different products. To simplify access to technical and performance information on their products, AMP began using CD-ROM disks. CD-ROMs allow users to quickly access large amounts of information from their personal computer workstation. AMP's CD-ROM reference catalogue of parts assists AMP employees, distributors, and customers with information access on key electronic components. Just think of the market share increase this can mean—how many new designs will AMP win simply because equipment designers had ready access to critical connector product information? This strategy relies on information that AMP already had on its products. What's more, there is ample opportunity to expand this strategy to incorporate other information databases critical to the needs of the company's customer base.

In the 1980s the best examples of collecting useful information about customers came from the airline industry's frequent flier programs. This did not involve very much in the way of new data collection so much as new ways of organizing information already collected through a high-power marketing system. By putting the marketing spin on these data-capturing programs and by rewarding customers for frequent use, the airlines were able to add an important layer of differentiation on top of a commodity service.

As in the airline industry, new information-based strategies can change the nature of the business. The frequent flier programs have changed the ways airlines market their products. They have also changed the nature of the marketing partnerships through combination of awards with hotels, car rentals, and credit cards. Both buying and selling patterns have changed.

Similar changes are in store for many other markets through the collection of customer information at the point of contact. Those who find what, when, where, and how to collect will be the marketing wizards of the 1990s. Successful high-tech companies will meet the challenges posed by these new ideas by capturing electronic representation of customer contact and converting this information to improve their customer's market share.

Business Partnerships Will Reshape Entire Industries

In 1992, the health care industry moved out in a big way to establish an information network. The National Electronic Information Corp. (NEIC) is a consortium of 60 firms paying health care bills. Medicare agreed to back a single standard for electronic data interchange and electronic funds transfer. NEIC then moved to build a network providing real-time links to doctors, hospitals, medical labs, and insurers. This new network will provide insurance coverage information in real time and—within seconds—will electronically bill the appropriate insurance company, avoiding paper-based transactions. Experts expect the annual savings for this paperless system to be on the order of $4 billion. In just a few years, the information flow between insurance companies, patients, and health care providers will be reshaped by an industry partnership targeted at creating a paperless system.

Work-in-process pipelines account for the greatest percentage of time in the industrial value chain. Electronic information-based markets have the ability to significantly reduce the length of these pipelines. With just-in-time manufacturing, companies eliminated much of the inventory lag time within their own value chain. Information-based electronic marketplaces have the ability to extend these just-in-time ideas and elements across an industry wide value chain.

All industry participants will be members of these electronic markets. Suppliers and consumers will access a common information infrastructure through their common desire to reduce their response time. The cumulative effect of response time reduction is directly measurable in dollars. Using these future networks, companies will better leverage resources, reduce acquisition costs, respond faster to customer demand, tailor custom response to customer requirements, and reduce inventory requirements. The best technology sellers of the 1990s will partner with customer participants at the outset of the formation of these networks.

Market dominant companies are well-positioned to be catalysts in the formation of these electronic markets. If they don't move out on an industry scale, others will form these markets instead, and they are an inevitable part of the 1990s. Your customer will want and need to help create such networks.

Businesses involved with these electronic markets will turn to the high-tech industry to provide goods and services to allow them to participate electronically. These companies will be collecting and utilizing information on a worldwide basis to differentiate themselves. They will use the electronic information available to them to reshape their value and the value of their product offering.

Selling smart means organizing your business partners into an effective selling entity focused on specific market development goals. Smart sellers anticipate information use changes within their customer's organization and work to become part of their customer's long-term information strategy.

Part V

Getting New Customers and Products While Keeping Existing Ones

The real measures for high-technology selling are your ability to get and keep new customers, your ability to expand existing customers, and your ability to sell new products quickly. New customers fuel growth. New customers bring new perspectives into your company's outlook. They can help you find important new ways of using your products and can give you ideas for creating new additions to your products. Your existing customer base may be your largest opportunity for continued success. Your new products represent your company's most important investments. All products have limited life spans. It's up to you to quickly create sales for your new products. The longer it takes to incubate the customer base for your new product, the less successful your company will be.

Chapter 11

Selling to Existing Customers

To many, selling to existing customers seems unnecessary. A lot of people think existing customers don't need the sales attention required by those who are not yet their customers. They ask, "Why should you have to sell to someone who is already your customer?" They'll start with the assumption that selling to existing customers is simple and then implement convoluted schemes to reduce the sales efforts and costs when working with their present customer base. Two years later, their company is in trouble—trouble that began as their existing customer base migrated away to other suppliers.

Existing customers buy the vast majority of products and services from high-tech companies. You should fall in love with your existing customer base. These are people that share your perspective with regard to your product. They have the exact demographics, characteristics, needs, and finances to be your customers. Not only were they your customers once, but they are also the best group to look at to be your customer many times in the future.

You can easily get caught up with the "new" of high-technology. We are so jaded by things that are new—new customers, new products, new designs, new software, new semiconductors, new information—that it is easy to forget the importance of existing accounts.

You and Your Customer
Base Have Something in Common

Your company saw a need in the market and created a product to fill it. Your existing customers had a need and bought your product to satisfy it. This relationship ties you together. It's up to you to decide where you go from here.

One way to proceed is to continue to look at how your customer's needs expand. What else does he need as he continues to use your products? In the short term, these needs may be pretty basic and can include things like updates, product refreshments, and maintenance. Over a longer period of time, you can probably identify different phases in which your customer's involvement with your product changes. These phases may represent major new opportunities to expand your relationship with your customer.

The same sort of thinking can apply to your reseller channel. The successes you've had with your resellers are important. As with your customer, you and your resellers share a perspective. You were looking for customers with certain profiles. Your reseller was able to attract these customers. As with a customer, your future relationship with your reseller has short- and long-term possibilities. Your resellers have their own plans on how they will be growing their businesses. You can capitalize on your future plans by coordinating your future expansion with that of your channel.

Your customers are smart. They made the decision once to buy your products. They're even willing to tell you what you can do to improve so that you get to the point where they'll buy from you again and again. It's up to you to seize this initiative.

Don't Make This Mistake

Again and again I run into companies that make the same mistake. They begin treating their existing customers as a birthright and take customer loyalty for granted. It's easy to see how this can happen. Most high-tech companies are run by people with little or no sales background. Most customers are dependent on their supplier as the sole source for upgrades over the short term. It seems logical then that a customer with no alternative will remain loyal—so why not take advantage of this situation?

Taking your customers' loyalty for granted manifests itself in many ways. I've seen companies that sell expensive software products to large end users believe that they can save sales expenses by hiring inexperienced sales people to handle their large installed base. Some companies will decrease their sales commissions for orders received from existing customers. (Instead of decreasing commissions, these companies should have raised commissions for orders received from new customers. Decreasing commissions sends a very strong negative message.) Often, a company thinking like this will eliminate its sales involvement from service and maintenance operations in an attempt to lower costs. Companies selling retail computer products will often ignore their product registration cards, never thinking that in their registered user base lies a treasure of opportunities.

More often than not, what's behind this is that somewhere in management someone thinks that the installed base of customers doesn't need quality sales attention. That's wrong. It's probably true that the sales plan you create for new accounts is not the one you will use for existing accounts. Your customer base may need a sales plan tailored to its needs. When you create a sales plan for new customers, revenue generation from the sales of new units is the driving factor—your measure is sales dollars per month. That's probably not true for your existing customers. If they are already using your product, then what is left to sell them? For these customers, you have to broaden your window of opportunity. Instead of looking at the customer and wondering how much monthly revenue they'll produce, it is better to look at a group of these customers and focus on their revenue generation over a multi-year time frame (see Figure 11-1).

Figure 11-1   Look at Your Customer's Revenue Production over Multiple Years

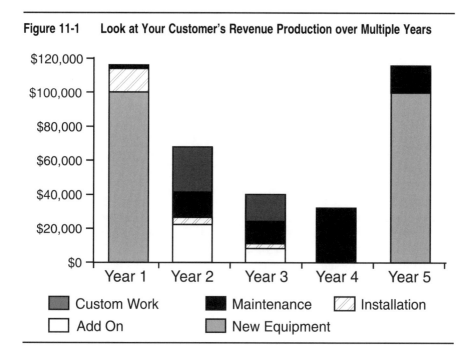

Looking at your existing customers in terms of a multi-year revenue stream gives you a better sense of long-term account management. If you are selling high-ticket items, the year after your initial customer purchase they may not be in a position to make another major procurement. You can still look to them to purchase other services from you such as maintenance or customization. A revenue stream perspective points you in the direction of managing revenue targets, not just product purchases.

When you manage your existing customer in terms of their revenue production across several years, you can develop a scenario of growth phases. Some phases involve new product purchases. There may be some important expansion phases. Some may be for customization services. Still others may involve installation and maintenance. Selling to your existing customers in terms of multiple phases over multiple years creates a planning partnership that's important to both of you. When you come out with new products, you can redo these planning phases as part of showing your customers your new products. As changes happen at your customers they'll invite you in to update your planning phases.

A long-term plan of four parts can be jointly developed with your existing customer:

Part I   Overview of the present situation

Part II   Selecting the relevant corporate goals that can be addressed as part of the planning process

Part III   Description of the long-term goal and a model of how these goals can be met

Part IV   Identification of the phases to reach the goal

From this starting point, you and your customer can agree on the growth phases relevant to your company and your product (see Figure 11-2).

Customers appreciate suppliers that operate in this way. After all, you are the expert on how a company can benefit from your product. You should be able to identify the most significant phases of using your product. It also puts you in a position of being side by side with your customers throughout their experience with your company. When it's finally time to replace your installed product, you'll be right there at the start of the process. Customers hate suppliers that sell them something and then are unseen for years until it's time to buy again.

Continuing to sell to your existing customer isn't just a strategy for high-ticket products sold directly to end users. This logic applies to anything that you sell. Remember, your customer has bought once. He will be

Figure 11-2   Working with Your Customer You Can Develop a Multi-Year Phased Approach

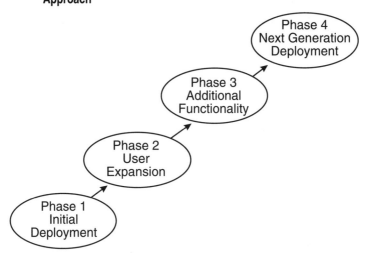

buying again, even if the next purchase will take place several years out. You're in the best position to set yourself up for the subsequent sale.

Take a simple example of a software company that is selling its product through retail. Of course, it encloses a registration card within the box. What can it do to get the most out of this card after it is returned? First off, it could probably put together a plan for setting up a continual relationship with this customer. The company can use the experience of previous customers to predict when this new customer will be needing new information, new service, or new updates. It can start a multi-year program with its customers designed to continually correspond with their new user. This could even be in some form of "official" organization like a user group run through the mail, or it can be on an ad hoc basis. By grouping all of its registered customers together the company can build an effective method for turning its relationship with customers from a one-time purchase to a revenue stream.

I learned a valuable lesson a long time ago—when you lose a customer to a competitor, the day that you should begin selling to him again is the day after your competitor delivered the product. Obviously this is a qualified customer as he just purchased a product. Since it is a high-tech product, there will eventually be the need to replace it. Plus, there is the good possibility that your competitor will make a mistake early on—she may mess up the installation, she may have underestimated the capacity needed, or do a terrible job servicing the account. I'd make it my job to keep in touch with this user's needs and be better prepared for the next purchase.

It's a good practice to put in place a long-term plan for your existing customer base. If you don't do it, someone else may do it for you. This same logic applies to your resellers. High-tech companies are notorious for signing up a reseller, selling a bunch of inventory and demo equipment, then leaving everything else up to the reseller. I don't know why resellers don't insist on some sort of performance guarantees before they pay their bills. I'm sure that many distributors have a Wall of Shame—high-tech products that were crammed down their throats by suppliers and never moved off the shelves. If you don't put a continuous support program together with your resellers, you are leaving yourself wide open to your competitor.

Selling to Existing Customers Is Not Easy

Many people think it's easy to go into an existing customer and walk out with an order. Quite often, management of high-tech companies with little sales experience will put their most junior sales people onto their largest accounts. If Exxon was your biggest customer accounting for millions a year in annual sales, would you put an inexperienced salesperson in charge of this relationship?

Believe it or not, it happens every day.

The reasons people think it's easy to sell to existing customers is because they think the customer has few options, now that they are a committed user. That kind of thinking will lead you to big trouble.

Selling to existing customers may not require much in the way of sales prospecting skills. In this way, developing new customers is the harder job. Nevertheless, the difficulty associated with new customer development by no means diminishes the complexity of selling to existing customers.

Your existing customers already using your products know the good, the bad, and the ugly of your company. To them your promises of service capability and maintenance levels are not rhetorical statements, they are their reality. For instance, if you have an 800 number to service your customer's questions, they can tell you exactly how long they are on hold each time they call. Your existing customer knows your company better than you do.

Existing users also know more about technology requirements than nonusers. So, when these customers need additional products and resources, their requirements can be quite complicated. After having used your products, they are more aware of what they need before they can make additional purchases.

If you are selling to large accounts, you'll want to expand your presence from the division currently using your product to additional divisions. Depending on the customer, this can be much more difficult than it sounds. Customers often have internal rivalries that can get in the way as you attempt to develop other users.

Another problem that complicates working with existing customers is that they encounter real-world difficulties working with your product. They may find it harder to use than they anticipated before they bought it. They may have bigger problems than they expected getting your product to fit into their businesses. Selling further things to these customers means first addressing the existing problems before suggesting they conquer new ground.

Personalities play a big role in all types of selling. Your customer's company may have a potpourri of personalities all clashing around your product. The early adopter that recommended your product may be a good long-term thinker but may not have the respect of the pragmatists who must keep your product running. Or people in another division may want to do something different from what their company is already doing. In all types of selling, personalities come to play a big role in the purchase decision. When selling to existing customers, personality issues seem to dominate.

Existing Customers Can Attract New Customers

Your biggest sales strength can be your successful customers. Early in your new product's life, you may be selling pizzazz. Later on, after your competitors have responded with new products of their own, you can begin to fall back on your installed accounts for strength. Your competition may have the latest features. You've got customers successfully using your products. Your strength is risk reduction.

You should start to build your reference account strengths early. Don't wait until the last minute to generate references. As soon as you sell to a new customer you should bring him into your community of reference accounts. There are many things you can do to make your reference accounts into a strong group that will serve to attract new users into the fold. One of the oldest is one of the best—user groups. In some cases you may be in a position to form your own. In other cases it may be better to form a subgroup within an existing group. You don't have to wait around for your home office to do this for you. Regional user groups are quite active throughout the industry and are often formed by local sales teams. A strong set of reference accounts helps build up entry barriers that your competitors will have difficulty crossing. Prospects often get the bulk of their input from existing users. Satisfied references can be the strongest factor influencing the growth of your markets. Word Perfect, one of the great success stories in the PC software business, owes much of its early growth to satisfied users influencing new purchases.

Your existing customers can also serve as a leading indicator for new trends occurring in your markets. Some of these users have proven their ability to act as early adopters. Years later, they may still be doing the same for your new products and those of your competitors. Your existing users can also help you find new extensions to your strategy that might have broad market appeal.

Look for Ways to Cultivate Your Existing Customers

I'm always on the lookout for new ways to work with existing customers. What works best for your company may not work well for others. There are four things that you would like your existing customers to do:

1. Continue to use your product

2. Expand their needs resulting in more purchases

3. Refer new prospects to your company

4. Provide feedback for your future plans

It's up to you to turn these goals into reality. You can structure a program to organize your existing accounts into a long-term sales asset helping you to increase their usage of your products and drawing new customers into your fold.

Smart sellers know that their existing customers are a valuable component in their future growth plans. They develop ways to turn their installed customer base into a strong asset that continues to purchase while they add new customers.

Chapter 12

Building New Customers and Selling New Products

New customers drive technology businesses. The shelf life of high-tech products is short because new products and major enhancements are constantly arriving. As soon as a new product hits the market, its future replacement is already on the drawing board (and maybe even leaked out to customers). Since you operate in a dynamo of product activity, new product selling absorbs a tremendous amount of your time and resources. Building customers for your new products is difficult, especially since selling to new customers produces uncertain results from substantial investments of time and resources. Nevertheless, your success at acquiring customers is vital to the health and welfare of your company. Your company will spend millions thinking about, researching, marketing, and manufacturing its new products. New products often grab the bulk of the available resources well before they are creating a sustainable return, making new product mix the most important opportunity cost decision your company can make. In order to achieve long-term, above average performance and to expand your business, your new products must successfully build new customers. Creating new customers for new technology products is fundamental to your success.

The terms "new products" and "new customers" cover a broad range. New products are major new additions to your company's product portfolio. New customers are new user populations that are experiencing your product for the first time, and can also include divisions within your existing customers that are working with you for the first time. If you are a brand new startup and have spent $5 million and the last couple of years

creating a product, you are probably dealing with a new product and selling to brand new customers. If you are a large established company like
Novell and have a new communications protocol to add to a file server, this
probably would not be considered a major new product. For this discussion,
we'll be concentrating on handling the major new product additions sold to
new customers.

Successfully bringing new customers into your user community
means doing a number of things right the first time, including profiling
prospects, locating prospects, anticipating value payoffs, accurately forecasting the results of your activity, and completing the sales cycle. What
makes working with new products difficult is that you must accurately
anticipate the results of your future actions without any experience with
your new product's sales process. It's like living in the future perfect
tense.

Suppose your company is in the personal computer software business
making time management software. Your company decides that the new
world of Personal Digital Assistants (PDAs) is important to its future and
spends two years developing a time management product for PDA users.
You know that you've got to put together your part of the sales plan. Look
at the list of things that you know and things that you don't know. You
know a lot about your present products, your present customers, what price
and promotions are appealing to your target customers, what reseller channels attract your prospects at the right time, where your competition is
successful, and where they are failing. If there are things you need to refine
about your model of existing customers, you can assemble a customer focus
group and get a tremendous amount of input. But that's your present product. For your new PDA-based product, you know much less. You are not
sure what price points will work. The PDA industry itself may not yet
understand how price sensitive its customers are. You are uncertain about
the overall value of your product to your customer and you may not know
how useful it actually will be based on the performance of the PDA units.
Furthermore, you are unsure of the important buying patterns among PDA
users. Will the majority of the future PDA purchases be driven by a corporate procurement around a specific project, or will they be individually
purchased? Within any single manufacturer's family of PDAs, which configurations will be the most important for you to support? You can only
predict likely buying channels for your future products. You don't know
which submarkets will move first to buy these products. You cannot predict
which resellers will be key. Unlike your answers to the questions about
your existing product line, you'll be guessing at the answers to each of these
questions.

You don't have much data from which to work. Inaccurate answers to these questions will lead you down false sales paths that waste your most valuable resource—time. It's easy to confuse the things you are sure of with those you are uncertain about. For instance, your sales team may be forecasting two different sales—one for your existing product and one for your new product line. Your existing product forecast would normally contain information garnered from your years of experience with the product line, reseller channel, and customer base. But your new product line forecast has tremendous uncertainty. First, the new product itself is an unknown and you've had no customer experience with it. There are also things that you do not know about the prospective customer base for these products, especially in the case of brand new customers buying your product. On top of this is the relationship between your present product line and your new products. Your sales time (and that of your resellers) will be split and your new product may pirate sales from your existing one. Nevertheless, long before you've had experience with your new product, you must produce extensive forecasts and predict your allocation of time and resources. Each time your guess is a little bit off, you may be tying up valuable future resources. The opportunity costs of guessing wrong are high. For instance, if you guess wrong about the value your product offers and your company prices it out of reach of the customer base that could move first and fastest, you'll lose precious submarket development time and may provide competitors with an unexpected blessing.

Selling to Early Adopters versus Selling to the General Market

Your new product sales go through two phases. In order to get customer acceptance for your ideas, someone must be first in line to use your product. With high-tech products, the early adopters of your products will be people that, for a variety of reasons, will experiment with your new product in the hopes that somehow it can benefit their company. These people do not need to see working reference accounts. Early adopters will be willing to see through the holes in your product line with the hope that your shortcomings will soon be filled in. These early adopters may even be willing to perform special product adaptations or customization themselves.

The motives of early adopters vary widely. Some are trying to push the technology envelope for their companies, and are willing to assume the risks of your new product to take advantage of your capability. Others share your long-term vision and are excited about your implementation. Still others really need the long-term benefits available from your technology and are willing to risk time and money and incubate the adaptation of your technology into their environment. Still others are just plain curious.

Regardless of the intention of the early adopters, they all have one thing in common—they are willing to work with your product before you have established working production users because they have something to gain from their individual perspectives. The early adopter sales process for your new product can be a protracted experience, though. Complex technology products have adoption cycles that can take years.

During the early adoption process, your company can gain invaluable experience regarding the suitability of your product implementation to your customer's business experience. It often occurs that the product your company built may have accurately anticipated certain needs but have left out some very important functions. When your early adopters start using your new product, these missing features start appearing and your company begins to understand the re-engineering needed to round out the product. This sort of thing is common in today's world because customer needs are so complex. Even the best product planners will miss important product features and functionality. Product success is an iterative process involving lots of customer feedback.

When you work with early adopters, its easy to forget that these initial users are different from your future general market customers. They don't wear badges reminding you that they are risk takers with respect to your product. Keep in mind that your early adopters are willing to risk their time and money because they share your vision of the business advantages that your product provides. They are willing to plug the holes in your product to get their advantages early because they feel that your risk/reward payback is high. Your general market customers will want the same rewards but won't want the risks. They'd rather spend their time working on other projects and wait until you level out your uncertainty factors by getting other customers into production. Your reference customers provide input to help your later market customers minimize their risk factors.

Early adoption of your product is impacted by the availability of other technology products. You need to understand where you are in the technology adoption food chain. Sometimes its obvious. For instance, when low-cost video conferencing terminals first arrived, another technology factor entered the equation. Video conference users had to also install dial-up, 56Kbps telephone lines. Both of these new products appeared simultaneously in the market. Video conferencing demand was an important factor justifying the telephone companies' investment in dial-up, 56Kbps services. The ubiquitous national availability of 56Kbps services influenced the availability of low-cost video conferencing terminals. The sellers of each of these technologies had to answer the concerns of their early adopters and make certain that the availability of their complementary products moved along as well. Their early adopters could not become reference production users until both technologies became available.

The situation is similar in the computer business. DEC's Alpha computers offer users a single processor family that spans PCs to high-end processing. Thus DEC offers a choice for companies buying different-sized computers. Since these new computers are useless without application software, DEC had to identify the software most needed by its customers and evangelize its processor family to the authors of these products. DEC's early adopters must experience the Alpha computer working with a variety of useful software packages that have been ported to the Alpha platform. Obviously, moving early adopters along to production usage is a tremendous task for a computer product line as broad as the Alpha processor family.

Each of your important submarkets has its own, unique, early adoption cycle. Your product may go through this process quickly in one vertical market while others are much slower. The reasons for these differences in adoption cycles range from technical, government approval to specific industry factors. The net effect, though, is that long after your new product is out, one vertical market may have many reference customers in production mode, another submarket may be just entering production, and a third vertical market may consist of early adopters.

Why do you care so much about differentiating early adopters from production users? Because the actions of your early adopters are not repeatable on a larger scale in the vertical market in which they operate. Their motivations are unique and rare. Yes, they have bought and paid for your product. Yes, you do wish they were like all other customers. No, they are the exception, not the rule. When an early adopter buys from you, she is taking a risk your general market customer will not take. You cannot expect your general market customer to take the same risks that your early adopters take.

The good news is that your early adopters generally do want to become production users. They are willing to spend time and money working with you to field-test your product. Early adopters are tremendously important to the success of your product. They can help you spot all of the "last mile" problems overlooked by your designers. They can list each hurdle in the way of production usage of your product. They also can be your value testers, helping you determine where you really make a contribution to your customer's business.

To move your early adopters into production you'll have to refine your product after introduction. Early adopters provide valuable feedback and discover things that your design and marketing teams overlooked. These first users will encounter obstacles that you'll have to overcome.

Some don't mind filling in the missing pieces themselves. For the mainstream market, it is up to you to round out your product offering so users go rapidly from purchase to production.

Moving through the early adopter phase into your mainstream customer base takes time. Your company first must come to terms with something it doesn't want to hear—that your new product is not yet ready for prime time. After all the time and money your company spent on creating, designing, producing, and launching your new product, no one wants to hear that there is still a lot more time and money needed to finish the product. Eventually though, people in your company will come to accept the reality that your new product needs more work to "finish up" for a larger audience.

Big problems occur when your sales groups incorrectly forecast high sales expectations from the experiences of the early adopters. You are probably familiar with a common scenario at many high-tech companies. A company introduces a new product at its major trade show. They get a lot of attention and a number of purchase orders from important customers. Their competition is scrambling. The sales team gets back from the trade show and says, "Wow, if we sold that much in just one month, imaging what we can do in a year!" They prepare a large forecast (AKA an aggressive forecast). Management is ecstatic. They ramp up and hire more people. A year later, everyone is depressed. New product sales have limped along. Early customers are having major problems getting the product into production environments. The sales staffing is too high and sales are too low. It's time to reduce head count.

This scene plays itself out regularly within high-tech companies. The problems are not with the quality of the product or the ability of the sales staff to close business. The problems stem from incorrectly predicting the time and difficulties associated with incubating new products in real live customer situations.

Be skeptical of a high-tech company predicting a huge jump in sales for a new product based on relatively little data. After launching a new product, sales are likely to be high due to the demand that built up during product development. A company must stimulate interest in its new product long before it is officially introduced. Two or three months after launch, reality begins to set in. Using these initial sales as the basis for long-term forecasting isn't sensible. Forecasting with the wrong data leads to bad strategic planning. If you forecast too low you won't have the right people on board and your competitors will pick up where you leave off. If you forecast too high you've got too many people and need more financing at the worst possible moment—after sales have dipped. So, where do you go to get the data to create more accurate sales predictions? If you can't use preliminary sales as a forecast basis, what can you use to create early product life sales forecasts that are 80 percent accurate?

Selling to New Customers versus Selling to Existing Users

Establishing new relationships takes time. Whether these relationships are new customers, new divisions within new customers, new submarkets, new international markets, new resellers, or new distributors, you've got to get to know your new business partners. When you are selling to someone you're familiar with, you know a lot about how he operates, how he makes decisions and his ability to keep on schedule and meet commitments. When you're selling to someone new, you're not familiar with her operation practices and your ability to predict her actions is diminished. The result of working with new customers is that you are less likely to accurately predict the future than when you are working with existing customers. Figure 12-1 illustrates this point.

The most reliable forecasts from a sales team should be for existing customers buying existing products. The highest risk forecasts will be those involving new products sold to new customers, or new submarkets, and through new distributors to new customers.

Figure 12-1   Forecast Accuracy Relates to Customer and Product Experience

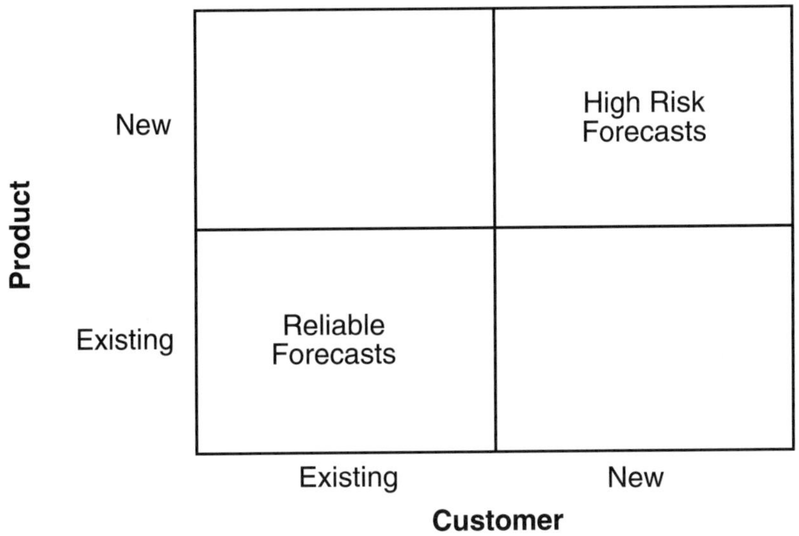

Your new product needs early adopters to become familiar with it and recommend its use to mainstream customers. In a similar manner, your new sales relationship succeeds when you have successfully developed an early adopter inside your prospective customer. This person becomes an inside salesperson evangelizing your company to others. This early adopter is instrumental in making your future sales relationship a success.

Building New Submarkets

Each important vertical market for your company has a unique set of hurdles to jump before you reach the market's mainstream customers. Prospects in one submarket may not care about functionality considered essential in other submarkets. Therefore, your success in other submarkets may be only slightly helpful in developing a new submarket.

When you are selling into a new submarket, you must remember where you are. If only a few leading edge customers purchased the product and if these customers are using it in a laboratory, then you are in the early adopter phase within this submarket. Your signpost for leaving this phase behind is the development of reference production users in your new submarket.

High-technology selling means executing your early adopter sales phase differently than your general market selling phase. A seller that treats its early adopter sales cycle the same as its production user sales cycle operates inefficiently and puts itself in jeopardy. Selling to early adopters means locating the few customers willing to spend time with you and take the risks. As we've seen, your early adopter sales may or may not be reproducible. By definition, early adopters are unusual because they take on high-risk products not ready for prime time. Early adopter selling means finding the right set of users from which to start cultivating this emerging customer base, putting programs in place to break through your product's shortcomings and moving these customers into production status.

Selling to your general market means finding your mainstream market. In this phase you'll put in place the processes to locate and sell to the larger audience of prospective customers. All of the important considerations involving your channel strategy, international roll-out plan, customer service model, and vertical market segmentation enter into this portion of your sales plan. Mainstream selling means that you'll be targeting broad customer segments to put sales prospects into your sales funnel for your sales channel to close. This is about winning orders.

When you're selling a brand new product, keep in mind that it's not yet ready for a large audience. The consequences of moving out too soon can be exasperating and expensive. You must manage this process to meet your long-term business objectives. When your company first starts to build its new product, a product plan and a marketing plan usually come together to shape your future business strategy. This is the time to prepare a sales plan. Most new product sales plans have two phases. The first is the sales plan for selling to the early adopters. The second is the plan for selling to the mainstream markets.

Shortening your new product's incubation period is your number one sales job. Success at this means:

1. Building an early adopter sales strategy well before your product is actually introduced into the market.

2. Executing and correcting your early adopter sales strategy after launch. Successful people set goals and measure their performance.

Sales Goals

Reducing the early adopter incubation period is the first goal for a new product sales team. This is an unusual goal. Most sales goals have to do with getting orders and shipping product. Not this one! The sooner your product goes through its incubation period and is accepted in its first production application, the sooner your mainstream customer base will turn on. If your mainstream customer base represents a $60 million annual sales opportunity in production, then each month of sales is valued at $5 million. That means $5 million removed from your future revenue stream each month your incubation period is extended. The extra time also gives your competitor the opportunity to bear down and beat you to the mainstream market.

As your second goal, you must find relevant early adopters in each of your near-term, vertical market segments. Not just any first customers will do. If your new product is relevant for banking, insurance, and financial services applications, getting early adopters in the wholesale inventory markets is inconsistent with your next phase sales plan. Even if you succeed in getting the inventory customer into production, you'll still need to incubate successes in these other vertical markets before they will develop mainstream usage. Smart sellers recognize the limitations of their early adopters and put in place programs that will shorten this product incubation period. This second goal reflects your long term vertical market penetration strategy.

Table 12-1   Sales Planning Checklist

Early Adopter Sales Plan		Mainstream Customer Sales Plan	
✓	Evangelize and sell complementary product providers	3	Prioritize vertical markets
✓	Profile relevant customers in each submarket	✓	Motivate sales partners
✓	Identify risk takers in each submarket	✓	Develop sales lead submarket generation strategy
✓	Develop a simple revenue forecast based on data from risk takers who will work with you	✓	Expand sales capacity
✓	Identify individuals in your sales channel that work with early adopters	✓	Turn on reseller channel

Your third goal is to make sure your channel strategy can actually work in the real world, after your product is ready for prime time. While you may not be using your channel participants during this incubation period, it may be appropriate to use this time to test out your channel strategy. For instance, instead of introducing your product in Europe during the early adopter sales phase, you may find it more consistent to postpone European sales in favor of shortening the U.S. adopter roll-out cycle. You can still use this time period to make sales progress in Europe by organizing your resellers, keeping them apprised of your first-phase successes and staging your European incubation period to keep its elapsed time short. Your final early adopter sales goal is the revenue that you expect from your early adopter sales strategy.

The data you need for your early adopter sales strategy often come from different sources than you expect. New product ideas have less sales information available simply because these markets do not yet exist. Marketing people love to form customer focus groups to generate input regard-

Early Adopter Sales Goals

Time Goals	1. Establish product incubation timeline
Sales Targets	2. Identify and quantify early adopter prospects and mainstream customers in each submarket
Channel Planning	3. Get the channel strategy plans in place and ready to roll out when the time is right

ing new products. That formula works when the product is a revision of one familiar to the participants. When the product is a wholly new concept, focus groups may be of little use. You'll find that you have to generate new information previously not available. Use Table 12-2 to check your early adopter input.

The sources for the input into your early adopter strategy are not unusual. You must cultivate and explore relevant information from multiple sources in order to determine how to create your new sales opportunities. You'll want to explore which prospective customers are most likely to want your new product, the reasons why they will want it and the amount of risk they will take. Your own design team will be of great help to you, especially if they are in communication with potential customers. Certain resellers, complementary product sellers, and specific salespeople can provide good information resources for you. Figure 12-2 shows how you can organize your plan for a new product.

Separating your early customer development mission from the mainstream sales goals allows you to focus on successfully bringing your product through its transition period. Once you succeed in converting your first customers into reference accounts, your sales role expands to the bulk market opportunity. Selling in the mainstream means qualifying the available sales prospects and turning your resellers on full blast. Now your new product is ready for prime time and you are able to capitalize on its larger market opportunity.

Your sales forecasting challenge is best met by dividing your forecast in two—an early adopter forecast and a mainstream customer forecast. This gives you a better idea of how and when your new product sales can grow. What's more, you'll be able to understand the prerequisites that control your sales growth. Early adopters are a unique breed. They don't need reference accounts, great documentation, packaging, advertising, service, or

Table 12-2   Early Adopter Input Planning Checklist

✓	Your design team
✓	Your leading-edge salespeople
✓	Your competitor's early adopters
✓	Resellers successful in the market arena
✓	Industry trade association members
✓	Niche trade publications

Figure 12-2   Sales Planning Process for a New Product

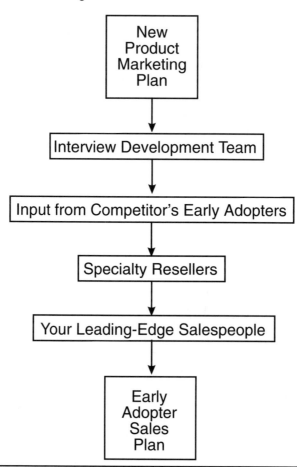

support. They usually are the visionaries within their company who are experimenting with new applications. Today's end-user technology management encourages this risk-taking as a way to achieve competitive advantage when one of their "skunk work" projects moves to full deployment. Sales to early adopters can result in a starter purchase in the hope that orders will follow after the pilot application rolls out to production. Technology companies can also get customization fees as early adopters identify and fund development of new functions. Early adopter revenue may be substantial—in the millions of dollars. Even so, keep in mind that early adopter sales are "one of a kind" situations and cannot reliably be projected into "typical" customer forecasts.

The second forecast is for the mainstream production user. These companies have a specific, well-known application and are searching for a solution set that will meet their needs. Mainstream customers have budgets for investigation, application development, pilot, and deployment. Buyers want to see successful reference accounts to better understand their risks. Having no industry reference accounts will increase their risk factor (and may also mean that your new product doesn't get to participate in this round). This customer team has a management commitment in place backed by a very visible budget. It wants to deliver a successful project to its customer.

Going from early adopters to production users is the most difficult problem for developing new accounts and bringing new products to market. When you are creating the first version of your product, it is difficult to understand all of the critical needs of your production user. Since you don't have any production users, you must predict all of the probable obstacles facing your potential production users. Focus groups are useless when no one has any real experience with your new vision. The reality of life in today's technology world is that you do the best job possible anticipating the needs of both types of users and build these into your product. A year or so later, after you worked with the early adopters, you may still be told by potential production users that they won't buy your product until additional functionality appears. If you are lucky, you can spend a little money and fix your weaknesses. However, you may have to face up to a pretty costly product "reinvention." That's not bad news, just reality. It becomes bad news when sales forecasts were incorrect and no one expected this to happen. A company in this position has overstretched its resources. Reality can also become bad news when early commitments need to be modified significantly and the company's management is emotional about going back to a customer and decommitting past promises. It becomes very bad news when the company needs unplanned financing. The good news, often unnoticed, is that at this point in the product's early existence, the company may have found a market! Mainstream customers are actually interested enough to suggest refinements.

It's crucial that you identify where you are in the sales development growth process. Just knowing that there are large dollars in the forecast isn't enough. If you have big accounts and they are all in the early adopter state, you know you must successfully manage their transition through production and that the future of these accounts is difficult to predict. Likewise, if your forecast contains existing customers with well-known budgets trying to expand existing production applications, you can decide how to proceed. In the former case, management should still be worried about stabilizing its product and customer base and coming to terms with the potential redesign activity. In the latter case, it may be time to put in place the proper infrastructure to increase customer production activity (service, installation, training).

Four models are useful for deciding where things are with a new product forecast. The first (Figure 12-3) shows the gap between early adopters and production users.

This forecast assumes that there will be a sales drop-off period while the product re-enters the design phase and the new features are built in. It's a great worst-case model because it assumes that sales drop off completely and there is a significant time period before the product is ready for your general customer.

The second type of forecast is called "right the first time." This forecast (Figure 12-4) assumes that your team "knows all" when it first creates your product. Everything works according to plan. Any unforeseen setbacks can be quickly fixed without impacting the plan. You can't even tell the difference as the company develops its later market. Everything looks like one smooth and easy ramp. If this company misses just a little, their situation can rapidly deteriorate. (The early drop-out rate of well-financed ventures into the PDA market proves that "crash and burn" continues to happen.)

This model worked well for many companies in the early 1980s when product designs were less complex and new customers were hungry for new products. It worked for Lotus and everyone wants to be just like Lotus. Why not?

The third forecast model (Figure 12-5) is the real road traveled by most of today's successful new products. They have a sales dip between the early

Figure 12-3   Gap between Early Adopters and Production Users

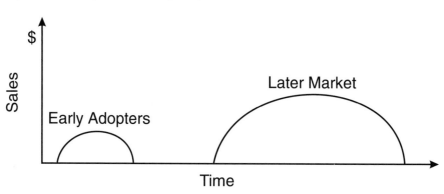

Figure 12-4   Right the First Time

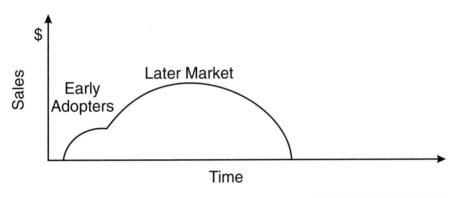

adopters buying product and their eventual production users. This company must spend time "reinventing" its product to suit its mainstream market requirements. During this time, sales are flat and may even dip slightly. Most likely this company's product can achieve success in three or four different vertical markets. The verticals that are the most successful become market production users early and help mitigate the dip period. The great unknown here is how long sales will be flat.

The last forecast model represents failure (Figure 12-6). This is pretty common for new software products. The company has an idea, develops the product, gets some early adopters along with some initial revenue. Product modifications are identified. Unfortunately, the company runs out of time and money before it can reenter the market. It could have been a great

Figure 12-5   Mixed Mode

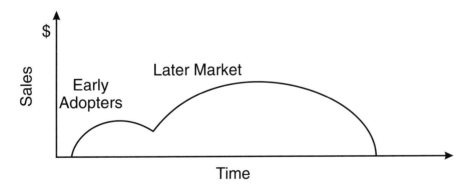

Figure 12-6   Failure

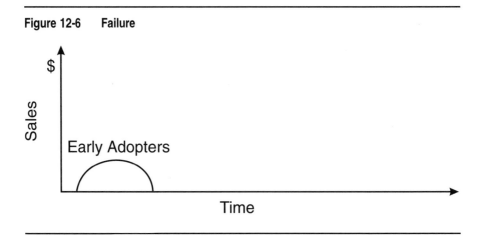

product and a great idea. What failed here may not have been the product, but their business plan.

Forecast Concerns

A major difficulty is that the most important planning document at this point in a new product launch is the sales forecast. Early on, your company has the least amount of data from which to project its sales. You are trying to forecast new products selling to new customers. There are a few rules that can guide you through this forecasting process:

1. Predicting early adopter buying patterns will drive you crazy. At best it's unpredictable. At worst, it's random. Just because these situations are early does not mean they are unimportant. The dollar amounts can be very high.

2. Predicting later market activity to an 80 percent confidence factor is possible.

You are dealing with real customers with real budgets. The risks are:

    a.   Customer application roll-outs slip
    b.   Your roll-out slips
    c.   Your own sales team misreads the data.

While you cannot reliably predict the results of any one account, at this stage you should be dealing with a handful of different accounts. A positive on one side cancels out a negative on the other.

Forecast Model #1 (Figure 12-3) is the best starting point for forecasting new product sales (probably because it assumes the worst case). When you're using Model #1, you're expecting a future sales quarter with little or no activity. You try to shorten as much of the early adopter market as you can. Your engineering group is standing by, ready to make any and every modification. Its development environment is set up to be flexible, so changes can be made quickly. The entire company is not disappointed when the decision to redesign major portions of the product is made. They take this in stride. Investors are aware of what is going on. No one is sweeping negative information under the rug. The future situations are:

1. The market doesn't develop quickly enough for the product to be reintroduced within the current financing scheme and this becomes a candidate for Model #4 (Figure 12-6).

2. The company is more successful than originally planned and it moves into Model #2 (Figure 12-4) or #3 (Figure 12-5). It's your job to reduce the early adopter incubation time period to make this happen.

The most important sales roles in a high-tech company are to

1. Develop new accounts

2. Successfully bring new products to market

Smart sellers know that when dealing with something new (customer or product) their ability to predict the future drops. Nevertheless, smart sellers allocate the right amount of resources at the right time to maximize the possible return on their sales investment.

Epilogue

Good Selling

When you close this book and go back to work there are three ideas that you can take with you:

1. Companies buy high-tech/high-ticket items to gain unique competitive advantage.

2. Your distinctive value differentiates your company and products in the marketplace. Distinctive value increases your market share and produces price premiums.

3. Your selling effectiveness increases when you form pervasive sales partnerships. The first group to partner with is your customer. Then you can extend these partnerships to your reseller channel and your complementary market providers.

Good selling.

Index